Advanced OS/2™ Presentation Manager Programming

Accredited

Thomas E. Burge

Joseph Celi, Jr.

John Wiley & Sons, Inc.

NEW YORK / CHICHESTER / BRISBANE / TORONTO / SINGAPORE

Associate Publisher: Katherine Schowalter
Senior Acquisitions Editor: Diane Cerra
Managing Editor: Jacqueline A. Martin
Composition: Coordinated by Greg Martel, Publication Services, Inc.

This text is printed on acid-free paper.

OS/2 is a registered trademark of International Business Machines Corporation. Other words in this publication in which the Author and Publisher believe trademark or other proprietary rights may exist have been designated as such by use of Initial Capital Letters. However, in so designating or failing to designate such words, neither the Author nor the Publisher intends to express any judgment on the validity or legal status of any proprietary right that may be claimed in the words.

This publication is designed to provide accurate and authoritative information in regard to the subject matter covered. It is sold with the understanding that the publisher is not engaged in rendering legal, accounting, or other professional service. If legal advice or other expert assistance is required, the services of a competent professional person should be sought. FROM A DECLARATION OF PRINCIPLES JOINTLY ADOPTED BY A COMMITTEE OF THE AMERICAN BAR ASSOCIATION AND A COMMITTEE OF PUBLISHERS.

Library of Congress Cataloging-in-Publication Data

Burge, Thomas E.
    Advanced OS/2 presentation manager programming / Thomas E. Burge, Joseph Celi, Jr.
        p.   cm.
    Includes index.
    ISBN 0-471-59198-X (alk. paper)
    1. Operating systems (Computers) 2. OS/2 (Computer file)
3. Presentation manager. I. Celi, Joseph, 1963– . II. Title.
QA76.76.O63B859   1993
005.4'3—dc20
                                                        93-7135
                                                        CIP

Printed in the United States of America
10 9 8 7 6 5 4 3 2 1

This book is dedicated to my parents and my brother for their help and support during the writing of this book.

–Thomas E. Burge

This book is dedicated to my wife, Susan, for her encouragement and understanding during the writing of this book. I would also like to dedicate this book to my children, Stephanie and Steven.

–Joseph Celi, Jr.

Foreword

On the evening of Tuesday, March 31, 1992, I had the honor of introducing IBM's advanced, 32-bit PC operating system, OS/2 Version 2.0, unquestionably the most significant release since the product's inception. The occasion was a special general meeting of the New York Personal Computer Users Group at the Marriott Marquis Hotel in Manhattan.

To mark this special event, a live satellite video link to the birthplace of OS/2, IBM's Boca Raton Programming Center, was established. Meeting attendees were given the opportunity to speak directly with the Boca team—a group clearly beaming with pride in their accomplishment. This excited, albeit tired, group answered questions from the audience and provided invaluable insight into the extraordinary thought and future-directed planning that accompanied all aspects of the OS/2 2.0 development effort.

I mention what took place on the evening of March 31, 1992, because it was an evening that I recall with great pride. It marked the culmination of a project in which IBM had invested heavily. Significant obstacles were overcome by good people who had also invested heavily of themselves—to the extent that, whatever was necessary to "get the job done," they did, regardless of obstacles. With the pessimists questioning their ability, the Boca team delivered a world-class product. It was a remarkable achievement.

Midway through the evening's presentation, one of the first OS/2 shrink-wrapped packages arrived and was displayed to an enthusiastic audience. During the year since OS/2 2.0 was introduced, more than two million copies of the product have been shipped, and OS/2 has gained worldwide acceptance as an operating system that provides unparalleled versatility, power, and protection.

The industry has embraced OS/2 as an easy-to-use and flexible operating system designed with an "eye toward the future." Under OS/2 you can have up to 240 virtual DOS sessions, each with custom configurations for individually governing a session. Existing 16-bit applications find less hostile environments in which to run because of fewer memory restrictions, crash protection, and efficiency boosts. And many 32-bit applications designed to take advantage of the OS/2 environment, over 1,200 as of this writing, have shipped already.

We at IBM continue to drive hard toward providing enhancements, improvements, and support, and to chart a long-range future for our OS/2 customers. OS/2 2.0 brought to the PC marketplace a 32-bit operating system endowed with rich feature sets previously unavailable in other operating systems, and our next release, OS/2 2.1, will bring to OS/2 important enhancements such as a new 32-bit graphics engine that will let OS/2 redraw a large file or save it to disk as much as 25 to 30 percent faster. In addition, OS/2 2.1 will provide an enhanced set of device drivers that take better advantage of hardware capabilities and enhancements.

Version 2.0 of OS/2 shipped with a new graphical user interface (GUI) called the Workplace Shell. The Workplace Shell "sits on top of" Presentation Manager (PM), meaning PM is a component that provides basic tools and features for the Workplace Shell. The OS/2 Presentation Manager has been expanded with new graphical controls and additional system calls to provide better support and faster development for programmers writing 32-bit applications.

What Thomas Burge and Joseph Celi have provided in this book is an advanced programmer's guide to the tools and features of PM. This book demonstrates that PM is a tremendously capable component of OS/2 that provides a rich set of flexible tools and features for creating applications that are intuitive and easy to use. By providing a healthy number of well-designed and unique examples, this book illustrates how PM frees programmers from the necessity of using a formal and rigid GUI.

Burge and Celi do a wonderful job of clearly demonstrating that understanding PM programming gives programmers an enormous "head start" in writing applications that are easy to use, provide creative user interfaces, and offer a large set of graphical controls that can be used in an almost unlimited number of configurations.

The authors address advanced topics of PM programming, including new PM features. They explain, often by use of example, how to take advantage of PM's extraordinary range of capabilities. The book is packed with example programs that not only cover advanced programming but also provide practical, time-saving techniques that can be incorporated easily into a wide variety of OS/2 programs.

The example programs that are presented in this book exemplify the versatility and adaptability that are the hallmarks of OS/2. By showing how controls can be altered, added, deleted, and custom designed, this book demonstrates how the "standard window" appearance provided by PM can, among other stunts, literally be "turned upside down"!

I trust you will enjoy this book, learn some new techniques, and find it a handy reference tool.

James A. Cannavino
IBM Senior Vice President and General Manager
Personal Systems
IBM Corporation
Somers, New York

March 31, 1993

Preface

Presentation Manager (PM) is a tremendously capable component of OS/2 that provides a rich set of flexible tools for creating applications that are intuitive and easy to use. Programmers will not find PM restricting them to a formal and rigid graphical user interface (GUI). To the contrary, PM gives programmers an enormous "head start" in writing programs that are easy to use, provide very creative and imaginative user interfaces, and provide a large set of graphical controls that can be used in an almost unlimited number of configurations.

With the March 1992 release of OS/2 Version 2.0, PM has been upgraded to use a 32-bit operating system and has been supplemented to provide an enhanced set of graphical controls. Coupled with OS/2's new Workplace Shell, the PM component of OS/2 2.0 offers a rich and powerful program development environment. The information presented in this book describes how to take full advantage of PM and its controls.

This book relates to 32-bit versions of OS/2, namely to Version 2.0 and subsequent versions. Among the many new features that were introduced with OS/2 2.0 is the ability to run applications written for a variety of operating systems simultaneously. DOS applications written a decade ago now can be run together with 16-bit and 32-bit OS/2 applications. Programmers can develop and test applications written for many different operating systems while still remaining in the OS/2 environment. Compiling and testing can be done while each application is fully protected from any mischievous actions that the code that is being debugged may inadvertently take.

OS/2 provides a splendidly flexible environment that has been designed to address the ever-increasing demands that are placed on personal computer software. PM programmers can take advantage of hundreds of system calls and features that are provided by OS/2 and its present and future extensions, including, for example, support for networking, multimedia, pen-based systems, and other new system features that will be added during years to come.

While this book is not intended to be an "all-encompassing" reference for Presentation Manager, it brings to light a robust selection of features that have very practical uses and will enhance the "look and feel" of programs running under OS/2.

ACKNOWLEDGMENTS

We wish to thank our many colleagues and friends who have helped us along the way. In particular, for their time and effort, we wish to thank Chris Andrew, Mark Benge, Dave Blaschke, Peter Brightbill, Claudette Caldwell, Dick Conklin, Donald Hobern, Charlene Joyce, Scott Kliger, Mindy Pollack, Alex Pollitt, Joanne Rearnkham, Robert Rose, James Taylor, Gordon Webster, and Julio Wong.

Thomas E. Burge
Joseph Celi, Jr.

April 1993

Contents

X CONTENTS

CHAPTER 1
Introduction

Even programmers who are familiar with Presentation Manager (PM) programming probably will not be familiar with all of the interesting, esoteric, and useful capabilities of PM that are demonstrated in this book. Some topics that are discussed in the following chapters have received little more than a paragraph of explanation in documentation and articles that have been written about OS/2.

This book uses example programs and detailed explanations to demonstrate the power, flexibility, and promise of PM. PM brings to personal computers such features as a complete graphics library, based on software that was originally used on mainframe-sized computers. A programmer can use PM to give an application a graphical user interface (GUI) that expresses a great deal of creativity and imagination. A delightful aspect of PM is that it requires very little code in contrast to the enormous amount of functionality that it can add to a program. Graphical controls, in the form of buttons, menus, and dialog boxes, are just some of the tools that PM can bring to applications written to run under OS/2.

One component of PM that this book focuses on is its window manager, which handles the GUI and contains the code needed to create and handle windows in a PM environment. A PM Application Programming Interface (API) gives access to many functions that are built into the window manager. Often referred to as "Win calls" because of the Win prefix of their function names, the window manager APIs give a programmer access to functions that the window manager routinely uses to manage windows, controls, and message handling.

Another major component of PM is a graphics engine, which can be controlled by a Graphical Programming Interface (GPI). The graphics engine gives PM the ability to draw lines, arcs, bitmaps, and other objects. The window manager relies on the graphics engine to paint the contents of its windows and controls. To customize the look of the PM controls, GPI calls are used in many of the examples in this book. There are too many GPI functions to cover all of them in this book. Any GPI calls that are used in this book are explained, but the explanations are typically limited to such information as you will need to understand how a particular GPI call is used to draw a part of a control.

Discussed in this book are the many programming features of PM that were introduced beginning with Version 2.0 of OS/2 and how they affect the writing of future PM programs. The new Workplace Shell and a new set of graphical controls that have been added to OS/2 are also discussed, in view of the extensive use that they make of PM. While IBM programmers at Cary, North Carolina, developed the new graphical controls, the Workplace Shell and other features of OS/2 2.0 were developed by IBM programmers at Boca Raton, Florida. The authors both participated in the work done at Boca Raton.

DEVELOPING OS/2 2.0

The development of OS/2 2.0 was a remarkable undertaking that has produced the most capable operating system presently available for use with personal computers. While the final version of the code that comprises OS/2 2.0 was developed and tested at the IBM Boca Programming Center (BPC), thousands of programmers from the United States, Canada, the United Kingdom, Japan, and many other countries contributed millions of lines of code to the product during the years of OS/2's development.

On March 31, 1992, the completed product, known as OS/2 Version 2.0, was placed onto "Golden Master" diskettes for manufacture and distribution. Version 2.0 is the first 32-bit release of OS/2. Many new features, including Workplace Shell, have given rise to new markets for the OS/2 operating system.

As has been mentioned in computer industry trade papers, OS/2 2.0 was known internally within IBM by the code name "Cruiser." While it was being developed, a picture of a cruise liner often identified areas where the offices and labs of OS/2 programmers were situated. The authors and other IBM programmers invested many late night hours to complete "Cruiser." Many of the programmers who contributed to Version 2.0 of OS/2 continue to work on projects that relate to future releases of this splendid operating system.

EXAMPLE CODE PRESENTED IN THIS BOOK

Example code is presented throughout this book to illustrate aspects of PM programming. Screen captures, which show programs at various stages of running, and associated source code listings are provided. If you already are familiar with PM programming, you will probably elect to turn to sections of this book that present examples that are of particular interest to you. Whether you skip around or read this book straight through, you will learn more about PM programming if you take an active part in writing, or at least modifying, some PM code.

COMPILERS AND TOOLS NEEDED

The examples in this book were compiled with tools from IBM's C Developer's WorkSet/2. Many other development tools are available and can be used to compile the example programs. As a minimum, you will need a C compiler and a resource compiler. If you want to use OS/2's ability to display help screens, you will also need what has been commonly referred to as a Help Manager compiler—which is known by the acronym "IPFC" for "Information Presentation Facility Compiler." Because the computer industry has a tendency to use acronyms, documentation that is provided with commercially available tool kits is likely to use the terms "RC compiler" for the resource compiler and "IPF compiler" for the Help Manager compiler.

The C/C++ Compiler

The code presented in this book has been compiled and tested with IBM's C Set/2 compiler, which is included with IBM's C Developer's WorkSet/2. However, a number of other C and C++ compilers are available for OS/2 and can be used just as easily. Old OS/2 compilers, which produce 16-bit code, are *not* able to take advantage of the 32-bit Application Program Interfaces (API) that became available with Version 2.0 of OS/2 and, therefore, will *not* properly compile the example code that is set out in this book. While 16-bit compilers can still be used to produce working 16-bit PM applications that will run under 32-bit OS/2, they will not make use of the new 32-bit APIs.

A process known as *thunking*, which translates addresses between the 16-bit format and OS/2's new 32-bit format, supports compatibility with 16-bit PM applications. Many computer articles have mistakenly referred to this process as "thinking," but the correct word is "thunking" (with a "u" instead of an "i"). Thunks are provided to take 16-bit addresses used by 16-bit applications and convert them into a proper format for 32-bit OS/2 to use with its 32-bit flat memory model. Some components built into 32-bit OS/2 still remain in a 16-bit format and require a *32-bit to 16-bit thunking layer* to handle function calls, which is the reverse of the normal *16-bit to 32-bit thunk*.

The names of the PM calls have gone substantially unchanged throughout OS/2's history; however, there are some minor differences between the functions used in 32-bit code and those used in 16-bit code. While a 16-bit program usually can be ported (with relatively few changes) to a 32-bit compiler, the reverse is not necessarily true. The examples in this book use many of PM's new features that are available *only* to 32-bit programs and will, therefore, require the use of a 32-bit C compiler. Major changes to OS/2's API set were made in the kernel calls that handle the new 32-bit flat memory model. Calls to allocate memory no longer deal with segments and are therefore much easier to use. Kernel calls to create threads and semaphores also have been considerably improved. As for PM's function calls, additions have been made to support new graphical controls. A few PM calls have been renamed to follow a more consistent naming convention.

The Resource Compiler

While many C compilers are available for OS/2 and can be used to write and port standard C programs, you will need a *resource compiler*, which places icons, bitmaps, and other resources into a program's executable file. Many of PM's functions use complex data structures that are stored in its executable file. Resources are accessed by calls made to the OS/2 kernel. Many PM calls are provided that simplify the use of resources unique to PM by handling a series of kernel functions automatically.

By using a resource compiler and the automated features that PM offers, a program does not have to deal with calls to the kernel to load resources. Resource compilers accept a special script language to describe a program's resources and translate these scripts into an equivalent set of data structures, which can be added to an OS/2 executable file.

You can avoid using a resource compiler for some of these data structures by placing them directly in your C code along with additional system calls to load the data properly as resources; however, this approach is very tedious to implement for even the simplest of resources (such as those that describe a menu template) and presents more than enough work to quickly discourage any programmer from trying to proceed without having at least a simple resource compiler close at hand.

Creating Text for Help Manager

OS/2 provides an ability to display detailed help screens with the use of its Help Manager facility. Programs such as OS/2's Tutorial make use of Help Manager to display text, bitmaps, and animation. Using a set of PM calls, a help file, produced by an Information Presentation Facility (IPF) compiler, can easily integrate help screens into your programs. Animation requires that extra code be written to utilize a set of Help Manager functions to display a series of bitmaps.

The IPF compiler uses its own tag language to describe how text and pictures are to appear in a Help Manager screen. Most tool kits that provide a resource compiler will also provide an IPF compiler, so if you purchase a resource compiler, you should not have to look for an IPF compiler as a separate package. The IPF tag language is relatively easy to learn, and the results it can provide in creating help screens will be found to be very rewarding.

HARDWARE CONFIGURATIONS

Any system that has OS/2 and a program developer's tool kit installed can be used as a development machine. Compilers tend to be greedy when it comes to using system memory, so, to improve the speed of your compiler, you may need to increase the amount of RAM your system has on board. The examples included in this book were compiled on a variety of machines, ranging from a slow, 16 MHz 80386-based machine with 8 MB of RAM to a faster, 25 MHz 80486 machine with 16 MB of RAM. The performance difference between these machines was noticeable, but the slower machine's performance was still quite acceptable.

If you are writing software that is primarily at a system level, you should consider using the OS/2 debugging kernel that is included in IBM's tool kit to help you debug your software. This special kernel gives you access to the system's inner workings, by communicating detailed information about each thread, and it allows you to trace through the operation of programs as they run. The debugging kernel uses one of the computer's serial ports and requires you to hook up another computer as a terminal through a null modem cable. The examples in this book do not require a debugging kernel, but the use of a debugging kernel does offer the advantage of giving you total control over the operation of an OS/2 system. As you explore and learn more about OS/2, you will want to consider using the debugging kernel.

"EVERYTHING BEGINS WITH A PENCIL"

Perhaps this old quote should be updated to read, "Everything begins with an editor." Like a pencil, an editor is so commonly used that it is easy to overlook the amount of time you will spend with it. When switching to a new environment, you have probably spent hours searching for a better editor; or, like many programmers, you found yourself putting up with the shortcomings and nuances of an available editor.

A basic text editor is one of the most important tools a programmer uses. If you are moving from DOS to OS/2, you should consider investing in a good OS/2 editor. OS/2 can easily run your favorite DOS editor in a full-screen session or in a PM window, but many of the companies selling DOS editors also offer OS/2 versions of the same editors.

One of the advantages of an OS/2 editor is the ability it gives you to rid yourself of the old DOS memory constraints. Many DOS editors have 64 kB limits to the file sizes that they can edit. Still other DOS editors that do not have this particular memory barrier nonetheless suffer from other limitations set by DOS. It is convenient, though not often necessary, to be able to work with large ASCII files that may reach a size measured in megabytes. For example, at IBM there is an ASCII file that lists every acronym IBMers have collected over the past twenty years. Though the file is three megabytes in size, even the most basic OS/2 editors have the ability to load and display it.

Users of OS/2 should take advantage of its capabilities. In the long run, putting up with the limitations of a DOS editor can become quite frustrating. OS/2 comes with two editors: the *System Editor* and the *Enhanced Editor*. The System Editor is OS/2's equivalent to DOS's EDLIN and was intended only for changing OS/2's config.sys and other simple files. The Enhanced Editor is a more capable application and has many features that can be configured by using an options menu. While the Enhanced Editor first starts in a rather "crippled" mode, with most of its features hidden to prevent novice users from becoming confused, all of its hidden functionality can be revealed by changing its default settings. The editors that were used to write the example code presented in this book are essentially derived from IBM's relatively old E3 editor.

CHAPTER 2
Programmer's Overview of the OS/2 Product

The OS/2 operating system has had many additions made to it during recent years, not the least of which are Workplace Shell and new graphical controls. While new components have been added, the architecture of PM and the way it makes use of the base operating system have remained much the same since its introduction.

Because OS/2 is so rich with features that programmers can use in creative and innovative ways, merely learning about the possibilities that PM and Workplace Shell offer can provide a sizable challenge. In this chapter some of the components of OS/2 and the functions they perform are described.

MAPPING OUT PM AND THE WORKPLACE SHELL

When programmers first heard of the Workplace Shell during the development of OS/2 2.0, rumors about an entirely new set of APIs for the shell caused some confusion and apprehension about how future PM programs should be written. However, such concerns were unfounded, for a clear line of demarcation has been defined between Workplace Shell and Presentation Manager, and the structure of PM programs has remained largely unchanged.

Starting with Version 2.0 of OS/2, Workplace Shell and Presentation Manager comprise separate, individual components that are each highly capable of carrying out their distinctly different duties. While versions of OS/2 released prior to the release of Version 2.0 included a "Desktop Manager" and windows that "grouped" icons representing programs that could be started, the introduction of Workplace Shell dramatically changed and expanded the shell of OS/2 to provide a powerful object-oriented desktop metaphor. The "Desktop Manager" and its "Group" windows are history. Their functions now are attended to by Workplace Shell.

Workplace Shell treats programs and files as "objects sitting on a desktop" or as "folders on a desktop." The new shell provided by Workplace Shell is greatly enhanced and has been rendered much easier to use by providing features that appeal to a wide variety of user preferences and tastes.

Workplace Shell is not a component of PM. Nor does Workplace Shell represent a "new version" of PM. Workplace Shell is a program that sits on top of PM and makes heavy use of almost every feature PM has available. PM, on the other hand, provides the window-handling and drawing capabilities of OS/2, along with controls such as menus, dialog boxes, and selector buttons.

Customizing the Workplace Shell

Unlike the "Desktop Manager" of old, Workplace Shell offers a design that can be handsomely customized to accommodate user preferences and tastes. While simple features, such as fonts and colors can be modified with ease, almost every significant feature of Workplace Shell can also be customized by replacing it with substitute code. Access to Workplace Shell functions that draw and manipulate its objects is readily provided by a set of *methods* that programmers can work with to provide custom features. A method is essentially a hook into the internal code of Workplace Shell, providing programmers with opportunities to modify, enhance, or even replace functions that are used by the shell. By changing the shell's methods, passwords can be added to access data contained in Workplace folders. Appropriate modification of Workplace Shell can also allow the application to disable the editing of certain files.

Workplace Shell methods are contained in a hierarchy of objects that are used to construct Workplace Shell. Each method is introduced in an object, and the method is then inherited by children of the object. Descendants can override the code that defines any inherited method if the programmer desires to alter or add to inherited methods. To use the hundreds of methods that are made available by Workplace Shell, an object must be created and registered with the shell so that it can inherit and use the methods that are associated with a selected one of the shell's many objects.

Methods Are Not APIs

The manner in which system APIs are called cannot be used to call Workplace Shell methods. Workplace Shell methods were the rumored "new set of APIs" that programmers who first heard of Workplace Shell worried about having to learn. While Workplace Shell methods may look somewhat like typical system calls when described in a technical reference, a special procedure is required to call Workplace Shell methods. Moreover, to help distinguish the names of Workplace Shell methods from system calls, each method is identified by a lowercase name that begins with a wp prefix.

If you want to use Workplace Shell methods, you will need to become familiar with a new component of OS/2 called the System Object Model (SOM), which maintains Workplace Shell's hierarchy of objects. To program Workplace Shell, you will need an understanding of SOM to learn how to create a new object and to learn how methods are inherited and modified. Programming Workplace Shell is a book-sized topic unto itself. However, a very brief overview of SOM is provided in the following section in the hope that it will be of some assistance to programmers who are new to OS/2.

SYSTEM OBJECT MODEL

The SOM component of OS/2 provides an object-oriented environment for organizing the objects of Workplace Shell into a hierarchy of parent–child relationships. Each object contains methods that can be used by it and by its children. SOM handles how an object's methods are accessed by other objects, through a series of properties that are common to most object-oriented environments. An object's children gain access to their parent's methods through a property called *inheritance*. However, a child can modify an inherited method by registering code with SOM to override the method.

The advantage of using SOM is the capability that it provides to change the behavior of code that is already compiled and stored in an executable format. How objects are to appear in SOM's hierarchy must be described by registering each object along with the identity of its parent and a list of the methods that the object uses and modifies. When an object makes a call to a method that has been modified, SOM redirects the call, if need be, to an appropriate object that has been registered for the requested method. Likewise, when a child calls a method that has been inherited from its parent, SOM redirects the call to the parent object.

A method call is actually a call to SOM that is redirected to a function that has been named when the method was registered. A method's behavior is changed by changing the name of the function that SOM calls to handle the method. Each Workplace Shell method represents an exported function contained in a dynamic link library (DLL) called PMWP.DLL. The functions that comprise PMWP.DLL should never be called directly, since that would bypass SOM. To write code that uses a Workplace Shell method, the code must be written in a format that will permit it to be compiled as a SOM object. To gain access to Workplace Shell methods, the object must be registered by using a system call that describes the object to the shell.

To initialize code that uses Workplace Shell methods, several calls are made to SOM to describe where the code fits in among SOM's objects. Registering an object and making a call to a method is a rather complicated process involving the SOM functions. To do Workplace Shell programming, a SOM compiler (actually, a preprocessor) is provided with IBM tool kits to replace tags, specially placed in your source code, with appropriate SOM functions.

FUTURE PM APPLICATIONS

The addition to OS/2 of Workplace Shell does not alter how PM programs are written. PM programs written years ago can still run under a version of OS/2 that incorporates the new shell.

A PM program can be written as a Workplace Shell object to provide access to the shell's hundreds of methods. In fact, writing a PM program as an object of Workplace Shell gives the PM program more control over how it will appear and how it will be used by the shell. Such things as the object's context menu and settings pages can be modified to contain items that are specific to the object's purpose.

To use Workplace Shell methods effectively, you need to understand how PM works. Many of the shell's methods simply represent a function for handling a window message or for altering a PM control. Almost all of PM's capabilities can be found in use by Workplace Shell. Without a reasonable understanding of PM, you will not be able to fully appreciate the significance of being able to override a particular method that is provided by Workplace Shell.

WINDOWS AND MESSAGES

PM uses a message-based system, wherein its windows and graphical controls react to messages that notify the windows and graphical controls of events that have taken place. The user's input to the system, and events that occur as windows interact with each other, are all converted into messages that windows of PM must answer. An advantage that results from using a message-based system is the ability to change a window's behavior by filtering its messages. PM uses this ability to implement its object-oriented system of handling windows.

Window Classes

PM uses an object-oriented technique to handle a library of window classes. There are over a dozen types of windows, such as buttons, menus, and scroll bars, that are registered public classes accessible to PM programs. A system call is provided to allow PM programs to add to the public classes and to register their own classes. PM uses a similar function call to register its public classes when the OS/2 system is loading.

A window class is identified by a *class name*. The behavior of a window class is defined by how its window procedure handles messages that are sent to it. It is possible to create a new class that is based on an existing window class. This involves a process called subclassing, which is one of the most important features used in PM programming. Many of the example programs in this book illustrate various techniques that can be used to subclass a window. As you become more familiar with PM, you will be able to reuse window classes for new and very different purposes.

Hooks

A *hook* provides a method of altering a function performed by PM that most programs normally do not need to change. Such functions as PM's internal message loops need to run as efficiently as possible, and hooks allow alterations to their data without sending a complex series of messages. To set up a hook, an address to a function that accepts a correct parameter list for the hook is registered with PM. If an internal PM function supports a hook, it will be designed to provide its data to a function that checks for hooks and that passes the data onto duly registered functions.

By using hooks, you can alter the keystrokes that a program receives or change the behavior of a dialog box. Hooks provide inside information about the manner in which PM handles keystrokes, mouse events, message loops, and many other pieces of data. Chapter 21 goes into the use of hooks in greater detail.

COMMON PM PROGRAMMING NOTATION

Throughout the code that makes up a PM program, you will find variable names that begin with a set of lowercase letters. These letters indicate the variable type and conform to a standard style of writing code called "Hungarian Notation." The purpose of this notation is to assist in keeping track of a variable's type and to avoid assigning two variables equal to each other if they have prefixes that do not match. For example, a lowercase "p" prefix indicates that a variable is a pointer. With so many variables used in writing programs, Hungarian Notation provides a helpful way of double checking yourself as you write code.

The idea of Hungarian Notation has been carried through the OS/2 header files, where suggested prefixes for the data structures are placed in comments alongside the `typedef` declarations. It is common practice to simply

TABLE 2.1 Commonly used variable prefixes used in PM code

p	Pointer
hwnd	Handle to a window
hab	Handle to an anchor block
hmq	Handle to a message queue
ptl	POINTL data structure, which stores an *x* and a *y* coordinate
rcl	RECTL data structure, which describes the boundaries of a rectangular area
fnwp	Window procedure
swp	SWP data structure, used to set a window's size and position
clsi	CLASSINFO data structure
fcd	FRAMECDATA data structure
qmsg	QMSG data structure, for storing a message being sent to a window

use a variable's prefix by itself as a variable name for temporary values. Table 2.1 lists many of the common prefixes you will see in PM programs.

CUA CONTROLS

With the introduction of OS/2 Version 2.0, a set of Common User Access (CUA) Controls has been added to PM. The controls provide sliders, notebooks, file dialogs, font dialogs, value sets, and containers. These controls are located in the file PMCTLS.DLL and provide a new extension to PM. You can use these controls in your programs to avoid writing your own dialogs and controls for such commonly performed tasks as prompting the user for the name of a file. Several chapters of this book describe in detail how you can write code to make use of these controls.

WRITING TUTORIALS WITH HELP MANAGER

The OS/2 product includes a tutorial with animation to explain to novices how to use the system. A series of bitmaps showing a hand moving a mouse and dragging objects is presented in the tutorial. The tutorial was written using a new feature of Help Manager called Dynamic Data Formatting (DDF). An entire set of Ddf calls are provided to place animation into help screens and to create stand-alone tutorials.

If you are writing a tutorial, you may want to consider looking into DDF and how an "application-controlled window" can be created. The IPF documentation contains information on how to use the IPF tag language, together with functions that are contained in a program or in a DLL for displaying bitmaps and for changing text. Your help screens can be set up to ask for a name and then to incorporate it into the help screen text.

USING THE C SET/2 COMPILER

The example programs provided in this book were compiled using the IBM C SET/2 compiler. There are many C compilers available for OS/2, and the compiler flags they use probably are different from the C Set/2 compiler flags.

To keep the complexity of compiling example programs to a minimum, as few as possible of the cryptic compiling flags have been used in the example programs that are presented in this book. If you have a C compiler other than C Set/2 compiler, an equivalent compiling flag should be used for the following C Set/2 compiling flags:

- /C+ Compile only, do not perform linking. The default (/C-) compiles and links.
- /Ge- Build a DLL file instead of the default (/Ge+), which builds an EXE file.
- /Gm+ Link the object code with the multithreaded version of the library being used. The default (/Gm-) links the object code with a single-threaded library.
- /Rn- Build the object code as a subsystem without the extra support code needed for the standard libraries.
- /O+ Set optimization on. The default (/O-) is no optimization.
- /Sp1 Pack data on one-byte boundaries. Other options are to pack data using 2-, 3-, or 4-byte boundaries.
- /Ss Accept double slash marks (//) as the beginning of comments. The default is to consider double slashes as a syntax error.
- /W3 Use the highest level of warnings.

CHAPTER 3
The Basic Code Template

Many programmers find it convenient to use code from an existing PM application as a basis for a new program. This technique of reusing code has led to the popularity of tool kits that include a simple program, called a *template*. A template for a PM program typically contains only such code as is needed to set up a standard window. In essence, a PM template is a "stripped down" PM program that a programmer copies and then supplements with code to produce a new application.

Templates give programmers a quick start in developing a new PM application. Each of the example PM programs provided in this book can be used as a template. However, you should keep in mind that the example programs presented herein frequently include extra sections of code that are intended to provide illustrations of specific features of PM and of PM programming.

If you are choosing a PM program for use as a template, it is best to select one that contains as few lines of code as possible, while at the same time providing code that corresponds as closely as possible to what you need to accomplish in order to set up a particular program. Unless a template's code contains almost exactly what you want, it usually is the case that the larger the template you select, the more lines of code you will need to delete or rewrite prior to compiling.

SETTING UP A PROGRAM

When first learning about developing PM applications, a programmer will commonly encounter comparisons between (1) the number of lines of code needed to print the text "hello world" using standard C libraries and (2) the significantly larger number of lines of code needed to display the same text in a PM window. Except for a simple PM function call that causes the text "hello world" to be displayed, the rest of the requisite PM code serves the purposes of setting up and displaying a standard window, within which the text is to be displayed. Such setup and display code can be thought of as constituting a body of "boilerplate" code that is present in almost every PM program.

Templates have become quite popular for use with PM programming due to the presence of essentially standard boilerplate sections of code that are required even in very simple PM programs and are also typically found in relatively complex PM programs. While non-PM programs that are written in C reflect a great diversity of writing styles, PM programs that are written in C often show a high degree of similarity and uniformity of style. The use of templates contributes to the uniformity and similarity of PM code.

PM templates provided with tool kits may vary in the size and number of the C files they use, but, regardless of how a so-called "standard template" is structured, it will almost always execute the following four stages:

- Setting up a message queue
- Registering any needed private window classes
- Creating windows based on public classes or on privately registered classes
- Handling a message loop until asked to stop

While templates often provide good assistance, they do not address all needs. Because the series of functions that a program goes through to register classes and to create windows can be implemented in a great many ways, there is no single template that can describe all of the possible combinations of PM calls that one can use to register classes and to create windows.

The templates you have at hand should not be permitted to dictate how you will write all of your PM programs. An example template is presented in this chapter. Also presented in this chapter are code excerpts that can be used to replace or to supplement code that is used in the template.

AN EXAMPLE TEMPLATE

To begin an exploration of PM programming, a basic code template, called TEMPLATE, is presented below. Figure 3.1 shows a standard window that is created by running the TEMPLATE program. TEMPLATE's source code is quite short and includes only such lines as are needed to create a very plain-looking window with a pair of menu items.

Although the window shown in Figure 3.1 is rather plain, the TEMPLATE program provides an important starting point for use in explaining the events that take place when a very basic PM program creates a window. The TEMPLATE program and accompanying alternative excerpts of code are utilized to explain some of the many options that PM has available to create a window of "standard" appearance.

The templates that are included with commercially available tool kits vary in complexity. They are sometimes divided into multiple C files, and

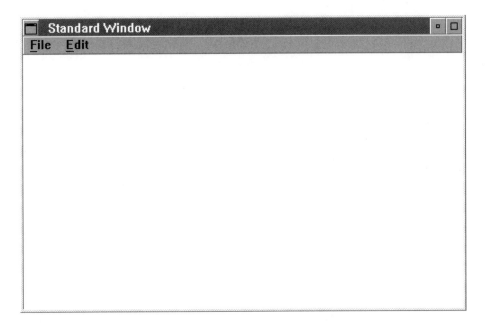

FIGURE 3.1   A TEMPLATE window just opened.

they usually include lines of comments to designate locations where the template code is intended to be supplemented. In contrast, the TEMPLATE program that follows was kept as simple as possible. Only the following six files are needed to compile it:

TEMPLATE.C

```
#define INCL_GPI
#define INCL_WIN
#include <os2.h>
#include "template.h"

/* prototypes */
INT main( VOID );
MRESULT EXPENTRY ClientWndProc( HWND, ULONG, MPARAM, MPARAM );

INT main( VOID )
{
    HAB    hab;
    HMQ    hmq;
    QMSG   qmsg;
    HWND   hwndFrame;
    HWND   hwndClient;
    CHAR   szTitleText[]  = "Standard Window";
    CHAR   szClientClass[] = "Client Window";
```

```
    ULONG flCreateFlags = FCF_TITLEBAR       /* create: title bar control      */
                        | FCF_SYSMENU        /*          system menu control   */
                        | FCF_MENU           /*              action bar         */
                        | FCF_MINMAX         /*              min and max buttons */
                        | FCF_SIZEBORDER     /* draw sizeborders               */
                        | FCF_SHELLPOSITION  /* shell decides window position  */
                        | FCF_TASKLIST       /* title added to switch list     */
                        | FCF_ICON;          /* frame has an icon              */

  hab = WinInitialize( 0 );  /* create anchor block handle for this session */
  hmq = WinCreateMsgQueue( hab, /* create message queue for this thread */
                    0 ); /* default to system queue size */

  WinRegisterClass( hab,               /* anchor block handle */
                    szClientClass,     /* class name */
                    ClientWndProc,     /* pointer to window procedure */
                    0,                 /* class style */
                    0 );               /* number of class data bytes */

  hwndFrame = WinCreateStdWindow(
                    HWND_DESKTOP,      /* parent */
                    WS_VISIBLE,        /* make window visible */
                    &flCreateFlags,    /* creation flags for frame window */
                    szClientClass,     /* client window class name */
                    szTitleText,       /* text placed in the title bar */
                    0,                 /* use default client window style   */
                                       /*   WS_VISIBLE is not needed here */
                    NULLHANDLE,        /* resource ID's are in rc file */
                    ID_FRAMEWND,       /* ID for frame window and its resources */
                    &hwndClient );     /* address to place client window handle */

  if (hwndFrame)
     while (WinGetMsg( hab, &qmsg, NULLHANDLE, 0, 0 ))
        WinDispatchMsg( hab, &qmsg );

  WinDestroyWindow( hwndFrame );    /* clean up */
  WinDestroyMsgQueue( hmq );
  WinTerminate( hab );

  return 0;
} /* end main */


MRESULT EXPENTRY ClientWndProc( HWND hwnd, ULONG msg, MPARAM mp1, MPARAM mp2 )
{
  switch (msg) {

  // place message handling here

  case WM_ERASEBACKGROUND:
     return (MRESULT)TRUE;
  default:
     return WinDefWindowProc( hwnd, msg, mp1, mp2 );
  } /* endswitch */
} /* ClientWndProc */
```

TEMPLATE.H

```
#define ID_FRAMEWND    1
#define MY_PULLDOWN1   101
#define MY_PULLDOWN2   102
#define MY_MENUITEM1   201
#define MY_MENUITEM2   202
#define MY_MENUITEM3   203
#define MY_MENUITEM4   204
#define MY_MENUITEM5   205
#define MY_MENUITEM6   206
```

TEMPLATE.RC

```
#include <os2.h>
#include "template.h"

ICON ID_FRAMEWND template.ico


MENU ID_FRAMEWND
    BEGIN
       SUBMENU "~File", MY_PULLDOWN1
          BEGIN
             MENUITEM "~New",   MY_MENUITEM1
             MENUITEM "~Open",  MY_MENUITEM2
             MENUITEM "~Close", MY_MENUITEM3
          END
       SUBMENU "~Edit", MY_PULLDOWN2
          BEGIN
             MENUITEM "Cu~t\tShift+Delete",    MY_MENUITEM4
             MENUITEM "~Copy\tCtrl+Insert",    MY_MENUITEM5
             MENUITEM "~Paste\tShift+Insert",  MY_MENUITEM6
          END
    END
```

TEMPLATE.DEF

```
NAME      TEMPLATE     WINDOWAPI

DESCRIPTION 'TEMPLATE OS/2 PM Example Program'

STUB        'OS2STUB.EXE'

DATA        MULTIPLE

STACKSIZE   16348
HEAPSIZE    16348

PROTMODE
```

TEMPLATE.MAK

```
all : template.exe

template.exe : template.obj  template.def template.res
        link386 /PM:PM template,,,,template.def;
        rc template.res

template.res : template.rc template.ico template.h
        rc -r template.rc

template.obj : template.c template.h
        icc /C /Ss /W3 .$*.c
```

TEMPLATE.ICO

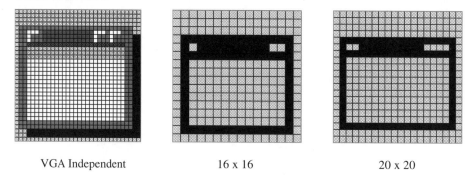

VGA Independent   16 x 16   20 x 20

TEMPLATE.ICO file containing various icons of different sizes.

UNDERSTANDING THE TEMPLATE PROGRAM

To understand the source code that comprises the TEMPLATE program, a few basic concepts, used by substantially all PM programs, need to be explained. While it is easy to oversimplify the content and functions that are associated with the code that comprises PM programs, doing this would constitute a disservice to the reader, for a great many of the features that make PM easier to program would be overlooked.

PM provides so many features that some programmers take the view that a whole new language of terms and expressions has been created just for PM. However, you do not need to learn "a whole new language" in order to make a great deal of powerful use of PM. The most important terms to focus on when learning about PM are those that are used to identify how a basic window is constructed.

PM has over 500 system calls, which can be assembled like building blocks in the programs you write, but if you learn the basics, you will know where to look for a particular API that probably provides the functionality you want. Because there are far too many functions to learn all at once, it is suggested that you begin by acquiring a feel for how PM works. As you advance, learn what you need to know about the APIs that you need to employ to add desired capabilities to your programs.

The Standard Window

The term *standard window* informally has been given a special meaning in the art of PM programming. It refers to a window that uses a *frame window* to give it a "standard" look and "standard" functionality.

A frame window, or *frame*, is one of PM's most interesting and complex classes of windows. A frame provides many of the basic features, such as a title bar, menus, and other controls, that are normally expected to appear in a PM window. Many of these controls actually are windows themselves, which the frame arranges in a manner that will be discussed in Chapter 4.

By using the default behavior of a frame window, a PM application can almost completely ignore the complexities of "how" the frame handles its controls to achieve a standard look and feel. For this reason, most PM programmers write their applications to set up a standard window (thus avoiding working directly with a frame).

It is quite typical for the code of a PM application to work exclusively with a window called the *client window*, which is positioned within the frame (among other standard controls, as is discussed in greater detail in Chapter 4). The client window, or *client*, is usually the largest of a frame's windows. The client provides the environment in which programs such as spreadsheets and word processors display documents to be edited.

Frame Windows

The *frame* surrounds a window's controls, such as its title bar, menus, buttons, and size borders. Except for the size borders, these controls are referred to by the term *frame controls*. As will be explained in greater detail in Chapter 4, each of the frame controls constitutes a separate window that communicates with the frame.

Even though size borders determine the shape and size of the frame window, they are not considered to be frame controls. A frame's size borders do not constitute a window or windows that are separate from the frame, nor do they send messages to the frame. The size borders are simply visible portions of a frame window that are painted and handled by the frame. The frame responds directly to any event that takes place over the size borders.

The Minmax Frame Control

Like size borders, a standard window's minmax button has not been considered to be a frame control. However, the minmax button differs in character from size borders in that the minmax button *does* constitute a separate window and therefore is not painted by the frame. Although it has been rumored that the minmax button is drawn by the frame, that rumor is patently untrue. The minmax button functions exactly like a standard window's system menu. Therefore, in this book, the minmax button is properly referred to as a frame control.

Both the system menu and the minmax button are actually menu windows with bitmaps of selector buttons that constitute menu items. The system menu window has only one item in it. The minmax button will vary in the number of items that are included on its menu, depending on the ability of its associated frame to be minimized or maximized. When a menu item is selected from one of the menu windows used for either the system menu or the minmax button, the appearance of a button being depressed is produced by replacing the button's "unpressed" bitmap with a bitmap of a "pressed" button. Unlike normal bitmap menu items, PM employs special built-in code to handle the replacement of the "unpressed" and "pressed" bitmaps that are used for the system menu and minmax buttons.

The significance of the fact that a minmax button constitutes a frame control has to do with the fact that the minmax button constitutes a window all by itself. The distinction between the frame controls, which are windows, and size borders, which are not windows, becomes important when you consider that any PM window can be resized and repositioned. Like any other window, each of the frame controls can be manipulated and arranged in substantially any preferred manner. However, since frame controls are controlled by the frame, if a nonstandard arrangement of frame controls is to be preserved, a special technique must be used to override the standard way in which the frame tries to position its controls.

Setting Up the Frame Controls

Frame controls often are set up automatically by the frame window. It is not unusual for programmers to take the functionality that is provided by the frame for granted and to write application code exclusively to handle the painting and controlling of the client window.

The client window and all of the frame controls are owned by (and are children of) the frame window. Whenever a standard window is resized, the frame is the window that is being directly changed. When a final size is selected, the frame repositions its children to comply with the new size. The process of changing the positions of a frame's children is called *formatting the frame*. It is this process that prevents the frame's controls from overlapping each other and from overlapping portions of the client window.

Standard windows are so commonly used that PM provides a special function, called `WinCreateStdWindow`, to create a frame window that has a selection of frame controls and an optional client window. The TEMPLATE program uses this API because it promotes simplicity in the required code by providing a large number of useful features with one simple call.

Client Windows

A client window's characteristics usually are so uniquely designed (to serve the needs of a particular application) that none of PM's public classes can be used as a basis for the client window. Therefore, client windows usually are members of a window class that will be privately registered by and for use with a particular program. Registering a private class gives a window total control over how every message that is sent to it is processed. Any unprocessed messages are sent to a default window procedure by a function that is provided by PM. The messages that signify major events, such as the creation of a window (WM_CREATE) or the painting of a window (WM_PAINT), are normally handled entirely by a client window's procedure and do not get forwarded to PM's default procedure.

Because most PM programs are written with their own client window procedure, PM provides special code that helps the frame to work smoothly with the client. Many of the messages that are sent by a frame's controls or by PM are resent to the client window. Sufficient access to the frame's messages is intentionally given to the client so that it can control the entire application's window. While some messages are not reported to the client, most programmers find that the amount of control that PM gives a client window is satisfactory to meet programming needs.

Instead of writing a private class for a client window, one of PM's public classes can be used; however, if a public class is used, the frame's method of handling its messages needs to be changed. PM's window classes, such as its list boxes and entry fields classes, require that their parents communicate with them through a set of special messages. The frame needs to be provided with code that will permit it to handle these special messages; otherwise, problems are likely to arise when the frame receives a series of unexpected and unknown messages.

A technique for modifying a frame to handle a public class as a client window is presented in the next chapter. In the present chapter, procedures that are commonly used in dealing with a standard window are explored.

THE TEMPLATE SOURCE CODE

TEMPLATE creates a standard PM window that includes a client window, title bar, system menu, action bar, size borders, and minmax buttons. By reviewing the content of the file TEMPLATE.C, you will see the APIs that are needed to set up a PM program and to create its application window.

Two functions, called main and ClientWndProc, are used in TEMPLATE.C. When a PM program written in C first starts, a series of PM calls must eventually be made, either directly or indirectly, by the program's main function. TEMPLATE.C's main function contains these required calls and sets up a window that uses ClientWndProc as a *window procedure* for its client window. A window's window procedure defines the methods that the window will use to draw itself and to react to PM messages.

The `ClientWndProc` function is an example of an extremely simple window procedure that draws a neutral-colored background and lets PM handle all other tasks.

WinInitialize

The first call made to PM must be to a function called `WinInitialize`. This API returns a handle to what is known as an *anchor block*. An anchor block is used frequently as a parameter by one or more of PM's functions. An anchor block is supposed to provide needed information about a thread that makes PM calls; however, OS/2 is able to determine the information it needs by referring to the identity of the thread, and therefore does not make use of anchor blocks. Anchor blocks were included in the design of PM principally to support other system architectures that may need additional information to run a ported version of PM.

Many example programs have been published that use a `NULLHANDLE` value in place of a required anchor block handle. This is *not* recommended and clearly offers the potential for causing problems if used with future versions of PM. Although it is tempting to refrain from worrying about the anchor block handle, it is quite simple to write a program to use anchor block handles in the recommended way. As a minimum, a global variable can be used to store and retrieve the anchor block handle when needed.

Besides returning an anchor block handle, `WinInitialize` attends to the setup of a PM environment for a program. If any problems are encountered during a thread's setup, a value of `NULLHANDLE` will be returned. As a part of `WinInitialize`'s function, a check is made to see that a program's stack size is at least as large as the specified minimum stack size. If needed, additional memory is allocated for the stack.

The recommended minimum stack size (16,384 bytes) is larger than the previously recommended size of 8,192 bytes specified for 16-bit PM applications. This recommended minimum stack size should be used because each system call may involve other calls to functions to complete their tasks. Each function call places still more values on a program's stack, so the recommended minimum stack size may genuinely be needed in circumstances that you would not expect to require such a large stack. The size of the stack can be specified in a module definition file (`.DEF` file) or on the command line when linking a program (default for the LINK386 program is 8Kb if size is not specified).

WinCreateMsgQueue

After `WinInitialize` is called, `WinCreateMsgQueue` is used to set up a message queue, which is required for a majority of PM's functions. The second parameter of `WinCreateMsgQueue` specifies the size of the message queue; however, this value normally is set to zero, indicating that a default size (10 messages) is allowed.

Reserving space for only 10 messages may not appear to be enough, especially if you consider that each time the mouse pointer moves across a window, hundreds of WM_MOUSEMOVE messages will be posted. But a message queue of 10 messages does tend to suffice for a normal window.

Mouse events and keyboard strokes are not stored in a PM application's queue. For performance reasons, PM avoids posting mouse and keyboard messages to the queue of a program by conducting a system queue check each time that a program checks its own queue.

Messages concerning timing events, semaphores, and selected menus are stored in a program's message queue. Because messages such as those from a timer have a potential to flood the program's message queue, when a new timer message is posted to a queue, any unprocessed timer messages are removed.

Many PM programs do not bother with setting up extra threads. However, if one or more extra threads are set up, keep in mind that each thread can set up its own message queue. For a thread to have the ability to create a window, it must have a message queue and be able to handle the dispatching of messages that are posted to the message queue.

WinRegisterClass

When a message queue is set up, window classes needed by a program are then registered by calling WinRegisterClass. TEMPLATE registers a private class for its client window, as shown in the following excerpt of code from TEMPLATE.C:

```
WinRegisterClass( hab,              /* anchor block handle */
                  szClientClass,    /* class name */
                  ClientWndProc,    /* pointer to window procedure */
                  0,                /* class style */
                  0 );              /* number of class data bytes */
```

This API requires a class name (szClientClass) and an address of a window procedure (ClientWndProc). The class name is entered into a hash table that is used by PM to search window classes quickly for the associated window procedure and for other needed information. A class name can take substantially any desired form, but it should avoid taking the form of a string that is composed of a pound sign (#) followed by up to five digits. Such a format is used by PM's public classes. If you avoid using this public class format for your private class names, potential problems will be avoided. From the TEMPLATE.C code provided earlier in this chapter, the szClientClass string "Client Window" was arbitrarily chosen.

If you were to register a private class with a name that matched the name of a public class, the public class would be altered privately for your program to use the window procedure address that you specify. Values supplied in the OS/2 header files and starting with a "WC_" prefix should be used if you wish to identify a public class. For example, WC_FRAME is used for the frame class, and WC_TITLEBAR is used for the title bar class.

In TEMPLATE's call to register a client, two zero values trail the list of parameters. The first zero indicates a default class style that is to be used for any window created that is of the szClientClass. The second zero is a parameter of WinRegisterClass that indicates the number of class data bytes the specified class requires for information that is unique to windows of the class szClientClass. Since the client class selected does not need any space reserved, a value of zero is used here.

If a class style value called CS_PUBLIC is to be used with WinRegister-Class, it must be registered when PM is loaded—in which case its window procedure must be set out in a DLL, as will be explained in Chapter 23, when the subject of registering a public class is addressed. For public classes, WinRegisterClass must be called while PM is being loaded and before it has created the desktop and other windows.

WinCreateStdWindow

All of the PM calls made thus far have been for TEMPLATE's one call to the API WinCreateStdWindow. This API accepts a relatively long list of parameters, as the following excerpt code demonstrates:

```
hwndFrame = WinCreateStdWindow(
        HWND_DESKTOP,      /* parent */
        WS_VISIBLE,        /* make window visible */
        &flCreateFlags,    /* creation flags for frame window */
        szClientClass,     /* client window class name */
        szTitleText,       /* text placed in the title bar */
        0,                 /* use default client window style    */
                    /*   WS_VISIBLE is not needed here */
        NULLHANDLE,        /* resource ID's are in rc file */
        ID_FRAMEWND,       /* ID for frame window and its resources */
        &hwndClient );     /* address to place client window handle */
```

The preceding call to WinCreateStdWindow returns a handle to a standard window's frame that contains a client of the class szClientClass. Any messages that need to be sent to the client will be received by a window procedure ClientWndProc which was registered with the client's class name. A message sent to the frame is received by a window procedure of PM that handles the frame class. During the processing of WinCreateStdWindow two messages, namely WM_CREATE and WM_ADJUSTWINDOWPOS, are sent to the frame and client windows. The ClientWndProc calls a default window procedure for each of these messages. This is in contrast to WM_CREATE, which, when sent to the frame, will initiate a complex series of actions.

Frame Creation Flags

When the frame receives a `WM_CREATE` message, it creates its frame controls and loads resources that are specified by the frame creation flags (FCF) in `flCreateFlags`. The FCF flags `FCF_TITLEBAR`, `FCF_SYSMENU`, `FCF_MENU`, `FCF_MINMAX`, `FCF_VERTSCROLL`, and `FCF_HORZSCROLL` are available to create frame controls. The `FCF_SIZEBORDER` flag tells the frame to expand its size around the frame controls in order to draw size borders of the frame.

While many FCF values are available, not all of them indicate the creation of a control. For instance, `FCF_ICON` and `FCF_ACCELTABLE` inform the frame to load and use an icon and an accelerator table, respectively. The value `FCF_TASKLIST` adds the name of the window to the Window List and sets the text for the frame's title bar.

TEMPLATE's use of the flags `FCF_ICON` and `FCF_MENU` specifies that resources exist and are to be used during the creation of the frame window. These resources are described in the `TEMPLATE.RC` file, and they all have the same ID number, namely `ID_FRAMEWND`. (Resources can have the same ID number as long as they are different types. An ID number and its type, taken together, uniquely identify a resource that is stored in an executable module.)

`TEMPLATE.EXE` is built with the compiled resources for an icon and menu. A value of `NULLHANDLE` is set in the foregoing `WinCreateStdWindow` call to indicate that `TEMPLATE.EXE`, rather than a DLL, should be searched for resources.

A frame will search one location for resources if it is given a resource ID. In the foregoing `WinCreateStdWindow` call, the resource ID is set equal to `ID_FRAMEWND`. Like the ID numbers that are used for the frame controls, the frame window can have an ID number of its own. The `WinCreateStdWindow` call happens to use the value `ID_FRAMEWND` as both a resource ID and as an ID for the frame. The frame ID could have been set to zero or to any other value; however, the approach described here is the way `WinCreateStdWindow` sets up a "standard" window.

Writing the Code for an FCF Flag

PM provides APIs that can be used to perform functions that are represented by each of the FCF values. It is easier to include FCF flags that make use of code that already has been compiled into the frame window's `WM_CREATE`-handling functions. Unless the resource to be used is not known when a window is created (such as a user-defined icon), always consider using the appropriate FCF flag.

The only other situation in which you are likely to encounter a need to use equivalent code to replace an FCF flag is in the handling of `FCF_ACCELTABLE`, `FCF_ICON`, and `FCF_MENU` for a dialog box. For reasons that are explained in greater detail in Chapter 5, these FCF flags cannot be used for dialog boxes because, unlike the other FCF flags, they depend on the loading of resources.

The FCF_ICON Flag

Loading an icon (FCF_ICON) could have been implemented in TEMPLATE by sending a WM_SETICON message with a handle to an icon returned from WinLoadPointer, as is illustrated in the following code:

```
HPOINTER hIcon;

hIcon = WinLoadPointer( HWND_DESKTOP, NULLHANDLE, ID_FRAMEWND), NULL );
WinSendMsg( hwndFrame, WM_SETICON, (MPARAM)hIcon, NULL );
```

Before the program terminates, a call should be made to WinDestroyPointer to release the resource. If a window had exclusive use of the icon, WinDestroyPointer would normally appear in code that is used to process the window's WM_DESTROY message.

The FCF_TASKLIST Flag

If your application needs control over the text that appears in the title bar and in the Window List, you can write code to replace the use of FCF_TASKLIST. Adding a window's name to the window list can be performed by making a call to WinAddSwitchEntry, as is illustrated in the following example:

```
SWCNTRL swctl;

swctl.hwnd = hwndFrame;
swctl.hwndIcon = NULLHANDLE;
swctl.hprog = NULLHANDLE;
swctl.idProcess = 0;
swctl.idSession = 0;
swctl.uchVisibility = SWL_VISIBLE;
swctl.fbJump = SWL_JUMPABLE;
strcpy( swctl.szSwtitle, "My Window List Title" );
WinAddSwitchEntry( &swctl );
```

This code places the string "My Window List Title" in the Window List, which shows the running programs. The SWCNTRL structure reserves enough space for swctl.szSwtitle to have a maximum length of MAXNAMEL (plus 1 for the terminating NULL character). If the window's name already is present in the Window List, WinChangeSwitchEntry needs to be used in place of WinAddSwitchEntry.

If you also need to control the text that appears in the title bar, the shell provides a suggested title that can be retrieved by WinQuerySessionTitle or its old equivalent `WinQueryTaskTitle`. The shell's title must be queried before the title bar is created, otherwise these two APIs will simply return the text that is contained in the title bar. `WinQuerySessionTitle` is the recommended API to use because it employs an anchor block handle as its first parameter. The rest of the parameters are identical to the parameters used for `WinQueryTaskTitle`.

After getting the shell's suggested title, create the application's window and title bar. Then make a call to `WinSetWindowText` in the manner that is shown in the code that follows:

```
CHAR  szTitleText[MAXNAMEL + 1];

WinQuerySessionTitle( hab,                      /* anchor block handle */
                      0,                        /* default to this session */
                      szTitleText,              /* address of string buffer */
                      sizeof(szTitleText) );    /* length of string buffer */

// Create the frame window (hwndFrame) with the title bar

WinSetWindowText( hwndFrame, szTitleText );  /* change the title bar text */
```

The FCF_SHELLPOSITION Flag

During the creation of a window, its height and width are always set to zero. While the size and position of a window can be specified in `WinCreateStdWindow`, TEMPLATE nonetheless places zeros where they are specified, because it uses `FCF_SHELLPOSITION`. At the end of the creation of TEMPLATE's window, the frame is set to a position that is specified by the shell. You can query and modify the shell's suggested position by calling `WinQueryTaskSizePos` and `WinSetWindowPos`. The code excerpt that follows uses this technique, which can be placed in `TEMPLATE.C` just after the call to `WinCreateStdWindow`:

```
SWP swp;  /* add a declaration for swp */

WinQueryTaskSizePos( hab, 0, &swp );

WinSetWindowPos( hwndFrame,          /* change the frame window's position */
                 HWND_TOP,           /* put window on top */
                 swp.x, swp.y,       /* position of lower left corner */
                 swp.cx, swp.cy,     /* width and height */
                 SWP_ACTIVATE        /* make window active */
                 | SWP_ZORDER        /* do not ignore HWND_TOP */
                 | SWP_MOVE          /* do not ignore swp.x and swp.y */
                 | SWP_SIZE          /* do not ignore swp.cx and swp.cy */
                 | SWP_SHOW );       /* set WS_VISIBLE and show window */
```

While the querying function can be carried out before any windows are created, `WinSetWindowPos` must be performed after window creation. If you are going to use this technique, you should remove `WS_VISIBLE` and `FCF_SHELLPOSITION` from the source code of TEMPLATE. The presence within your code of these two functions ought not cause problems; thus, if you want to experiment, you can leave them in. By leaving them in, you will see `WinCreateStdWindow` create and, because of `WS_VISIBLE` display, TEMPLATE's window, followed by a sudden "jerking" movement of the window.

The movement of the window results from the `WinQueryTaskSizePos` call and the `WinSetWindowPos` call both making the same calls when `FCF_SHELLPOSITION` is used. Because an application can create two or more main windows, `WinQueryTaskSizePos` tries to prevent overlap by incrementing the last suggested position that it has provided. (As the suggested window positions move across the screen, the position selected will eventually be reset back to the very left of the screen.) When viewed during operation, a sudden jerking movement is what one tends to see.

Leaving `WS_VISIBLE` in the code you use will result in a window being displayed before it has been properly positioned. A flag in `WinSetWindowPos`, called `WM_SHOW`, would have caused the window to be displayed *after* it had been properly placed. Including `WS_VISIBLE` and `FCF_SHELLPOSITION` in the foregoing code causes a wasted series of system calls to be made, and the end result does not have a very professional appearance.

Why Not an FCF_CLIENT Flag?

Every child window of the frame has its own FCF flag except the client window. With all of the FCF flags available, why is there no `FCF_CLIENT` creation flag?

The `WinCreateStdWindow` function was intended to provide an easy-to-use solution for creating a frame having a client window. To implement an `FCF_CLIENT` flag, more data, such as the client's class name, would have to be provided to the frame window for it to process its `WM_CREATE` message. If a programmer also wanted to set other features of a client window, such as window style, the `WM_CREATE` message would need to be supplemented with even more data.

The PM solution is to provide the `WinCreateStdWindow` API, which accepts the client's class name and window style. Default values are used for such other properties as can be set for the client window.

WinCreateWindow and WinCreateStdWindow

Inside the code of PM is a function that is so basic that PM itself uses it. The function implements the API called `WinCreateWindow`—an API that can be used to create every window that appears on the desktop. Frames, clients, menus, title bars, scroll bars, and many other classes of windows can all be created if the proper class name and control data are set.

WinCreateStdWindow actually calls WinCreateWindow twice; and, if WS_VISIBLE is set in the frame's window style, WinShowWindow is called. The following code illustrates the inner workings of the WinCreateStdWindow call made in TEMPLATE.C:

```
FRAMECDATA fcd;

fcd.cb = sizeof(FRAMECDATA);   /* length of structure */
fcd.flCreateFlags =  FCF_TITLEBAR       /* create: title bar control    */
                  | FCF_SYSMENU        /*             system menu control  */
                  | FCF_MENU           /*              action bar */
                  | FCF_MINMAX         /*              min and max buttons  */
                  | FCF_SIZEBORDER     /* draw sizeborder   */
                  | FCF_SHELLPOSITION  /* shell decides window position */
                  | FCF_TASKLIST       /* title added to switch list    */
                  | FCF_ICON;          /* frame has an icon  */
fcd.hmodResources = NULLHANDLE;   /* refer to this exe file */
fcd.idResources   = ID_FRAMEWND;  /* identifier for the frame */

hwndFrame   = WinCreateWindow(
            HWND_DESKTOP,     /* parent window is the desktop */
            WC_FRAME,         /* use public frame class */
            szTitleText,      /* text added to title bar */
            0,                /* window style */
            0, 0, 0, 0,       /* ignored, FCF_SHELLPOSITION was set */
            NULLHANDLE,       /* no owner window */
            HWND_TOP,         /* place on top of Desktop's children */
            ID_FRAMEWND,      /* ID number for frame resources */
            &fcd,             /* data unique for frame windows */
            NULL );           /* no presentation parameters */

hwndClient = WinCreateWindow(
            hwndFrame,        /* parent window is the frame */
            szClientClass,    /* use privately registered client class */
            NULL,             /* window name not used by client */
            0,                /* window style */
            0, 0, 0, 0,       /* ignored, client window */
            hwndFrame,        /* owner window is the frame */
            HWND_BOTTOM,      /* standard z-order for a client window */
            FID_CLIENT,       /* ID number recognized by the frame */
            NULL,             /* no control data */
            NULL );           /* no presentation parameters */

WinShowWindow( hwndFrame, TRUE );  /* show the frame window */
```

The only things that are skipped in the code just listed are error checking (to see that the frame was created) and a check to determine whether the WS_VISIBLE flag is turned on or off. If WS_VISIBLE is not set, the call to WinShowWindow is skipped.

One of the aspects to keep in mind in creating any window is the question of when to make it visible. Many of the examples shown in later chapters depend on their windows not being displayed until they have been modified. In many cases, if a window were displayed before modifications were complete, the window would appear incorrectly, because its frame formatting or some other aspect was completed too soon for the modifications to take effect.

WS_VISIBLE

WS_VISIBLE is the only window style (WS) flag that has been used so far. There are several class styles (CS flags), which are used in combination to form a value that is ORed with the WS flags that are used in the window style. The CS flags that are registered with WinRegisterClass define a default style regardless of whether a window style of zero was used. Because a window class cannot be given a default class style to make it visible, a CS_VISIBLE flag is not included. As is shown by the "inner workings" of WinCreateStdWindow (see the code example just presented), a CS_VISIBLE style would cause problems by allowing a class of windows to have a default style that makes the windows visible during the time they are being created.

When a window is created, a WM_ADJUSTWINDOWPOS message is sent after WM_CREATE. When the frame window is not visible, WM_ADJUSTWINDOWPOS is ignored. If WS_VISIBLE is set, the frame will respond to the message by formatting its frame controls to fit within the borders of the frame window. If a client window is created after the WM_ADJUSTWINDOWPOS message is sent, the frame will not be aware of the existence of the client until the frame is formatted again. A WM_UPDATEFRAME could be sent to notify the frame of the existence of a new child window. Alternatively, WinSetWindowPos could be used to force the frame to format its child windows once again.

Message Loops

After TEMPLATE has created a standard window, a while loop is used to call an API named WinGetMsg. This loop is known as a *message loop*. It handles messages that are posted to it by calling WinDispatchMsg. The message loop ends when a WM_QUIT message is posted and WinGetMsg responds by returning FALSE, thereby breaking the loop.

WinGetMsg

One of the least explained API calls in PM, and yet one of the most important, is WinGetMsg. This API not only receives messages that are posted to a program's queue but also handles many other details for a program. Since many PM programmers would cringe at seeing yet another rendition of the difference between "sending" and "posting" messages, the following section is presented simply to point out the many actions that take place when WinGetMsg is called.

A thing to keep in mind in reviewing the sections that follow is that WinGetMsg not only "gets" posted messages but also provides a way for a window procedure to handle the messages that are "sent."

Sending and Posting Messages

`WinSendMsg` and `WinPostMsg` are two of the most commonly used PM calls for sending or posting a message to a window. A message can be sent to a window procedure directly or can be *posted* to a program's message queue. When `WinSendMsg` is called, it will wait for a reply from the window to which it has sent a message. `WinPostMsg` does not wait for a reply; rather, it simply places its message into the message queue of the window.

PM associates a window and a message queue by means of a thread that created both the window and its message queue. For a thread to have created a window it must also have created a message queue. TEMPLATE only has one thread, and its message queue will receive all messages that are posted to its standard window. PM allows other threads to create windows; however, they, too, must create their own message queues.

When `WinSendMsg` is used to communicate with a window of another thread or with another running program, the calling thread is suspended until the receiving thread that owns the window gives a reply. The reason for suspending the calling thread is that the receiving thread has exclusive access to the code that handles its windows. Suspension of the calling thread ensures that it waits for a response, and it saves CPU cycles while the thread waits. A thread that uses `WinSendMsg` to provide one of its own window procedures with a message will simply be making a function call to the window procedure's address. In such a case, no threads are suspended to wait for a reply.

Using WinGetMsg to Run a Message Loop

Since a thread has exclusive access to the data and the code that handles a window and its message queue, the thread must spend its time running both its message loop (to handle posted messages) and its window procedures (to receive messages that were sent directly to the window procedure).

In order for PM to use an API such as `WinSendMsg` to send messages, it has to be able to "grab" control of a thread that has exclusive access to its window procedures. When a thread makes a call to `WinGetMsg` in its message loop, PM takes control of the thread and not only returns a posted message but also handles such messages as may have been sent to one of the thread's window procedures.

ERROR CHECKING

While you experiment with example PM programs, you might add a frame creation flag and forget to add its associated resource to the resource file. For instance, you might add `FCF_MENU` to the list of flags and forget to copy a menu template into your program's RC file. When the frame is being created, it will search for a menu template and, not finding one, will return an error.

If an error is encountered by one of PM's `Win` APIs, a value of `FALSE` will be returned. In `TEMPLATE.C`, only one line of code is included to check for an error when TEMPLATE sets up its application window. The line of code is located just before the message loop starts and consists of the `if` statement shown here:

```
if (hwndFrame)
    while (WinGetMsg( hab, &qmsg, NULLHANDLE, 0, 0 ))
        WinDispatchMsg( hab, &qmsg );
```

The `if` statement checks to assure that the handle of the frame window is not `NULL`. If it is `NULL`, the frame window was not created, and the program should not be permitted to enter the message loop.

Without a window for the user to close, a `WM_QUIT` message cannot be posted to the message queue. `WM_QUIT` is posted when a `WM_CLOSE` message is sent to the frame, indicating that the user wishes to close the window. Without a `WM_QUIT` message, the program will be stuck in its message loop with no visible window or mention in PM's switch list. The only ways out of this are to send a message to the thread or to kill the thread's process. While utilities can be written to do these things, many programmers will find themselves shutting down their systems to kill the program. To prevent such a nuisance, a simple `if` statement is added to check the existence of a frame handle before entering the message loop. By this arrangement, if a mistake prevents the frame from being created, the program gracefully exits.

CHANGING HOW PM SIZES AND POSITIONS WINDOWS

While the manner in which `FCF_SHELLPOSITION` can be implemented with two PM calls has been explained, many programs require more than just the standard size and position that are used by TEMPLATE's window. The sections that follow present ways to customize the sizes and positions of windows.

WinSetWindowPos

The `WinSetWindowPos` function can be used as one of the APIs that implements code to emulate the use of an `FCF_SHELLPOSITION` flag. The `WinSetWindowPos` function uses a set of "SWP" flags to specify which properties of a window are to be changed. In Table 3.1, the SWP flags are listed, and their relationship to the parameters used in `WinSetWindowPos` is described.

When `WinSetWindowPos` is called to manipulate a window, the API goes through its given list of SWP flags and removes any flags that will not change the window. If the `SWP_SIZE` flag is set, and if the width and height that are set out in the parameter list are found to be the same as the window's present

TABLE 3.1   Description of SWP flags available for use in `WinSetWindowPos`

`SWP_ACTIVATE`	Make the window active.
`SWP_DEACTIVATE`	Deactivate the window.
`SWP_HIDE`	Make the window invisible.
`SWP_MINIMIZE/` `SWP_MAXIMIZE`	Minimize/maximize the window. `SWP_MOVE` and `SWP_SIZE` are required
`SWP_MOVE`	Change the position of window's lower left corner to coordinate (x,y).
`SWP_NOADJUST`	When resizing the window, do not send it a `WM_ADJUSTWINDOWPOS`.
`SWP_RESTORE`	Change the window from a minimized or maximized state to its restored position. `SWP_MOVE` and `SWP_SIZE` are not needed, unless you wish to specify a restored position.
`SWP_SHOW`	Make the window visible on the desktop.
`SWP_SIZE`	Change the window size using parameters width and height.
`SWP_ZORDER`	Change the window's Z-order.

size, there is no need to go through the series of messages to alter the window's size. In this case, the `SWP_SIZE` flag is removed so that the specified width and height are ignored.

A common misuse of `WinSetWindowPos` arises when `WinCreateWindow` is called to set up a frame window followed by a client window. While it is tempting to believe that code is needed to position the client between the size borders of the frame, the frame handles this automatically when the frame is formatted. Even if the client is not visible, the frame will set its position and make it visible when the frame is displayed for the first time.

WinShowWindow

The `WinShowWindow` can show or hide a window and its children, depending on a Boolean value that is used as its second parameter. The following is an example of calling `WinShowWindow`:

```
WinShowWindow( hwnd, TRUE );  /* show the window */
```

If the second parameter were `FALSE`, the window (hwnd) would be made invisible. It is interesting to note that `WinShowWindow` is nothing more than a call to `WinSetWindowPos` with either `SWP_SHOW` or `SWP_HIDE` being used appropriately. The following code performs the same function as showing a window with `WinShowWindow`:

```
WinSetWindowPos( hwnd, NULLHANDLE, 0, 0, 0, 0, SWP_SHOW );
```

Maximizing and Minimizing Windows

It is not possible to set flags to create a frame window in a maximized or minimized state with `WinCreateStdWindow` or `WinCreateWindow`. If you try to use the window styles `WS_MAXIMIZE` and `WS_MINIMIZE`, these styles will be removed from the window style as PM creates the window.

To have TEMPLATE's window appear in a maximized state, remove `WS_VISIBLE` from the window style and add the following code after the `WinCreateStdWindow` call has been made:

```
SWP swp;   /* add a declaration for swp */

/* get the window position when restored */
WinQueryWindowPos( hwndFrame, &swp );

/* Make the window maximized */
WinSetWindowPos( hwndFrame,            /* change the frame window's position */
              NULLHANDLE,              /* ignored, SWP_ZORDER not set */
              swp.x, swp.y,            /* position of lower left corner */
              swp.cx, swp.cy,          /* width and height */
              SWP_MAXIMIZE             /* make window maximized */
              | SWP_MOVE               /* do not ignore swp.x and swp.y */
              | SWP_SIZE               /* do not ignore swp.cx and swp.cy */
              | SWP_SHOW );            /* set WS_VISIBLE and show window */
```

In the code excerpt just presented, the parameters for the size and position specify how the window is to appear as if it were restored. The `FCF_SHELLPOSITION` could have been removed to allow `WinQueryWindowPos` to be replaced with `WinQueryTaskSizePos`.

If you wish to have the window appear minimized, simply replace the `SWP_MAXIMIZE` with `SWP_MINIMIZE`. To restore the window, make a call to `WinSetWindowPos` as shown in the following example:

```
WinSetWindowPos( hwndFrame,            /* change the frame window's position */
              NULLHANDLE,              /* ignored, SWP_ZORDER not set */
              0, 0,                    /* position ignored */
              0, 0,                    /* width and height ignored */
              SWP_RESTORE );           /* restore the window */
```

WinCalcFrameRect

There is a relationship between the size of the frame and client windows. `WinCalcFrameRect` calculates the size of one of these windows, given the size of the other.

If you want to change the size of the frame to have a client window of a particular size and shape, the `WinCalcFrameRect` API can calculate the size and position needed for a frame to surround a client window. The following code uses `WinCalcFrameRect` to set TEMPLATE's frame into a shape that makes the client window a square:

```
SWP swp;        /* add a declarations for swp and rcl */
RECTL rcl;

WinQueryWindowPos( hwndClient, &swp );

WinSetRectEmpty( hab, &rcl ); /* clear rcl structure */

/* get the minimum of the client's height or width */
if (swp.cx > swp.cy) {
   rcl.xRight = swp.cy;
   rcl.yTop   = swp.cy;
} else {
   rcl.xRight = swp.cx;
   rcl.yTop   = swp.cx;
}

WinCalcFrameRect( hwndFrame, &rcl, FALSE ); /* get the size of the frame */

WinSetWindowPos( hwndFrame,          /* change the frame window's position */
                 NULLHANDLE,         /* ignored, SWP_ZORDER not set */
                 0, 0,               /* position ignored, SWP_MOVE not set */
                 rcl.xRight - rcl.xLeft,  /* new width  */
                 rcl.yTop - rcl.yBottom,  /* new width  */
                 SWP_SIZE            /* do not ignore width and height */
                 | SWP_SHOW );       /* set WS_VISIBLE and show window */
```

To use the code set out here, insert it after `WinCreateStdWindow`, and remove the `WS_VISIBLE` flag from `WinCreateStdWindow`. Do not remove `FCF_SHELLPOSTION` from the TEMPLATE program, because the flag sets a window size and position for the TEMPLATE window. The above code assumes that the window has already been given a size and position.

`WinCalcFrameRect`'s third parameter indicates which window's shape is to be calculated. In the code shown in this section, a value of FALSE is used to indicate that the frame's shape is to be calculated. The FALSE value also indicates that the second parameter (`&rcl`) points to a structure that describes the client area's shape.

The example code presented here is concerned only with changing the width and height of the frame and client. The values in the `rcl` variable describe a client window that has its lower left corner at coordinates (0,0) and its upper right corner at coordinates at (`swp.cy,swp.cy`) or (`swp.cx.swp.cx`), depending on which of the two values of `swp.cy` and `swp.cx` is the minimum.

CHAPTER 4
Getting a Handle on PM Windows

In the previous chapter, a technique for creating windows was described that will satisfy the needs of most applications. However, if you want to have more control over the way your windows look and function, you will want to make direct calls to `WinCreateWindow`.

During the writing of PM programs, you will probably find it handy to use a utility that lists all of the windows that currently comprise your PM desktop, together with a list of the class names and positions of such windows. When experimenting with and changing the code of a sample program, one commonly wants to see this information. Moreover, information of this type is especially helpful to have at hand during the debugging of code.

An example PM program, called WINLIST, is discussed in this chapter. It is a utility program that can be used to display desktop window information in a list box. WINLIST is a short but capable utility and is compiled from code that provides a number of examples of how "nonstandard" window code is created using `WinCreateWindow`. The source code from which the WINLIST utility is compiled is set out in the latter half of this chapter. Portions of the WINLIST source code provide examples that illustrate such techniques as programming a list box and registering a private version of the frame class.

THE WINLIST PROGRAM

As is depicted in Figure 4.1, the WINLIST program starts by displaying what looks to be a standard window having vertical and horizontal scroll bars. However, the client area of this newly opened window is, in actuality, a list box window.

After the WINLIST program starts, the list box window will contain one item labeled "<Desktop Window>" followed by the desktop's class name,

FIGURE 4.1   A WINLIST window that has just been opened.

position, width, and height, as is shown in Figure 4.1. By double clicking on the one listed item, descriptions of the desktop's children are added to the list. Each of these added items can also be expanded by double clicking on them to add descriptions of any children they may have to the display. A typical expanded WINLIST listing is shown in Figure 4.2.

The WINLIST program uses only a selected few of the APIs that have the `WinQuery` prefix. Thus, the resulting display includes only the text, class name, size, and position of each window for which information is displayed. Because PM provides over 50 functions to query different properties of a window, WIN-LIST sets out only a fraction of the information that could be made available. Nonetheless, the WINLIST utility serves nicely as an illustration to help explain a number of points, including how PM handles its hierarchy of windows.

PM'S WINDOW HIERARCHY

PM controls the order in which windows are stacked on top of each other. The hierarchy of PM's windows is called the "Z-order," referring to an imaginary "z-axis" that extends perpendicular to the plane of the screen. The position that a particular window occupies along the z-axis (that is, the Z-order) determines the order in which windows are drawn above and below the particular window.

PM always maintains the desktop as the "lowermost" or "bottommost" window. When referring to a group of windows that have a common "parent," the terms "child," "children," and "siblings" often are used. The parent–child

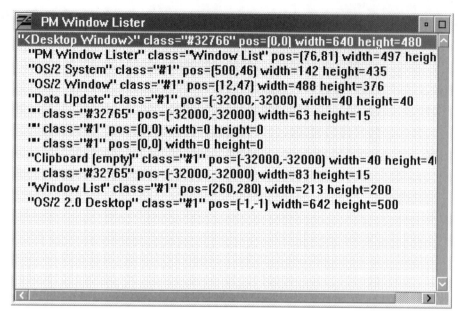

FIGURE 4.2 An expanded WINLIST listing.

relationship will be mentioned many times when dealing with PM programs, as will sibling peer-to-peer relationships.

The functions `WinCreateWindow` and `WinSetWindowPos` accept a parameter that sets a Z-order for the display of associated child and parent windows. A window's Z-order can be set at the time of creation of the window and changed when needed. The only windows that have a Z-order that cannot be changed by a simple call to `WinSetWindowPos` are a frame's control windows.

All of the frame controls of a window, such as the window's title bar and system menu, constitute children of the frame window and have a particular Z-order, which is maintained by PM. Although the frame controls are positioned such that they do not overlap, they do not all coexist in a common plane; rather, the Z-order determines the arrangement of these items in layers, like transparencies overlaid one atop another on an overhead projector.

The character of the Z-order of the components of a PM desktop can easily be determined by using the WINLIST utility. By double clicking on the item that describes the WINLIST window itself, one can view a list of frame controls that make up WINLIST and the order in which they are arranged.

Public Window Classes

All of PM's class names follow the format of a pound sign followed by up to five digits. WINLIST's window contains four child windows. The first three of these children are the title bar, system menu, and minmax buttons. The client window is the fourth—and always last—in the list.

TABLE 4.1 Some of PM's control classes and their associated strings

Commonly Used WC Values	Strings Displayed by WINLIST
WC_BUTTON	#3
WC_CONTAINER	#37
WC_FRAME	#1
WC_LISTBOX	#7
WC_MENU	#4
WC_TITLEBAR	#9

PM has over a dozen public window classes. In Table 4.1, a list is provided of some of PM's window classes and class name strings that typically can be identified by using the WINLIST program. The class name strings that appear in the right column of Table 4.1 may differ in future versions of PM. Thus, Table 4.1 should be regarded as providing an example of a typical display that may result from use of the WINLIST program.

If you use WINLIST to view the children of a frame, you will note that PM places client windows at the bottom of the list of frame controls. PM preserves this default order each time a frame window is resized or repositioned. The reason for the default order is to ensure that, as a display is being redrawn, it will be redrawn in a logical manner. Because frame controls, such as the title bar and system menu, can redraw themselves quickly, it makes sense for these items to be redrawn first. Because client windows tend to be among the slowest of a frame's children to redraw themselves, it makes sense to redraw these items last. If a reverse order were to be adopted that caused the client windows to be redrawn before the frame controls, areas where frame controls are to appear in the resulting display might appear empty for longer than is desirable.

The Z-order determines the order in which windows will be painted. Client windows are arranged in a Z-order listing that calls for frame controls to be drawn first and for client windows to be drawn last. PM's Z-order for drawing a frame's controls can be changed, but not by a simple call to `WinSetWindowPos`. Changes made to a frame control's Z-order, which are typically are made by rearranging its siblings, are undone when the frame window is resized or repositioned.

While the manner in which frame controls are formatted will be discussed later, you can use the WINLIST utility to view the many different windows that make up what you may have thought were "simple" application windows.

CREATING YOUR OWN CLASSES OF WINDOWS

Creating a standard window with `WinCreateStdWindow` requires that its frame window be a member of PM's frame window class. By using `WinCreateWindow` as an alternative API, your programs can utilize any needed window class and can thereby eliminate many lines of code that otherwise would be needed to get around limitations that are associated with the `WinCreateStdWindow` API.

The application window that is displayed by WINLIST is an instance of a privately registered class. Unlike a public window class, only the WINLIST program has access to this new class. All other running programs are unaware that this private class has been registered.

In the WINLIST utility, the public frame window class is used as a starting point for creating a new, privately registered WINLIST class. The new class has standard frame controls that include a system menu, a title bar, a minimize button, a maximize button, and size borders. What makes WINLIST "nonstandard" is that a list box is created as the client window and is set up during the processing of the frame's `WM_CREATE` message. An item that includes size and position information about the desktop window is added to the list box before the processing of `WM_CREATE` is completed.

CHANGING THE FRAME WINDOW

Because WINLIST constructs its windows by using a list box as a client, the code that comprises the WINLIST utility requires a modified frame window that knows how to handle a list box.

List boxes are controlled by messages that are sent to and from their parents. A list box needs to receive messages in order to initially place items in its list, and it sends back messages to report on any actions that a user might have taken to manipulate the listed items. Messages from a list box are sent in the form of `WM_CONTROL` messages. A parent window interprets messages from a list box and sends messages back to the list box.

PM's public frame class does not expect to receive messages from a list box. By default, PM's public frame class will ignore any `WM_CONTROL` messages that it receives from a list box, by returning a zero value. When assembling nonstandard application windows from PM's public classes, it is important to understand how they interact with their incoming and outgoing messages.

Some of PM's windows use `WM_COMMAND` messages instead of `WM_CONTROL` messages. If one of these windows were to be made into a frame's client window, the frame might mistake the client's `WM_COMMAND` messages as having originated with one of its frame controls, such as a system menu or an action bar. The frame expects to receive `WM_COMMAND` messages only from its controls. By default, the frame will handle `WM_COMMAND` messages by resending them to the client window for further processing (even though the client window that receives the resent message may be the entity that originated the message).

Problems encountered with messages are usually resolved by modifying the way in which the frame handles its messages. For example, message handling by the frame will need to take into account such situations as the WINLIST program, wherein a list box constitutes the client window. Assembling components of various windows of PM to create nonstandard application windows is a proper and very efficient way of writing PM programs. The way WINLIST changes its frame window to deal with problems that result from message handling is by registering a private frame class derived from PM's class of frame windows.

WHY USE A PRIVATE CLASS FOR A FRAME WINDOW?

A window that bases its behavior on another class is referred to as a "subclass." WINLIST's new frame class is an example of a subclass, because its behavior is based on (that is derived from) the behavior of the frame window class.

There are many ways in which the behavior of WINLIST's frame window could have been changed. Registering a new class is just one of the techniques that could have been used. Another way to create a subclass is by first creating a normal frame window, then modifying its behavior using an API called `WinSubclassWindow`. The technique of changing a window after it has been created is called "subclassing" and will be discussed later in this book. In the WINLIST program, the APIs for setting up windows, which were discussed in the previous chapter, will be used.

A very commonly used technique for handling a control is to employ `WinSubclassWindow` to modify the frame. A Workplace Shell folder exemplifies the use of such a technique. A Workplace Shell folder, is quite simply, a frame window that has a container control as a client window. The container control, like WINLIST's list box, sends messages to its parent frame window and requires messages that a normal PM frame would not supply. To handle container messages, the folder frame window is subclassed.

PROPER WINDOW STRUCTURE

When writing a PM program such as WINLIST, it is important to modify the frame window. Taking this approach provides a highly capable program while minimizing code.

A common mistake is to try to avoid modifying the frame window. Typically the approach that is mistakenly taken is to use a standard window and make the list box a child of the client window. To give the window the same appearance as the WINLIST program, the list box would need to be positioned to cover the client window entirely. This approach results in the list box communicating to a client window and not to a frame window incapable of handling its messages.

Problems with this cumbersome approach include the need to write the extra code that is required in order to create the appearance of the WINLIST program, as well as the waste of a client window that is completely covered by the list box. Moreover, repositioning of the list box window is not handled automatically, as it is in WINLIST (where advantage is taken of the frame's features by letting the modified frame position the list box as if it were a client window).

SOURCE CODE OF THE WINLIST PROGRAM

The source code of the WINLIST program provides examples that illustrate how to register a subclass and how to create windows with `WinCreateWindow`. Six files are listed below that are used to compile the `WINLIST.EXE` program.

WINLIST.C

```
#define INCL_GPI
#define INCL_WIN
#include <os2.h>
#include <stdlib.h>
#include <string.h>
#include "winlist.h"


/* function prototypes */
INT main( VOID );
MRESULT EXPENTRY WindowProc( HWND, ULONG, MPARAM, MPARAM );
SHORT AddToMyListBox( HWND, HWND, SHORT, SHORT );


/* structures */
typedef struct _MYLISTITEM {
   HWND    hwnd;
   SHORT   level;
} MYLISTITEM;


/* global variables */
HAB  hab;
CLASSINFO  fci;
MYLISTITEM desktop = { HWND_DESKTOP, 0 };


INT main( VOID )
{
   HMQ  hmq;
   QMSG qmsg;
   CHAR szMyFrameClass[] = "Window List";
   HWND hwndFrame;
   FRAMECDATA fcd;
   fcd.cb = sizeof(FRAMECDATA);  /* length of structure */
   fcd.flCreateFlags =  FCF_TITLEBAR      /* create: title bar control     */
                     | FCF_SYSMENU       /*          system menu control   */
                     | FCF_MINMAX        /*          min and max buttons    */
                     | FCF_SIZEBORDER    /* draw sizeborders                */
                     | FCF_SHELLPOSITION /* shell decides window position */
                     | FCF_TASKLIST      /* title added to switch list    */
                     | FCF_ICON;         /* frame has an icon             */
   fcd.hmodResources = NULLHANDLE;  /* refer to this exe file */
   fcd.idResources   = ID_WINLIST;  /* identifier for the frame's resources */

   hab = WinInitialize( (ULONG)NULL );
   hmq = WinCreateMsgQueue( hab, 0 );

   WinQueryClassInfo( hab, WC_FRAME, &fci );

   fci.flClassStyle &= ~CS_PUBLIC;
```

```
    WinRegisterClass( hab,                   /* anchor block handle */
                   szMyFrameClass,           /* class name */
                   WindowProc,               /* pointer to window procedure */
                   fci.flClassStyle,         /* class style */
                   fci.cbWindowData );       /* number of class data bytes */


    hwndFrame  = WinCreateWindow(
                   HWND_DESKTOP,    /* parent window is the desktop */
                   szMyFrameClass,  /* class name */
                   "PM Window Lister",   /* text added to title bar */
                   0,               /* window style */
                   0, 0, 0, 0,      /* ignored, FCF_SHELLPOSITION was set */
                   NULLHANDLE,      /* no owner window */
                   HWND_TOP,        /* place on top of Desktop's children */
                   ID_WINLIST,      /* ID number for frame resources */
                   &fcd,            /* data unique for frame windows */
                   NULL );          /* no presentation parameters */


    WinShowWindow( hwndFrame, TRUE );

    if (hwndFrame)
       while (WinGetMsg( hab, &qmsg, NULLHANDLE, 0, 0 ))
          WinDispatchMsg( hab, &qmsg );

    WinDestroyWindow( hwndFrame );
    WinDestroyMsgQueue( hmq );
    WinTerminate( hab );

    return 0;
} /* end main */

MRESULT EXPENTRY WindowProc( HWND hwnd, ULONG msg, MPARAM mp1, MPARAM mp2 )
{
    static HWND hwndClient;

    switch (msg) {
    case WM_CREATE:
       /* call the frame class window procedure */
       (*fci.pfnWindowProc)( hwnd, msg, mp1, mp2 );


       /* create a list box as a client window */
       hwndClient = WinCreateWindow(
                   hwnd,            /* parent window is the frame */
                   WC_LISTBOX,      /* class name */
                   NULL,            /* window name not used by list boxes */
                   LS_NOADJUSTPOS   /* window style */
                   | LS_HORZSCROLL,
                   0, 0, 0, 0,      /* ignored, frame positions this window */
                   hwnd,            /* the frame window is the owner */
                   HWND_BOTTOM,     /* standard z-order for a client window */
                   FID_CLIENT,      /* ID number recognized by the frame */
                   NULL,            /* no control data */
                   NULL );          /* no presentation parameters */
```

```
            /* Mention the Desktop in the list box */
            AddToMyListBox( hwndClient, HWND_DESKTOP, 0, 0 );

            break;

    case WM_CONTROL:
      { HWND   hwndParent;
        HWND   hwndNext;
        HENUM henum;
        SHORT Index;
        SHORT Level;
        MYLISTITEM * pItem;

        /* only interested in an LN_ENTER message from client window */
        if ((SHORT1FROMMP(mp1) == FID_CLIENT)&&(SHORT2FROMMP(mp1) == LN_ENTER))
        {
            Index = SHORT1FROMMR( WinSendMsg( hwndClient, LM_QUERYSELECTION,
                                              NULL, NULL ));
            pItem = (MYLISTITEM *)WinSendMsg( hwndClient, LM_QUERYITEMHANDLE,
                                              MPFROMSHORT( Index ), NULL );
            Index++; /* insert after the item selected */
            Level = pItem->level + 1; /* indent the text */
            hwndParent = pItem->hwnd;

            /* remove and add items without redrawing */
            WinEnableWindowUpdate( hwndClient, FALSE );

            /* existing items of child windows may be outdated, remove them */
            /*     also we do not want the list box to grow out of control    */
            while (SHORT1FROMMR( WinSendMsg( hwndClient, LM_QUERYITEMCOUNT,
                                             NULL, NULL)) > Index)
                if ((pItem = (MYLISTITEM *)WinSendMsg( hwndClient,
                                                       LM_QUERYITEMHANDLE,
                                                       MPFROMSHORT( Index),
                                                       NULL ))->level >= Level)
                {
                    WinSendMsg(hwndClient, LM_DELETEITEM, MPFROMSHORT(Index), NULL);
                    free( pItem );
                } else
                    break;/* the remaining windows are not children of hwndParent */

            /* add items about existing windows */
            henum = WinBeginEnumWindows( hwndParent );
            while ((hwndNext = WinGetNextWindow( henum )) != NULLHANDLE)
                AddToMyListBox( hwndClient, hwndNext, Index++, Level);
            WinEndEnumWindows (henum);

            /* show the updated list box */
            WinShowWindow( hwndClient, TRUE );
        } /* endif */
      } break;

    default:
        return (*fci.pfnWindowProc)( hwnd, msg, mp1, mp2 );
    } /* endswitch */
```

```
      return FALSE;
} /* end of WindowProc */


SHORT AddToMyListBox( HWND hwnd, HWND hwndTarget, SHORT Index, SHORT Level )
{
   MYLISTITEM * pItem;
   CHAR    szWindowText[99];
   CHAR    szClassName[99];
   PSZ     pszBuffer = NULL;
   PSZ     psz;
   SWP     swp;
   SHORT   i, rc;

   if (hwndTarget == HWND_DESKTOP) {
      pItem = &desktop;
      strcpy( szWindowText, "<Desktop Window>" );
   } else {
      pItem = malloc( sizeof(MYLISTITEM) );
      if (!pItem)
         goto InvalidHandle;
      pItem->hwnd  = hwndTarget;
      pItem->level = Level;
      WinQueryWindowText( hwndTarget, sizeof(szWindowText), szWindowText );
   } /* endif */

   if (!WinQueryClassName(  hwndTarget, sizeof(szClassName), szClassName ))
      goto InvalidHandle;

   if (!WinQueryWindowPos(  hwndTarget, &swp ))
      goto InvalidHandle;
   pszBuffer = malloc( Level + 300 );
   if (!pszBuffer)
      goto InvalidHandle;

   for (i=0, psz=pszBuffer; i<(3*Level); i++, psz++)
      *psz = ' ';
   sprintf( psz, "\"%s\" class=\"%s\" pos=(%ld,%ld) width=%ld height=%ld",
            szWindowText, szClassName, swp.x, swp.y, swp.cx, swp.cy );
   rc=(SHORT)WinSendMsg( hwnd, LM_INSERTITEM, MPFROMSHORT( Index ), pszBuffer );
   WinSendMsg( hwnd, LM_SETITEMHANDLE, MPFROMSHORT( Index ), pItem );
   free( pszBuffer );

   return rc;

InvalidHandle:
   free( pszBuffer );
   free( pItem );

   return FALSE;
} /* end of AddToMyListBox */
```

WINLIST.H

```
#define ID_WINLIST 1
```

WINLIST.RC

```
#include "winlist.h"
ICON ID_WINLIST winlist.ico
```

WINLIST.DEF

```
NAME      WINLIST      WINDOWAPI

DESCRIPTION 'WINLIST OS/2 PM Example Program'

STUB         'OS2STUB.EXE'

DATA         MULTIPLE

STACKSIZE    16348
HEAPSIZE     16348

PROTMODE
```

WINLIST.MAK

```
all : winlist.exe

winlist.exe : winlist.obj  winlist.def winlist.res
        link386 /PM:PM winlist,,,,winlist.def;
        rc winlist.res

winlist.res: winlist.rc winlist.ico winlist.h
        rc -r winlist.rc

winlist.obj:winlist.c winlist.h
        icc /C /Ss /W3 .\$*.c
```

WINLIST.ICO

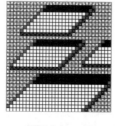
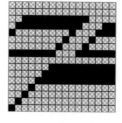
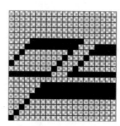

VGA Independent   16 x 16   20 x 20

WINLIST.ICO file containing various icons of different sizes.

LOOKING AT THE WINLIST SOURCE CODE

During the initialization of the WINLIST program, a private frame subclass is registered that filters all WM_CONTROL messages from the list box and calls PM's frame window procedure to handle the rest. An API called WinQueryClassInfo is called to get the address of PM's frame window procedure. The address is stored in a CLASSINFO data structure called fci and is referred to by using the value fci.pfnWindowProc. Filtering messages before resending them to another window procedure is a common technique in PM programming and appears frequently in the example code that is presented in this book.

In the previous chapter, mention was made of the fact that PM has an area of data that is set aside for each window. Such a data area contains an identification number, window text, and other items of information that compose the structure that is used by PM. A window class can be registered with additional space for data to be appended to PM's default window data structure. The appended window data is called "class data." Only code that understands the format in which class data is stored can correctly access and use this appended window data.

When a window is created, PM allocates memory that corresponds to the size of its window data structure plus the number of class data bytes specified for the window's class. The WinCreateWindow API accepts a pointer to a data structure, called the "control data," that describes enough information about the window that is being created to initialize its class data. During the processing of the WM_CREATE message, a window will initialize its class data by using information from control data that is passed by WinCreateWindow. The structure containing the control data can take substantially any format the programmer who designs the new window class prefers. The frame class, on the other hand, was designed to refer to a FRAMECDATA structure during WM_CREATE.

While the OS/2 operating system is loading, PM registers its public classes. As is the case with many of PM's windows, the frame class is registered as having class data that requires that its window data structure be expanded. It is common for programs to take advantage of querying and changing a frame window's class data.

In WINLIST, a variable called fcd is set up as a FRAMECDATA type. Frame windows require a pointer to a FRAMECDATA type that is passed as a part of the WM_CREATE message sent by WinCreateWindow. This pointer is a parameter that is given to WinCreateWindow and must point to a valid FRAMECDATA data structure; otherwise, the frame window procedure will signal an error during the WM_CREATE message. If the value TRUE is returned as an error signal, this means that the frame and its controls were not duly created. A NULL is a valid value for the pointer to a frame's control data. The use of a NULL pointer value will cause the frame to use a default FRAMECDATA structure that has no FCF flags set and will not create any frame controls.

For WINLIST to create a window that uses PM's frame window procedure, WinQueryClassInfo is used to find the size of the frame's class data, the frame default class style, and the address of the frame's window procedure. `WinQueryClassInfo` places all of this information into WINLIST's `CLASSINFO` data structure, `fci`. The size of the class data (`fci.cbWindowData`) and a slightly modified class style (`fci.flClassStyle`) are used to register WINLIST's new frame class.

The frame's class style (`fci.flClassStyle`) is modified by the following line of code to remove the `CS_PUBLIC` flag:

```
fci.flClassStyle &= ~CS_PUBLIC;
```

After `WinQueryClassInfo` initially has been called, the content of `fci.flClassStyle` equals the result of the ORing together of flags `CS_PUBLIC`, `CS_FRAME`, `CS_HITTEST`, `CS_SYNCPAINT`, and `CS_CLIPSIBLINGS`. The `CS_PUBLIC` flag needs to be removed since the new frame class is to be private to WINLIST. Most programs simply use the `CS` values they need and do not bother with `fci.flClassStyle`.

The Client Window

When the frame window is created, a `WM_CREATE` message is sent to a function in WINLIST, called `WindowProc`. The `WM_CREATE` message is handled by calling PM's frame window procedure, and then using `WinCreateWindow` to create a client list box. A frame window keeps track of its frame controls and its client by using identification numbers (IDs) that can be specified in `WinCreateWindow`. In order for the list box to constitute a client window, it must have the ID value of `FID_CLIENT`. Otherwise, the frame will not recognize the list box and will not position it properly.

The window style used for the list box is the result of ORing together the values of two flags known as `LS_NOADJUSTPOS` and `LS_HORZSCROLL`. `LS_NOADJUSTPOS` prevents the list box from changing its height to be evenly divisible by the height of a line of text—which prevents the list box from being called on to display the tops or bottoms of items that do not entirely fit into the list box. `LS_HORZSCROLL` simply adds a horizontal scroll bar to the list box.

Before the `WM_CREATE` message is completed, a function in WINLIST known as `AddToMyListBox` is called. The `AddToMyListBox` function adds items to the list box and operates to ensure that a description of the desktop window is the uppermost item so that the item can be easily accessed to update the entire list of windows. The `WM_CREATE` message is then returned, and the `WinCreateWindow` completes the creation of WINLIST's frame window. A call to `WinShowWindow` causes WINLIST's completed window to be displayed on the desktop. If the frame and its client were created using the style flag `WS_VISIBLE`, a process by which an item is added to the list box will be displayed on the desktop. To avoid the distraction caused by WINLIST's displaying the creation of a frame and a list box, it ordinarily is preferable to complete the creation of the frame and list box before displaying them.

Enumerating Windows

When the user chooses an item in the list box that describes a window, a `WM_CONTROL` message is sent to the `WindowProc` function. The APIs known as `WinBeginEnumWindows` and `WinGetNextWindow` are used to access any children of the selected window. `AddToMyListBox` is used to query each child's window text, class name, position, and size.

The `WinBeginEnumWindow` API takes as a parameter a handle to a window, and it creates a list of the window's children. This API causes PM to allocate just enough memory to store the list of children. A handle, of type `HENUM`, that identifies the list is returned. To gain access to any items in the list, the API `WinGetNextWindow` must be called with the `HENUM` value returned by `WinBeginEnumWindow`. `WinGetNextWindow` starts by returning the handle to the topmost child window (that is, the child window that is at the forefront of the display). Subsequent calls will return handles to child windows as `WinGetNextWindow` moves successively down the list of child windows until a `NULLHANDLE` value is returned. The `NULLHANDLE` value indicates that `WinGetNextWindow` has moved back to the top of the list and is ready to go through the list again in the same order as before.

It is important to remember that enumerating a window's children will capture and store a list of windows as they are found to exist at a particular instant in time. As `WinGetNextWindow` goes through its list, it may return an invalid handle if the associated window has been closed. Since `WinGetNextWindow` does not update the list as windows are closed or opened, a check needs to be made to determine whether a window handle is valid to determine whether an associated window still exists.

When your program has ceased to need the information that is provided by enumerating a window's children, you will want to remember to call `WinEndEnumWindows` so that PM deallocates memory that was reserved for storing the list of children.

THE OBJECT WINDOW

The WINLIST program can give the impression that all windows are descendants of the desktop; however, such is not the case. Another window, known as the "object window," is not a child of the desktop. The object window is utilized by PM to conveniently hide windows that frequently appear for short periods of time.

When the pull-down menus of an action bar are displayed and then hidden, they are not being created and destroyed. Rather, the pull-down menus are having their parents switched between the desktop and the object window. Changing parents is a more efficient method for selectively presenting pull-down menus than is the alternative of creating and destroying the menus. When an action bar is created, it will allocate all of the resources it needs by creating its pull-down menus all at once. The object window is where such menus are conveniently stored.

If you would like to view the children of the object window by using the WINLIST program, you should be warned that sending a message to an object window may hang your system. Object windows are notorious for being ill-behaved. The threads that are used to handle object windows may be blocked on semaphores, waiting to be brought back to the desktop. If WINLIST uses WinSendMsg or an API that sends a message, it will wait indefinitely for a reply. Object windows that are blocked on a semaphore cannot reply, and a deadlock will result. The object windows should use an API known as WinWaitMuxWaitSem to avoid causing a deadlock. Many object windows do not use this API and will instead make a call to the kernel, thereby disabling themselves from replying to messages.

It is possible to use WINLIST to explore the object window's children safely by changing two lines of source code. First, "comment out" the call to the WinQueryWindowText function, which is located in AddToMyListBox. The WinQueryWindowText happens to send a WM_QUERYWINDOWPARAMS message in order to get its information, and since messages represent problems to object windows, you will need to keep this line from being compiled into the program. Second, change the value of HWND_DESKTOP located at the beginning of WINLIST.C to HWND_OBJECT. This will provide the appropriate handle for the object window that is being queried. The resulting line of code should read as follows:

```
MYLISTITEM desktop = { HWND_OBJECT, 0 };
```

CHAPTER 5
Using Dialog Boxes

PM provides support for creating and handling special frame windows, called *dialog boxes,* that can contain large numbers of PM's controls for displaying and retrieving data. The controls of a dialog box can be automatically created and positioned by giving PM a *dialog template* that describes both the character of the controls that are to be created and how the controls are to be displayed.

Most PM programs use dialog boxes to briefly display or request information. However, with a few modifications a dialog box can be used as a program's main window.

One advantage that a dialog box has over a standard window is that complex arrays of controls can be created using dialog templates. Unless dialog templates are used, many lines of code are required both to create each individual control and to position it properly among other controls.

Another advantage obtained from using a dialog box is that the code that defines the default dialog window procedure contains needed keyboard interface code built in. Therefore, keystrokes such as those of cursor control keys can *easily* be given the needed ability to move a cursor among an array of dialog box controls. Similarly, the built-in keyboard interface code provides dialog boxes with a standard way to use the keyboard to access PM's controls.

CREATING A DIALOG BOX

Several methods are available to create a dialog box. Differences among the methods tend to center on the subjects of (1) how a dialog box's message queue is to be handled and (2) when the dialog is to be displayed. An API called `WinDlgBox` provides the simplest way of handling the creation of a single dialog box. However, the simplicity of using one API to create, display, and handle a dialog box brings with it several limitations. Other APIs are available that provide methods for creating dialog boxes that are not encumbered by limitations.

Types of Dialog Boxes

The `WinDlgBox` API creates what is referred to as a *modal dialog box*. A modal dialog box receives all user input that is sent to the program that created it. `WinDlgBox` disables the other windows of the dialog box's program and prevents them from receiving any user input. Creating a modal dialog box prohibits a user from continuing to use a program without first handling the request that is made by the dialog box. Error messages and other important notices are typically displayed using a modal dialog box.

During the time that a modal dialog is being displayed on the PM desktop, the user will *not* be able to alter any other windows of the associated program. However, the user *will* be able to switch to and use other programs.

Another type of dialog box that is permitted by PM is called a *system modal dialog box*. A powerful feature of a system modal dialog box is that it absolutely prohibits a user from accessing any window that otherwise would be accessible on the desktop. Due to the extreme character of the restrictions that system modal dialog boxes can impose on a user, they should only be used to handle the most severe errors.

Dialog Templates

A dialog box will normally contain several child windows, which act as a set of controls to receive data. A dialog box does not have a client window, so its controls are placed in the area where a client window normally would appear. The controls of a dialog box can be laid out by the use of a dialog template. A dialog box and its child windows can be created one at a time by repeatedly calling the `WinCreateWindow` API, but this is a tedious process. `WinCreateWindow` should be used to create the components of a dialog box individually done *only* if the positions of the components are not known until after a program has been started. Since most dialog boxes use an unchanging layout for their components, their appearance usually can be stored in a "read only" format, such as is provided by a dialog template.

A dialog template represents a complex data structure that can be described in an easy-to-understand format that is used by a resource compiler. The first step in making use of a dialog box is to load its template from an associated executable file or from DLL resources. This step can be skipped if the dialog template is directly written as a C data structure. However, as experienced programmers will readily appreciate, writing code to initialize complex C data structures is an arduous undertaking, and the presence of such structures within C code renders the C code difficult to maintain.

Dialog Boxes

Dialog boxes are subclassed frame windows. The window procedure of a dialog box will call the normal frame window procedure to handle unprocessed messages. A dialog box differs from a frame window in the way it behaves while being created, while dealing with keystrokes, and while being destroyed. Because a dialog box is subclassed, it does not receive a WM_CREATE message. Instead, the normal frame procedure receives the WM_CREATE message and sends a WM_INITDLG message to the dialog box.

A dialog box lacks the ability that a frame window has to automatically load an action bar, an accelerator table, and an icon. Added code is required to load and make use of such things as an icon. The way a dialog box is closed also distinguishes it from a frame window. For example, a dialog box closes itself when the "Escape" button of the keyboard is pressed. To use a dialog box as a program's main window, such properties as the automatic closing of a window when the "Escape" key is pressed need to be modified.

The WinDlgBox API

The WinDlgBox API is typically used to create a dialog box that will appear on the desktop only briefly. Such dialog boxes are typically used to request information or to provide notice. WinDlgBox contains code to load a dialog template, display the dialog box, handle a message loop, and destroy the dialog box. Since WinDlgBox handles its own messages, it intercepts keyboard and mouse messages that were intended to be sent to the message queue of the calling program. Intercepting messages is one of the ways in which WinDlgBox emulates the behavior of a modal dialog box.

In an example program PRODINFO (the source code of which is presented later), the WinDlgBox API handles the creation of what the Common User Access (CUA) rules recently have defined as a *product information box*. To save time and typing space, most programmers still call this box by a much more acceptable term, namely an *about box*.

Figure 5.1 shows two windows created by the PRODINFO program. The program's main window is a dialog box that presents two large buttons labeled "Product Information" and "OK." The "Product Information" button was used to create the second window of Figure 5.1, which displays PRODINFO's about box. The "OK" button serves simply to exit the program.

An about box needs to be displayed for only a short period of time. This makes it a perfect candidate for the WinDlgBox API. The PRODINFO program shows how to use WinDlgBox and also illustrates a technique to create a dialog box as an application's main window.

The PRODINFO program requires the following six files to be compiled:

PRODINFO.C

```
#define INCL_WIN
#include <os2.h>
#include "prodinfo.h"


/* function prototypes */
INT main( VOID );
```

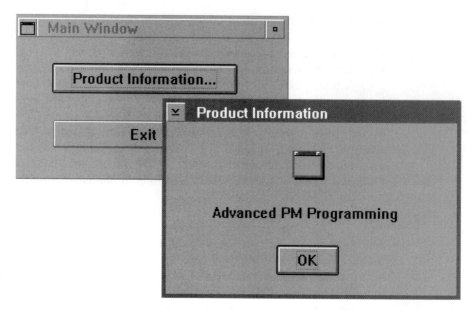

FIGURE 5.1   The two windows that can be created with the PRODINFO program.

```
MRESULT EXPENTRY MyDlgProc( HWND, ULONG, MPARAM, MPARAM );
MRESULT EXPENTRY MyProdInfo( HWND, ULONG, MPARAM, MPARAM );


/* global variables */
HPOINTER hIcon;


INT main( VOID )
{
   HAB   hab;
   HMQ   hmq;
   HWND  hwndDlg;
   QMSG  qmsg;
   SWP   swp;

   hab = WinInitialize( 0 );

   hmq = WinCreateMsgQueue( hab, 0 );

   hIcon = WinLoadPointer( HWND_DESKTOP, 0, ID_ICON );

   hwndDlg = WinLoadDlg( HWND_DESKTOP,       /* parent              */
                   HWND_DESKTOP,             /* owner               */
                   (PFNWP)MyDlgProc,         /* dialog window proc   */
                   0,                        /* module handle        */
                   ID_DLG1,                  /* dialog template ID   */
                   NULL);                    /* no app data          */
```

```
   WinSendMsg( hwndDlg, WM_SETICON, (MPARAM)hIcon, NULL );

   /* find where system would place dialog box */
   WinQueryTaskSizePos( hab, 0, swp );

   /* place dialog box at position given by the shell */
   WinSetWindowPos( hwndDlg,          /* change the dialog window's position */
                    NULLHANDLE,       /* ignored, SWP_ZORDER not set */
                    swp.x, swp.y,     /* position of lower left corner */
                    0, 0,             /* ignored SWP_SIZE not set */
                    SWP_SHOW          /* show dialog box */
                    | SWP_MOVE );     /* do not ignore swp.x and swp.y */

   if ( hwndDlg )
      while (WinGetMsg( hab, &qmsg, NULLHANDLE, 0, 0 ))
         WinDispatchMsg( hab, &qmsg );

   WinDestroyWindow( hwndDlg );    /* clean up */
   WinDestroyMsgQueue( hmq );
   WinTerminate( hab );

   return 0;

} /* end of main */


MRESULT EXPENTRY MyDlgProc( HWND hwnd, ULONG msg, MPARAM mp1, MPARAM mp2 )
{

   switch ( msg ) {

      case WM_COMMAND:
         switch (LOUSHORT( mp1 )) {

            case ID_ABOUT:
               WinDlgBox( HWND_DESKTOP,      /* parent window handle    */
                          hwnd,              /* set owner               */
                          MyProdInfo,        /* dialog procedure        */
                          NULLHANDLE,        /* module handle           */
                          ID_DLG2,           /* dialog identifier       */
                          NULL);             /* initialization data     */
               break;

            case ID_EXIT:
               WinPostMsg( hwnd, WM_QUIT, 0, 0 );
               return FALSE;

         }
         break;

      case WM_CLOSE:
         WinPostMsg( hwnd, WM_QUIT, 0, 0 );
         return FALSE;
```

```
        default:
            return WinDefDlgProc( hwnd, msg, mp1, mp2 );

    }

    return (MRESULT)FALSE;
} /* end of MyDlgProc */


MRESULT EXPENTRY MyProdInfo( HWND hwndDlg, ULONG msg, MPARAM mp1, MPARAM mp2 )
{
    switch ( msg ) {

    case WM_INITDLG:
      { HWND      hwndSysMenu;
        MENUITEM  mi;
        USHORT    MenuID;
        SHORT     PresentItem = 0;
        INT       NumberOfItems;

        hwndSysMenu = WinWindowFromID( hwndDlg, FID_SYSMENU );
        WinSendMsg( hwndSysMenu,
                    MM_QUERYITEM,
                    MPFROM2SHORT( SC_SYSMENU, FALSE ),
                    (MPARAM)&mi );
        NumberOfItems = (INT)WinSendMsg( mi.hwndSubMenu,
                                         MM_QUERYITEMCOUNT,
                                         NULL,
                                         NULL );
        while (NumberOfItems--) {
            MenuID = (USHORT)WinSendMsg( mi.hwndSubMenu,
                                MM_ITEMIDFROMPOSITION,
                                MPFROM2SHORT( PresentItem, TRUE ),
                                NULL );

            switch (MenuID) {
            case SC_CLOSE:
            case SC_MOVE:
                PresentItem++;
                break;
            default:
                WinSendMsg( mi.hwndSubMenu,
                            MM_DELETEITEM,
                            MPFROM2SHORT( MenuID, TRUE ),
                            0 );
            }
        }
      } break;

    default:
        return WinDefDlgProc( hwndDlg, msg, mp1, mp2 );
    }

    return (MRESULT)FALSE;
} /* end of MyProdInfo */
```

PRODINFO.H

```
#define ID_ICON   200

#define ID_DLG1   201
#define ID_ABOUT  202
#define ID_EXIT   203
#define ID_DLG2   204
#define ID_TEXT   205
```

PRODINFO.RC

```
#include <os2.h>
#include "prodinfo.h"

ICON ID_ICON prodinfo.ico

DLGTEMPLATE ID_DLG1 LOADONCALL MOVEABLE DISCARDABLE
BEGIN
    DIALOG   "Main Window", ID_DLG1, -1, 10, 170, 64, 0,
             FCF_SYSMENU | FCF_TITLEBAR | FCF_MINBUTTON | FCF_TASKLIST
    BEGIN
        DEFPUSHBUTTON "Product Information...", ID_ABOUT, 23, 38, 119, 14,
                                                              WS_GROUP

        PUSHBUTTON    "Exit", ID_EXIT, 23, 12, 119, 14
    END
END

DLGTEMPLATE ID_DLG2 LOADONCALL MOVEABLE DISCARDABLE
BEGIN
    DIALOG "Product Information", ID_DLG2, 13, 14, 185, 80, 0,
             FCF_SYSMENU | FCF_TITLEBAR
    BEGIN
        ICON          ID_ICON, ID_ICON, 79, 53, 21, 16, WS_GROUP
        CTEXT         "Advanced PM Programming", ID_TEXT, 29, 32, 118, 10
        DEFPUSHBUTTON "OK", DID_OK, 70, 9, 40, 14
    END
END
```

PRODINFO.DEF

```
NAME        PRODINF WINDOWAPI

DESCRIPTION 'Dialog Box Example'
CODE        MOVEABLE
DATA        MOVEABLE MULTIPLE

HEAPSIZE    10240
STACKSIZE   24576
```

PRODINFO.MAK

```
all : prodinfo.exe

prodinfo.exe : prodinfo.obj prodinfo.def prodinfo.res
        link386 /PM:PM prodinfo,,,,prodinfo.def;
        rc prodinfo.res

prodinfo.res: prodinfo.rc prodinfo.h
        rc -r prodinfo.rc

prodinfo.obj: prodinfo.c prodinfo.h
        icc /C /Ss /W3 .\$*.c
```

PRODINFO.ICO

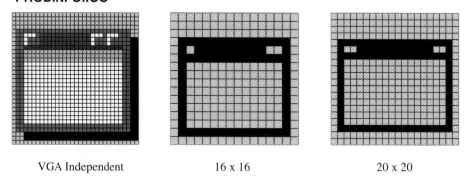

VGA Independent   16 x 16   20 x 20

PRODINFO.ICO file containing various icons of different sizes.

THE PRODINFO PROGRAM

When the "Product Information" button is pressed, a WM_COMMAND message is handled by the main window procedure called MyDlgProc. The main window procedure calls WinDlgBox to create the PRODINFO about box. Keyboard and mouse messages are received by WinDlgBox until the about box button labeled "OK" is pressed to close the about box.

The function provided by the WinDlgBox API can be emulated with a series of Win calls: WinLoadDlg, WinProcessDlg, and WinDestroyWindow. The following is an example of how a WinDlgBox call issued from within PRODINFO can be constructed by using only a few PM calls:

```
hwndDlg = WinLoadDlg( HWND_DESKTOP,/* set the parent as the desktop */
                      hwnd,        /* set owner as the main window */
                      MyDlgProc,   /* address of window procedure */
                      NULLHANDLE,  /* use .EXE fill for resources */
                      ID_ABOUTBOX, /* ID of the dialog box resource */
                      NULL );      /* no control data */
WinProcessDlg( hwndDlg ); /* handle keyboard and mouse events */
WinDestroyWindow( hwndDlg );
```

The `WinLoadDlg` API loads a dialog template and uses it to create a dialog box and associated child windows. Most templates will not use the window style `WS_VISIBLE`; therefore, `WinLoadDlg` will not display a dialog box. `WinProcessDlg` handles the display of the dialog box and receives mouse and keyboard events. When the about box has been dismissed, the `WinDestroyWindow` API handles the destruction of the dialog box.

CLOSING A DIALOG BOX

The about box created by the PRODINFO program has a button labeled "OK." This button has a window ID number that is referred to by the name `DID_OK` (`DID` is an abbreviation for Dialog Identification). When the "OK" button is pressed, a `WM_COMMAND` message is posted containing the `DID_OK` value. The default dialog procedure interprets the `DID_OK` value as signaling that the user has finished with the present dialog box and that the dialog should be closed. As a part of closing the dialog box, the default dialog procedure calls the `WinDismissDlg` API. This API hides the dialog box and gives its owner window the focus.

If a dialog box is being used as an application's main window, the dialog box will not have an owner window to give focus to when it is closed. A program being closed should give the focus to the session that started the program. For most applications, the session that was used to start a program is another program, such as OS/2's `CMD.EXE`, or a shell, such as Workplace.

An application such as the PRODINFO program, that uses a dialog box as a main window needs to modify the default dialog procedure to give the focus to the appropriate window. This is done by closing the dialog window without calling the `WinDismissDlg` API. The `WinDismissDlg` API must be avoided, because it will give the incorrect session the focus as it tries to assign the focus to an owner window. Instead of giving the focus to the session that started a program, `WinDismissDlg` gives the focus to an unrelated session.

To avoid calling the `WinDismissDlg`, a program must prevent the default dialog procedure (`WinDefDlgProc`) from processing certain messages. `WinDefDlgProc` handles certain messages inappropriately for a main window, by calling `WinDismissDlg`. The messages that need special handling are command messages sent with either `DID_OK` or `DID_CANCEL` as message parameters, as well as the `WM_CLOSE` message.

A `WM_COMMAND` message with a `DID_CANCEL` value is very much like a command message with a `DID_OK` value in that each of these messages is handled by calling `WinDismissDlg`. Like the `DID_OK` value, `DID_CANCEL` can be used as a window ID for a dialog control. When selected, a control with a `DID_CANCEL` ID sends command messages in the same format as a control with a `DID_OK` ID does, except that `DID_CANCEL` replaces `DID_OK` as the value that was sent with the message. Another difference between `DID_CANCEL` and `DID_OK` is that the default dialog procedure will send a `DID_CANCEL` command message when certain keystrokes have occurred. Unlike `DID_OK`, a dialog box will send itself a message to close the dialog box when the "Escape" button is pressed.

The default method for handling the command messages for DID_OK and DID_CANCEL is suitable for most dialog boxes. However, the way these messages are handled needs to be altered when a dialog box is being used as a main window. The PRODINFO main window is a modified dialog box that overrides actions that are taken when the messages WM_COMMAND and WM_CLOSE are received. The values DID_OK or DID_CANCEL that are sent using a WM_COMMAND message are handled by simply giving the message a return code of FALSE. DID_OK and DID_CANCEL are returned to prevent them from being processed by the default dialog procedure (WinDefDlgProc). If WM_COMMAND messages are not intercepted, the WinDefDlgProc procedure will cause a dialog box to act inappropriately for an application's main window. For instance, the "Escape" button on the keyboard should not be empowered to close an application's main window.

The PRODINFO program sets up and runs its main window by using WinLoadDlg and a while statement as a message loop. For the PRODINFO program to close properly, the message loop must receive a WM_QUIT message when a WM_CLOSE message is received. If the WM_CLOSE message is not intercepted, the WinDefDlgProc API will handle the message by calling the WinDismissDlg API.

It is appropriate for the PRODINFO program to post a WM_QUIT message in response to WM_CLOSE messages, because PRODINFO is using its own message loop (the while statement that calls WinGetMsg). However, posting a WM_QUIT message is not appropriate if the PRODINFO program uses the WinProcessDlg or WinDlgBox API to handle its main window rather than using its own message loop. The WinProcessDlg and WinDlgBox APIs create their own message loop and interpret WM_QUIT messages by calling WinDismissDlg.

If WinProcessDlg or WinDlgBox is to be used to handle an application's main window, WM_CLOSE messages should not be handled by posting a WM_QUIT message. Instead, WM_CLOSE should be handled with the following code:

```
case WM_CLOSE:
   WinDestroyWindow( hwnd) ;
   break;
```

This code destroys the main window and avoids having WinProcessDlg or WinDlgBox make a call to WinDismissDlg. Another way of processing WM_CLOSE would be to set a FF_DLGDISMISSED flag as a part of the window style of the main window. Both the WinProcessDlg and WinDlgBox APIs use a message loop that continues until the dialog box is either destroyed or given a FF_DLGDISMISSED style flag. Setting the FF_DLGDISMISSED style flag essentially performs the function of WinDismissDlg without hiding the dialog box and inappropriately setting the focus to another window.

The following code sets a `FF_DLGDISMISSED` flag when a `WM_CLOSE` message is received:

```
case WM_CLOSE:
{   USHORT us;
    us =  WinQueryWindowUShort( hwnd, QWS_FLAGS );
    us|= FF_DLGDISMISSED;
    WinSetWindowUShort( hwnd, QWS_FLAGS, us );
}   return FALSE;
```

PRODINFO's Main Window

The PRODINFO main window is set up using `WinLoadDlg` followed by a message loop. By providing a message loop, the `main` function in `PRODINFO.C` can be expanded to include code to create more windows. If the message loop were replaced with a call to `WinProcessDlg`, additional calls to set up more windows could not be made from the `main` function without first destroying the dialog box that is handled by `WinProcessDlg`.

A shortcoming of dialog boxes is that the frame creation flags that handle such things as the automatic loading of an icon are not supported. The flags `FCF_ICON`, `FCF_ACCELTABLE`, and `FCF_MENU` can be specified in a dialog template, but PM simply removes these flags from among the other frame creation flags.

If a dialog box is to have an icon, an action bar or an accelerator table, the dialog box must load such items itself. The PRODINFO program uses the `WinLoadPointer` API and sends a `WM_SETICON` message to load its icon and to associate its icon with its dialog window. The following two lines of code from the PRODINFO program load an icon and associate it with the main window:

```
hIcon = WinLoadPointer( HWND_DESKTOP, 0, ID_ICON );
WinSendMsg( hwndDlg, WM_SETICON, (MPARAM)hIcon, NULL );
```

CHANGING THE SYSTEM MENU

A dialog box will often add or delete menu items in its system menu. It is typical for a dialog box to remove selected items from the system menu because the dialog box cannot use the selected items. Since most dialog boxes cannot be minimized or maximized, the menu items in the system menu for such actions are automatically disabled by PM. The items that are automatically disabled appear "grayed out" and clutter the system menu. The only items that are not grayed out are typically the "Move" and "Close" menu items.

To remove all the disabled menu items and leave a system menu that contains only the items "Move" and "Close," a dialog box can be instructed to delete the unneeded menu items. The system menu is designed to receive MM_DELETEITEM messages to remove each unneeded item. To correctly find and remove unneeded menu items, a dialog box must send MM_DELETEITEM messages to the correct submenu of the system menu.

The system menu is actually made up of two menus. One menu is the button that appears in the upper left corner of standard windows. This menu's only menu item is a bitmap with the appearance of a button. The other window is a submenu of the button menu; that is, it is the pull-down menu that appears when the button is pressed. The pull-down menu contains the items that manipulate a frame window. The commonly used expression "modifying the system menu" refers not to changing the button menu but rather to modifying the pull-down menu.

The PRODINFO about box deletes all menu items from its system menu except the items "Move" and "Close." These items have the menu ID numbers SC_MOVE and SC_CLOSE. PRODINFO's window procedure (MyDlgProc), which handles the about box has additional code for changing the system menu when a WM_INITDLG message is received.

The system menu's pull-down has the menu ID number SC_SYSMENU, which is used to query the pull-down's menu handle. Using the handle, messages are sent directly to the pull-down menu. The following code shows how the PRODINFO program removes menu items from the system menu of its about box:

```
{ HWND        hwndSysMenu;
  MENUITEM    mi;
  USHORT      MenuID;
  SHORT       PresentItem = 0;
  INT         NumberOfItems;

  hwndSysMenu = WinWindowFromID( hwndDlg, FID_SYSMENU );
  WinSendMsg( hwndSysMenu,
              MM_QUERYITEM,
              MPFROM2SHORT( SC_SYSMENU, FALSE ),
              (MPARAM)&mi );
  NumberOfItems = (INT)WinSendMsg( mi.hwndSubMenu,
                                   MM_QUERYITEMCOUNT,
                                   NULL,
                                   NULL );
  while (NumberOfItems--) {
     MenuID = (USHORT)WinSendMsg( mi.hwndSubMenu,
                                  MM_ITEMIDFROMPOSITION,
                                  MPFROM2SHORT( PresentItem, TRUE ),
                                  NULL );
     switch (MenuID) {
     case SC_CLOSE:
     case SC_MOVE:
        PresentItem++;
        break;
```

```
        default:
            WinSendMsg( mi.hwndSubMenu,
                        MM_DELETEITEM,
                        MPFROM2SHORT( MenuID, TRUE ),
                        0 );
    }
  }
}
```

CHAPTER 6
Colors

PM provides a device-independent way of writing code that takes the fullest available advantage of a graphics adapter's capabilities. The availability of a graphics adapter's capabilities is determined by its display driver, some of which are more capable than others.

Introduced with OS/2 2.0 is an ability to use 32-bit display drivers that enhance PM's capabilities. A palette manager now permits 32-bit display drivers to change an adapter's palette so that an optimal color scheme is created that meets the specific needs of a foreground application. PM also has an ability to support background applications that request a custom palette. The requested custom palette is made available by PM's doing something of a juggling act to provide palettes simultaneously to foreground and background applications.

All of PM's controls rely on being able to choose from a variety of colors. The techniques that PM's controls use to select colors are important to understand when writing code that makes use of PM's controls. Although selecting the colors to use when drawing within a window is a subject that more properly belongs in a book that deals with the topic of GPI programming, PM's controls make so much use of color selection that the topic of color selection needs to be discussed in this book.

SELECTING A COLOR

In PM programming there are two available modes that may be used to select a color for drawing in a window: *index mode* and *RGB mode*. Depending on the mode being used, APIs that take a parameter that describes a color will expect to receive either an *index,* which is selected from a table of available colors (index mode), or a direct description of a color in a format known as an *RGB value* (RGB mode).

A table of available colors, called a *logical color table* or simply a *color table,* is used in index mode. The colors that are identified in color tables can be set up by a program or by a default logical color table that is supplied by PM. In RGB mode no color tables are needed, because when an RGB value is specified, the specification already contains enough information to describe a particular color directly.

LOGICAL COLOR TABLES

PM maintains a consistent color scheme by using a default color table to provide PM applications with an easy-to-access set of colors. The default color table uses RGB values that remain constant for different graphics adapters regardless of their capabilities to display colors. Different graphics adapters typically have different ranges of colors defined by their associated physical color tables. An adapter's lack of available colors may cause even some default colors to appear to be identical when presented on a display that is driven by such an adapter.

A default logical color table is initially assigned to any PM program that begins to use PM's drawing functions. The default logical color table is displayed in Table 6.1.

PM has a predefined set of color indexes, which are identified by a CLR_ prefix and are listed in Table 6.1. The predefined color indexes each describe a commonly used color, the RGB values for which are also listed in Table 6.1. If the color needs of an application are satisfied by PM's default colors, there is no need for the application to set up its own color table. The application simply uses a CLR_ value to specify a desired color.

TABLE 6.1 The default logical color table that is provided by PM

Definition	Index	RGB Value in Hex
CLR_BACKGROUND	0L	0x00ffffff
CLR_BLUE	1L	0x000000ff
CLR_RED	2L	0x00ff0000
CLR_PINK	3L	0x00ff00ff
CLR_GREEN	4L	0x0000ff00
CLR_CYAN	5L	0x0000ffff
CLR_YELLOW	6L	0x00ffff00
CLR_NEUTRAL	7L	0x00000000
CLR_DARKGRAY	8L	0x00808080
CLR_DARKBLUE	9L	0x00000080
CLR_DARKRED	10L	0x00800000
CLR_DARKPINK	11L	0x00800080
CLR_DARKGREEN	12L	0x00008000
CLR_DARKCYAN	13L	0x00008080
CLR_BROWN	14L	0x00808000
CLR_PALEGRAY	15L	0x00cccccc

TABLE 6.2 Additional logical color indexes

Definition	Index	RGB Value in Hex
CLR_FALSE	−5L	0x00000000
CLR_TRUE	−4L	0x00ffffff
CLR_DEFAULT	−3L	0x00ffffff
CLR_WHITE	−2L	0x00ffffff
CLR_BLACK	−1L	0x00000000

In addition to the predefined color indexes of Table 6.1, each PM application also has available for its use a number of additional color indexes, which are set out in Table 6.2. The added color indexes in Table 6.2 are not included among the indexes of the default color table. Rather, they are predefined by the operating system and cannot be changed by an application.

In essence, a color table is an array of RGB values that can be referenced indirectly by using one or more values chosen from a listed set of color indexes. Such RGB values as correspond to a particular color index are stored in an RGB2 data structure, which has the following format:

```
typedef struct _RGB2 {
    BYTE bBlue;
    BYTE bGreen;
    BYTE bRed;
    BYTE fcOptions;
} RGB2;
```

The RGB2 data structure describes a color by using a byte to store intensity levels of the three primary colors: red, green, and blue. Specified intensities of each of the three primary colors can range from 0 to 255, with the result that any one color is selected from a palette of 16,777,216 colors.

PRESENTATION SPACES

For an application to begin drawing a window, it must first set up a *presentation space* within the window. A window can have a *cached-micro, micro,* or *normal* presentation space. A thorough discussion of the distinctions that exist among these three types of presentation spaces, and which type of presentation space is best to select for a particular use within a particular application, is more suitable for books that are devoted principally to the topic of PM graphics programming. Accordingly, these topics will be discussed here only to the extent that it is necessary and appropriate to do so.

Most windows use the simplest of the three types of presentation spaces, namely, a cached-micro presentation space. However, some of the techniques that are presented in this book may require a more powerful type of presentation space. Reasons will be briefly explained for selecting one of the two more powerful types of presentation spaces in case a more capable presentation space is needed.

WORKING IN INDEX MODE

When an application first creates a presentation space, it is given the default color table that is shown in Table 6.1. The application can modify its color table by calling the `GpiCreateLogColorTable` API, which also can be used to switch between index mode and RGB mode for selecting colors.

When in the index mode, applications use a color index value to designate a color to use for painting their windows. A color index is an offset into a color table that maps an index to a corresponding RGB value. Table 6.1 presents a color table that shows the default color index values used by PM. Table 6.1 also lists the RGB values that are associated with the listed default color indexes.

You can change the RGB value for any color index in a color table by using the `GpiCreateLogColorTable` API. Such entries can be added to and removed from a color table as may be needed; however, there is a limit to the number of entries that can be added. The largest index into a logical color table that the system allows can be queried by using the `DevQueryCaps` API with a `CAPS_COLOR_INDEX` flag.

When using `GpiCreateLogColorTable` to make changes in the contents of a color table, keep in mind that the changes that are made apply only to a designated presentation space. If you are using a cached-micro presentation space to process a `WM_PAINT` message, your changes will be lost once you release the presentation space. Therefore, if you need to preserve the state of a color table while processing many messages, you should select a micro presentation space or a normal presentation space instead of a cached-micro presentation space.

Displaying a Color Table

An example program, called the LCT program (the source code for which is listed in the following section), displays all of the colors that are available using the predefined indexes of Tables 6.1 and 6.2. The client window that is set up by the LCT program is divided into equally sized rectangles to display the rainbow of colors that are described in PM's default color table.

The client's window procedure in the LCT program handles the task of displaying the rainbow of colors when it receives a `WM_PAINT` message. The code that handles `WM_PAINT` messages goes through the list of PM's predefined color index values, starting with the first-listed index, `CLR_FALSE`, and ending with the last-listed index, `CLR_PALEGRAY`. A horizontal rectangle is drawn using each color index. The result is a window striped with rectangles that show each available color.

WinBeginPaint

An API called `WinBeginPaint` is used to obtain a cached-micro presentation space to process `WM_PAINT` messages. The following excerpt of code from the LCT program shows the call that is made:

```
hps = WinBeginPaint( hwnd, NULLHANDLE, &rcl );
```

The cached-micro presentation space is automatically set up with PM's default logical color table using index mode. A call to `WinEndPaint` will release the presentation space when the processing of the `WM_PAINT` message has been completed. Because a cached-micro presentation space has been used, changes to the color table will be lost at this point. If you want to retain these changes for use with the next `WM_PAINT` message, the `NULLHANDLE` value will need to be changed to a presentation space handle obtained from a call to `GpiCreatePS`, which is done when a window is created.

The presentation space obtained from `WinBeginPaint` is automatically set up in the index mode. The mode determines how PM interprets the third parameter used in the API that paints the LCT program's colored rectangles, namely `WinFillRect`.

In the index mode, PM assumes that a color index will be used for all APIs that require a color as one of their parameters. However, if the RGB mode is set, PM assumes that color parameters will be specified by using an RGB color value. These color parameters could also take the form of an index into a logical device palette, but only if the application is using palette management.

THE LCT PROGRAM'S SOURCE CODE

The LCT program is a very short program with most of its code devoted to handling the `WM_PAINT` and `WM_SIZE` messages. The LCT program was compiled from the following files:

LCT.C

```
#define INCL_WIN
#define INCL_GPI
#define INCL_DEV
#include <os2.h>
#include "lct.h"


/* prototypes */
INT main( VOID );
MRESULT EXPENTRY ClientWndProc( HWND, ULONG, MPARAM, MPARAM );
```

```
INT main (VOID)
{
   HAB    hab;
   HMQ    hmq;
   HWND   hwndFrame;
   HWND   hwndClient;
   CHAR   szClientClass[] = "Client Window";
   QMSG   qmsg;
   ULONG  flCreateFlags = FCF_TITLEBAR        /* create: title bar control  */
                        | FCF_SYSMENU         /*         system menu control */
                        | FCF_MINMAX          /*         min and max buttons  */
                        | FCF_SIZEBORDER      /* draw sizeborders            */
                        | FCF_SHELLPOSITION   /* shell decides window position */
                        | FCF_TASKLIST        /* title added to switch list  */
                        | FCF_ICON;           /* frame has an icon           */

   hab = WinInitialize( 0 );

   hmq = WinCreateMsgQueue( hab, 0 );

   WinRegisterClass( hab,                     /* anchor block handle */
                     szClientClass,           /* class name */
                     ClientWndProc,           /* pointer to window procedure */
                     CS_SIZEREDRAW,           /* class style */
                     0 );                     /* number of class data bytes */

   hwndFrame = WinCreateStdWindow(
                     HWND_DESKTOP,                    /* Desktop window is parent   */
                     WS_VISIBLE,                      /* window styles              */
                     &flCreateFlags,                  /* frame control flag         */
                     szClientClass,                   /* client window class name   */
                     "Default Logical Color Table",   /* title bar text             */
                     0,                               /* no special class style     */
                     NULLHANDLE,                      /* resource is in .EXE file   */
                     ID_FRAME_RES,                    /* frame window identifier    */
                     &hwndClient);                    /* client window handle       */

   if ( hwndFrame )
      while (WinGetMsg( hab, &qmsg, NULLHANDLE, 0, 0 ))
         WinDispatchMsg( hab, &qmsg );

   WinDestroyWindow( hwndFrame ); /* clean up */
   WinDestroyMsgQueue( hmq );
   WinTerminate( hab );

   return 0;
} /* end of main */


MRESULT EXPENTRY ClientWndProc( HWND hwnd, ULONG msg, MPARAM mp1, MPARAM mp2 )
{
   static SHORT cxClient, cyClient;        /* size of the client window        */

   switch( msg ) {
```

```
      case WM_PAINT:
        { HPS    hps;
          RECTL  rectl;
          ULONG  ulyStart, ulyInc, ulyExtra;
          LONG   i;

          hps = WinBeginPaint( hwnd, 0L, &rectl );

          ulyStart = (LONG)cyClient;                /* start at the top */
          ulyInc = (LONG)cyClient / NUM_INDICES;    /* row size in pels */
          ulyExtra = (LONG)cyClient % NUM_INDICES;  /* extra pels        */

          for (i = CLR_FALSE; i <= CLR_PALEGRAY; i++) {
             rectl.xLeft = 0;
             rectl.xRight = (LONG)cxClient;
             rectl.yTop = ulyStart;
             rectl.yBottom = ulyStart-ulyInc;

             ulyStart -= ulyInc;            /* reset start for next time around */

               if (ulyExtra) {              /* distribute any remaining rows */
                  rectl.yBottom--;
                  ulyStart--;
                  ulyExtra--;
               }

             WinFillRect(hps, &rectl, i);
          }

        WinEndPaint( hps );
        } break;

      case WM_SIZE:
          cxClient = SHORT1FROMMP(mp2);
          cyClient = SHORT2FROMMP(mp2);
          break;

      case WM_ERASEBACKGROUND:
          /* return TRUE to request PM to paint the window background */
          return (MRESULT)( TRUE );

      default:
          return WinDefWindowProc( hwnd, msg, mp1, mp2 );

      }

      return (MRESULT)FALSE;
} /* end of ClientWndProc */
```

LCT.H

```
#define ID_FRAME_RES      100

#define NUM_INDICES       ((CLR_PALEGRAY-CLR_FALSE)+1)
```

LCT.RC

```
#include <os2.h>
#include "lct.h"

ICON    ID_FRAME_RES lct.ico
```

LCT.DEF

```
NAME LCT WINDOWAPI

DESCRIPTION 'Logical Color Table Example Program'

CODE    MOVEABLE
DATA    MOVEABLE MULTIPLE

HEAPSIZE  10240
STACKSIZE 24576
```

LCT.MAK

```
all : lct.exe

lct.exe : lct.obj lct.def lct.res
        link386 /PM:PM lct,,,,lct.def;
        rc lct.res

lct.res : lct.rc lct.ico lct.h
        rc -r lct.rc

lct.obj : lct.c lct.h
        icc /C /Ss /W3 .$*.c
```

LCT.ICO

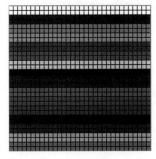

VGA Independent

LCT.ICO file, containing the icon for the LCT program.

WORKING IN RGB MODE

An RGB value can be used to specify a color directly instead of using an index into a color table. Most applications are satisfied with the default colors; however, applications that want to exploit color beyond the colors that are provided by system defaults can set up custom color tables or can switch to RGB mode. RGB mode yields a color palette of 16,777,216 unique colors and supplies much more flexibility than is offered by using the color tables of index mode.

The `GpiCreateLogColorTable` API is used to switch a presentation space into RGB mode. An example program called CIRCLES (the source code for which is presented later) demonstrates how an application's presentation space can be put into the RGB mode. The program displays three intersecting circles, each drawn with one of the primary colors, red, green, and blue. The three circles are drawn so that their colors blend together where they overlap.

The CIRCLES program illustrates the possible combinations of colors that can be formed by blending a user-defined set of the three primary colors. The centermost area, where all three circles overlap, shows the RGB color that results from combining all three primary colors. The three other overlapping areas show the RGB colors that result when two of the three primary colors are blended.

Figure 6.1 shows two of the windows that are created by the CIRCLES program. One window contains the three intersecting circles. The other window is a dialog box that provides a set of three PM controls called *spin buttons*. Each

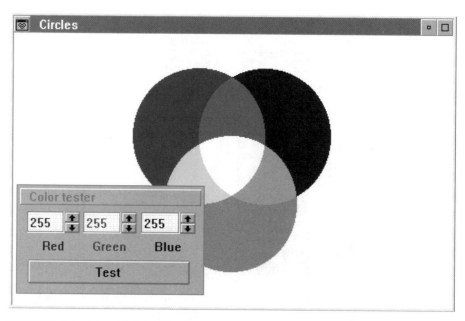

FIGURE 6.1   The CIRCLES program as it appears when started.

of the three spin buttons is associated with a separate one of the three circles. The spin buttons each store a value, ranging from 0 to 255, that represents the light intensity of the primary color of its associated circle. The primary color intensities that are used to draw the intersecting circles can be altered by changing the values that appear in the circles' associated spin buttons. The result of the changed intensities can be viewed by pressing the button labeled "Test." The "Test" button causes the three circles to be drawn with the newly set red, green, and blue intensity values.

The following listings show the code used to create the CIRCLES program:

CIRCLES.C

```
#define INCL_GPI
#define INCL_WIN
#include <os2.h>
#include "circles.h"

/* prototypes */
INT main( VOID );
MRESULT EXPENTRY ClientWndProc( HWND, ULONG, MPARAM, MPARAM );
MRESULT EXPENTRY MyDlgProc( HWND, ULONG, MPARAM, MPARAM );


/* global variables */
HAB       hab;
HWND      hwndClient;
POINTL    aPtl[3];
SHORT     Radius;
ARCPARAMS arcp = { 1, 1, 0, 0 };
LONG aColors[] = { 0x00FF0000L, 0x0000FF00L, 0x000000FFL };
                  /* red           green         blue */



INT main( VOID )
{
    HMQ  hmq;
    QMSG qmsg;
    HWND hwndFrame;
    HWND hwndDlg;
    static CHAR szClientClass[] = "Client Window";
    ULONG flCreateFlags = FCF_TITLEBAR       /* create: title bar control   */
                   | FCF_SYSMENU       /*          system menu control  */
                   | FCF_MINMAX        /*          min and max buttons   */
                   | FCF_SIZEBORDER    /* draw sizeborders              */
                   | FCF_SHELLPOSITION /* shell decides window position */
                   | FCF_TASKLIST      /* title added to switch list     */
                   | FCF_ICON;         /* frame has an icon              */

    hab = WinInitialize( 0 );
    hmq = WinCreateMsgQueue( hab, 0 );

    WinRegisterClass( hab,             /* anchor block handle */
                  szClientClass,  /* class name */
```

```
                      ClientWndProc,  /* pointer to window procedure */
                      CS_SIZEREDRAW | CS_SYNCPAINT,  /* class style */
                      0 );            /* number of class data bytes */

    hwndFrame = WinCreateStdWindow(
                  HWND_DESKTOP,   /* parent */
                  0,              /* use default frame window style */
                  &flCreateFlags, /* creation flags for frame window */
                  szClientClass,  /* client window class name */
                  "Circles",      /* text added to title */
                  0,              /* use default client window style */
                  NULLHANDLE,     /* resource ID's are in rc file */
                  ID_CIRCLES,     /* ID for frame window */
                  &hwndClient );  /* address to place client window handle */

    if (hwndFrame) {
        WinShowWindow( hwndFrame, TRUE );

        hwndDlg = WinLoadDlg( HWND_DESKTOP,       /* Parent */
                              hwndFrame,          /* Owner */
                              (PFNWP)MyDlgProc,
                              NULLHANDLE,
                              ID_DLGBOX,
                              NULL );
        if ( hwndDlg)
            while (WinGetMsg( hab, &qmsg, NULLHANDLE, 0, 0 ))
                WinDispatchMsg( hab, &qmsg );
    }

    WinDestroyWindow( hwndFrame );
    WinDestroyMsgQueue( hmq );
    WinTerminate( hab );

    return 0;
} /* end of main */


MRESULT EXPENTRY ClientWndProc( HWND hwnd, ULONG msg, MPARAM mp1, MPARAM mp2 )
{
    static HDC hdc;
    static HPS hps;
    static SIZEL sizl = { 0, 0 };

    switch (msg) {

    case WM_SIZE:
      { SHORT x,y, xTrans, yTrans;

        x = (SHORT)( SHORT1FROMMP( mp2 ) / 4 );
        y = (SHORT)( SHORT2FROMMP( mp2 ) / 4 );
        Radius = ( x > y ? y : x );
        xTrans = (SHORT)( ( SHORT1FROMMP( mp2 ) - 3*Radius )/2 );
        yTrans = (SHORT)( ( SHORT2FROMMP( mp2 ) - 3*Radius )/2 );
```

```
      aPtl[0].x = Radius + xTrans;                  aPtl[0].y = 2*Radius + yTrans;
      aPtl[1].x = (SHORT)(1.5*Radius) + xTrans;  aPtl[1].y =   Radius + yTrans;
      aPtl[2].x = 2 * Radius + xTrans;             aPtl[2].y = 2*Radius + yTrans;

      arcp.lQ = arcp.lP = Radius;
    } break;

  case WM_PAINT:
    { RECTL rcl;
      SHORT i;

      hps = WinBeginPaint( hwnd, NULLHANDLE, &rcl );
      WinFillRect( hps, &rcl, CLR_BLACK );

      GpiCreateLogColorTable( hps, 0, LCOLF_RGB, 0, 0, NULL );
      GpiSetArcParams( hps, &arcp );

      GpiSetMix( hps, FM_OR );

      for (i=0; i<3; i++) {
          GpiMove( hps, &aPtl[i] ) ;
          GpiSetColor( hps, aColors[i] );
          GpiFullArc( hps, DRO_FILL, MAKEFIXED(1,0) );
      } /* endfor */

      WinEndPaint(hps);
    } break;

  default:
    return WinDefWindowProc( hwnd, msg, mp1, mp2 );
  }
  return FALSE;
} /* end of ClientWndProc */


MRESULT EXPENTRY MyDlgProc( HWND hwnd, ULONG msg, MPARAM mp1, MPARAM mp2 )
{
  switch(msg) {

    case WM_INITDLG:
        WinSendDlgItemMsg( hwnd, ID_RED_SPIN, SPBM_SETLIMITS,
                           MPFROMLONG( 255 ), MPFROMLONG( 0 ));
        WinSendDlgItemMsg( hwnd, ID_GREEN_SPIN, SPBM_SETLIMITS,
                           MPFROMLONG( 255 ), MPFROMLONG( 0 ));
        WinSendDlgItemMsg( hwnd, ID_BLUE_SPIN, SPBM_SETLIMITS,
                           MPFROMLONG( 255 ), MPFROMLONG( 0 ));
        WinSendDlgItemMsg( hwnd, ID_RED_SPIN, SPBM_SETCURRENTVALUE,
                           MPFROMLONG( 255 ), MPFROMLONG( 0 ));
        WinSendDlgItemMsg( hwnd, ID_GREEN_SPIN, SPBM_SETCURRENTVALUE,
                           MPFROMLONG( 255 ), MPFROMLONG( 0 ));
        WinSendDlgItemMsg( hwnd, ID_BLUE_SPIN, SPBM_SETCURRENTVALUE,
                           MPFROMLONG( 255 ), MPFROMLONG( 0 ));
        break;
```

```
    case WM_COMMAND:
       switch (SHORT1FROMMP( mp1 )) {

         case ID_TEST:
           { ULONG ulRed, ulGreen, ulBlue;
             WinSendDlgItemMsg( hwnd, ID_RED_SPIN, SPBM_QUERYVALUE,
                                MPFROMP( &ulRed ),
                                MPFROM2SHORT( 0, SPBQ_ALWAYSUPDATE ) );
             WinSendDlgItemMsg( hwnd, ID_GREEN_SPIN, SPBM_QUERYVALUE,
                                MPFROMP( &ulGreen ),
                                MPFROM2SHORT( 0, SPBQ_ALWAYSUPDATE ) );
             WinSendDlgItemMsg( hwnd, ID_BLUE_SPIN, SPBM_QUERYVALUE,
                                MPFROMP( &ulBlue ),
                                MPFROM2SHORT( 0, SPBQ_ALWAYSUPDATE ) );
             aColors[0] = ( ulRed   << 16 );
             aColors[1] = ( ulGreen << 8 );
             aColors[2] = ( ulBlue );
             WinInvalidateRect( hwndClient, NULL, FALSE );
           } break;

         default:
             return (MRESULT)FALSE;
       }
       break;

    default:
       return( WinDefDlgProc( hwnd, msg, mp1, mp2 ));
  }

  return FALSE;
} /* end of MyDlgProc */
```

CIRCLES.H

```
#define ID_CIRCLES       1
#define ID_DLGBOX        263
#define ID_RED_SPIN      264
#define ID_GREEN_SPIN    265
#define ID_BLUE_SPIN     266
#define ID_RED_TEXT      267
#define ID_GREEN_TEXT    268
#define ID_BLUE_TEXT     269
#define ID_BOX           270
#define ID_TEST          271
```

CIRCLES.RC

```
#include <os2.h>
#include "circles.h"

ICON ID_CIRCLES circles.ico
```

```
DLGTEMPLATE ID_DLGBOX LOADONCALL MOVEABLE DISCARDABLE
BEGIN
    DIALOG "Color tester", ID_DLGBOX, 10, 10, 135, 46, WS_VISIBLE,
        FCF_TITLEBAR | FCF_NOMOVEWITHOWNER
    BEGIN
        CONTROL         "", ID_RED_SPIN,    3, 31, 40, 12, WC_SPINBUTTON,
                        SPBS_NUMERICONLY | SPBS_MASTER | SPBS_SERVANT |
                        SPBS_JUSTDEFAULT | WS_GROUP | WS_TABSTOP |
                        WS_VISIBLE
                        PRESPARAMS PP_FOREGROUNDCOLORINDEX, CLR_DARKRED
                        PRESPARAMS PP_HILITEFOREGROUNDCOLORINDEX, CLR_DARKRED
        CONTROL         "", ID_GREEN_SPIN, 46, 31, 40, 12, WC_SPINBUTTON,
                        SPBS_NUMERICONLY | SPBS_MASTER | SPBS_SERVANT |
                        SPBS_JUSTDEFAULT | WS_GROUP | WS_TABSTOP |
                        WS_VISIBLE
                        PRESPARAMS PP_FOREGROUNDCOLORINDEX, CLR_DARKGREEN
                        PRESPARAMS PP_HILITEFOREGROUNDCOLORINDEX, CLR_DARKGREEN
        CONTROL         "", ID_BLUE_SPIN,  89, 31, 40, 12, WC_SPINBUTTON,
                        SPBS_NUMERICONLY | SPBS_MASTER | SPBS_SERVANT |
                        SPBS_JUSTDEFAULT | WS_GROUP | WS_TABSTOP |
                        WS_VISIBLE
                        PRESPARAMS PP_FOREGROUNDCOLORINDEX, CLR_DARKBLUE
                        PRESPARAMS PP_HILITEFOREGROUNDCOLORINDEX, CLR_DARKBLUE
        CTEXT           "Red",   ID_RED_TEXT,    3, 20, 40, 8
                        PRESPARAMS PP_FOREGROUNDCOLORINDEX, CLR_DARKRED
        CTEXT           "Green", ID_GREEN_TEXT, 46, 20, 40, 8
                        PRESPARAMS PP_FOREGROUNDCOLORINDEX, CLR_DARKGREEN
        CTEXT           "Blue",  ID_BLUE_TEXT,  89, 20, 40, 8
                        PRESPARAMS PP_FOREGROUNDCOLORINDEX, CLR_DARKBLUE
        PUSHBUTTON      "Test", ID_TEST, 3, 3, 123, 14
    END
END
```

CIRCLES.DEF

```
NAME CIRCLES WINDOWAPI

DESCRIPTION 'Circles Example Program'

CODE    MOVEABLE
DATA    MOVEABLE MULTIPLE

STACKSIZE    16348
HEAPSIZE     16348
```

CIRCLES.MAK

```
all : circles.exe

circles.exe : circles.obj circles.def circles.res
        link386 /PM:PM circles,,,,circles.def;
        rc circles.res
```

```
circles.res: circles.rc circles.ico circles.h
        rc -r circles.rc

circles.obj:circles.c circles.h
        ICC.EXE /C /Ss /W3 .\$*.c
```

CIRCLES.ICO

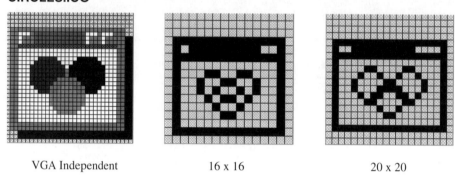

VGA Independent   16 x 16   20 x 20

CIRCLES.ICO file, containing various icons of different sizes.

DRAWING IN RGB MODE

The CIRCLES program was specifically designed to demonstrate how applications can use the RGB color mode. The circles that are drawn by the CIRCLES program use the GpiFullArc API after a special attribute is set to blend the circles' colors together in regions where the circles overlap. Before drawing the circles, GpiSetMix is used to set the foreground mix attribute to FM_OR. The mix attribute FM_OR will OR any pixels that are being drawn with the color already located at the pixel's position.

To get the proper effect of blending the colors of the circles together, it was necessary to first paint the client window black. If the client window were allowed to be a color other than black, the FM_OR mix attribute would blend the three circles' colors with the color of the client window. Thus, the resulting colors would *not* represent the desired color combinations.

If the default color of white were used to paint the client window before the circles were drawn, the color of the circles being drawn would be blended into the white and render the circles indistinguishable from the white color of the client window. This is due to the fact that the FM_OR mixing cannot alter a pixel that is painted white (since all of the pixel's bits are set to a value of one). Setting the client window's color to black sets each pixel to a value of zero, which permits each pixel to be changed as may be needed to permit the overlapping circles to be displayed when the nonzero colors of the circles are ORed with the zero-value black background.

Another preparatory step that is taken before drawing the three circles is to set the color table into the RGB mode. This is accomplished with the following call to `GpiCreateLogColorTable`:

```
GpiCreateLogColorTable( hps, 0, LCOLF_RGB, 0, 0, NULL );
```

The first parameter that is used by `GpiCreateLogColorTable` is the presentation space handle, namely `hps`. Next are the options flags. A zero value was used because neither of the following available option flags was needed:

- `LCOL_RESET`—a flag that resets the color table to its default state before updating it
- `LCOL_PURECOLOR`—a flag that indicates not to use dithering to simulate a color that is unavailable

Next, the `LCOLF_RGB` parameter is used to set an RGB mode. If an index mode were selected (as by specifying either of the flags `LCOLF_INDRGB` or `LCOLF_CONSECRGB`), additional data describing a color table would be required to appear as the last three parameters. However, since the flag `LCOLF_RGB` was used to set an RGB mode, the last three parameters can be ignored.

Before each of the three circles is drawn, the `GpiSetColor` API is used to set the foreground color to one of the primary colors, depending on the circle being drawn. The actual drawing of the circles is handled by the following code:

```
for (i=0; i<3; i++) {
    GpiMove( hps, &aPtl[i] ) ;
    GpiSetColor( hps, aColors[i] );
    GpiFullArc( hps, DRO_FILL, MAKEFIXED(1,0) );
}
```

An array, called `aPtl`, is set up with the positions to place the circles each time CIRCLES's window is resized. `GpiFullArc` is used with the `DRO_FILL` option to create circles that are filled in with the color set by `GpiSetColor`.

PHYSICAL COLOR TABLES

Each graphics adapter has its own physical color table that lists the actual colors the adapter can use to draw its pixels. The physical color table can be retrieved with the `GpiQueryRealColors` API. This API is similar to `GpiQueryLogColorTable` in that a table of RGB values along with the corresponding color indexes can also be obtained. `GpiQueryRealColors` can return the RGB values that are currently loaded into the palette of a graphics adapter or other physical device.

If the `LCOLOPT_INDEX` flag was set when the `GpiQueryRealColors` API was called, the corresponding color indexes will also be returned. By default, there are only 16 color indexes, ranging from `CLR_BACKGROUND` (0) to

CLR_PALEGRAY (15). If the system supports more than sixteen colors, all RGB values in the physical color table that do not correspond to one of the predefined color index values will be reported as having a color index of CLR_NOINDEX (negative 254). Applications can set color index values above CLR_PALEGRAY to correspond to any of the physical palette's RGB values not set by PM.

The color table information returned by the GpiQueryRealColors API reflects the state of a device's physical palette at the time of the call. The device's physical color palette can be changed by applications through the new palette manager functions, which will be discussed later.

COLOR DITHERING

PM applications can work with 24-bit RGB values, which yield a color palette of 16,777,216 entries. If a graphics adapter does not support 24 bits to describe each pixel, PM creates an illusion of having more colors available by using a technique called *dithering*.

Dithering uses several colors together to create the look of a color that is not actually available in the physical device palette. By filling an area with pixels of alternating colors a desired color can be approximated. An example of using this technique is filling an area with varying amounts of black and white pixels to create various shades of gray on a monochrome system.

PM applications can turn off dithering by restricting the display of color to "pure" colors that actually are available. A color table can be set up that excludes dithered colors, by using a flag called LCOL_PURECOLOR flag in the flOptions field of the GpiCreateLogColorTable API.

PALETTE MANAGER

Introduced with OS/2 Version 2.0 is a collection of APIs referred to as the *palette manager*. The APIs of the palette manager allow applications to manipulate the palette of a physical device to provide for custom color requirements. For example, if a video display is capable of running at 8 bits per pixel, this permits 256 unique colors to be available for use at any given time.

PM's display drivers try to set a physical device, such as a graphics adapter, to have a palette of colors that covers an entire spectrum of visible color. If a physical palette handles only a small number of colors, only a few shades of each primary color will be stored in the physical palette. Most colors of the spectrum will need to be drawn using dithering.

Problems with using a limited palette can be seen by displaying a bitmap using many shades of a single primary color. The default palette loaded by a PM device driver will try to make available as many colors as possible. A bitmap using many different shades of blue may not appear clear, principally because too many of the pure colors that are available in a physical palette are being used for other colors such as red and green. By default, the shades of blue in the bitmap that are not available in the physical device palette will be nearest fit to a color that is available in the default device palette. Using the palette manager APIs, one can tune the physical palette to accommodate the color requirements of a bitmap or application program.

Palette management is very hardware-specific and is not always available. The number of colors available for a system using one to four bits per pixel is not large enough to use a palette manager. Support for such small palettes simply does not make sense and is not supported in OS/2. At the other extreme, when a 16- to 24-bit-per-pixel video mode (referred to as a *direct color mode*) is used, a color is specified by the RGB value without the need for a palette; hence, the palette manager is not supported when a direct color mode is in use.

The palette manager is intended to serve video displays that run at 8 bits per pixel. At 8 bits per pixel you have access to 256 colors, which is enough to keep the standard PM colors intact while allowing applications some flexibility to adjust the physical palette to meet their color needs.

Programming the Palette Manager

To use the palette manager, the PM display driver must have built-in functions to provide support for the palette manager APIs. Support for the palette manager can be tested by using the DevQueryCaps API with a CAPS_ADDITIONAL_GRAPHICS index. The API returns a value that has a bit called CAPS_PALETTE_MANAGER set when palette manager APIs are supported by the system.

The following is a list of the palette manager's available APIs:

- GpiCreatePalette An API that creates a logical palette by using an array of RGB2 values and returns a handle to the newly created logical palette. A logical palette is not automatically associated into a presentation space. Before the logical palette can be used, the GpiSelectPalette API must be called to associate the logical palette with a presentation space. A logical palette must be realized by calling the WinRealizePalette API.
- GpiSelectPalette An API that associates a logical palette, referenced by the HPAL data type, with a presentation space. You can specify a NULLHANDLE to select the default palette.
- WinRealizePalette An API that realizes a logical palette into the physical hardware palette. If a window has the focus when it calls this API, the PM display driver will give it highest priority when it allocates slots from the real physical device palette. This API causes a broadcast of the WM_REALIZEPALETTE message, and it invalidates the whole desktop if any of the system default colors were changed during the realization of a palette.

- `GpiAnimatePalette` An API that changes the RGB values of palette indexes that have been marked as *animating indexes*. During `GpiCreatePalette`, palette indexes are marked as animating by setting the `PC_RESERVED` flag in the `fcOptions` field of the `RGB2` structure. Animating indexes are normally used when the RGB color values need to be changed often. Palette slots marked with this bit will not be shared with other palette manager applications.
- `GpiSetPaletteEntries` An API that changes the RGB values of a previously defined logical palette. The updated palette must be realized in order for these changes to be reflected into the physical device palette.
- `GpiQueryPalette` An API that returns the logical palette currently selected into the presentation space.
- `GpiQueryPaletteInfo` An API that returns the palette information for a given logical palette.
- `GpiDeletePalette` An API that deletes a logical palette as long as it is not currently selected into a presentation space.

The PALETTE Program

An example program called PALETTE (the source code for which is presented here) creates a logical palette consisting of 128 entries. It begins with a palette containing 128 shades of blue. The client window is divided into 128 columns, and `WinFillRect` is used to fill each column with a color from its palette. A pull-down menu labeled "Colors" can change the color shades in the logical palette to one of the following colors: red, green, blue, and gray.

The PALETTE program's source code is listed in the following six files:

PALETTE.C

```
#define INCL_WIN
#define INCL_GPI
#define INCL_DEV
#define INCL_DOS
#include <os2.h>
#include "palette.h"


/* prototypes */
INT main( VOID );
MRESULT EXPENTRY ClientWndProc( HWND, ULONG, MPARAM, MPARAM );


/* globals */
HAB hab;
RGB2 Palette[128];
```

```
INT main (VOID)
{
    HMQ     hmq;
    HWND    hwndFrame;
    HWND    hwndClient;
    QMSG    qmsg;
    CHAR    szClientClass[] = "Client Window";
    ULONG   flCreateFlags = FCF_TITLEBAR       /* create: title bar control   */
                          | FCF_SYSMENU        /*         system menu control */
                          | FCF_MENU           /*         action bar          */
                          | FCF_MINMAX         /*         min and max buttons  */
                          | FCF_SIZEBORDER     /* draw sizeborders            */
                          | FCF_SHELLPOSITION  /* shell decides window position */
                          | FCF_TASKLIST       /* title added to switch list  */
                          | FCF_ICON;          /* frame has an icon           */

    hab = WinInitialize( 0 );

    hmq = WinCreateMsgQueue( hab, 0 );

    WinRegisterClass( hab,                 /* anchor block handle */
                      szClientClass,       /* class name */
                      ClientWndProc,       /* pointer to window procedure */
                      CS_SIZEREDRAW,       /* class style */
                      0 );                 /* number of class data bytes */

    hwndFrame = WinCreateStdWindow(
                HWND_DESKTOP,          /* desktop window is parent    */
                WS_VISIBLE,            /* window styles               */
                &flCreateFlags,        /* frame control flag          */
                szClientClass,         /* client window class name    */
                "Palette Example",     /* no window text              */
                0,                     /* no special class style      */
                NULLHANDLE,            /* resource is in .EXE file    */
                ID_FRAME_RES,          /* frame window identifier     */
                &hwndClient);          /* client window handle        */

    if ( hwndFrame )
        while (WinGetMsg( hab, &qmsg, NULLHANDLE, 0, 0 ))
            WinDispatchMsg( hab, &qmsg );

    WinDestroyWindow( hwndFrame );     /* clean up */
    WinDestroyMsgQueue( hmq );
    WinTerminate( hab );

    return 0;
} /* end of main */


MRESULT EXPENTRY ClientWndProc( HWND hwnd, ULONG msg, MPARAM mp1, MPARAM mp2 )
{
    static HDC    hdc;                      /* device context handle    */
    static HPS    hps;                      /* presentation space handle */
```

```
static HPAL   hpal;                   /* palette handle          */
static SHORT  cxClient, cyClient;  /* size of the client window */

/* variables to keep handy for storing temporary values */
static ULONG  ulClrChanged;           /* count of colors changed  */
static LONG   i;                      /* used for array indexing  */

switch( msg ) {

case WM_CREATE:
 { SIZEL pagesize = { 0L, 0L }; /* presentation page size    */
   LONG lReturn;

    /* Since we are using a cached-micro PS, we can simply use this
     *    call to obtain a handle to the display device context.
     */
   hdc = WinOpenWindowDC( hwnd );

   DevQueryCaps( hdc,
                 CAPS_ADDITIONAL_GRAPHICS,
                 (LONG)1,
                 &lReturn );

   if (!(lReturn & CAPS_PALETTE_MANAGER))
       WinMessageBox( HWND_DESKTOP,              /* parent window handle */
                      hwnd,                      /* owner window handle  */
                      "No Palette Support",      /* MsgBox Text          */
                      "Palette Program",         /* MsgBox Title Text    */
                      0,                         /* MsgBox Window ID     */
                      MB_ENTER | MB_WARNING); /* MsgBox window style  */

   hps = GpiCreatePS ( hab,
                       hdc,
                       &pagesize,
                       PU_PELS |
                       GPIT_MICRO |
                       GPIA_ASSOC );


    /* Set up the RGB values in our logical palette (alLogPal).
     * Our logical palette is an array of 65 LONGs which contain
     * the RGB values. Each color is a 4 byte integer, with a value
     * (F*16777216) + (R*65536) + (G*256) + B
     */
   for (i = 0; i < 128; i++) {
       Palette[i].bBlue = (BYTE)i;
       Palette[i].bGreen = Palette[i].bRed = Palette[i].fcOptions = 0;
   } /* endfor */

   hpal = GpiCreatePalette( hab,
                            LCOL_PURECOLOR,
                            LCOLF_CONSECRGB,  /* array of RGB values */
                            128,              /* count of elements    */
                            (PULONG)&Palette );
```

```
   GpiSelectPalette( hps, hpal );

   WinRealizePalette( hwnd, hps, &ulClrChanged );

 } break;

case WM_COMMAND:

   switch (SHORT1FROMMP( mp1 )) {

      case IDM_BLUE:
      case IDM_RED:
      case IDM_GREEN:
      case IDM_GRAY:

         if ( SHORT1FROMMP(mp1) == IDM_BLUE ) {
            for (i = 0; i < 128; i++) {
               Palette[i].bBlue = (BYTE)i;
               Palette[i].bGreen = Palette[i].bRed
                  = Palette[i].fcOptions = 0;
            } /* endfor */
         }

         else if (SHORT1FROMMP( mp1 ) == IDM_RED) {
            for (i = 0; i < 128; i++) {
               Palette[i].bRed = (BYTE)i;
               Palette[i].bGreen = Palette[i].bBlue
                  = Palette[i].fcOptions = 0;
            } /* endfor */
         }

         else if (SHORT1FROMMP( mp1 ) == IDM_GREEN) {
            for (i = 0; i < 128; i++) {
               Palette[i].bGreen = (BYTE)i;
               Palette[i].bRed = Palette[i].bBlue
                  = Palette[i].fcOptions = 0;
            } /* endfor */
         }

         else if (SHORT1FROMMP( mp1 ) == IDM_GRAY) {
            for (i = 0; i < 128; i++) {
               Palette[i].bBlue = Palette[i].bGreen =
               Palette[i].bRed = (BYTE)i;
               Palette[i].fcOptions = 0;
            } /* endfor */
         }

         GpiSetPaletteEntries( hpal,
                              LCOLF_CONSECRGB, /* array of RGB values */
                              0,               /* starting index      */
                              128,             /* count of elements   */
                              (PULONG)&Palette );
```

```
            WinRealizePalette( hwnd, hps, &ulClrChanged );
            WinInvalidateRect( hwnd, NULL, FALSE );
            break;

        default:
            return WinDefWindowProc( hwnd, msg, mp1, mp2 );
    }
    break;

case WM_ERASEBACKGROUND:
    return (MRESULT)(TRUE);

case WM_PAINT:
  { RECTL         rcl;

    WinBeginPaint( hwnd, hps, &rcl );

    for (i = 0; i < 128; i++) {
        rcl.yBottom = 0;
        rcl.yTop = cyClient;
        rcl.xLeft = i * (LONG)cxClient/128;
        rcl.xRight = (i + 1) * (LONG)cxClient/128;

        WinFillRect( hps, (PRECTL)&rcl, i );

    } /* endfor */

    WinEndPaint( hps );
  } break;

case WM_SIZE:
    cxClient = SHORT1FROMMP( mp2 );
    cyClient = SHORT2FROMMP( mp2 );
    break;

case WM_REALIZEPALETTE:
    if (WinRealizePalette( hwnd, hps, &ulClrChanged ))
        WinInvalidateRect( hwnd, NULL, FALSE );
    break;

case WM_DESTROY:
    GpiDestroyPS( hps );
    DevCloseDC( hdc );
    break;

default:
    return WinDefWindowProc( hwnd, msg, mp1, mp2 );
}

return (MRESULT)FALSE;
} /* end of ClientWndProc */
```

PALETTE.H

```
#define ID_FRAME_RES   100

#define IDM_COLORS     200
#define IDM_BLUE       201
#define IDM_RED        202
#define IDM_GREEN      203
#define IDM_GRAY       204
```

PALETTE.RC

```
#include <os2.h>
#include "palette.h"


ICON    ID_FRAME_RES palette.ico

MENU    ID_FRAME_RES PRELOAD
BEGIN
  SUBMENU "~Colors", IDM_COLORS
  BEGIN
    MENUITEM "Blue",  IDM_BLUE,  MIS_TEXT
    MENUITEM "Red",   IDM_RED,   MIS_TEXT
    MENUITEM "Green", IDM_GREEN, MIS_TEXT
    MENUITEM "Gray",  IDM_GRAY,  MIS_TEXT
  END
END
```

PALETTE.DEF

```
NAME PALETTE WINDOWAPI

DESCRIPTION 'Palette Manager Example Program'

CODE    MOVEABLE
DATA    MOVEABLE MULTIPLE

HEAPSIZE  10240
STACKSIZE 24576
```

PALETTE.MAK

```
all : palette.exe

palette.exe : palette.obj palette.def palette.res
        link386 /PM:PM palette,,,,palette.def;
        rc palette.res
```

```
palette.res : palette.rc palette.ico palette.h
        rc -r palette.rc

palette.obj : palette.c palette.h
        icc /C /Ss /W3 . $*.c
```

PALETTE.ICO

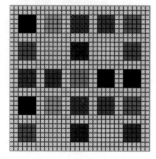

VGA Independent

PALETTE.ICO file, containing the icon for the PALETTE program.

Some systems will not support the palette manager's APIs. To determine if the palette manager functions are available, PALETTE makes a call to DevQueryCaps when it handles a WM_CREATE message. The following code is an excerpt of the call made to DevQueryCaps:

```
DevQueryCaps( hdc,
             CAPS_ADDITIONAL_GRAPHICS,
             (LONG)1,
             &lReturn );

if (!(lReturn & CAPS_PALETTE_MANAGER))
    WinMessageBox( HWND_DESKTOP,              /* parent window handle */
                   hwnd,                      /* owner window handle  */
                   "No Palette Support",      /* MsgBox Text          */
                   "Palette Program",         /* MsgBox Title Text    */
                   0,                         /* MsgBox Window ID      */
                   MB_ENTER | MB_WARNING );   /* MsgBox window style  */
```

The first parameter (hdc) is obtained by calling the WinOpenWindowDC API. Using the CAPS_ADDITIONAL_GRAPHICS index, the last parameter (lReturn) receives a set of flags describing any additional graphics functions that are supported. A CAPS_PALETTE_MANAGER flag is present in lReturn if the palette manager APIs are supported.

If the palette manager is supported, a micro presentation space is created and associated with the screen device context (`hdc`) previously obtained by `WinOpenWindowDC`. A micro presentation space is used because the cached-micro presentation spaces are not efficient when dealing with the palette manager. Using a micro presentation space, the logical palette needs to be selected into the presentation space only once, unless there is a need to change it. Using a cached-micro presentation space, one would continually have to select the logical palette into the presentation space every time a new cached-micro presentation space is obtained.

PM will also broadcast a `WM_REALIZEPALETTE` message to determine the palette needs for all palette-aware applications. Using a cached-micro presentation space, an application will always need to carry out the additional step of calling `GpiSelectPalette` before `WinRealizePalette`. This additional step is inefficient and can be avoided by using a micro presentation space.

After PALETTE sets up the micro presentation space, it initializes an array of `RGB2` data structures, containing 128 shades of blue. Using this array, `GpiCreatePalette` is called to obtain a handle to a palette (`HPAL`) for PALETTE's logical palette.

During a `WM_PAINT` message, PALETTE divides the client window into 128 columns and uses `WinFillRect` to fill each column with a unique shade of blue from our `Palette` array of `RGB2`s. Once a palette is selected into a presentation space, colors can be referenced by using an index into the logical palette. The RGB color that will be used is a value that corresponds to that index taken from the currently selected palette.

The WM_REALIZEPALETTE Message

The `WM_REALIZEPALETTE` message is generated by PM under several different circumstances. This message is there to help both the application and the operating system. An application should realize its palette during this message. If the number of remapped indexes returned from the `WinRealizePalette` call is greater than zero, the application should repaint itself, because its colors may be out of date.

The `WM_REALIZEPALETTE` message also helps PM find out if there are any palette-aware applications still around. All palette-aware applications should handle this message. The default message handler will realize the default palette during the processing of this message.

Changing Palette Values

If the user selects one of the four choices that are available on the "Colors" pull-down menu, the contents of PALETTE's logical palette will be changed to one of the four available options. The available options are Red, Green, Blue, and Gray.

The logical palette used by the PALETTE program is changed by updating the palette structure (`Palette`) and calling the `GpiSetPaletteEntries` API. This API requires a handle to a palette and a pointer to a structure describing a palette. The `HPAL` that the PALETTE program is working with is already associated with the presentation space, so the `GpiSelectPalette` API does not need to be reused—one of the many advantages that result from using micro presentation spaces when working with the palette manager. To realize the updated palette, `WinRealizePalette` is called, and the client area is repainted by invalidating the client window.

CHAPTER 7
Presentation Parameters

PM's controls are designed to refer to a set of values called *presentation parameters* for the colors and fonts they should use. Presentation parameters allow programmers to change the default colors and the fonts of any PM control without having to change the code that handles the painting of the control's window. The system font and color scheme that is used in PM's buttons and menus can be replaced to provide new and different appearances.

Figure 7.1 shows an example of the radical changes you can make to the appearance of PM's controls by setting presentation parameters. The window shown in the figure belongs to an example program called PRESPARM, which is presented in this chapter to illustrate how presentation parameters are used and how a control receives data that specifies its presentation parameters.

WHY USE PRESENTATION PARAMETERS?

Presentation parameters serve a very practical purpose. They provide a very powerful and very flexible means for changing the appearance of PM's controls.

Many uses to which presentation parameters will be put during the years to come were probably not even imagined when PM was written. With this possibility kept in mind, it will be seen that the large fonts that can be displayed by the program shown in Figure 7.1 serve more as a demonstration of what can be done using presentation parameters than as an example of what presently is seen as having a practical application.

Actually, there are many practical applications for the use of presentation parameters. For instance, a program that has many menu items in its action bar may want to use a slightly smaller font to aid in fitting more items across

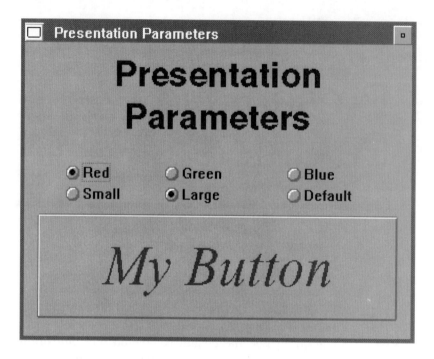

FIGURE 7.1   The window of an example program, called PRESPARM, that uses presentation parameters.

the width of its window. Another example of using presentation parameters is to allow users to replace the system font with a larger font that is easier to read. Similarly, the use of presentation parameters can permit a data entry program to change font colors used in a set of entry fields to red, indicating that the data that is presented in these fields needs to be updated or given special attention. As these examples illustrate, presentation parameters empower PM's controls and PM programs with a very great deal of flexibility.

Table 7.1 shows a list of available presentation parameters. The names of the various presentation parameters are descriptive, and the uses to which their associated values are to be put are quite clear. Note that each control concerns itself with only a few of the values that are set out in Table 7.1. Therefore, to change the appearance of a control, you will need to find the values that a particular control queries and uses. For instance, a static text control concerns itself only with colors that are specified by parameters `PP_FOREGROUNDCOLOR`, `PP_FOREGROUNDCOLORINDEX`, `PP_BORDERCOLOR`, and `PP_BORDERCOLORINDEX`. Setting any of the dozens of other parameters that are listed in Table 7.1 will have no effect on a static text control.

What a set of presentation parameters really provides is a "database" of recommended values for controls to use. However, if the data in the "database" is not queried by a control, the control will not be affected by a presentation parameter recommendation. Because PM's static text control explicitly queries

TABLE 7.1   The PP_ values available from PM

PP_FOREGROUNDCOLOR	1L
PP_FOREGROUNDCOLORINDEX	2L
PP_BACKGROUNDCOLOR	3L
PP_BACKGROUNDCOLORINDEX	4L
PP_HILITEFOREGROUNDCOLOR	5L
PP_HILITEFOREGROUNDCOLORINDEX	6L
PP_HILITEBACKGROUNDCOLOR	7L
PP_HILITEBACKGROUNDCOLORINDEX	8L
PP_DISABLEDFOREGROUNDCOLOR	9L
PP_DISABLEDFOREGROUNDCOLORINDEX	10L
PP_DISABLEDBACKGROUNDCOLOR	11L
PP_DISABLEDBACKGROUNDCOLORINDEX	12L
PP_BORDERCOLOR	13L
PP_BORDERCOLORINDEX	14L
PP_FONTNAMESIZE	15L
PP_FONTHANDLE	16L
PP_RESERVED	17L
PP_ACTIVECOLOR	18L
PP_ACTIVECOLORINDEX	19L
PP_INACTIVECOLOR	20L
PP_INACTIVECOLORINDEX	21L
PP_ACTIVETEXTFGNDCOLOR	22L
PP_ACTIVETEXTFGNDCOLORINDEX	23L
PP_ACTIVETEXTBGNDCOLOR	24L
PP_ACTIVETEXTBGNDCOLORINDEX	25L
PP_INACTIVETEXTFGNDCOLOR	26L
PP_INACTIVETEXTFGNDCOLORINDEX	27L
PP_INACTIVETEXTBGNDCOLOR	28L
PP_INACTIVETEXTBGNDCOLORINDEX	29L
PP_SHADOW	30L
PP_MENUFOREGROUNDCOLOR	31L
PP_MENUFOREGROUNDCOLORINDEX	32L
PP_MENUBACKGROUNDCOLOR	33L
PP_MENUBACKGROUNDCOLORINDEX	34L
PP_MENUHILITEFGNDCOLOR	35L
PP_MENUHILITEFGNDCOLORINDEX	36L
PP_MENUHILITEBGNDCOLOR	37L
PP_MENUHILITEBGNDCOLORINDEX	38L
PP_MENUDISABLEDFGNDCOLOR	39L
PP_MENUDISABLEDFGNDCOLORINDEX	40L
PP_MENUDISABLEDBGNDCOLOR	41L
PP_MENUDISABLEDBGNDCOLORINDEX	42L

PP_FOREGROUNDCOLOR, setting this parameter will have the desired effect of informing a static text control which color it should use to draw its text.

Many PM programs are written such that they make use only of system colors (SYSCLR_ index values) to draw their windows' borders, background, and text. These programs lack the flexibility to implement color scheme changes unless the entire PM environment and all of its controls are changed by altering system colors. Presentation parameters, on the other hand, have the advantage of being able to alter the colors that are used in a selected window, with the colors being changed one by one as may be desired.

INHERITING PRESENTATION PARAMETERS

When a PM window is created, it *inherits* a table of presentation parameters from its *owner window*. However, if a newly created window does not have an owner, then no presentation parameters are inherited.

As is shown by the parameter names that are listed in Table 7.1, presentation parameters store recommended colors for use in many of the common situations that a program may encounter. Also included in Table 7.1 is a default font (PP_FONTNAMESIZE) that a PM program uses when it draws text in a window (unless an alternate font is specified). By setting PP_FONTNAMESIZE, the system font that is usually used will be replaced.

Many windows have no need to bother with querying or changing inherited presentation parameters. Controls are usually the only window classes that make use of presentation parameters, and even a control typically will refer to only three or four parameters from the set of inherited presentation parameters. Because an attempt to store all of the parameters that are listed in Table 7.1 would require a sizable block of memory, windows are *not* set up such that each window has its own table to list all of its available presentation parameters.

To conserve resources, PM permits each window to list only additions and changes that have been made to the presentation parameters that the particular window inherited from its owner. When a window specifies a noninherited presentation parameter value, extra memory is allocated to store the parameter's value. Parameters can be added or deleted at any time during the existence of a window; if a window is destroyed, the memory that was allocated to store its presentation parameters is released.

Most windows use parameters that were inherited from their owner windows. A parameter that is being used by a particular window can be queried by using the WinQueryPresParams API. This API will determine whether the window has the parameter being queried in its list of parameters. If no matching parameter is found, the API will go on to check the owner's list of parameters for a match. Failing to find a match there, the API will proceed up the chain of owner windows until it finds a matching parameter that is listed by an owner window or until the API finally returns a zero to indicate that no match was found. By taking the approach of checking each window along the owner chain, PM avoids allocating extra memory if a window simply makes use of its inherited presentation parameters.

To check whether a window has listed any parameters of its own, the WinQueryPresParams API can be used with a flag called QPF_NOINHERIT to indicate that only the window's noninherited parameters are to be checked and that all inherited parameters are to be ignored. By the use of the QPF_NOINHERIT flag, the API will be instructed to return the value of a matching noninherited parameter or to return a value of zero if no match was found.

SETTING PRESENTATION PARAMETERS

The setting and removal of presentation parameters can be handled by the APIs `WinSetPresParam` and `WinRemovePresParam`, respectively. These APIs can be called at any time and will handle the needed allocation and deallocation of memory to store the presentation parameters of a window. A window's presentation parameters can also be specified during the creation of a window. That process allows one or more presentation parameters to be set without using the `WinSetPresParam` API.

THE PRESPARM PROGRAM

This example program, referred to by the title PRESPARM, displays a large button labeled "My Button" near the bottom of its window. The size and color of the font that labels the "My Button" button can be changed by using two sets of radio buttons that are located just above the "My Button" button.

Code listings that are used to compile the PRESPARM program follow:

PRESPARM.C

```c
#define INCL_GPI
#define INCL_WIN
#include <os2.h>
#include "presparm.h"


/* function prototypes */
INT main( VOID );
MRESULT EXPENTRY MyDlgProc( HWND, ULONG, MPARAM, MPARAM );


INT main( VOID )
{
   HAB  hab;
   HMQ  hmq;
   QMSG qmsg;
   HWND hwndDlg;
   SWP  swp;

   hab = WinInitialize( 0 );
   hmq = WinCreateMsgQueue( hab, 0 );

   hwndDlg = WinLoadDlg( HWND_DESKTOP,  /* set the desktop as parent */
                    NULLHANDLE,    /* no owner */
                    MyDlgProc,     /* address of dialog procedure */
                    NULLHANDLE,    /* use .EXE fill for resources */
                    ID_DLGBOX,     /* ID of the dialog box resource */
                    NULL );        /* no */

   /* find where system would place dialog box */
   WinQueryTaskSizePos( hab, 0, &swp );
```

```
        /* place dialog box at position given by the shell */
    WinSetWindowPos( hwndDlg,        /* change the dialog window's position */
                    NULLHANDLE,      /* ignored, SWP_ZORDER not set */
                    swp.x, swp.y,    /* position of lower left corner */
                    0, 0,            /* ignored SWP_SIZE not set */
                    SWP_SHOW         /* show dialog box */
                    | SWP_MOVE );    /* do not ignore swp.x and swp.y */

    if (hwndDlg)
        while (WinGetMsg( hab, &qmsg, NULLHANDLE, 0, 0 ))
            WinDispatchMsg( hab, &qmsg );

    WinDestroyWindow( hwndDlg );
    WinDestroyMsgQueue( hmq );
    WinTerminate( hab );

    return 0;
} /* end of main */


MRESULT EXPENTRY MyDlgProc( HWND hwnd, ULONG msg, MPARAM mp1, MPARAM mp2 )
{
    static HWND hwndButton;
    static CHAR szSmall[] = "8.Helvetica";
    static CHAR szLarge[] = "40.Times New Roman Italic";
    static RGB2 aRGB[] = {    0,    0, 0xFF,  0, /* red */
                              0, 0xFF,    0,  0, /* green */
                           0xFF,    0,    0,  0  /* blue */
                         };

    switch (msg) {

    case WM_INITDLG:
        /* set an icon for the dialog */
        WinSendMsg( hwnd,
                    WM_SETICON,
                    (MPARAM)WinQuerySysPointer( HWND_DESKTOP,
                                                SPTR_APPICON,
                                                FALSE ),
                    NULL);

        /* set ID_LARGE as presently selected */
        WinSendDlgItemMsg ( hwnd,
                            ID_LARGE,
                            BM_SETCHECK,
                            MPFROM2SHORT( TRUE, 0 ),
                            NULL );

        /* set ID_RED as presently selected */
        WinSendDlgItemMsg ( hwnd,
                            ID_RED,
                            BM_SETCHECK,
                            MPFROM2SHORT (TRUE, 0),
                            NULL );
```

```
      /* store the handle to "My Button" */
      hwndButton = WinWindowFromID( hwnd, ID_BUTTON );
      break;

   case WM_CONTROL:
      switch (SHORT1FROMMP( mp1 )) {
      case ID_RED:
      case ID_GREEN:
      case ID_BLUE:
          WinSetPresParam( hwndButton,
                           PP_FOREGROUNDCOLOR,
                           4, /* don't use sizeof( RGB ), too small == 3 */
                           (PVOID)&aRGB[ SHORT1FROMMP(mp1) - ID_RED ] );
          break;
      case ID_SMALL:
          WinSetPresParam( hwndButton,
                           PP_FONTNAMESIZE,
                           strlen( szSmall ) + 1,
                           (PVOID)szSmall );
          break;
      case ID_LARGE:
          WinSetPresParam( hwndButton,
                           PP_FONTNAMESIZE,
                           strlen( szLarge) + 1,
                           (PVOID)szLarge );
          break;
      case ID_DEFAULT:
          WinRemovePresParam( hwndButton,
                              PP_FONTNAMESIZE );
          break;
      default:
          return WinDefDlgProc( hwnd, msg, mp1, mp2 );
      }
      break;

   case WM_COMMAND:
      return (MRESULT)FALSE;

   case WM_CLOSE:
      WinPostMsg( hwnd, WM_QUIT, 0, 0 );
      return FALSE;

   default:
      return WinDefDlgProc( hwnd, msg, mp1, mp2 );
   }

   return (MRESULT)FALSE;
} /* end of MyDlgProc */
```

PRESPARM.H

```
#define ID_DLGBOX       101
#define ID_SMALL        102
#define ID_LARGE        103
```

```
#define ID_DEFAULT     104
#define ID_RED         105
#define ID_GREEN       106
#define ID_BLUE        107
#define ID_TEXT1       108
#define ID_TEXT2       109
#define ID_BUTTON      110
```

PRESPARM.RC

```
#include <os2.h>
#include "presparm.h"

DLGTEMPLATE ID_DLGBOX LOADONCALL MOVEABLE DISCARDABLE
BEGIN
    DIALOG "Presentation Parameters", ID_DLGBOX, 0, 0, 250, 138, 0,
        FCF_TITLEBAR | FCF_SYSMENU | FCF_MINBUTTON | FCF_TASKLIST
    BEGIN
        CTEXT          "Presentation",  ID_TEXT1,  8, 108, 234, 25
                       PRESPARAMS PP_FOREGROUNDCOLORINDEX, CLR_BLUE
                       PRESPARAMS PP_FONTNAMESIZE, "25.Helvetica Bold"
        CTEXT          "Parameters",    ID_TEXT2,  8,  88, 234, 25
                       PRESPARAMS PP_FOREGROUNDCOLORINDEX, CLR_BLUE
                       PRESPARAMS PP_FONTNAMESIZE, "25.Helvetica Bold"
        AUTORADIOBUTTON "Red",    ID_RED,    27, 72, 45, 10, WS_TABSTOP
                                                           | WS_GROUP
        AUTORADIOBUTTON "Green",  ID_GREEN,  92, 72, 45, 10, WS_TABSTOP
        AUTORADIOBUTTON "Blue",   ID_BLUE,  170, 72, 45, 10, WS_TABSTOP

        AUTORADIOBUTTON "Small",  ID_SMALL,  27, 62, 45, 10, WS_TABSTOP
                                                           | WS_GROUP
        AUTORADIOBUTTON "Large",  ID_LARGE,  92, 62, 45, 10, WS_TABSTOP
        AUTORADIOBUTTON "Default", ID_DEFAULT, 170, 62, 45, 10, WS_TABSTOP
        PUSHBUTTON      "My Button", ID_BUTTON, 8, 8, 234, 50
                       PRESPARAMS PP_FOREGROUNDCOLOR, 0x00ff0000
                       PRESPARAMS PP_FONTNAMESIZE,"40.Times New Roman Italic"
    END
END
```

PRESPARM.DEF

```
NAME      PRESPARM    WINDOWAPI

DESCRIPTION 'Presentation Parameters Example'

STUB      'OS2STUB.EXE'

DATA      MULTIPLE

STACKSIZE   16348
HEAPSIZE    16348

PROTMODE
```

PRESPARM.MAK

```
all : presparm.exe

presparm.exe : presparm.obj  presparm.def presparm.res
        link386 /PM:PM presparm,,,,presparm.def;
        rc presparm.res

presparm.res: presparm.rc presparm.h
        rc -r presparm.rc

presparm.obj:presparm.c presparm.h
        icc /C /Ss /W3 .\$*.c
```

CHANGING PRESPARM'S APPEARANCE

The PRESPARM window is a dialog box that is created by using a dialog template included in the `PRESPARM.RC` file. Lines of code, each of which begins with "PRESPARAMS," were added to the dialog template to set up various presentation parameters for the controls of the "My Button" button automatically.

Two sets of radio buttons are displayed in the PRESPARM window to make changes to the presentation parameters of the "My Button" button. Changes are made dynamically by using the `WinSetPresParam` and `WinRemovePresParam` APIs. The first set of radio buttons is used to change the color of the text "My Button." The second set of radio buttons uses the labels "Small," "Large," and "Default" and changes the size of the font in which the text will appear.

To get the default font, the "Default" radio button uses the `WinRemove-PresParam` API to destroy the presentation parameter `PP_FONTNAMESIZE`, which provides an alternate font that can be substituted for the normal system font. After `PP_FONTNAMESIZE` is removed, the text "My Button" is displayed in the default system font.

WinQueryPresParams

During the creation of one of PM's controls, several queries will be made for presentation parameters that recommend colors for use in certain situations. A control such as the static control will search for a value that is associated with such presentation parameters as `PP_FOREGROUNDCOLOR` and `PP_FOREGROUNDCOLORINDEX`. If no presentation parameter has been specified, the static control uses a system color that is identified by the index `SYSCLR_WINDOWSTATICTEXT`. The function that is used by PM's controls to query their presentation parameters is internal to PM and is compiled into

PMWIN.DLL. To query a window's presentation parameters, PM programs use the WinQueryPresParams API.

Most of the presentation parameters that are listed in Table 7.1 can be divided into associated pairs, wherein one parameter represents an RGB value and the other an index value. For instance, PP_ACTIVECOLOR, an RGB value, is associated with PP_ACTIVECOLORINDEX, which is an index value. Because most parameters belong to a pair of parameters, WinQueryPresParams is designed to search for two parameters at a time. The following is an example of a call made to WinQueryPresParams:

```
WinQueryPresParams(
    hwnd,           /* handle of window being queried */
    PP_ACTIVECOLOR,
    PP_ACTIVECOLORINDEX,
    pIDfound, /* will receive the id of the value found */
    cbLength, /* maximum number of bytes, pValueFound can store */
    pValueFound,  /* place to store the value found */
    0 );            /* no flags */
```

In this example the second and third parameters specify that a search is to be made for PP_ACTIVECOLOR and PP_ACTIVECOLORINDEX. Since PP_ACTIVECOLOR is mentioned first in issuing the search instruction, the API tries to find a match for it before searching for PP_ACTIVECOLORINDEX. However, since this example function call does not use QPF_NOINHERIT as a flag in the last parameter, the window's entire chain of owner windows will be queried, if needed, in an effort to find a match for PP_ACTIVECOLOR or PP_ACTIVECOLORINDEX.

If a matching parameter is found during such a search, the value of the matching parameter is stored at an address that is specified by pValueFound, and pIDfound will be given either the value PP_ACTIVECOLOR or PP_ACTIVECOLORINDEX to indicate the type of value that was found. The variable cbLength tells the API the maximum number of bytes of usable memory pointed to by pValueFound. If the parameter's value is larger than the number of bytes cbLength specifies, extra data is truncated. Because the API will return the length of the presentation parameter it has found, the truncation of data can be checked for by comparing the returned length with cbLength.

Most controls will not bother to query for the PP_FONTNAMESIZE presentation parameter. Unlike other presentation parameters, the PP_FONTNAMESIZE parameter sets a control's default font regardless of whether the control queries the parameter. The control's only concern may be to query the height of the font in order to properly draw its text. However, querying the height of the font involves using GPI calls, not the WinQueryPresParams API.

SETTING PRESENTATION PARAMETERS

A window's presentation parameters can be set when the window is created or modified by using `WinSetPresParam`. The simplest way to set a window's presentation parameters is to have the window described by a resource template that appears in an RC file and use `PRESPARAMS` statements. The `PRESPARM` program uses `PRESPARAMS` statements that are located in the `PRESPARM.RC` file to set its control's presentation parameters.

When a resource template is used to create a window in accordance with a specified set of parameters, it is the equivalent of calling the `Win-CreateWindow` API with a desired set of parameters placed in a `PRESPARAMS` data structure, which contains an array of `PARAM` data structures. Each `PARAM` data structure describes one presentation parameter.

The following lines of code illustrate the `PRESPARAMS` and `PARAM` data structures:

```
typedef struct _PRESPARAMS {
    ULONG cb;  /* number of PARAM structures in aparm[] */
    PARAM aparm[1]; /*
} PRESPARAMS;  /* recommended abbreviation: pres */

typedef struct _PARAM {
    ULONG id; /* PP_ value identifying parameter */
    ULONG cd; /* number of bytes needed to store value in ab[] */
    BYTE ab[1];
} PARAM; /* recommended abbreviation: param */
```

The following `PUSHBUTTON` statement from the `PRESPARM.RC` file sets up the button labeled "My Button" with its requisite presentation parameters:

```
PUSHBUTTON   "My Button", ID_BUTTON, 8, 8, 234, 50
             PRESPARAMS PP_FOREGROUNDCOLOR, 0x00ff0000
             PRESPARAMS PP_FONTNAMESIZE, "40.Times New Roman Italic"
```

The function performed by this code for setting up the "My Button" button could alternatively be implemented by calling the `WinCreateWindow` API to create the button when a `WM_INITDLG` message is handled. The `WinCreateWindow` call would require that one `PRESPARAMS` data structure and two `PARAM` data structures be set up to describe the font and the color that are to be used. Most programmers will find it more convenient simply to use a resource template instead of using the `WinCreateWindow` call to create a control. Setting up the `PRESPARAMS` structure without using a template can become quite tedious.

If you don't use a resource template for setting up a window, the `WinSetPresParam` API can be used. The following is an excerpt from the PRESPARM program that handles changing the font size of the "My Button" button when the radio button labeled "Large" is selected:

```
case ID_LARGE:
   WinSetPresParam( hwndButton,
                    PP_FONTNAMESIZE,
                    strlen( szLarge ) + 1,
                    (PVOID)szLarge );

   break;
```

`WinSetPresParam` does not require large data structures such as `PRESPARAMS` and `PARAM`. Rather, to use the `WinSetPresParam` API you need only a handle to a window, the `PP_` value, the size of the data, and the data itself.

PRESENTATION PARAMETER MESSAGES

Three messages concern presentation parameters: `WM_SETWINDOWPARAMS`, `WM_QUERYWINDOWPARAMS`, and `WM_PRESPARAMCHANGED`. Most controls simply let a default window procedure handle `WM_SETWINDOWPARAMS` and `WM_QUERYWINDOWPARAMS`. A control concerns itself with one of these messages only when the control needs to be informed that its window text has been changed. `WM_SETWINDOWPARAMS` message is sent every time a window's text is updated.

Most controls will answer the `WM_PRESPARAMCHANGED` message by checking the change made and calling `WinInvalidateRect` to force PM to redraw the control. Redrawing the control will handle any font or color changes that have been made. Unlike most controls, PM's menu control cannot simply redraw itself if `PP_FONTNAMESIZE` was changed. A different font will change the size of each menu item and may require a larger menu window to contain the items. To handle this problem, the menu sends a `WM_UPDATEFRAME` message to its frame if a larger window size is needed. The message forces the frame to reposition its frame controls to give the menu a larger window size.

WORKING WITH PRESENTATION PARAMETERS

Because a window may use a combination of default values, system colors, and presentation parameters, conflicts may arise between presentation parameters and other set values. For instance, if the foreground color is set without checking whether it matches the background color, text may be rendered invisible. Likewise, setting a font with `PP_FONTNAMESIZE` may cause text to no longer fit within the confines of a window.

The PRESPARM program sizes its controls by using dialog box coordinates, which are relative to the size of the system font. The fonts that are selected for use in the button labeled "My Button" will vary slightly in size from system to system; this is due in large measure to slight differences in the size of system fonts. Giving a window enough size to handle slight variations between the relative size of a font and its associated system font should satisfy most programs.

CHAPTER 8
Bitmaps

Bitmaps provide PM with an efficient way to perform such functions as drawing images and moving images from place to place on a display screen. While PM supports the drawing of bitmaps to a variety of output devices, this chapter focuses on the use that PM makes of the window manager to provide screen-displayed controls.

The window manager of PM uses bitmaps to move a window from one screen location to another by copying the bitmap image of the window where it presently exists at one location and then reproducing the copied bitmap image at another location to which the window is to be moved. Screen-displayed PM controls use bitmaps to provide a quick visual response to mouse and keyboard input. Examples are radio buttons and scroll bars, which use bitmaps to provide quickly drawn three-dimensional buttons that appear as though they have been physically "pressed" when they are selected.

UNDERSTANDING BITMAPS

The quality of the image that is produced by displaying a bitmap can vary quite substantially depending on the character of the system that is used to effect the display. While a particular bitmap may call for a wide range of colors to appear when the bitmap is drawn, the device that is used to draw the bitmap may not have the particular colors that the bitmap requests.

To give bitmaps as much device independence as possible, PM attends to such color conversions as are needed to provide the best possible display of a bitmap on a particular system, and it attends to other format considerations that need to be taken into account in running a PM application. A set of powerful APIs are provided to create, draw, and manipulate bitmaps. They can be used to handle such concerns as the aspect ratio and the color capabilities of a display.

A bitmap is a series of bits that describes a raster image. Each pel, or pixel, used in forming an image is represented by a predetermined number of bits. PM supports device-independent bitmap formats that use 1, 4, 8, or 24 bits per

104

pixel. The number of bits per pixel that is used by a selected format defines the number of unique colors that are available to incorporate into a bitmap. A 24-bits-per-pixel bitmap has the most capable format that is made available by PM. It offers 16,777,216 unique colors.

While PM can display such complex images as 24-bit color bitmaps, the actual quality and character of the image that is displayed will be determined in large measure by the color capabilities of the system being used to effect the display. The aspect ratio of a monitor can also constitute an important factor in determining the quality of a displayed bitmap. Many present-day systems are limited by the available color selections of their displays or by their aspect ratios.

If a particular system cannot provide all of the colors that are called for in a bitmap that is to be displayed, PM will try to provide unavailable colors, either by dithering or by "nearest fitting" available colors as substitutes for unavailable colors. The capability of PM to work with a particular display or other output device to dither or "nearest fit" substitute colors depends in large measure on the extent to which the device driver that governs the operation of a particular output device will cooperate with and permit PM to exercise its capabilities.

THE NEW BITMAP DATA STUCTURES

With the introduction of OS/2 Version 2.0, bitmap support has been enhanced, and many of the data structures that relate to bitmap graphics have been extended to accommodate bitmap enhancements. The extended data structures have names that are similar to the original data structures (the data structures that were used by earlier versions of OS/2) except that the numeral "2" has been placed at the ends of the names of the extended data structures. Although the older (16-bit) data structures still are supported by PM, this chapter and its examples principally treat the newer enhanced (32-bit) data structures.

THE BMP FILE STRUCTURE

A bitmap typically is stored in a file having a name that ends with a .BMP extension. PM uses a standard format for .BMP files to allow bitmaps to be accessible by PM applications. The ICONEDIT utility, which is provided with the OS/2 operating system, is an example of an application that works with .BMP files. The ICONEDIT utility allows the user to create a new bitmap or to modify an existing bitmap and will work with bitmaps that arc in the old (16-bit) or the new (32-bit) formats.

PM supports two types of .BMP files, each with its own file format. The two types of .BMP files are BFT_BMAP and BFT_BITMAPARRAY. The BFT_BMAP file type is used for a .BMP file that defines a single bitmap. The BFT_BITMAPARRAY file type is used for a .BMP file that contains an array of bitmaps. The differences between these two bitmap file types are subtle and are discussed in subsequent sections of this chapter.

BFT_BMAP Bitmap Files

The BFT_BMAP type of file that is used to store a single bitmap is made up of three sections that contain, respectively, a BITMAPFILEHEADER2 data structure, a color table, and bitmap data. The three sections that make up a BFT_BMAP bitmap file are illustrated in Figure 8.1.

The BITMAPFILEHEADER2 data structure that is used in a BFT_BMAP type file is defined in a header file named PMBITMAP.H, which contains the bitmap-related data structures and definitions. The BITMAPFILEHEADER2 data structure is defined as follows:

```
typedef struct _BITMAPFILEHEADER2 { /* suggested abbreviation: bfh2 */
    USHORT      usType;
    ULONG       cbSize;
    SHORT       xHotspot;
    SHORT       yHotspot;
    ULONG       offBits;
    BITMAPINFOHEADER2 bmp2;
} BITMAPFILEHEADER2;
```

The information that is contained in the BITMAPFILEHEADER2 data structure contains information that is relevant only to the size and format of the file. The usType field designates the .BMP file type which, in this case, is BFT_BMAP. The cbSize field contains the total size of the BITMAPFILEHEADER2 structure in bytes. Based on the value of the cbSize field, applications can determine if the BMP file is using the newer 32-bit or the older 16-bit data structure. The xHotspot and yHotspot fields do not apply to bitmaps and are used principally when the BITMAPFILEHEADER2 data structure describes an icon or a

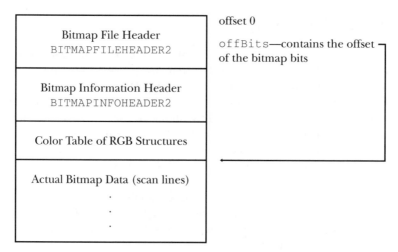

FIGURE 8.1   Bitmap file format for BFT_BMAP type files.

pointer file, which uses hotspot fields. The `offBits` field is the offset from the start of the file to the bitmap data.

A bitmap information header (`BITMAPINFOHEADER2`) data structure is embedded in the `BITMAPFILEHEADER2` data structure. The `BITMAPINFOHEADER2` data structure contains information about the physical characteristics of the bitmap. The following shows the format of the `BITMAPINFOHEADER2` data structure:

```
typedef struct _BITMAPINFOHEADER2 { /* suggested abbreviation: bmp2 */
    ULONG   cbFix;
    ULONG   cx;
    ULONG   cy;
    USHORT  cPlanes;
    USHORT  cBitCount;
    ULONG   ulCompression;
    ULONG   cbImage;
    ULONG   cxResolution;
    ULONG   cyResolution;
    ULONG   cclrUsed;
    ULONG   cclrImportant;
    USHORT  usUnits;
    USHORT  usReserved;
    USHORT  usRecording;
    USHORT  usRendering;
    ULONG   cSize1;
    ULONG   cSize2;
    ULONG   ulColorEncoding;
    ULONG   ulIdentifier;
} BITMAPINFOHEADER2;
```

Immediately following the `BITMAPINFOHEADER2` data structure is a color table, which describes the colors that are used by the bitmap. The color table takes the form of an array of `RGB2` structures. When using color bitmaps with 4 or 8 bits per pixel, the bits constitute indexes to palettes of 16 or 256 entries, respectively. At 24 bits per pixel, the bits represent actual RGB values, so when a 24-bit-per-pixel format is used, there is no need to provide a color table, because all of the needed information about each color is included in the 24-bit-per-pixel format itself.

Immediately following the color table are the bits that represent each pixel in the bitmap. The `offBits` field of the `BITMAPFILEHEADER2` data structure contains the offset from the beginning of the file to the location of the bitmap bits. The number of bits per pixel is determined by the `cBitCount` field of the `BITMAPINFOHEADER2` data structure. The listings of pixels each start at the lower left-hand corner of the bitmap.

The number of bits used to describe each row of a bitmap is always a multiple of 32. For example, if an 8-bit-per-pixel bitmap with 7 columns per row is being used, 56 bits are needed to describe each row; however, to comply with the conventions of PM, the nearest greater multiple of 32 bits, namely 64 bits, will be used for each row. The last 8 bits in the 64 bits of each row have no meaning; rather, they are provided simply as place holders.

When working with bitmap files, the cbFix field of the BITMAPINFO-HEADER2 structure must be checked to determine whether the bitmap that is to be referenced is set out in the new (32-bit) format or in the old (16-bit) format. The cbFix field is a ULONG value that contains the size of the bitmap header data structure in bytes. If the cbFix field is greater than the size of a BITMAPINFOHEADER structure, the bitmap is in the new extended format used by 32-bit versions of OS/2.

BFT_BITMAPARRAY Bitmap Files

A BFT_BITMAPARRAY type bitmap file is very similar to a BFT_BMAP bitmap file except that the BFT_BITMAPARRAY type allows several bitmaps to be stored in one file. The several bitmaps that make up a BFT_BITMAPARRAY type bitmap file ordinarily are intended to describe substantially the same image; however, each bitmap is optimized for the color and resolution capabilities of a particular graphics adapter, such as a VGA or an XGA adapter.

The only difference between the format of a BFT_BITMAPARRAY file and the format of a BFT_BMAP file is that a BITMAPARRAYFILEHEADER2 data structure is placed before each BITMAPFILEHEADER2 data structure. The following describes the BITMAPARRAYFILEHEADER2 data structure:

```
typedef struct _BITMAPARRAYFILEHEADER2{/* suggested abbreviation: bafh2 */
    USHORT     usType;
    ULONG      cbSize;
    ULONG      offNext;
    USHORT     cxDisplay;
    USHORT     cyDisplay;
    BITMAPFILEHEADER2 bfh2;
} BITMAPARRAYFILEHEADER2;
```

The offNext field of the BITMAPARRAYFILEHEADER2 structure contains an offset (measured from the start of the associated file) to the next bitmap that is described with its own BITMAPARRAYFILEHEADER2 data structure. Components that are used to construct a BFT_BITMAPARRAY file are shown in Figure 8.2.

THE BMPVIEW PROGRAM

An example program, called BMPVIEW, the source code for which is presented later in this chapter, inputs the contents of a user-selected BMP file and presents bitmap header information in the BMPVIEW client window. Figure 8.3 shows an example of BMPVIEW displaying information about a bitmap file. The header information that is presented in the client window is an assembly of BITMAPARRAYFILEHEADER2, BITMAPFILEHEADER2

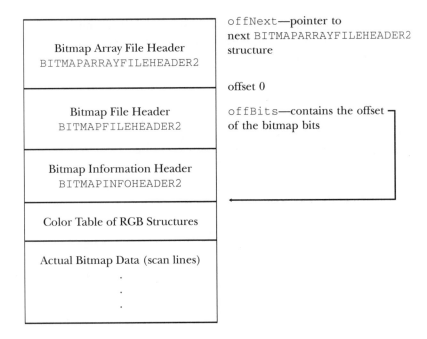

FIGURE 8.2 BFT_BITMAPARRAY type BMP file format.

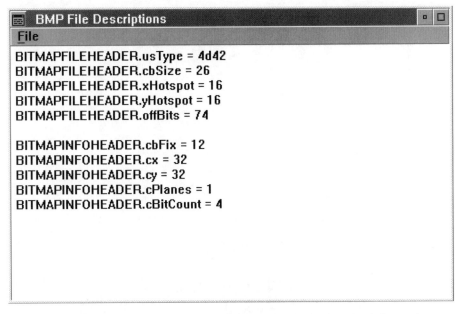

FIGURE 8.3 An example of the BMPVIEW, displaying header information.

and `BITMAPINFO2` data structures. BMPVIEW handles `BFT_BMAP` and `BFT_BITMAPARRAY` type bitmap files and their associated older and newer bitmap data structures.

The BMPVIEW program is compiled from the following six files:

BMPVIEW.C

```
#define INCL_WIN
#define INCL_GPI
#include <os2.h>
#include "bmpview.h"


/* prototypes */
INT main( VOID );
MRESULT EXPENTRY ClientWndProc( HWND, ULONG, MPARAM, MPARAM );
BOOL GetBMPFile( HWND );
VOID DisplayMessage( HWND, PSZ );
VOID ShowBMPInfo( HWND, LONG, SHORT );
VOID ShowBMPInformation( PBYTE, HWND );
VOID ShowBMPArrayFileHeader( PBITMAPARRAYFILEHEADER, HWND, HPS);
VOID ShowBMPFileHeader( PBITMAPFILEHEADER, HWND, HPS );
VOID ShowBMPInfoHeader( PBITMAPINFOHEADER, HWND, HPS );
VOID ShowBMPInfoHeader2( PBITMAPINFOHEADER2, HWND, HPS );


/* globals */
CHAR    szFileName[CCHMAXPATH];
CHAR    szBuffer[50];
SHORT   sClientY;
LONG    lLineHeight;
POINTL  pt;


INT main( VOID )
{

    HAB    hab;
    HWND   hwndFrame;
    HMQ    hmq;
    HWND   hwndClient;
    CHAR   szClientClass[] = "Client Window";
    QMSG   qmsg;
    ULONG  flCreateFlags = FCF_TITLEBAR        /* create: title bar control    */
                         | FCF_SYSMENU         /*          system menu control */
                         | FCF_MENU            /*          action bar          */
                         | FCF_MINMAX          /*          min and max buttons */
                         | FCF_SIZEBORDER      /* draw sizeborders             */
                         | FCF_SHELLPOSITION   /* shell decides window position */
                         | FCF_TASKLIST        /* title added to switch list   */
                         | FCF_ICON;           /* frame has an icon            */

    hab = WinInitialize( 0 );
```

```
   hmq = WinCreateMsgQueue( hab, (0 );

   WinRegisterClass( hab,                /* anchor block handle */
                     szClientClass,      /* class name */
                     ClientWndProc,      /* pointer to window procedure */
                     CS_SIZEREDRAW,      /* class style */
                     0 );                /* number of class data bytes */

   hwndFrame = WinCreateStdWindow(
                   HWND_DESKTOP,                 /* Desktop window is parent   */
                   WS_VISIBLE,                   /* window styles              */
                   &flCreateFlags,               /* frame control flag         */
                   szClientClass,                /* client window class name   */
                   "BMP File Descriptions",      /* title bar text             */
                   0,                            /* no special class style     */
                   NULLHANDLE,                   /* resource is in .EXE file    */
                   ID_FRAME_RES,                 /* frame window identifier    */
                   &hwndClient                   /* client window handle       */
                   );

   if ( hwndFrame )
       while (WinGetMsg( hab, &qmsg, NULLHANDLE, 0, 0 ))
           WinDispatchMsg( hab, &qmsg );

   WinDestroyWindow( hwndFrame ); /* clean up */
   WinDestroyMsgQueue( hmq );
   WinTerminate( hab );

   return 0;
} /* end of main */


MRESULT EXPENTRY ClientWndProc( HWND hwnd, ULONG msg, MPARAM mp1, MPARAM mp2 )
{
   static BOOL fReady = FALSE;

   switch (msg) {

   case WM_CREATE:
    { HPS  hps;
      FONTMETRICS fm;

      hps = WinGetPS( hwnd );
      GpiQueryFontMetrics(hps, (LONG)sizeof fm, &fm );
      lLineHeight = fm.lMaxBaselineExt;
      WinReleasePS( hps );
    } break;

   case WM_COMMAND:

       switch (SHORT1FROMMP( mp1 )) {

           case IDM_OPEN:
               if ( GetBMPFile( hwnd ) ) {
                   fReady = TRUE;
```

```
                    ShowBMPInfo( hwnd, lLineHeight, sClientY );
                } else
                    DisplayMessage( hwnd, "Error reading bitmap" );

            break;

          default:
              return WinDefWindowProc( hwnd, msg, mp1, mp2 );
        }
    break;

  case WM_ERASEBACKGROUND:
      /* return TRUE to request PM to paint the window background */
      return (MRESULT)TRUE;

  case WM_PAINT:

    { HPS hps;
      RECTL rctl;

      if (fReady) {
          hps = WinBeginPaint( hwnd, NULLHANDLE, &rctl );
          ShowBMPInfo( hwnd, lLineHeight, sClientY );
          WinEndPaint( hps );
      }
    } break;

  case WM_SIZE:
      sClientY = SHORT2FROMMP( mp2 );
      break;

  default:
      return WinDefWindowProc( hwnd, msg, mp1, mp2 );
  }

  return (MRESULT)FALSE;
} /* end of ClientWndProc */


APIRET GetBMPFile( HWND hwndClient )
{
  FILEDLG FileDlg;
  HWND hwndDlg;
  BOOL rc = FALSE;

  memset( &FileDlg, 0, sizeof(FILEDLG) );  /* Init all fields to zero */

  FileDlg.cbSize = sizeof(FILEDLG);

  FileDlg.fl = FDS_HELPBUTTON | FDS_CENTER | FDS_OPEN_DIALOG;

  FileDlg.pszTitle = "Open a BMP file";

  strcpy( FileDlg.szFullFile, "*.bmp" );
```

```
        /* display the file dialog */
        hwndDlg = WinFileDlg( HWND_DESKTOP, hwndClient, (PFILEDLG)&FileDlg );

        /* upon successful return of a file, open it for reading */
        if ( hwndDlg && (FileDlg.lReturn == DID_OK) ) {

            strcpy( szFileName, FileDlg.szFullFile );
            return TRUE;
        } else
            return FALSE;

} /* end of GetBMPFile */


VOID ShowBMPInfo( HWND hwndClient, LONG lCharBoxY, SHORT sTotalY)
{

    HFILE       FileHandle;
    ULONG       ulAction;
    FILESTATUS  FileInfo;
    PBYTE       pFileBegin = NULL;   /* beginning of bitmap file data */
    ULONG       cbRead;              /* number of bytes read by DosRead. */
    APIRET      rc;                  /* API return code */

    rc = DosOpen( szFileName,              /* file name                  */
                  &FileHandle,             /* get file handle            */
                  &ulAction,               /* get status of file         */
                  0,                       /* ignored, used to set file size */
                  FILE_NORMAL,             /* file attribute bits        */
                  FILE_OPEN,               /* open flags                 */
                  OPEN_ACCESS_READONLY
                  | OPEN_SHARE_DENYNONE,   /* open mode                  */
                  NULL );                  /* no EA buffer               */

    if (rc) {
        sprintf( szBuffer, "DosOpen failed with a rc of %ld", rc );
        DisplayMessage( hwndClient, szBuffer );
        return;
    }

    rc = DosQueryFileInfo( FileHandle,
                           FIL_STANDARD, /* file information level */
                           &FileInfo,
                           sizeof(FileInfo));

    if (rc) {
        sprintf( szBuffer, "DosQueryFileInfo failed with a rc of %ld", rc );
        DisplayMessage( hwndClient, szBuffer );
        return;
    }

    rc = DosAllocMem( (PPVOID)&pFileBegin,
                      (ULONG)FileInfo.cbFile,
                      (ULONG)PAG_READ | PAG_WRITE | PAG_COMMIT );
```

```
   if (rc) {
      sprintf( szBuffer, "DosAllocMem failed with a rc of %ld", rc );
      DisplayMessage( hwndClient, szBuffer );
      return;
   }

   rc = DosRead( FileHandle,
                 (PVOID)pFileBegin,
                 FileInfo.cbFile,
                 &cbRead );

   if (rc) {
      sprintf( szBuffer, "DosRead failed with a rc of %ld", rc );
      DisplayMessage( hwndClient, szBuffer );
      return;
   }

   ShowBMPInformation( pFileBegin, hwndClient );

   DosFreeMem( pFileBegin );
   DosClose( FileHandle );

} /* end of ShowBMPInfo */


VOID ShowBMPInformation( PBYTE pFileBegin, HWND hwndClient )
{

   HPS hps;
   PBITMAPARRAYFILEHEADER pBitmapArrayFileHeader;
   PBITMAPFILEHEADER pBitmapFileHeader;
   PBITMAPINFOHEADER2 pBitmapInfoHeader2;

   hps = WinGetPS( hwndClient );
   GpiErase( hps );
   pt.x = 5;
   pt.y = (LONG)sClientY - lLineHeight;

   if (*((PUSHORT)pFileBegin) == BFT_BITMAPARRAY) {

      pBitmapArrayFileHeader = (PBITMAPARRAYFILEHEADER)pFileBegin;

      ShowBMPArrayFileHeader( pBitmapArrayFileHeader, hwndClient, hps );

      pFileBegin = (PBYTE)&pBitmapArrayFileHeader->bfh;
   }

   pBitmapFileHeader = (PBITMAPFILEHEADER)pFileBegin;

   if (pBitmapFileHeader->usType == BFT_BMAP) {

      ShowBMPFileHeader( pBitmapFileHeader, hwndClient, hps );

      pBitmapInfoHeader2 = (PBITMAPINFOHEADER2)&pBitmapFileHeader->bmp;
```

```
        if (pBitmapInfoHeader2->cbFix == sizeof(BITMAPINFOHEADER))
            ShowBMPInfoHeader( (PBITMAPINFOHEADER)pBitmapInfoHeader2,
                               hwndClient,
                               hps );

        else if (pBitmapInfoHeader2->cbFix == sizeof(BITMAPINFOHEADER2))
            ShowBMPInfoHeader2( pBitmapInfoHeader2, hwndClient, hps );

    } else {
        sprintf( szBuffer, "Bitmap type %x not recognized!",(PUSHORT)pFileBegin );
        DisplayMessage( hwndClient, szBuffer );
    }

    WinReleasePS( hps );
} /* end of ShowBMPInformation */


VOID ShowBMPArrayFileHeader( PBITMAPARRAYFILEHEADER pArrayHeader,
                             HWND hwndClient,
                             HPS hps )
{

    sprintf( szBuffer, "BITMAPARRAYFILEHEADER.usType = %x",
             pArrayHeader->usType );
    GpiCharStringAt( hps, &pt, strlen( szBuffer ), szBuffer );

    pt.y -= lLineHeight;
    sprintf( szBuffer, "BITMAPARRAYFILEHEADER.cbSize = %ld",
             pArrayHeader->cbSize );
    GpiCharStringAt( hps, &pt, strlen( szBuffer ), szBuffer );

    pt.y -= lLineHeight;
    sprintf( szBuffer, "BITMAPARRAYFILEHEADER.offNext = %ld",
             pArrayHeader->offNext );
    GpiCharStringAt( hps, &pt, strlen( szBuffer ), szBuffer );

    pt.y -= lLineHeight;
    sprintf( szBuffer, "BITMAPARRAYFILEHEADER.cxDisplay = %d",
             pArrayHeader->cxDisplay );
    GpiCharStringAt( hps, &pt, strlen( szBuffer ), szBuffer );

    pt.y -= lLineHeight;
    sprintf( szBuffer, "BITMAPARRAYFILEHEADER.cyDisplay = %d",
             pArrayHeader->cyDisplay );
    GpiCharStringAt( hps, &pt, strlen( szBuffer ), szBuffer );

    pt.y -= lLineHeight*2;

} /* end of ShowBMPArrayFileHeader */


VOID ShowBMPFileHeader( PBITMAPFILEHEADER pBMapFileHdr,
                        HWND hwndClient,
                        HPS hps )
{
```

```
    sprintf( szBuffer, "BITMAPFILEHEADER.usType = %x", pBMapFileHdr->usType );
    GpiCharStringAt( hps, &pt, strlen( szBuffer ), szBuffer );

    pt.y -= lLineHeight;
    sprintf( szBuffer, "BITMAPFILEHEADER.cbSize = %ld", pBMapFileHdr->cbSize );
    GpiCharStringAt( hps, &pt, strlen( szBuffer ), szBuffer );

    pt.y -= lLineHeight;
    sprintf( szBuffer, "BITMAPFILEHEADER.xHotspot = %d",
             pBMapFileHdr->xHotspot );
    GpiCharStringAt( hps, &pt, strlen( szBuffer ), szBuffer );

    pt.y -= lLineHeight;
    sprintf( szBuffer, "BITMAPFILEHEADER.yHotspot = %d",
             pBMapFileHdr->yHotspot );
    GpiCharStringAt( hps, &pt, strlen( szBuffer ), szBuffer );

    pt.y -= lLineHeight;
    sprintf( szBuffer, "BITMAPFILEHEADER.offBits = %ld",
             pBMapFileHdr->offBits);
    GpiCharStringAt( hps, &pt, strlen( szBuffer ), szBuffer );

    pt.y -= lLineHeight*2;

} /* end of ShowBMPFileHeader */


VOID ShowBMPInfoHeader( PBITMAPINFOHEADER pBMapInfoHdr,
                        HWND hwndClient,
                        HPS hps )
{

    sprintf( szBuffer, "BITMAPINFOHEADER.cbFix = %ld", pBMapInfoHdr->cbFix );
    GpiCharStringAt(hps, &pt, strlen( szBuffer ), szBuffer );

    pt.y -= lLineHeight;
    sprintf( szBuffer, "BITMAPINFOHEADER.cx = %d", pBMapInfoHdr->cx );
    GpiCharStringAt(hps, &pt, strlen( szBuffer ), szBuffer );

    pt.y -= lLineHeight;
    sprintf( szBuffer, "BITMAPINFOHEADER.cy = %d", pBMapInfoHdr->cy );
    GpiCharStringAt(hps, &pt, strlen( szBuffer ), szBuffer );

    pt.y -= lLineHeight;
    sprintf( szBuffer, "BITMAPINFOHEADER.cPlanes = %d", pBMapInfoHdr->cPlanes);
    GpiCharStringAt(hps, &pt, strlen( szBuffer ), szBuffer );

    pt.y -= lLineHeight;
    sprintf( szBuffer, "BITMAPINFOHEADER.cBitCount = %d",
             pBMapInfoHdr->cBitCount );
    GpiCharStringAt( hps, &pt, strlen( szBuffer ), szBuffer );

} /* end of ShowBMPInfoHeader */
```

```
VOID ShowBMPInfoHeader2( PBITMAPINFOHEADER2 pBMapInfoHdr,
                         HWND hwndClient,
                         HPS hps)
{

   sprintf( szBuffer, "BITMAPINFOHEADER2.cbFix = %ld", pBMapInfoHdr->cbFix );
   GpiCharStringAt(hps, &pt, strlen( szBuffer ), szBuffer );

   pt.y -= lLineHeight;
   sprintf( szBuffer, "BITMAPINFOHEADER2.cx = %d", pBMapInfoHdr->cx );
   GpiCharStringAt( hps, &pt, strlen( szBuffer ), szBuffer );

   pt.y -= lLineHeight;
   sprintf( szBuffer, "BITMAPINFOHEADER2.cy = %d", pBMapInfoHdr->cy );
   GpiCharStringAt( hps, &pt, strlen( szBuffer ), szBuffer );

   pt.y -= lLineHeight;
   sprintf( szBuffer, "BITMAPINFOHEADER2.cPlanes = %d",
            pBMapInfoHdr->cPlanes );
   GpiCharStringAt( hps, &pt, strlen( szBuffer ), szBuffer );

   pt.y -= lLineHeight;
   sprintf( szBuffer, "BITMAPINFOHEADER2.cBitCount = %d",
            pBMapInfoHdr->cBitCount );
   GpiCharStringAt( hps, &pt, strlen( szBuffer ), szBuffer );

} /* end of ShowBMPInfoHeader2 */


VOID DisplayMessage( HWND hwndOwner, PSZ pszText )
{

   WinMessageBox ( HWND_DESKTOP,
                   hwndOwner,
                   pszText,
                   "BMP Example",
                   0,
                   MB_OK );
} /* end of DisplayMessage */
```

BMPVIEW.H

```
#define ID_FRAME_RES 100

#define IDM_FILE     101
#define IDM_OPEN     102
```

BMPVIEW.RC

```
#include <os2.h>
#include "bmpview.h"
```

```
ICON ID_FRAME_RES bmpview.ico

MENU     ID_FRAME_RES
BEGIN
    SUBMENU "~File", IDM_FILE
    BEGIN
        MENUITEM "~Open", IDM_OPEN
    END
END
```

BMPVIEW.DEF

```
NAME BMPVIEW WINDOWAPI

DESCRIPTION 'Bitmap File Description Example Program'

CODE    MOVEABLE
DATA    MOVEABLE MULTIPLE

HEAPSIZE  10240
STACKSIZE 24576
```

BMPVIEW.MAK

```
all : bmpview.exe

bmpview.exe : bmpview.obj bmpview.def bmpview.res
        link386 /PM:PM bmpview,,,,bmpview.def;
        rc bmpview.res

bmpview.res : bmpview.rc bmpview.ico bmpview.h
        rc -r bmpview.rc

bmpview.obj : bmpview.c bmpview.h bmpview.mak
        icc /C /Ss /W3 .$*.c
```

BMPVIEW.ICO

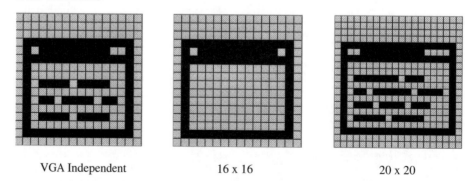

VGA Independent   16 x 16   20 x 20

BMPVIEW.ICO file, containing various icons of different sizes.

BITMAP HANDLES

PM applications can identify a bitmap by using a bitmap handle of the type `HBITMAP`. A bitmap handle is used to allow a PM application to draw a bitmap in a specified presentation space or to query information about the bitmap. Because there are a finite number of bitmap handles available to PM applications, a PM application should delete bitmap handles that are no longer needed, using the `GpiDeleteBitmap` API.

OS/2 SYSTEM BITMAPS

PM provides a set of *system bitmaps,* which are available to all PM applications. PM uses system bitmaps to provide its minmax buttons, scroll bar buttons, system menu buttons, and other controls. Many other bitmaps are available, such as those that depict disk drives, folders, files, and programs.

An application loads a system bitmap by making a call to the `WinGetSysBitmap` API. Each of the system bitmaps has a unique identifier that is prefixed by the character `SBMP_`; `WinGetSysBitmap` returns a bitmap handle to an application after loading the bitmap from a stored resource. The following is a sample call made to `WinGetSysBitmap` to load a "disk drive" bitmap:

```
hbmDrive = WinGetSysBitmap( HWND_DESKTOP, SBMP_DRIVE );
```

LOADING BITMAPS FROM RESOURCES

By adding `BITMAP` statements to the RC file of a PM application, bitmaps that are stored in a `BMP` format can be incorporated into an application's read-only resources. Each `BITMAP` statement requires only an ID number to give APIs a way of identifying needed `BMP` data.

A bitmap stored in a read-only resource can be loaded into memory by using the `GpiLoadBitmap` API with the bitmap ID number. During loading, a bitmap is converted by PM into a format that is usable by the display. The following is an example of the use of `GpiLoadBitmap` to load a bitmap that is associated with a resource ID named `ID_MYBITMAP`:

```
hbmMyBmp = GpiLoadBitmap(
              hps,           /* presentation space handle */
              NULLHANDLE,    /* use .EXE file resources */
              ID_MYBITMAP,   /* resource ID number */
              0L,            /* no set width (avoid stretching) */
              0L );          /* no set height (avoid stretching) */
```

The first parameter (hps) of this API describes a presentation space that is used to describe a format in which the ID_MYBITMAP bitmap is to be stored. Unlike other Gpi calls that write graphic images to a presentation space as their first parameter, GpiLoadBitmap uses a presentation space only to query its associated output device for a format that is to be used to store the bitmap. When a bitmap is to be used with a PM control or window, the presentation space that is used in a call to GpiLoadBitmap is associated with the display, *not* with a printer or other output device. The handle hps typically is set by using the WinGetPS API, which returns a presentation space handle that is caused to be automatically associated with the display.

The foregoing example uses a NULLHANDLE for the second parameter. NULLHANDLE tells PM to look for the ID_MYBITMAP bitmap resource in the executable file of the program that called GpiLoadBitmap. A handle to a module such as a DLL could have been used in place of NULLHANDLE.

The last two parameters of GpiLoadBitmap are used to stretch or compress the image of the bitmap. In the example presented above, both values of the last two parameters are set to zero to inform PM that no stretching or compressing of the bitmap is desired.

CREATING BITMAPS DYNAMICALLY

An application program can create a bitmap dynamically by calling the GpiCreateBitmap API, which returns a bitmap handle that can be used to draw a specified bitmap or to query information about the bitmap. An example program, CREATE24, the source code for which is presented in this section, creates a 24-bit-per-pixel bitmap and displays it. The bitmap that is created and displayed is a 3-row by 8-column bitmap that has alternating colors and consists of a total of 12 pixels. CREATE24 stretches the bitmap to the size of the client window by setting the DBM_STRETCH flag in a WinDrawBitmap API call.

The following six files were used to compile the CREATE24 example program:

CREATE24.C

```
#define INCL_WIN
#define INCL_GPI
#include <os2.h>
#include "create24.h"


/* prototypes */
INT main( VOID );
MRESULT EXPENTRY ClientWndProc( HWND, ULONG, MPARAM, MPARAM );


/* globals */
HAB   hab;
RGB aRGB[] = { /* bitmap data for a 3-row by 8-column bitmap */
```

```
      /* 3rd row (bottom)      */
      /*  bBlue  BGreen  bRed  */
        { 0xFF,       0,      0 },
        {    0,       0,   0xFF },
        {    0,    0xFF,      0 },
        { 0xFF,       0,      0 },
        {    0,       0,   0xFF },
        {    0,    0xFF,      0 },
        { 0xFF,       0,      0 },
        {    0,       0,   0xFF },
      /* 2nd row (middle)       */
      /*  bBlue  BGreen  bRed  */
        {    0,    0xFF,      0 },
        { 0xFF,       0,      0 },
        {    0,       0,   0xFF },
        {    0,    0xFF,      0 },
        { 0xFF,       0,      0 },
        {    0,       0,   0xFF },
        {    0,    0xFF,      0 },
        { 0xFF,       0,      0 },
      /* 1st row (top)          */
      /*  bBlue  BGreen  bRed  */
        {    0,       0,   0xFF },
        {    0,    0xFF,      0 },
        { 0xFF,       0,      0 },
        {    0,       0,   0xFF },
        {    0,    0xFF,      0 },
        { 0xFF,       0,      0 },
        {    0,       0,   0xFF },
        {    0,    0xFF,      0 },
      };


INT main( VOID )
{
   HMQ    hmq;
   HWND   hwndFrame;
   HWND   hwndClient;
   CHAR   szClientClass[] = "Client Window";
   QMSG   qmsg;
   ULONG  flCreateFlags = FCF_TITLEBAR       /* create: title bar control    */
                        | FCF_SYSMENU        /*          system menu control */
                        | FCF_MINMAX         /*            min and max buttons */
                        | FCF_SIZEBORDER     /* draw sizeborders             */
                        | FCF_SHELLPOSITION  /* shell decides window position */
                        | FCF_TASKLIST       /* title added to switch list   */
                        | FCF_ICON;          /* frame has an icon            */

   hab = WinInitialize( 0 );

   hmq = WinCreateMsgQueue( hab, 0 );

   WinRegisterClass( hab,              /* anchor block handle */
                   szClientClass,  /* class name */
```

```
                        ClientWndProc,   /* pointer to window procedure */
                        CS_SIZEREDRAW,   /* class style */
                        0 );             /* number of class data bytes */

   hwndFrame = WinCreateStdWindow(
                   HWND_DESKTOP,           /* Desktop window is parent  */
                   WS_VISIBLE,             /* window styles             */
                   &flCreateFlags,         /* frame control flag        */
                   szClientClass,          /* client window class name  */
                   "24-Bit Bitmap Example", /* title bar text           */
                   0,                      /* no special class style    */
                   NULLHANDLE,             /* resource is in .EXE file   */
                   ID_FRAME_RES,           /* frame window identifier    */
                   &hwndClient );          /* client window handle       */

   if (hwndFrame)
      while (WinGetMsg( hab, &qmsg, NULLHANDLE, 0, 0 ))
         WinDispatchMsg( hab, &qmsg );

   WinDestroyWindow( hwndFrame );   /* clean up */
   WinDestroyMsgQueue( hmq );
   WinTerminate( hab );

   return 0;
} /* end of main */


MRESULT EXPENTRY ClientWndProc( HWND hwnd, ULONG msg, MPARAM mp1, MPARAM mp2 )
{
   static HBITMAP hbm;              /* bit map handle          */
   static SHORT cxClient, cyClient; /* size of the client window  */

   switch (msg) {
    case WM_CREATE:
     { BITMAPINFOHEADER2 bmih;
         BITMAPINFO2 bmi;
         HPS hps;

         /* set all values in bmih and bmi structures to zero */
         memset( &bmih, 0, sizeof(BITMAPINFOHEADER2) );
         memset( &bmi, 0, sizeof(BITMAPINFO2) );

         bmih.cbFix = sizeof(BITMAPINFOHEADER2);
         bmi.cbFix = sizeof(BITMAPINFOHEADER2);

         bmi.cx = bmih.cx = 8;
         bmi.cy = bmih.cy = 3;
         bmi.cPlanes = bmih.cPlanes = 1;
         bmi.cBitCount = bmih.cBitCount = 24;

         /* length of the bitmap storage data in bytes */
         bmi.cbImage = bmih.cbImage = 8*3*4;

         /* X resolution of target device */
         bmi.cxResolution = bmih.cxResolution = (LONG)cxClient;
```

```
        /* Y resolution of target device */
        bmi.cyResolution = bmih.cyResolution = (LONG)cyClient;


        /* color encoding */
        bmi.ulColorEncoding = bmih.ulColorEncoding = BCE_RGB;


        hps = WinGetPS( hwnd ) ;


        hbm = GpiCreateBitmap (
                hps,
                (PBITMAPINFOHEADER2)&bmih,  /* bitmap header */
                CBM_INIT,
                (PBYTE)aRGB,
                (PBITMAPINFO2)&bmi) ; /* bitmap header plus color table */


        if (!hbm)
        {   ERRORID err;
            CHAR szBuffer[50];


            err = WinGetLastError( hab );
            sprintf( szBuffer, "GpiCreateBitmap %lx error", err );
            WinMessageBox( HWND_DESKTOP,             /* parent window handle */
                        hwnd,                        /* owner window handle  */
                        szBuffer,                    /* MsgBox Text          */
                        "RGB Bitmap Example",        /* MsgBox Title Text    */
                        0,                           /* MsgBox Window ID     */
                        MB_ENTER | MB_WARNING ); /* MsgBox window style  */
            return (MRESULT)TRUE;
        }


        WinReleasePS(hps);
    } break;

    case WM_PAINT:
    { HPS hps;
        RECTL rcl;


        hps = WinBeginPaint( hwnd, 0L, &rcl );


        rcl.xLeft = 0;
        rcl.xRight = (LONG)cxClient;
        rcl.yBottom = 0;
        rcl.yTop = (LONG)cyClient;


        WinDrawBitmap( hps,
                    hbm,
                    NULL,           /* PRECTL (NULL = draw whole bitmap) */
                    (PPOINTL)&rcl,  /* bitmap destination                */
                    0L,             /* foreground color                  */
                    0L,             /* background color                  */
                    DBM_STRETCH );  /* stretch bmap to coordinates in pt */


        WinEndPaint( hps );
    }  break;
```

```
    case WM_SIZE:
        cxClient = SHORT1FROMMP( mp2 );
        cyClient = SHORT2FROMMP( mp2 );
        break;

    default:
        return WinDefWindowProc( hwnd, msg, mp1, mp2 );
  }

  return (MRESULT)FALSE;
} /* end of ClientWndProc */
```

CREATE24.H

```
#define ID_FRAME_RES 100
```

CREATE24.RC

```
#include <os2.h>
#include "create24.h"

ICON ID_FRAME_RES create24.ico
```

CREATE24.DEF

```
NAME CREATE24 WINDOWAPI

DESCRIPTION 'Bitmap Example Program'

CODE    MOVEABLE
DATA    MOVEABLE MULTIPLE

HEAPSIZE  10240
STACKSIZE 24576
```

CREATE24.MAK

```
all : create24.exe

create24.exe : create24.obj create24.def create24.res
        link386 /PM:PM create24,,,,create24.def;
        rc create24.res

create24.res : create24.rc create24.ico create24.h
        rc -r create24.rc

create24.obj : create24.c create24.h
        icc /C /Ss /W3 .$*.c
```

CREATE24.ICO

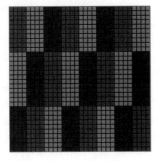

VGA Independent

CREATE24.ICO file, containing the icon used for the CREATE24 program.

THE CREATE24 PROGRAM

CREATE24 creates a bitmap using GpiCreateBitmap during the processing of a WM_CREATE message. The following excerpt from CREATE24.C shows how the bitmap is created:

```
hbm = GpiCreateBitmap( hps,
                       (PBITMAPINFOHEADER2)&bmih,
                       CBM_INIT,
                       (PBYTE)aRGB,
                       (PBITMAPINFO2)&bmi );
```

The parameter that follows the presentation space handle in this code is a pointer to a BITMAPINFOHEADER2 data structure named bmih. The bmih data structure determines the format that is used by the newly created bitmap. The C runtime library function memset is used to initialize all fields in the data structure to zero. Since default values for the optional BITMAPINFOHEADER2 fields are always zero, only the fields that apply to the CREATE24 program are filled.

The cbFix field in the bmih structure is set to the total size (in bytes) of the fixed portion of the BITMAPINFOHEADER2 data structure. PM uses the cbFix field to determine whether the extended (32-bit) or older (16-bit) data structure is being used. The cx and cy fields of bmih describe the height and width of the bitmap, which in the example above is 8 (pixels) by 3 (pixels). The cPlanes field is initialized to 1 (plane) and the cBitCount field is initialized to 24 (bits per pixel).

The third parameter of GpiCreateBitmap is the flag options field. The CBM_INIT flag is set to indicate that the next two fields are to be used to initialize the bitmap that is being created.

The fourth parameter is a pointer to data that comprises the actual bitmapped image. In the above example, a format of 24 bits per pixel is being used. An array of RGB values is set up to define bitmap colors. The RGB structure uses three bytes to specify a color. The color values that are loaded into the aRGB array sets up a bitmap of alternating red, green, and blue pixels.

The last parameter is a pointer to a BITMAPINFO2 structure. This structure is identical to the BITMAPINFOHEADER2 structure except it has appended to it an array of RGB2 values. In most cases a color table will immediately follow the BITMAPINFO2 structure. The BITMAPINFO2 structure is defined as having one entry available for a color table. Most color tables will require more than one entry. To set up a BITMAPINFO2 structure large enough to hold a color table, a pointer of type PBITMAPINFO2 is set to point at a block of memory that is large enough to hold the BITMAPINFO2 structure and the color table. In CREATE24, a 24-bit-per-pixel bitmap format is used; therefore, no color table is needed.

The GpiCreateBitmap API will return a bitmap handle that is used to draw the bitmap when the CREATE24 program handles WM_PAINT messages. Using the WinDrawBitmap API, the bitmap is stretched to the size of the client window.

GpiBitBlt

PM relies heavily on a function, supplied by the graphics engine, called a bitblt (bit block transfer, pronounced "bit blit"). This function is used by PM to copy bitmaps that are stored in memory or displayed on screen. Such common actions as moving a window on the desktop rely on the capabilities and speed that the graphics engine exhibits in handling bitblt operations. While a bitblt can be viewed as a memory-copying function, a bitblt also supports features for handling the copying and merging of bitmaps when drawing either to memory or the screen.

PM provides the GpiBitBlt and WinDrawBitmap APIs as its most commonly used bitblt functions. GpiBitBlt is the "workhorse" API that handles the operation of "blitting" a bitmap from a source location to a destination location. The WinDrawBitmap API is another bitblt function that is easier to use than GpiBitBlt, but it contains only a subset of the features that are available with GpiBitBlt.

THE BLTER PROGRAM

The BLTER program demonstrates the power of the GpiBitBlt API. BLTER utilizes the CUA file dialog to allow the user to select any bitmap file. The open-file dialog is activated when the user selects the "Open" menu item. Once a bitmap file has been selected by the user, BLTER reads it in and displays it on the screen. The bitmap will be drawn to fit exactly into area of the client window.

By choosing items from the pull-down menus, a user can select the parameters that are used by the call to GpiBitBlt that displays the bitmap. A pull-down menu labeled "Orientation" sets parameters that are used to invert the bitmap. A pull-down menu labeled "ROP" sets a parameter that describes how the loaded bitmap is drawn onto the background. The background color can be selected with the "Background" menu.

The menu labeled "ROP" lists available methods that can be used to draw the loaded bitmap. The "ROP" label stands for "raster operation" and refers to the ROP_ values that describe the types of operations that GpiBitBlt can perform when drawing bitmaps. The GpiBitBlt API is capable of drawing a bitmap that results from merging up to three bitmaps together. The ROP values are used to indicate to the GpiBitBlt API how the three bitmaps are to be merged. By default the BLTER program uses the ROP_SRCCOPY value as a parameter. The ROP_SRCCOPY value indicates that the loaded bitmap is simply to be drawn, without modification, at the destination location (the client window). Other ROP_ values listed in the ROP menu perform more complicated operations involving a pattern bitmap that is used by the BLTER program and a background color that is set by the Background menu.

The source code for the BLTER example program is listed in the following six files.

BLTER.C

```
#define INCL_WIN
#define INCL_GPI
#include <os2.h>
#include "blter.h"


/* function prototypes */
INT main( VOID );
MRESULT EXPENTRY ClientWndProc( HWND, ULONG, MPARAM, MPARAM );
VOID GetAndStoreBMP( HWND, HPS );
VOID DisplayMessage ( HWND, PSZ );
VOID CheckMenuItem( HWND, SHORT *, SHORT );


/* global variables */
HAB     hab;
HWND    hwndFrame;
HBITMAP hbm = 0;
POINTL  apts[4];
LONG    aROP[] = { ROP_SRCCOPY,
                   ROP_SRCPAINT,
                   ROP_SRCAND,
                   ROP_SRCINVERT,
                   ROP_SRCERASE,
                   ROP_NOTSRCCOPY,
```

```
                        ROP_NOTSRCERASE,
                        ROP_MERGECOPY,
                        ROP_MERGEPAINT,
                        ROP_PATCOPY,
                        ROP_PATPAINT,
                        ROP_PATINVERT,
                        ROP_DSTINVERT,
                        ROP_ZERO,
                        ROP_ONE
                    };
ULONG aCLR[] = { CLR_BLACK,
                 CLR_RED,
                 CLR_GREEN,
                 CLR_BLUE,
                 CLR_WHITE
                };


INT main( VOID )
{

    HMQ   hmq;
    HWND  hwndClient;
    QMSG  qmsg;
    CHAR  szClientClass[] = "Client Window";
    ULONG flCreateFlags = FCF_TITLEBAR       /* create: title bar control     */
                        | FCF_SYSMENU        /*         system menu control   */
                        | FCF_MENU           /*         action bar            */
                        | FCF_MINMAX         /*         min and max buttons    */
                        | FCF_SIZEBORDER     /* draw sizeborders             */
                        | FCF_SHELLPOSITION  /* shell decides window position */
                        | FCF_TASKLIST       /* title added to switch list    */
                        | FCF_ICON;          /* frame has an icon            */

    hab = WinInitialize( 0 );

    hmq = WinCreateMsgQueue( hab, 0 );

    WinRegisterClass( hab,            /* anchor block handle */
                      szClientClass,  /* class name */
                      ClientWndProc,  /* pointer to window procedure */
                      CS_SIZEREDRAW,  /* class style */
                      0 );            /* number of class data bytes */

    hwndFrame = WinCreateStdWindow(
                    HWND_DESKTOP,            /* Desktop window is parent      */
                    WS_VISIBLE,              /* window styles                 */
                    &flCreateFlags,          /* frame control flag            */
                    szClientClass,           /* client window class name      */
                    "GpiBitBlt Tester",      /* title bar text                */
                    0,                       /* no special class style        */
                    NULLHANDLE,              /* resource is in .EXE file       */
                    ID_FRAME_RES,            /* frame window identifier       */
                    &hwndClient );           /* client window handle          */
```

```
    if ( hwndFrame )
        while (WinGetMsg( hab, &qmsg, NULLHANDLE, 0, 0 ))
            WinDispatchMsg( hab, &qmsg );

    WinDestroyWindow( hwndFrame ); /* clean up */
    WinDestroyMsgQueue( hmq );
    WinTerminate( hab );

    return 0;
} /* end of main */


MRESULT EXPENTRY ClientWndProc( HWND hwnd, ULONG msg, MPARAM mp1, MPARAM mp2 )
{
    static SHORT    sClientX, sClientY;    /* client window X and Y dimensions */
    static SHORT    sOrient = IDM_NORMAL;  /* use normal orientation */
    static SHORT    sROP    = IDM_SRCCOPY; /* use ROP_SRCCOPY */
    static SHORT    sCLR    = IDM_BLACK;   /* target color */
    static HPS      hpsMemory;
    static HDC      hdcMemory;

    switch( msg ) {

        case WM_CREATE:
          { SIZEL sizl;

            hdcMemory = DevOpenDC(
                            hab,
                            OD_MEMORY,
                            "*",
                            0L,
                            NULL,
                            NULLHANDLE );

            sizl.cx = sizl.cy = 0 ;

            hpsMemory = GpiCreatePS(
                            hab,
                            hdcMemory,
                            &sizl,
                            PU_PELS | GPIF_DEFAULT | GPIT_MICRO | GPIA_ASSOC );

            apts[2].x = apts[2].y = 0;

          } break;

        case WM_COMMAND:

            /* if it is an ROP menu item */
            if ((SHORT1FROMMP(mp1) >= IDM_SRCCOPY)
                  && (SHORT1FROMMP( mp1 ) <= IDM_ONE) ) {
                CheckMenuItem( WinWindowFromID( hwndFrame, FID_MENU),
                               &sROP,
                               SHORT1FROMMP( mp1 ) );
                WinInvalidateRect(hwnd, NULL, FALSE);
```

```
        /* else if it is an Orientation menu item */
        } else if ((SHORT1FROMMP( mp1 ) >= IDM_NORMAL)
                && (SHORT1FROMMP( mp1 ) <= IDM_INVERTXY)) {
            CheckMenuItem( WinWindowFromID( hwndFrame, FID_MENU),
                        &sOrient,
                        SHORT1FROMMP( mp1 ) );
            WinInvalidateRect( hwnd, NULL, FALSE );

        /* else if it is a Background menu item */
        } else if ((SHORT1FROMMP( mp1 ) >= IDM_BLACK)
                && (SHORT1FROMMP( mp1 ) <= IDM_WHITE)) {
            CheckMenuItem( WinWindowFromID( hwndFrame, FID_MENU),
                        &sCLR,
                        SHORT1FROMMP(mp1) );
            WinInvalidateRect( hwnd, NULL, FALSE );

        /* else if it is the Open menu item */
        } else if (SHORT1FROMMP( mp1 ) == IDM_OPEN) {
                GetAndStoreBMP( hwnd, hpsMemory );
                WinInvalidateRect( hwnd, NULL, FALSE );

        /* else no match */
        } else
            return WinDefWindowProc( hwnd, msg, mp1, mp2 );
        break;

case WM_ERASEBACKGROUND:
    return (MRESULT)TRUE;

case WM_PAINT:
 { HPS hps;
   RECTL rcl;

   hps = WinBeginPaint( hwnd, NULLHANDLE, &rcl );

   WinFillRect( hps, &rcl, aCLR[sCLR - IDM_BLACK] );

   GpiSetPattern( hps, PATSYM_DIAG1 );

   switch (sOrient) {

       case IDM_NORMAL:
           apts[0].x = apts[0].y = 0;      /* Target X left and Y bot  */
           apts[1].x = (LONG)sClientX;     /* Target X right           */
           apts[1].y = (LONG)sClientY;     /* Target Y top             */
           break;

       case IDM_INVERTX:
           apts[0].y = 0;                  /* Target Y bottom          */
           apts[1].y = (LONG)sClientY;     /* Target Y top             */
           apts[0].x = (LONG)sClientX;     /* Target X left            */
           apts[1].x = 0;                  /* Target X right           */
           break;
```

```
                case IDM_INVERTY:
                    apts[0].x = 0;                      /* Target X left         */
                    apts[1].x = (LONG)sClientX;         /* Target X right        */
                    apts[0].y = (LONG)sClientY;         /* Target Y bottom       */
                    apts[1].y = 0;                      /* Target Y top          */
                    break;

                case IDM_INVERTXY:
                    apts[0].x = (LONG)sClientX;         /* Target X right        */
                    apts[0].y = (LONG)sClientY;         /* Target Y top          */
                    apts[1].x = apts[1].y = 0;          /* Target X left and Y bot */
                    break;
            }

        GpiBitBlt( hps,
                   hpsMemory,
                   4L,
                   (PPOINTL)apts,
                   aROP[ sROP - IDM_SRCCOPY ],
                   BBO_IGNORE);

        WinEndPaint( hps );

        } break;

    case WM_SIZE:
        sClientX = (LONG)SHORT1FROMMP( mp2 );
        sClientY = (LONG)SHORT2FROMMP( mp2 );
        break;

    case WM_DESTROY:
        GpiDestroyPS( hpsMemory );
        DevCloseDC( hdcMemory );
        GpiDeleteBitmap( hbm );
        break;

    default:
        return WinDefWindowProc( hwnd, msg, mp1, mp2 );
    }

    return (MRESULT)FALSE;
} /* end of ClientWndProc */


VOID GetAndStoreBMP( HWND hwndClient, HPS hpsMem )
{
    FILEDLG      FileDlg;
    HWND         hwndDlg;
    HFILE        FileHandle;
    ULONG        ulAction;
    ULONG        cbRead;
    FILESTATUS   FileInfo;
    PBYTE        pFileBegin = NULL; /* beginning of bitmap file data */
    HPS          hps;
```

```
PBITMAPFILEHEADER2 pbfh2;
PBITMAPINFOHEADER2 pbmp2;
CHAR szBuffer[50];
APIRET  rc;
ERRORID err;

memset( &FileDlg, 0, sizeof(FILEDLG) );

FileDlg.cbSize  = sizeof(FILEDLG);
FileDlg.fl      = FDS_HELPBUTTON | FDS_CENTER | FDS_OPEN_DIALOG;
FileDlg.pszTitle = "Open A BMP File";

strcpy( FileDlg.szFullFile, "*.bmp" );

hwndDlg = WinFileDlg( HWND_DESKTOP, hwndClient, (PFILEDLG)&FileDlg );

rc = DosOpen( FileDlg.szFullFile,
              &FileHandle,
              &ulAction,
              0,
              FILE_NORMAL,
              FILE_OPEN,
              OPEN_ACCESS_READONLY | OPEN_SHARE_DENYNONE,
              NULL );

if (rc) {
   sprintf( szBuffer, "DosOpen failed" );
   DisplayMessage( hwndClient, szBuffer );
   return;
}

rc = DosQueryFileInfo( FileHandle,
                       FIL_STANDARD,
                       &FileInfo,
                       sizeof(FileInfo)p);
if (rc) {
   sprintf( szBuffer, "DosQueryFileInfo failed" );
   DisplayMessage( hwndClient, szBuffer );
   return;
}

rc = DosAllocMem((PPVOID) &pFileBegin,
                 (ULONG)  FileInfo.cbFile,
                 (ULONG)  PAG_READ | PAG_WRITE | PAG_COMMIT);

if (rc) {
   sprintf( szBuffer, "DosAllocMem failed" );
   DisplayMessage( hwndClient, szBuffer );
   return;
}

rc = DosRead( FileHandle,
              (PVOID) pFileBegin,
              FileInfo.cbFile,
              &cbRead );
```

```
   if (rc) {
       sprintf( szBuffer, "DosRead failed" );
       DisplayMessage( hwndClient, szBuffer );
       return;
   }

   if (*((PUSHORT)pFileBegin) == BFT_BITMAPARRAY)
       pbfh2 =(PBITMAPFILEHEADER2)&((PBITMAPARRAYFILEHEADER2)pFileBegin)->bfh2;
   else
       pbfh2 =(PBITMAPFILEHEADER2)pFileBegin;

   pbmp2 = &pbfh2->bmp2;    /* pointer to info header (readability) */

   hps = WinGetPS( hwndClient );

   if (hbm)
       GpiDeleteBitmap( hbm );

   hbm = GpiCreateBitmap(
           hps,
           pbmp2,                   /* BITMAPINFOHEADER2 */
           CBM_INIT,                /* options */
           (PBYTE)pFileBegin        /* address of bitmap data */
           + pbfh2->offBits,
           (PBITMAPINFO2)pbmp2 );   /* structure for color and format */

   WinReleasePS( hps );

   if (!hbm) {
       err = WinGetLastError( hab );
       sprintf( szBuffer, "GpiLoadBitmap failed with a rc of %ld", err );
       DisplayMessage( hwndClient, szBuffer );
   }

   GpiSetBitmap( hpsMem, hbm );        .

   if (pbmp2->cbFix == sizeof(BITMAPINFOHEADER2)) {
       apts[3].x = pbmp2->cx;
       apts[3].y= pbmp2->cy;
   } else {
       apts[3].x = (LONG)((PBITMAPINFOHEADER)pbmp2)->cx;
       apts[3].y = (LONG)((PBITMAPINFOHEADER)pbmp2)->cy;
   }

   DosFreeMem( pFileBegin);
   DosClose( FileHandle);
} /* end of GetAndStoreBMP */


VOID DisplayMessage ( HWND hwndOwner, PSZ pszText )
{

   WinMessageBox( HWND_DESKTOP,
                  hwndOwner,
                  pszText,
```

```
                    "GpiBitBlt Example",
                    0,
                    MB_OK );
} /* end of DisplayMessage */


VOID CheckMenuItem( HWND hwndMenu, SHORT *psPrev, SHORT sNew )
{
   WinSendMsg( hwndMenu,
               MM_SETITEMATTR,
               MPFROM2SHORT( *psPrev, TRUE ),
               MPFROM2SHORT( MIA_CHECKED, 0 ));
   *psPrev = sNew;
   WinSendMsg( hwndMenu,
               MM_SETITEMATTR,
               MPFROM2SHORT( *psPrev, TRUE ),
               MPFROM2SHORT ( MIA_CHECKED, MIA_CHECKED ));
} /* end of CheckMenuItem */
```

BLTER.H

```
#define ID_FRAME_RES      100

#define IDM_FILE          101
#define IDM_OPEN          102

#define IDM_ROP           201
#define IDM_SRCCOPY       202
#define IDM_SRCPAINT      203
#define IDM_SRCAND        204
#define IDM_SRCINVERT     205
#define IDM_SRCERASE      206
#define IDM_NOTSRCCOPY    207
#define IDM_NOTSRCERASE   208
#define IDM_MERGECOPY     209
#define IDM_MERGEPAINT    210
#define IDM_PATCOPY       211
#define IDM_PATPAINT      212
#define IDM_PATINVERT     213
#define IDM_DSTINVERT     214
#define IDM_ZERO          215
#define IDM_ONE           216

#define IDM_ORIENT        301
#define IDM_NORMAL        302
#define IDM_INVERTX       303
#define IDM_INVERTY       304
#define IDM_INVERTXY      305

#define IDM_BACKGROUND    401
#define IDM_BLACK         402
#define IDM_RED           403
#define IDM_GREEN         404
#define IDM_BLUE          405
#define IDM_WHITE         406
```

BLTER.RC

```
#include <os2.h>
#include "blter.h"

ICON     ID_FRAME_RES blter.ico

MENU     ID_FRAME_RES
BEGIN
   SUBMENU  "~File",  IDM_FILE, MIS_TEXT
   BEGIN
      MENUITEM "~Open...",     IDM_OPEN
   END
   SUBMENU  "~ROP",  IDM_ROP, MIS_TEXT
   BEGIN
      MENUITEM "ROP_SRCCOPY",        IDM_SRCCOPY,, MIA_CHECKED
      MENUITEM "ROP_SRCPAINT",       IDM_SRCPAINT
      MENUITEM "ROP_SRCAND",         IDM_SRCAND
      MENUITEM "ROP_SRCINVERT",      IDM_SRCINVERT
      MENUITEM "ROP_SRCERASE",       IDM_SRCERASE
      MENUITEM "ROP_NOTSRCCOPY",     IDM_NOTSRCCOPY
      MENUITEM "ROP_NOTSRCERASE",    IDM_NOTSRCERASE
      MENUITEM "ROP_MERGECOPY",      IDM_MERGECOPY
      MENUITEM "ROP_MERGEPAINT",     IDM_MERGEPAINT
      MENUITEM "ROP_PATCOPY",        IDM_PATCOPY
      MENUITEM "ROP_PATPAINT",       IDM_PATPAINT
      MENUITEM "ROP_PATINVERT",      IDM_PATINVERT
      MENUITEM "ROP_DSTINVERT",      IDM_DSTINVERT
      MENUITEM "ROP_ZERO",           IDM_ZERO
      MENUITEM "ROP_ONE",            IDM_ONE
   END
   SUBMENU  "~Orientation",  IDM_ORIENT, MIS_TEXT
   BEGIN
      MENUITEM "~Normal",            IDM_NORMAL,, MIA_CHECKED
      MENUITEM "Invert ~X",          IDM_INVERTX
      MENUITEM "Invert ~Y",          IDM_INVERTY
      MENUITEM "~Invert X and Y",    IDM_INVERTXY
   END
   SUBMENU  "~Background",  IDM_BACKGROUND, MIS_TEXT
   BEGIN
      MENUITEM "~Black",   IDM_BLACK,, MIA_CHECKED
      MENUITEM "~Red",     IDM_RED
      MENUITEM "~Green",   IDM_GREEN
      MENUITEM "B~lue",    IDM_BLUE
      MENUITEM "~White",   IDM_WHITE
   END
END
```

BLTER.DEF

```
NAME BLTER WINDOWAPI

DESCRIPTION 'GpiBitBlt Example'
```

```
CODE      MOVEABLE
DATA      MOVEABLE MULTIPLE

HEAPSIZE  10240
STACKSIZE 24576
```

BLTER.MAK

```
all : blter.exe

blter.exe : blter.obj blter.def blter.res
        link386 /PM:PM blter,,,,blter.def;
        rc blter.res

blter.res : blter.rc blter.ico blter.h
        rc -r blter.rc

blter.obj : blter.c blter.h
        icc /C /Ss /W3 ./$*.c
```

BLTER.ICO

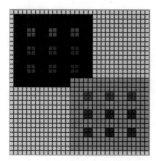

VGA Independent

BLTER.ICO file, containing the icon used for the BLTER program.

Using GpiBitBlt

The GpiBitBlt API has many options that can be chosen by setting its parameters. The BLTER program allows the user to set values that are used for two of the GpiBitBlt parameters. Even though the set of options that the BLTER program exercises is limited, they can still make the GpiBitBlt API perform a large number of operations. The following code excerpt shows the GpiBitBlt call that is used by the BLTER program:

```
GpiBitBlt( hps,
           hpsMemory,
           4L,
           (PPOINTL)apts,
           aROP[sROP - IDM_SRCCOPY],
           BBO_IGNORE );
```

The fourth and fifth parameters of the GpiBitBlt API are the two parameters that the user sets by using the pull-down menus of the BLTER program. The fourth parameter describes the orientation of the bitmap being drawn. The fifth parameter describes how a source, a destination, and a pattern bitmap are merged together. Depending on the choice of parameters, the function performed by the GpiBitBlt API can vary from a simple bitmap copy operation to a complex manipulation of bitmaps.

When an application works with GpiBitBlt, it actually uses three bitmaps: a source bitmap, a destination bitmap, and a pattern bitmap. The source bitmap is identified by the second parameter. The destination bitmap is the image that is stored in the target presentation space (identified by the first parameter) that is altered by GpiBitBlt. The pattern bitmap is a monochrome or color bitmap that is associated with the target presentation space by a call to GpiSetPattern.

The three bitmaps used by GpiBitBlt can be manipulated with one of 256 available ROPs, specified by the fifth parameter. The most common ROPs are given predefined labels prefixed with ROP_, and are listed as a part of the ROP menu of the BLTER program.

Each ROP has an 8-bit hex value assigned to it. The assigned hex value is not a random value; rather, each ROP value is derived from the result of a Boolean operation performed on the source, destination, and pattern bitmaps. A ROP value describes a part of a truth table that the GpiBitBlt API uses to merge the bits from the three bitmaps.

Instead of dealing with an entire source bitmap and an entire destination bitmap, GpiBitBlt can deal with subsets of the source and destination bitmaps. Furthermore, the GpiBitBlt API permits a bitmap to be stretched, compressed, and rotated. These choices are specified by the fourth parameter of GpiBitBlt, which is an array (apts) of up to four points that describes the rectangular areas of the source and destination bitmaps that are to be used. The first two points of the array specify the lower left and upper right corners of the destination bitmap; the last two points specify the lower left and upper right corners of the source bitmap.

The orientation and size of a bitmap can be altered substantially as desired by setting values in the apts array. If the array describes a destination rectangle that is of a different size than the source rectangle, the source bitmap is stretched or compressed to accommodate needed size changes. The orientation of the bitmap being drawn can be inverted in one or both of the X and Y directions by manipulating the X and Y values of the destination rectangle.

Depending on the complexity of the bitblt operation, not all of the points listed in the apts array may need to be used. If no stretching or compressing of a bitmap is desired, the array can specify just three points, namely the lower left and upper right corners of the destination rectangle, and the starting position of the source bitmap. Such a specification will cause the source bitmap to be drawn, without change, into the destination rectangle that is specified by the first two of the three points. The third parameter of GpiBitBlt is used to indicate the number of points that are used in the array that is identified by the fourth parameter. The most commonly used values are 3 and 4. A value of 2 can be used when the fifth parameter is set to ROP_PATCOPY. The two specified points define a destination rectangle, which is to be filled with a pattern.

The last parameter of the GpiBitBlt API is used for one of the available option flags. These flags tell GpiBitBlt how to handle a situation in which the destination rectangle is smaller than the source rectangle. In this case, the source bitmap needs to be compressed, and some columns, rows, or both will need to be combined. When two rows or columns are to be combined into one, the following option flags tell GpiBitBlt how to handle the merge:

- BBO_AND   Causes GpiBitBlt to combine adjacent rows and columns using the logical AND operation.
- BBO_OR   Causes GpiBitBlt to combine adjacent rows and columns using the logical OR operation.
- BBO_IGNORE   Causes GPI to discard rows or columns to reduce the size of a bitmap.

The BBO_IGNORE flag is most commonly used for color bitmaps. The BBO_AND and BBO_OR flags are typically used with monochrome bitmaps, because the colors they produce are often unpredictable and frequently are found not to correspond to a desirable bitmap color scheme.

CHAPTER 9
Subclassing PM Windows

PM maintains a data structure to describe the properties of each window. Among the components of a window's data structure is the address of a window procedure, which defines how the window will react to incoming messages. If the programmer changes the address so that it points to an alternate window procedure, all incoming messages that were intended to be received by the window procedure at the old address are redirected to the alternate window procedure located at the changed address. By using this technique, the behavior that a window exhibits in reacting to the messages it receives can be redefined. The technique of changing a window's data structure to use an alternate window procedure is known as *subclassing*.

Subclassing gives programmers great flexibility to change existing window classes. Subclassing is *not* considered "sloppy patch work," nor is it looked down upon as being a bad programming technique. To the contrary, PM and its controls are *designed* to be subclassed so that their appearance and functionality can be modified quite easily when needed.

SUBCLASSING WINDOW PROCEDURES

PM's window classes were designed with subclassing in mind, so that a simple subclassing window procedure can be used to intercept and redirect incoming messages, and so that desired alternate reactions to messages can be obtained without requiring extensive amounts of new code to carry out these impressive objectives.

A subclassing window procedure typically modifies the behavior that a window exhibits in response to receiving a few selected messages. In many instances, the effect of subclassing is both to simply pass a majority of received messages on to the original window procedure to be processed in the usual way because such messages are not of interest, and to ensure that the alternate window procedure acts on selected messages in desired ways.

A subclassing window procedure should not call an API such as `WinDefWindowProc` to handle unprocessed messages. Rather, the original (subclassed) window procedure should be treated as a default procedure for receiving and acting on forwarded messages so that the subclassed window can handle typical "housekeeping" tasks.

A message that is processed by a subclassing window procedure may involve calling the original window procedure and then modifying the results of the action taken by the original window. Alternatively, the entire original window procedure can be bypassed by having a subclassing window procedure entirely process every aspect of a selected message.

Since messages represent functions that a window is capable of handling, the ability of a control to be subclassed depends to a significant extent on how well the particular control makes use of the message-based architecture of PM. A well-designed control can be subclassed easily, because it is set up to deal with a variety of messages that may require specialized treatment tailored to correspond to the character of the particular message received. The greater the number of messages that are associated with a particular control, the greater is the range of possibilities that exists for altering the control by subclassing.

Messages can provide access to the internal functions of a window. The design of the window should require that the window even send messages to itself in order to access the window's internal functions. Maintaining this practice ensures that each internal function can be replaced or altered by changing the way the window handles incoming messages. While requiring a window to send messages to itself may appear to be inefficient compared to making a direct call to an internal function, a well-designed window or control *must* follow this procedure if it is to be effectively subclassed. If a window procedure violates this rule (by failing to make use of messages to access its internal functions), it sacrifices possibilities that otherwise could be exploited by subclassing.

WHEN TO USE SUBCLASSING

Subclassing, regardless of when it is done, will always miss at least the first few messages that were used to create the window that is being subclassed. If it is critical to assure that absolutely no messages are missed by a particular window procedure, alternatives to subclassing can be used. For example, a relatively complex approach that can be taken is to register the particular window procedure as a new window class (a subject that is discussed in Chapter 4), so that the particular window procedure will receive even the first few messages that are sent when a window is created.

While steps can be taken, as just described, to ensure that initial messages sent to a particular window procedure are not "missed," in most instances the missing of a few of the initial messages is not found to cause a problem, even if subclassing is being used to alter a window's appearance. One of the reasons that the "missing" of initial messages normally does not cause problems is that many of the first messages that are sent during the creation of a window are ignored by such windows as frames, especially if the window being created is still invisible. Another reason is that some of the messages that were missed are resent when the window is made visible. By making a window visible *after* it has been subclassed, an opportunity is given to a subclassing window procedure to receive messages that relate to such actions as the setting of the window's size and position. Thus, subclassing can have the effect of altering a window even before it is displayed.

Such messages as WM_CREATE will not be resent when a window finally is displayed. This is because a subclassing window procedure is not permitted to receive a WM_CREATE message. In many cases, failure to receive a WM_CREATE message is not a problem; however, if a WM_CREATE message *must* be received by a window procedure, the correct approach is not to use subclassing but rather to register a new class of window.

EXAMPLES OF SUBCLASSED PM WINDOWS

PM and Workplace Shell make extensive use of subclassing. Dialog boxes and the folders of Workplace Shell are examples of subclassed frame windows. A dialog box is formed by creating a frame window and then subclassing the newly created window, by substituting the window procedure of a dialog box for the window procedure that a frame window normally uses.

During the creation of a dialog box, a WM_CREATE message will be sent by PM to the frame window before the dialog procedure is sent to subclass the frame. PM sends a WM_INITDLG message to a dialog procedure as a replacement for the missing WM_CREATE message.

The folders of the Workplace Shell are examples of subclassed frame windows that have a container as a client window. A folder is constructed by creating a frame window and by subclassing the newly created frame window. The frame is subclassed to cause a window procedure to intercept messages that a container sends to its parent—messages that a normal frame would not expect to receive from its client window.

TELLING PM TO SUBCLASS A WINDOW

An API called WinSubclassWindow is used to subclass a window. This API uses the handle of a window that is being subclassed and the address of a subclassing window procedure. WinSubclassWindow returns the address of the original window procedure, which the subclassing window procedure will need in order to forward any unprocessed messages to the original window procedure.

To undo the subclassing of a window, WinSubclassWindow can be called once again, but this time with the address of the original window procedure. The original window procedure's address replaces the subclassing window procedure, so that the behavior of the window is returned to normal.

The address of a window procedure is stored in an associated data structure that is maintained for each window by PM. APIs that can directly change a window's data can be used to implement substantially the same function that `WinSubclassWindow` performs. A call to `WinSubclassWindow` is similar to calling `WinQueryWindowPtr` to get the address of the original window procedure, followed by calling `WinSetWindowPtr` to set a new address pointing to the subclassing window procedure that is to be substituted.

The following code uses the `WinQueryWindowPtr` and `WinSetWindowPtr` APIs with the parameter `QWP_PFNWP` to query the address of the window procedure of a window with handle `hwnd` and to replace it with a pointer to a subclassing window procedure:

```
OriginalWndProc = (PFNWP)WinQueryWindowPtr( hwnd, QWP_PFNWP );
WinSetWindowPtr( hwnd, QWP_PFNWP, (PVOID)NewWndProc );
```

In this example code, the `WinQueryWindowPtr` API retrieves the address of the window procedure that is being used by the window `hwnd` and stores it in a pointer called `OriginalWndProc`. The `WinSetWindowPtr` API changes the address to point to a subclassing window procedure labeled `NewWndProc`.

The foregoing example does not handle some of the internal steps that the `WinSubclassWindow` API carries out. One of the steps skipped is a check that the API makes as to whether the process doing the subclassing owns the window with handle `hwnd`. A rule of subclassing is that only the process that has set up a window can later be used to subclass it. If a process attempts to use `WinSubclassWindow` to subclass a window that has been set up by another process, `WinSubclassWindow` will return a `NULL` pointer to signal that an error has occurred.

CHANGING THE WAY A WINDOW IS RESIZED

A typical use for subclassing is to change the way that a frame window's size borders operate. When a user starts to resize a frame window, a tracking rectangle is displayed. The tracking rectangle appears in the shape and position of the borders of a window that is being repositioned, and it serves to enable a user's keyboard or mouse to manipulate the shape and position of the rectangle. The final shape of the rectangle and its position on the screen determine the new shape and position that the frame window will take.

THE TRCKRECT PROGRAM

By subclassing a frame window, it is possible to change how a tracking rectangle operates and to set any restrictions that need to be imposed on the frame window, such as a minimum window size. The lines that are used to draw the

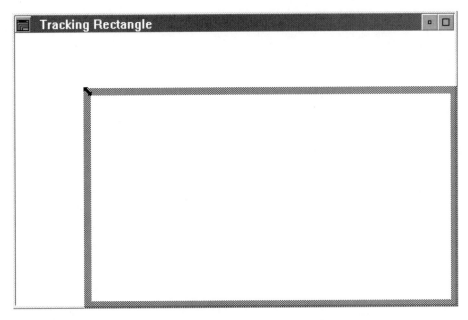

FIGURE 9.1   The subclassed tracking rectangle of TRCKRECT.

tracking rectangle show the size and thickness of the borders of the window. A minimum size is imposed on the window to prevent it from being made too small to fit a system menu, title bar, and minmax buttons.

Figure 9.1 shows a tracking rectangle that can be produced by an example program called TRCKRECT, the source code for which is presented in this section. TRCKRECT subclasses its frame window to double the thickness of the lines that are used to draw its tracking rectangle and to double the "minimum size" that the window must occupy.

The following six files list the source code that is compiled to provide the example program TRCKRECT:

TRCKRECT.C

```
#define INCL_GPI
#define INCL_WIN
#include <os2.h>
#include "trckrect.h"


/* prototypes */
INT main( VOID );
MRESULT EXPENTRY NewFrameWndProc( HWND, ULONG, MPARAM, MPARAM );
MRESULT EXPENTRY ClientWinProc( HWND, ULONG, MPARAM, MPARAM );
```

```
/* global variables */
PFNWP OldFrameWndProc = NULL;


INT main( VOID )
{
   HAB  hab;
   HMQ  hmq;
   QMSG qmsg;
   HWND hwndFrame;
   HWND hwndClient;
   static CHAR szClientClass[] = "Client Window";
   ULONG flCreateFlags = FCF_TITLEBAR      /* create: title bar control   */
                       | FCF_SYSMENU       /*          system menu control */
                       | FCF_SIZEBORDER    /*          sizeborders         */
                       | FCF_MINMAX        /*          min and max buttons  */
                       | FCF_SHELLPOSITION /* shell decides window position */
                       | FCF_TASKLIST      /* title added to switch list   */
                       | FCF_ICON;         /* frame has an icon            */

   hab = WinInitialize( 0 );
   hmq = WinCreateMsgQueue( hab, 0 );

   WinRegisterClass( hab,            /* anchor block handle */
                  szClientClass,  /* class name */
                  ClientWinProc,  /* pointer to window procedure */
                  CS_SIZEREDRAW,  /* class style */
                  0 );            /* number of control data bytes */

   hwndFrame = WinCreateStdWindow(
                  HWND_DESKTOP,    /* parent          */
                  0,               /* window style */
                  &flCreateFlags,  /* creation flags for frame window     */
                  szClientClass,   /* client window class name            */
                  "Tracking Rectangle",  /* title bar text                */
                  0,               /* use default client window style     */
                                   /*    WS_VISIBLE is not needed here     */
                  NULLHANDLE,      /* resource ID's are in rc file        */
                  ID_TRCKRECT,     /* ID for frame window and its resources */
                  &hwndClient );   /* address to place client window handle */

   OldFrameWndProc = WinSubclassWindow( hwndFrame, NewFrameWndProc );

   WinShowWindow( hwndFrame, TRUE );

   if ( hwndFrame )
      while (WinGetMsg( hab,&qmsg, NULLHANDLE, 0, 0 ))
         WinDispatchMsg( hab, &qmsg );

   WinDestroyWindow( hwndFrame );  /* clean up */
   WinDestroyMsgQueue( hmq );
   WinTerminate( hab );

   return 0;
} /* end main */
```

```
MRESULT EXPENTRY NewFrameWndProc( HWND hwnd, ULONG msg, MPARAM mp1, MPARAM mp2 )
{
   switch (msg) {

   //
   // message handling for modifying the frame's properties
   //

   case WM_QUERYTRACKINFO:
     /* let original frame window procedure fill the TRACKINFO structure */
      OldFrameWndProc( hwnd, msg, mp1, mp2 );

     /* modify the data in the TRACKINFO structure */
      ((PTRACKINFO)mp2)->cxBorder *= 2; /* double thickness of the lines */
      ((PTRACKINFO)mp2)->cyBorder *= 2;
      ((PTRACKINFO)mp2)->ptlMinTrackSize.x *= 2; /* double the minimum size */
      ((PTRACKINFO)mp2)->ptlMinTrackSize.y *= 2;

      return (MRESULT)TRUE; /* continue with repositioning window */

   default:
      /* call original frame window procedure */
      return (MRESULT)(*OldFrameWndProc)( hwnd, msg, mp1, mp2 );
   }

   return (MRESULT)FALSE;
} /* NewFrameWndProc */


MRESULT EXPENTRY ClientWinProc( HWND hwnd, ULONG msg, MPARAM mp1,MPARAM mp2 )
{
   switch (msg) {

   case WM_ERASEBACKGROUND:
      /* have the frame paint the client window */
      return (MRESULT) TRUE;

   default:
      return WinDefWindowProc( hwnd, msg, mp1, mp2 );
   }

   return (MRESULT)FALSE;
} /* ClientWinProc */
```

TRCKRECT.H

```
#define ID_TRCKRECT 1
```

TRCKRECT.RC

```
#include <os2.h>
#include "trckrect.h"

ICON ID_TRCKRECT trckrect.ico
```

TRCKRECT.DEF

```
NAME    TRCKRECT    WINDOWAPI

DESCRIPTION 'Subclassing Example Program'

STUB        'OS2STUB.EXE'

DATA        MULTIPLE

STACKSIZE   16348
HEAPSIZE    16348

PROTMODE
```

TRCKRECT.MAK

```
all : trckrect.exe

trckrect.exe : trckrect.obj trckrect.def trckrect.res
        link386 /PM:PM trckrect,,,,trckrect.def;
        rc trckrect.res

trckrect.res: trckrect.rc trckrect.ico trckrect.h
        rc -r trckrect.rc

trckrect.obj:trckrect.c trckrect.h
        icc /C /Ss /W3 .\$*.c
```

TRCKRECT.ICO

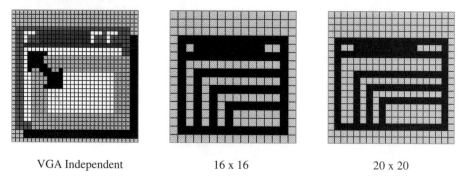

VGA Independent   16 x 16   20 x 20

TRCKRECT.ICO file, containing various icons of different sizes.

LOOKING AT THE TRCKRECT SOURCE CODE

In the TRCKRECT program, the `WinCreateStdWindow` API is called to create a frame window with size borders. Once the window is created, `WinSubclassWindow` is called to set a window procedure called `NewFrame-`

WndProc to receive all messages that are sent to the frame. If any further alterations need to be made to the frame window or any of its children, code that implements these alterations would be placed just before the call to WinShowWindow that appears after WinSubclassWindow.

It is typical to see the WinCreateWindow and WinCreateStdWindow APIs followed by a call to WinSubclassWindow and then to WinShowWindow. If WS_VISIBLE is used in either of the APIs that create a window, the window will be displayed before the subclassing window procedure has been given a chance to intercept messages. Knowing when to display a window that is being created can be quite important, especially if subclassing is being done to change the window's appearance.

The drawing and sizing of a tracking rectangle is handled by an API called WinTrackRect. When a frame detects that a menu option or size border is indicating an attempt to size its window, the frame sends itself a WM_TRACKFRAME message. By sending itself such a message, a subclassing window procedure can intercept such attempts as may be made to start sizing a window. The function NewFrameWndProc is called to handle each of the frame's messages, but it does not interfere with WM_TRACKFRAME messages; instead, it allows the frame to handle such messages.

When a frame receives a WM_TRACKFRAME message, it sets up a TRACKINFO data structure, which is required by the WinTrackRect API. A TRACKINFO structure tells WinTrackRect how the tracking rectangle is to be drawn and repositioned. A TRACKINFO structure also specifies a minimum and maximum size, as well as other features for a tracking rectangle. The frame will call the WinTrackRect API once it has filled a TRACKINFO data structure with the information needed to describe the properties of a tracking rectangle.

The information in a TRACKINFO structure is initialized as a result of the frame's having sent another message to itself called WM_QUERYTRACKINFO. The processing of this self-sent message simply alters the contents of the TRACKINFO data structure. WM_QUERYTRACKINFO is the only message that the NewFrameWndProc procedure intercepts; all other messages are sent to the OldFrameWndProc procedure. When NewFrameProc handles WM_QUERYTRACKINFO messages, OldFrameWndProc is called and the fields contained in a TRACKINFO structure are initialized. NewFrameWndProc then modifies selected properties of the tracking rectangle which are used when the frame next calls WinTrackRect.

USING SUBCLASSING

The technique of subclassing is used in many of the example programs that are provided in this book. The TRCKRECT program illustrates the fact that a PM window normally sends several messages, even if the task being carried out is as simple as the resizing of a window. Each message performs a specific function that allows a very narrow aspect of a program to be singled out and changed when needed. For example, the TRCKRECT program is only interested in changing how its frame sets the values in a TRACKINFO structure; therefore, only the message that is used to set the structure was changed in the TRCKRECT program.

A good design for a window or control recognizes which functions should be supported by a message. Without a WM_QUERYTRACKINFO message, the TRCKRECT program would have to replace the entire handling of the WM_TRACKFRAME message with its own code. A part of the needed code would attend to the setting of the TRACKINFO data structure and to the calling of the WinTrackRect API. The code would almost duplicate code that already is present in the frame window procedure to handle window sizing; the difference in the code would be the data used to set the TRACKINFO structure. The writing of code to implement the handling of a WM_TRACKFRAME message can be avoided because the frame uses an extra message (WM_QUERYTRACKINFO) for the important task of setting the data contained in the TRACKINFO data structure.

CHAPTER 10
Menus

PM uses the menu window class to provide many of its most commonly used controls. Menu windows are used to implement system menu buttons, minmax buttons, action bars, pull-down menus, and pop-up menus. Because most of these same controls are used in standard windows that are handled by the frame class, frame windows are designed to work closely with menu windows to provide standard windows that are easy to program.

A new type of menu that was introduced with OS/2 Version 2.0 is called a *conditional cascade menu*. Conditional cascade menus allow a default choice to be made available, so that a commonly chosen item in a submenu does not require the submenu to be displayed if the item already has been set as the default choice. Workplace Shell makes considerable use of conditional cascade menus for opening its folders and files.

Many features offered by menu class windows are not used either by PM or by Workplace Shell. One of these features, namely *owner-drawn menus,* allows an owner window to control the appearance of items that are presented in a menu window. Using an owner-drawn menu in an action bar can provide a menu with a very distinctive appearance. For example, the appearance of the action bar can be altered so that it functions as a *tool bar*—a control that steadily is gaining in popularity for use with a wide variety of applications.

An owner-drawn menu is normally handled by a frame window. Menus use a set of messages to communicate with frame windows concerning owner-drawn menus. Owner-drawn menus represent just one instance of how a menu class window can be customized and can work in harmony with a frame class window.

CONDITIONAL CASCADE MENUS

Unlike an action bar, both pull-down and pop-up menus can include items that have several levels of submenus, which are referred to by the terms *cascade menus* and *conditional cascade menus.*

149

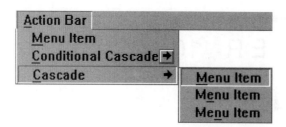

FIGURE 10.1   Example of a cascade menu with no default selection values.

A cascade menu will appear when its associated item in its parent menu is selected. Unlike cascade menus, conditional cascade menus do not appear when their associated parent menu item is selected. A conditional cascade menu will appear only if a special "mini-button," located in its associated parent menu, is pressed. In case the mini-button is not pressed, the conditional cascade menu has a default item, which will be chosen when its associated parent menu item is selected. If another selection (other than a default value) is desired, the mini-button can be pressed to display the conditional cascade menu, which sets out all of its selectable menu items. In a conditional cascade menu, default selections are identified by check marks that appear adjacent to the displayed default values.

The use of a conditional cascade menu saves the extra step of having a submenu appear so that the user can choose an item from among choices that are presented in the submenu. A submenu becomes a conditional cascade menu by having one of its items set up as a default, which is automatically selected when the associated parent menu item is selected. If an alternate (nondefault) item in the submenu needs to be selected, a mini-button that appears in the parent menu can be pressed to display the submenu.

Figure 10.1 shows a typical cascade menu. Figure 10.2 shows a conditional cascade menu and its parent menu. In Figure 10.2, the displayed list of available items was obtained by pressing a mini-button located in the parent menu.

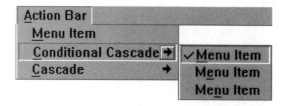

FIGURE 10.2   Example of a conditional cascade menu, with the default item designated by a check mark.

Creating a Conditional Cascade Menu

The following code excerpt can be placed into an RC file to create the conditional cascade menu shown in Figure 10.2:

```
MENU ID_MENUEXAMPLE
    BEGIN
        SUBMENU "~Action Bar", MY_PULLDOWNMENU1
            BEGIN
                SUBMENU  "~Conditional Cascade", MY_CASCADE1
                    BEGIN
                        MENUITEM "~Menu Item 1",   MY_ITEM1
                        MENUITEM "M~enu Item 2",   MY_ITEM2
                        MENUITEM "Me~nu Item 3",   MY_ITEM3
                    END
            END
    END
```

This code simply sets up a submenu as a traditional cascade menu. To turn the submenu into a conditional cascade menu, the submenu's window style is set with the MS_CONDITIONALCASCADE flag. Another required step is to send a message that identifies a default item.

The following code illustrates the steps that are needed to change the cascade menu that is described in the foregoing menu template into a conditional cascade menu:

```
hwndMenu = WinWindowFromID( hwndFrame, FID_MENU );

WinSendMsg( hwndMenu,
            MM_QUERYITEM,
            MPFROM2SHORT( MY_CASCADE1, TRUE ),
            MPFROMP( &menuitem ) );

ulMenuStyle = WinQueryWindowULong( menuitem.hwndSubMenu, QWL_STYLE );

WinSetWindowULong( menuitem.hwndSubMenu,
                   QWL_STYLE, ulMenuStyle | MS_CONDITIONALCASCADE );

WinSendMsg( menuitem.hwndSubMenu, MM_SETDEFAULTITEMID,
                       MPFROMSHORT( MY_ITEM1 ), NULL );
```

This code assumes that the variables hwndFrame and hwndMenu are of type HWND and that hwndFrame is the handle of the frame window that is associated with the action bar containing the cascade menu. The variable hwndMenu is set equal to the handle of the action bar. The hwndMenu variable is used in a message that both queries information about the cascade menu that is being changed and places information received in response to the query into a data structure called `menuitem`.

The variable `menuitem` is used to query the cascading menu's window style. The window style `MS_CONDITIONALCASCADE` is added to the window style, and the `WinSetWindowULong` API sets the cascade menu's new window style.

The final step taken in the foregoing code is to set the default item. A `MM_SETDEFAULTITEMID` message is sent to designate the first item (`MY_ITEM1`) as constituting a default. This message completes the changes that are needed to turn a cascade menu into a conditional cascade menu that has a check mark appearing to the left of its first menu item.

OWNER-DRAWN MENUS

Menu-class windows will typically attend to the drawing of the menu items that they display. However, a menu item can be designated as an *owner-drawn menu item* to give its owner window the ability to control the drawing of the item when the item is displayed on a menu. By giving a menu item the menu style `MIS_OWNERDRAW`, a menu window will surrender drawing control to its owner window. Menus that contain owner-drawn menu items are referred to by the term *owner-drawn menus*.

Owner-drawn menus give a program virtually complete control over how a menu and the items drawn on it should appear. An owner-drawn menu will still handle many functions automatically, such as setting the best positions for menu items to fit within the confines of a menu window. However, the menu items of an owner-drawn menu are not drawn by the menu window itself.

THE OWNRMENU PROGRAM

An example program called OWNRMENU (the source code for which is presented in this section) shows how the appearance of an action bar can be entirely changed with the use of owner-drawn menus. In Figure 10.3, an example is provided of the OWNRMENU window and its action bar.

The following six files were used to compile the OWNRMENU program:

OWNRMENU.C

```
#define INCL_GPI
#define INCL_WIN
#include <os2.h>
#include <string.h>
```

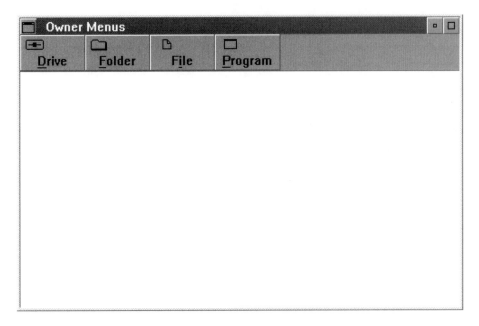

FIGURE 10.3 An example of a window and owner menus that are created by the OWNRMENU program.

```
#include "ownrmenu.h"
#define LAST_BTN 3


/* function prototypes */
INT main( VOID );
MRESULT EXPENTRY ClientWndProc( HWND, ULONG, MPARAM, MPARAM );
MRESULT EXPENTRY newFrameProc( HWND, ULONG, MPARAM, MPARAM );
VOID SetupForButtons( HAB, HWND );
VOID DrawButton( POWNERITEM );


/* globals */
HAB    hab;
HWND   hwndFrame;
PFNWP  oldFrameProc;
SHORT BtnBorderX;
SHORT BtnBorderY;
SHORT BtnHeight;
SHORT BtnWidth;
SHORT BtnMidX;
SHORT BtnMidY;
SHORT BtnTextHeight = 0;
HBITMAP hbmBtnCorner;
struct _BtnList {
    char *BtnLabel;
    HBITMAP Btnhbm;
```

```
} BtnList[] = {
   "~Drive",    0,
   "~Folder",   0,
   "F~ile",     0,
   "~Program", 0
}; /* end BtnList */
ULONG BmpList[] = { SBMP_DRIVE,
                    SBMP_FOLDER,
                    SBMP_FILE,
                    SBMP_PROGRAM };


INT main( VOID )
{
   HMQ   hmq;
   QMSG  qmsg;
   HWND hwndClient;
   static CHAR szClientClass[] = "MyButtonControls";
   ULONG flCreateFlags = FCF_TITLEBAR       /* create: title bar control    */
                       | FCF_SYSMENU        /*            system menu control */
                       | FCF_MENU           /*            action bar         */
                       | FCF_MINMAX         /*            min and max buttons */
                       | FCF_SIZEBORDER     /* draw sizeborders             */
                       | FCF_SHELLPOSITION  /* shell decides window position */
                       | FCF_TASKLIST       /* title added to switch list   */
                       | FCF_ICON;          /* frame has an icon            */

   hab = WinInitialize( 0 );
   hmq = WinCreateMsgQueue( hab, 0 );

   WinRegisterClass( hab,              /* anchor block handle */
                     szClientClass,    /* class name */
                     ClientWndProc,    /* pointer to window procedure */
                     CS_SIZEREDRAW,    /* class style */
                     0 );              /* number of class data bytes */

   hwndFrame = WinCreateStdWindow(
                     HWND_DESKTOP,     /* parent */
                     WS_VISIBLE,       /* frame window style */
                     &flCreateFlags,   /* creation flags for frame window */
                     szClientClass,    /* client window class name */
                     "Owner Menus",    /* text added to title */
                     0,                /* client window style */
                     NULLHANDLE,       /* resource ID's are in rc file */
                     ID_OWNRMENU,      /* ID for frame window */
                     &hwndClient );    /* address to place client window handle */

   oldFrameProc = WinSubclassWindow( hwndFrame, newFrameProc );

   if ( hwndFrame )
      while ( WinGetMsg( hab, &qmsg, NULLHANDLE, 0L, 0L ))
         WinDispatchMsg( hab, &qmsg );
```

```
    WinDestroyWindow( hwndFrame );
    WinDestroyMsgQueue( hmq );
    WinTerminate( hab );

    return 0;
} /* end main */


MRESULT EXPENTRY newFrameProc(HWND hwnd, ULONG msg, MPARAM mp1, MPARAM mp2)
{
    switch(msg) {
    case WM_TRANSLATEACCEL:
     { PQMSG pqmsg;
       USHORT us, id;

       if ((MRESULT)(*oldFrameProc)( hwnd, msg, mp1, mp2 ))
           return (MRESULT)TRUE;
       else {

           /* newFrameProc's mp1 parameter is a pointer to a QMSG structure */
           pqmsg = (PQMSG)mp1;

           /* the QMSG structure has a WM_CHAR mp1 message we want a part of */
           us = (USHORT)pqmsg->mp1;

           /* check if KC_KEYUP is off and KC_ALT is on */
           if ( !(us & KC_KEYUP) && (us & KC_ALT) ) {
               /* check for our owner-drawn menu's mnemonics */
               switch (SHORT1FROMMP( pqmsg->mp2 )) {
               case 'D': case 'd':
                   id = ID_DRIVE;
                   break;
               case 'F': case 'f':
                   id = ID_FOLDER;
                   break;
               case 'I': case 'i':
                   id = ID_FILE;
                   break;
               case 'P': case 'p':
                   id = ID_PROGRAM;
                   break;
               default:
                   return FALSE;
               } /* end switch */
               if ((SHORT)WinSendMsg( WinWindowFromID( hwnd, FID_MENU ),
                           MM_QUERYSELITEMID,
                           MPFROM2SHORT(  0, FALSE ),
                           MPFROM2SHORT(  0, 0 ) ) != MIT_NONE)
                   return FALSE;

               WinSendMsg( WinWindowFromID( hwnd, FID_MENU ) //>=ID_DRIVE)
                           MM_SELECTITEM,
                           MPFROM2SHORT( id, FALSE ),
                           MPFROM2SHORT(  0, FALSE ) );
```

```
               pqmsg->msg  = WM_NULL;
               pqmsg->hwnd = NULLHANDLE;
               pqmsg->mp1  = MPVOID;
               pqmsg->mp2  = MPVOID;

               return (MRESULT)TRUE;
            } /* end if */
         } /* end if */
       } return FALSE;
   default:
      return (MRESULT)(*oldFrameProc)( hwnd, msg, mp1, mp2 );
   } /* endswitch */
   return FALSE;
} /* end newFrameProc */


MRESULT EXPENTRY ClientWndProc(
   HWND hwnd,
   ULONG msg,
   MPARAM mp1,
   MPARAM mp2 )
{
   HWND hwndMenu;
   HPS hps;
   int i;

   switch (msg) {
   case WM_CREATE:
      SetupForButtons( hab, hwnd );
      hwndMenu = WinWindowFromID( hwndFrame, FID_MENU );
      break;
   case WM_MEASUREITEM:
      ((POWNERITEM)mp2)->rclItem.xRight = BtnWidth;
      ((POWNERITEM)mp2)->rclItem.yTop   = BtnHeight;
      return (MRESULT)BtnHeight;
   case WM_DRAWITEM:
      DrawButton( (POWNERITEM)mp2 );
      return (MRESULT)TRUE;
   case WM_COMMAND:
      if ( SHORT1FROMMP( mp2 ) == CMDSRC_MENU )
         WinAlarm( HWND_DESKTOP, WA_NOTE );
      break;
   case WM_ERASEBACKGROUND:
      return (MRESULT) TRUE;
   case WM_DESTROY:
      GpiDeleteBitmap( hbmBtnCorner );
      for (i = 1; i <= LAST_BTN; i++)
         GpiDeleteBitmap( BtnList[i].Btnhbm );
      break;
   default:
      return (MRESULT)WinDefWindowProc( hwnd, msg, mp1, mp2 );
   } /* endswitch */
   return (MRESULT)FALSE;
} /* end of ClientWndProc */
```

```
VOID SetupForButtons( HAB hab, HWND hwnd )
{
   BITMAPINFOHEADER2 bmpinfo2;
   BITMAPINFOHEADER bmpinfo;
   SHORT MaxBmpHeight = 0;
   SHORT MaxBmpWidth  = 0;
   SHORT MaxStrWidth  = 0;
   SHORT AveCharWidth;
   FONTMETRICS font;
   HBITMAP hbmOld;
   SIZEL szl;
   POINTL ptl;
   RECTL rctl;
   HDC hdcMem;
   HPS hps;
   int StrLen;
   int i;

   /* get the system font's size */
   hps = WinGetPS( hwnd );
      GpiQueryFontMetrics( hps, (LONG)sizeof(font), &font );
   WinReleasePS( hps );
   BtnTextHeight = font.lMaxBaselineExt;
   AveCharWidth = font.lAveCharWidth;

   /* get the system bitmaps */
   for (i = 0; i <= LAST_BTN; i++) {
      BtnList[i].Btnhbm = WinGetSysBitmap( HWND_DESKTOP, BmpList[i] );
      GpiQueryBitmapParameters( BtnList[i].Btnhbm, &bmpinfo );
      if (bmpinfo.cy > MaxBmpHeight)
         MaxBmpHeight = bmpinfo.cy;
      if (bmpinfo.cx > MaxBmpWidth)
         MaxBmpWidth = bmpinfo.cx;
      if ((StrLen = strlen(BtnList[i].BtnLabel)) > MaxStrWidth)
         MaxStrWidth = StrLen - 1; /* subtract one for the tilde character */
   }

   /* Convert MaxStrWidth from the number of characters to the number */
   /* of pixels wide the string needs                                 */
   MaxStrWidth = MaxStrWidth * AveCharWidth;

   /* get the nominal-border widths SV_CXBORDER and SV_CYBORDER       */
   BtnBorderX = WinQuerySysValue( HWND_DESKTOP, SV_CXBORDER );
   BtnBorderY = WinQuerySysValue( HWND_DESKTOP, SV_CYBORDER );

   /* set the buttons height and width */
   BtnHeight = 7*BtnBorderY + MaxBmpHeight + BtnTextHeight;
   BtnWidth  = 6*BtnBorderX + 4*AveCharWidth +
               (MaxBmpWidth > MaxStrWidth ? MaxBmpWidth : MaxStrWidth);

   /* calculate the size of the middle section */
   BtnMidX = BtnWidth - 2*BtnBorderX;
   BtnMidY = BtnHeight - 2*BtnBorderY;
```

```
   /* draw a bitmap for the buttons upper right and lower left corners */
   hdcMem = DevOpenDC( hab,
                       OD_MEMORY,
                       "*",
                       0L,
                       NULL,
                       NULLHANDLE );

   szl.cx = szl.cy = 0;
   hps = GpiCreatePS( hab,
                      hdcMem,
                      &szl,
                      PU_PELS
                      | GPIF_DEFAULT
                      | GPIT_MICRO
                      | GPIA_ASSOC );

   bmpinfo.cbFix     = 12L;
   bmpinfo.cx        = BtnBorderX;
   bmpinfo.cy        = BtnBorderY;
   bmpinfo.cPlanes   = 1;
   bmpinfo.cBitCount = 1;
   hbmBtnCorner      = GpiCreateBitmap( hps,
                                        (PBITMAPINFOHEADER2)&bmpinfo,
                                        0,
                                        NULL,
                                        NULL );

   hbmOld = GpiSetBitmap( hps,
                          hbmBtnCorner );

   /* clear the background */
   GpiErase( hps );

   /* create the diagonal meeting between the light and shaded colors */
   GpiSetColor( hps, CLR_FALSE );
   GpiBeginPath( hps, 1L ); /* since we have a micro-PS, use paths */
   ptl.x = 0;
   ptl.y = 0;
   GpiMove( hps, &ptl ); /* start at the lower left corner */

   ptl.x = BtnBorderX;
   GpiLine( hps, &ptl ); /* go along the bottom to the lower right corner */

   ptl.y = BtnBorderY;
   GpiLine( hps, &ptl ); /* go up to the upper right corner */

   GpiCloseFigure( hps );
   GpiEndPath( hps );
   GpiFillPath( hps, 1, FPATH_ALTERNATE );

   hbmOld = GpiSetBitmap( hps, NULLHANDLE );

   GpiDestroyPS( hps ); /* release handle to memory presentation space */
   DevCloseDC( hdcMem ); /* release handle to memory Device Controller */
} /* end of SetupForButtons */
```

```
VOID DrawButton( POWNERITEM pitm )
{
    HPS hps;
    SHORT ButtonID;
    BOOL BtnDown;

    LONG ColorTop = SYSCLR_BUTTONLIGHT;
    LONG ColorBottom = SYSCLR_BUTTONDARK;
    POINTL ptl;
    RECTL rctl;
    SHORT x, y;

    hps = pitm->hps;
    ButtonID = pitm->idItem - ID_BASE;
    BtnDown = pitm->fsAttribute & MIA_HILITED;

    /* location of the lower left corner of the button */
    x = pitm->rclItem.xLeft;
    y = pitm->rclItem.yBottom;

    pitm->fsAttribute = pitm->fsAttributeOld
        &= ~(MIA_CHECKED | MIA_HILITED | MIA_FRAMED);

    if (BtnDown) {
        ColorTop = SYSCLR_BUTTONDARK;
        ColorBottom = SYSCLR_BUTTONLIGHT;
    }

    /* draw the left edge */
    rctl.xLeft   = x;
    rctl.yBottom = y + BtnBorderY;
    rctl.xRight  = x + BtnBorderX;
    rctl.yTop    = rctl.yBottom + BtnMidY;
    WinFillRect) hps, &rctl, ColorTop );

    /* draw the right edge */
    rctl.xLeft   = x + BtnBorderX + BtnMidX;
    rctl.xRight  = x + BtnWidth;
    WinFillRect( hps, &rctl, ColorBottom );

    /* draw the top edge */
    rctl.xLeft   = x;
    rctl.yBottom = y + BtnBorderY + BtnMidY;
    rctl.xRight  = x + BtnBorderX + BtnMidX;
    rctl.yTop    - y + BtnHeight;
    WinFillRect( hps, &rctl, ColorTop );

    /* draw the bottom edge */
    rctl.xLeft   = x + BtnBorderX;
    rctl.yBottom = y;
    rctl.xRight  = x + BtnWidth;
    rctl.yTop    = y + BtnBorderY;
    WinFillRect( hps, &rctl, ColorBottom );

    /* draw the middle section */
    rctl.xLeft   = x + BtnBorderX;
```

```
    rctl.yBottom = y + BtnBorderY;
    rctl.xRight  = x + BtnBorderX + BtnMidX;
    rctl.yTop    = y + BtnBorderY + BtnMidY;
    WinFillRect( hps, &rctl, SYSCLR_BUTTONMIDDLE );

    /* bitblt in the corners */
    ptl.x = x; ptl.y = y;
    WinDrawBitmap( hps, hbmBtnCorner, NULL, &ptl,
                   ColorTop, ColorBottom, DBM_NORMAL );
    ptl.x = x + BtnWidth - BtnBorderX; ptl.y = y + BtnHeight - BtnBorderY;
    WinDrawBitmap( hps, hbmBtnCorner, NULL, &ptl,
                   ColorTop, ColorBottom, DBM_NORMAL );

    /* Draw the unique part of the part */
    if (BtnDown) {
        x += BtnBorderX; y -= BtnBorderY;
    } /* endif */
    rctl.xLeft   = x + 3*BtnBorderX;
    rctl.yBottom = y + 3*BtnBorderY;
    rctl.xRight  = x + BtnWidth - 3*BtnBorderX;
    rctl.yTop    = rctl.yBottom + BtnTextHeight;
    WinDrawText( hps,
                 -1,
                 BtnList[ButtonID].BtnLabel,
                 &rctl,
                 SYSCLR_MENUTEXT,
                 SYSCLR_BUTTONMIDDLE,
                 DT_CENTER | DT_VCENTER | DT_MNEMONIC);

    ptl.x = x + 3*BtnBorderX + 1; ptl.y = rctl.yTop + BtnBorderY;
    WinDrawBitmap( hps, BtnList[ButtonID].Btnhbm, NULL, &ptl,
                   SYSCLR_MENUTEXT, SYSCLR_BUTTONMIDDLE, DBM_NORMAL );
} /* end of DrawButton */
```

OWNRMENU.H

```
#define ID_OWNRMENU  1

#define ID_DRIVE   301
#define ID_FOLDER  302
#define ID_FILE    303
#define ID_PROGRAM 304
#define ID_BASE ID_DRIVE
```

OWNRMENU.RC

```
#include <os2.h>
#include "ownrmenu.h"

ICON ID_OWNRMENU ownrmenu.ico

MENU ID_OWNRMENU
   BEGIN
```

```
        SUBMENU "", ID_DRIVE,     MIS_OWNERDRAW
          BEGIN
            MENUITEM "Change drive letter...", 400
            MENUITEM "Query drive size",       401
            MENUITEM "Display directory",       402
          END
        SUBMENU "", ID_FOLDER,    MIS_OWNERDRAW
          BEGIN
            MENUITEM "Create folder...",        403
            MENUITEM "Move folder...",          404
            MENUITEM "Display contents",        405
          END
        SUBMENU "", ID_FILE,      MIS_OWNERDRAW
          BEGIN
            MENUITEM "Create file...",          406
            MENUITEM "Move file...",            407
            MENUITEM "Display contents",        408
          END
        SUBMENU "", ID_PROGRAM,   MIS_OWNERDRAW
          BEGIN
            MENUITEM "Find program...",         410
            MENUITEM "Run program...",          411
            MENUITEM "Query details",           412
          END
    END
```

OWNRMENU.DEF

```
NAME     OWNRMENU     WINDOWAPI

DESCRIPTION 'Owner Drawn Menu Example'

STUB        'OS2STUB.EXE'

DATA        MULTIPLE

STACKSIZE   16348
HEAPSIZE    16348

PROTMODE
```

OWNRMENU.MAK

```
all : ownrmenu.exe

ownrmenu.exe : ownrmenu.obj ownrmenu.def ownrmenu.res
        link386 /PM:PM ownrmenu,,,,ownrmenu.def;
      rc ownrmenu.res

ownrmenu.res: ownrmenu.rc ownrmenu.ico ownrmenu.h
      rc -r ownrmenu.rc

ownrmenu.obj:ownrmenu.c ownrmenu.h
      icc /C /Ss /W3 .\$*.c
```

OWNRMENU.ICO

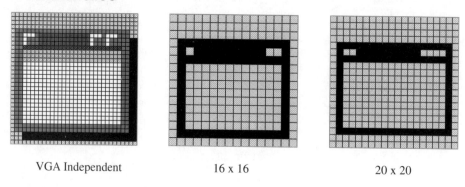

VGA Independent   16 x 16   20 x 20

OWNRMENU.ICO file, containing various icons of different sizes.

OWNER-DRAWN MENU ITEMS

When a menu contains an owner-drawn menu item, it will surrender control over the size and appearance of that item to its owner window. The menu must use messages to give the owner window access to draw its menu item within the owner window at the proper times. When a menu window is displayed for the first time, it sends a WM_MEASUREITEM message to its owner menu to query the owner about the height and width of each of its owner-drawn menu items. While height and width information normally is calculated by a menu, in the case of owner-drawn menu items the owner window is required to calculate the space requirements.

A WM_MEASUREITEM message contains the menu ID of an item that is being measured. The OWNRMENU program replies to a WM_MEASUREITEM message that is sent to it by placing the height and width of the menu item in the RECTL structure that the second message parameter of the WM_MEASUREITEM message points to. The following code shows how the OWNRMENU program handles WM_MEASUREITEM messages:

```
case WM_MEASUREITEM:
    ((POWNERITEM)mp2)->rclItem.xRight = BtnWidth;
    ((POWNERITEM)mp2)->rclItem.yTop   = BtnHeight;
    return (MRESULT)BtnHeight;
```

For the OWNRMENU program, the height (BtnHeight) and width (BtnWidth) are common to all five of its owner-drawn items. If the menu items were to vary in size, the OWNRMENU program could check the ID given by the first message parameter of the WM_MEASUREITEM message to determine which menu item is referred to by the message.

Once a menu window has calculated the sizes of its menu items and has queried for the sizes of any owner-drawn menu items that are to appear on the menu, the menu window will position each item within a rectangular space that is large enough to contain the item. When the items are being drawn, an owner window will receive a WM_DRAWITEM message indicating the location of a rectangle that defines a space that has been allocated to receive the image of an owner-drawn menu item. WM_DRAWITEM is sent each time the menu needs to redraw its items and each time that a menu item has been altered by changing its menu attributes (MIA_CHECKED and MIA_HILITED are the most commonly changed menu attributes).

Three-Dimensional Buttons

The OWNRMENU program uses a set of five owner-drawn menu items in its action bar. These items appear as three-dimensional buttons, which take on a "pressed" look when they are selected. The three-dimensional appearance of the menu items results from the use of a shaded border that surrounds each item. The border is drawn using a white color along its top and left sides and a dark gray color along its right and bottom sides. Figure 10.4 shows an example of how such buttons would appear if their borders were expanded.

Although the frame is the owner of the action bar wherein the buttons appear, the frame is also the owner of the client window that attends to the processing of the WM_MEASUREITEM and WM_DRAWITEM messages. To give client windows more control over their frame windows, a frame window will not process either of these messages. Instead, a frame will forward these messages to the

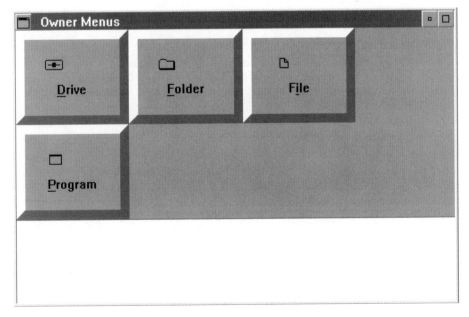

FIGURE 10.4   The OWNRMENU buttons with their borders expanded.

client window for processing. Sending the client window messages concerning owner-drawn menus serves as a convenience to programmers. A frame could be subclassed so that owner-drawn messages are handled by the frame and are not forwarded to its client.

A disadvantage of using owner-drawn menus is their lack of support for keyboard functions that non–owner-drawn menus provide. Most menu items are assigned a keystroke, called a mnemonic, that, if pressed, highlights a menu item. An owner-drawn menu ignores such mnemonic capabilities as may be available to the menu template that was used in constructing a particular owner-drawn menu.

The OWNRMENU program has additional code that gives its owner-drawn menus support for mnemonics. When a keyboard event occurs, PM sends the foreground window a `WM_TRANSLATEACCEL` message that identifies the combination of keyboard buttons that has been pressed. If the keystroke matches a menu's mnemonic, then the menu item that is associated with the keystroke will be highlighted and its submenu will be displayed.

The OWNRMENU program subclasses its frame window to intercept `WM_TRANSLATEACCEL` messages that signal possible mnemonics. The OWNR-MENU action bar ignores these messages and does not try to find a menu item that is associated with one or more keystrokes. By supplying code that is needed to compare a keystroke with a table of mnemonics, the OWNRMENU program emulates the normal behavior of non–owner-drawn menus. If a keystroke is found to match a mnemonic, a message is sent to an action bar that displays a submenu that has the mnemonic-associated item highlighted.

CHAPTER 11
Accelerator Tables

PM applications use *accelerator tables* to store a list of *accelerators,* which assign keystrokes to select available menu items. An accelerator is a "shortcut" that provides quick access to a menu item that may be "buried" in several levels of submenus. By simply loading an accelerator table, a PM application can assign accelerators to its most commonly chosen menu items, thereby giving the user a quick and easy way to select the menu items with a single keystroke.

In essence, an accelerator is a "relationship" that is established between a keystroke and a message that is to be sent when that keystroke is intercepted. The function of an accelerator table is to store a set of accelerator relationships. PM provides applications with a *system accelerator table* of commonly used keystrokes; however, it is not unusual for an application to set up its own accelerator table to establish additional accelerators or to "override" default accelerators that have been provided by PM.

PM implements accelerators by intercepting keystrokes as they are sent to an application and comparing the intercepted keystrokes with those listed in the accelerator tables that are used by the application and by PM. If an accelerator is assigned to an intercepted keystroke, PM replaces the keystroke with the message that is specified by the accelerator table; this message is equivalent to the selection of an item from the application's menus.

ACCELERATOR KEYSTROKES

Each accelerator assigns a keystroke to a menu selection by replacing a WM_CHAR message that is associated with the keystroke with a substitute WM_COMMAND, WM_SYSCOMMAND, or WM_HELP message indicating a menu selection. The type of message that an accelerator will use to replace a WM_CHAR message depends on what kind of menu item is assigned to the accelerator.

An accelerator needs to precisely emulate the messages that are posted when a menu item is selected. Menu items can post either a WM_COMMAND, a

WM_SYSCOMMAND, or a WM_HELP message when selected. A selected menu item typically posts a WM_SYSCOMMAND message if the item was selected from a system menu. However, if the item selected was in an action bar, it typically posts a WM_COMMAND message. A WM_HELP message ordinarily is not posted in response to the selection of a menu item; rather, it is posted by a menu window to indicate that a menu item has been selected by using the F1 keyboard key.

Replacing WM_CHAR Messages

PM applications are kept informed of keyboard keys that are pressed by receiving WM_CHAR messages that identify each keystroke. PM places messages that reflect keyboard input on the system queue, which is frequently checked by each PM application.

A PM message placed on the system queue is stored in a QMSG data structure. Altering the data contained within a message's QMSG data structure can change the information that the message relays. For example, a QMSG structure that represents a keystroke message can be changed to represent a menu selection message. Accelerators rely on an ability to change messages on the system queue in order to "trick" a PM application into handling a menu selection that actually did not occur.

The following code illustrates the format that is used to store information in a QMSG data structure:

```
typedef struct _QMSG {
    HWND       hwnd;
    ULONG      msg;
    MPARAM     mp1;
    MPARAM     mp2;
    ULONG      time;
    POINTL     ptl;
} QMSG;
```

The QMSG data structure contains information that describes a message. It specifies the identity of the window (hwnd) that was active at the time that the message was created as well as the type of the message (msg). Message parameters (mp1 and mp2) express information that is specific to the type of message being sent. By changing the information that is stored in a QMSG structure about a message, the entire meaning of the message can be altered as desired.

PM uses the WinTranslateAccel API to alter WM_CHAR messages to represent menu selections. A WM_CHAR message is given to WinTranslateAccel in the form of a pointer to a QMSG structure. If the message represented by the QMSG structure matches an accelerator listed in a designated accelerator table, WinTranslateAccel alters the information in the QMSG structure. The QMSG structure either may remain a WM_CHAR message or may be altered to represent a menu selection message (WM_COMMAND, WM_SYSCOMMAND, or WM_HELP).

WinGetMsg and WinPeekMsg

The APIs `WinGetMsg` and `WinPeekMsg` provide PM with the ability to implement accelerators. `WM_CHAR` messages are stored on the system queue and, like other system queue messages, are accessed by PM applications through the use of either of the APIs `WinGetMsg` or `WinPeekMsg`. These two APIs contain the code that gives PM the ability to change `WM_CHAR` messages as prescribed by accelerator tables. These two APIs will change a `WM_CHAR` message to a menu selection message if an associated accelerator exists. The `WinPeekMsg` API is intended only to "peek" at the contents of the next available message; however, it is important to note that `WinPeekMsg` *does* change `WM_CHAR` messages in the same manner as `WinGetMsg`.

The `WinGetMsg` and `WinPeekMsg` APIs can be instructed to search the system queue for particular types of messages using a *filter*. A filter specifies the type of messages that an application will accept from the system queue. A message not matching the requirements will be skipped, and the API will go on to test the next message that is presented in the system queue.

The use of filters complicates the efforts that `WinGetMsg` and `WinPeekMsg` make to translate `WM_CHAR` messages into menu selection messages. When `WinGetMsg` or `WinPeekMsg` is used with a filter to retrieve a message from the system queue, a given filter may accept a `WM_CHAR` message; however, the message that results from the translation procedure may no longer be acceptable to the filter. If the translated message is not acceptable, it is left on the system queue, and the next message is checked.

The `WinGetMsg` and `WinPeekMsg` APIs do not receive certain keystrokes that are reserved for PM. So-called "system keystrokes," such as Ctrl-Esc, Alt-Esc, and Ctrl-Alt-Delete, are intercepted by PM before `WM_CHAR` messages are created, thereby making system keystrokes unavailable for use by an accelerator.

To translate `WM_CHAR` messages, `WinGetMsg` and `WinPeekMsg` send a `WM_TRANSLATEACCEL` message to the window that is associated with the `WM_CHAR` message. A `WM_TRANSLATEACCEL` message includes a pointer to the `QMSG` structure of the `WM_CHAR` message. The window receiving a `WM_TRANSLATEACCEL` message must call the `WinTranslateAccel` API to access not only its own accelerator table but also the system accelerator table.

If a `WM_CHAR` message is not translated by `WinGetMsg` or `WinPeekMsg` sending a `WM_TRANSLATEACCEL` message, the `WM_CHAR` message will be used as the next available message on the system queue. However, if the `WM_CHAR` message is translated, the translated message must be a message that is acceptable to the message filter being used; otherwise, the message will be left on the system queue and the next acceptable message will be used.

The WM_TRANSLATEACCEL Message

A frame window typically will receive `WM_TRANSLATEACCEL` messages that are sent to a program. The frame window will call the `WinTranslateAccel`

API to perform any changes to the `WM_CHAR` message that may be called for by an accelerator table that may have been loaded by the frame.

If the `WM_CHAR` message remains unchanged by this `WinTranslate-Accel` call, the *action bar* will be given an opportunity to alter the `WM_CHAR` message. To give an action bar a `WM_CHAR` message to alter, a frame will send the action bar a `WM_TRANSLATEMNEMONIC` message, which includes a pointer to the `WM_CHAR` message. An action bar will alter the `WM_CHAR` message if the keystroke described matches a mnemonic that is present in the action bar. While action bars do not make use of accelerator tables, `WM_CHAR` messages are nonetheless treated in substantially the same manner that would result if a call were made to `WinTranslateAccel`.

If the `WM_CHAR` message still remains unchanged after a frame has sent a `WM_TRANSLATEMNEMONIC` message, `WinTranslateAccel` is used again to check the system accelerator table. To perform such a check, a `NULLHANDLE` value is used in the call that is placed to `WinTranslateAccel` (in place of a handle to an application accelerator table). This achieves the desired result, because the `WinTranslateAccel` API knows to interpret a `NULLHANDLE` value as an instruction to check the system accelerator table.

When a frame has completed the processing of a `WM_TRANSLATEACCEL` message, the frame provides a return code of `FALSE` or `TRUE` depending on whether any changes were made in the `WM_CHAR` message. If no changes were made, the return code is `FALSE`. If a return code of `TRUE` is provided, this indicates that the `WM_CHAR` message has been altered.

A `WM_TRANSLATEACCEL` message typically originates either from the `WinGetMsg` or the `WinPeekMsg` API's handling of a `WM_CHAR` message that has been found on the system queue. When a `WM_TRANSLATEACCEL` message is given a return code of `FALSE`, the `WinGetMsg` or `WinPeekMsg` API that sent the `WM_TRANSLATEACCEL` message will pass the `WM_CHAR` message on to the application as the next available message. If a return code of `TRUE` is given, the API that sent the message must check to determine whether the altered `WM_CHAR` message is still acceptable to the filter (if any) that the API is using.

The WM_TRANSLATEMNEMONIC Message

Between a frame's independent checks of its accelerator table and of the system accelerator table, the frame window sends a `WM_TRANSLATEMNEMONIC` message to its action bar (a window whose ID is `FID_MENU`) if one is present. A `WM_TRANSLATEMNEMONIC` message is in the same format that is used by a `WM_TRANSLATEACCEL` message and is, therefore, handled in the same manner.

Some tool kits may not have the `WM_TRANSLATEMNEMONIC` message defined in their header files. The following code will define `WM_TRANSLATEMNEMONIC` if the tool kit header files are missing the needed #define macro definition:

```
#ifndef WM_TRANSLATEMNEMONIC
#define WM_TRANSLATEMNEMONIC  0x0195
#endif
```

Most applications do not subclass a WM_TRANSLATEMNEMONIC message. Instead, if a frame needs to be subclassed to change the way accelerators are handled, the WM_TRANSLATEACCEL message normally is altered.

Subclassing the WM_TRANSLATEACCEL Message

To subclass the WM_TRANSLATEACCEL message it is important to have its WM_CHAR message altered if a return code of TRUE is to be used. This is because an infinite loop might occur if either WinGetMsg or WinPeekMsg receives an improper return code as the result of sending a WM_TRANSLATEACCEL message to a subclassing window procedure.

WinGetMsg and WinPeekMsg handle a return code of TRUE from a WM_TRANSLATEACCEL message by checking the message with the filter they are using (expecting the WM_CHAR message to be another type of message). If the WM_CHAR message remains unchanged, WinGetMsg and WinPeekMsg will send another WM_TRANSLATEACCEL message to translate the WM_CHAR message. The subclassing procedure that improperly used a TRUE return code will be called again. An infinite loop results if the subclassing procedure uses a return code of TRUE again without altering the WM_CHAR message.

A WM_CHAR message can be changed to a message that selects a menu item or to a WM_NULL message. Changing to a WM_NULL message entirely removes the WM_CHAR message and has substantially the same effect as if the WM_CHAR message was never generated.

The WM_NULL message should be set up with the following code (pmsg is the pointer to the WM_CHAR QMSG structure being changed):

```
pmsg->msg  = WM_NULL;
pmsg->hwnd = NULLHANDLE;
pmsg->mp1  = MPVOID;
pmsg->mp2  = MPVOID;
```

Changing a WM_CHAR message using this code prevents a keystroke from being processed. The WM_NULL value instructs PM to skip the original WM_CHAR entirely and to use the next available message on the system queue.

If a program subclasses a frame window and processes one or more WM_TRANSLATEACCEL messages, a WM_CHAR message should be handled only if it refers to a key being pressed. That is, when processing a WM_TRANSLATEACCEL message, a value of FALSE should be used as the return code if the KC_KEYUP flag is present in the first parameter of the WM_CHAR message. The WinTranslateAccel handles keystrokes when a button is pressed, not when it is released. If a program does not use WinTranslateAccel, the KC_KEYUP flag should be checked.

CHAPTER 12
Slider Controls

A *slider* control is one of the new Common User Access (CUA) controls that have been introduced in OS/2 Version 2.0. A slider is typically used to prompt the user to choose a value for a given variable from within a predefined range. The slider provides a visual indication of where the variable is set within the range of available values.

In this chapter an example program called MOUSEPTR is presented, which uses a slider control to adjust the tracking speed of the mouse pointer. In releases of OS/2 that predate Version 2.0, a scroll bar is used instead of a slider. Scroll bars are relatively simple controls that are useful to assist with such simple tasks as scrolling the contents of a window. However, scroll bars lack many of the more sophisticated features that are provided by a slider control.

A very simple form of slider, known as a *progress indicator,* provides the capability to display the current status of a changing value graphically (without allowing the displayed value to be changed by the user). A progress indicator is demonstrated in an example program called PROGRESS, presented later in this chapter.

COMPONENTS OF A SLIDER CONTROL

A slider is constructed using several components that can each be sized, positioned, and drawn in a selected style. One component, common to all slider controls, is referred to as the *slider shaft:* a bar of uniform width that defines a length that is used by the slider control to define a set of discrete positions (incremental values). A *slider arm* is movable along the shaft and serves the function of setting (selecting) a value within the range of available values that is represented by the length of the shaft. Components known as *tick marks*

170

are equally spaced along the length of the shaft to designate discrete values that the slider arm can be used to select. A *detent* is a special mark that can be placed at any desired position along the shaft (even at locations between tick marks); clicked on, it instantly sets the position of the slider arm. Labels for tick marks, referred to as *scale text* or *tick text,* may be positioned adjacent to the tick marks at desired locations along the shaft. Still another component is a set of two *slider buttons* for moving the slider arm selectively in either direction between adjacent tick marks. These various slider components can be used as needed, hidden, or omitted, and they can be constructed in a variety of ways to provide flexibility.

In Figure 12.1 the MOUSEPTR program is shown with a typical slider control displayed. The slider arm is shown occupying a midpoint position along the length of the shaft. A detent (an arrow-like symbol) also occupies a midshaft position to indicate the setting of a default value. Scale text is provided near end and center positions of the shaft. A pair of buttons, for moving the slider arm among the marked positions, is located near the right end of the slider shaft. To change the position of the slider arm, the user can push either of the buttons to move the slider arm in a corresponding direction from tick mark to tick mark. Alternatively, the user can use the mouse or arrow keys of the keyboard to set the position of the slider arm.

The scale text shown in Figure 12.1 indicates how changing the position of the slider arm along the shaft changes the tracking speed of the mouse pointer. Setting the arm at a "Slow" position instructs the mouse pointer to move correspondingly slowly across the screen. Setting the arm at a "Fast"

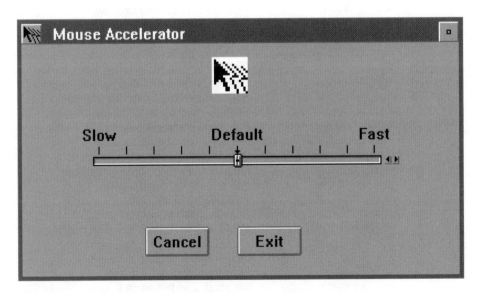

FIGURE 12.1   The MOUSEPTR program with its slider control.

position sets the mouse pointer to move correspondingly faster. A detent is labeled to confirm that it designates a default value that the slider arm will select unless instructed to do otherwise.

SLIDER CONTROL STYLES

A set of slider *style flags* are provided to permit default characteristics of a slider to be set. Slider characteristics that can be selected and changed by setting slider style flags are listed in Table 12.1.

Slider style flags can be used to specify such characteristics as the positions and orientations of slider components. If needed slider style flags are not set, PM uses a set of default values to determine the position, orientation, and character of components of a slider.

Because many of the components of a slider are optional (they can be hidden or omitted), the appearance of the resulting slider and the character of the function that it is capable of performing can be significantly changed. For example, if the slider arm and slider buttons are eliminated, the function and appearance of the slider that results is that of an "indicator," not a "control." Later in this Chapter a program called "PROGRESS" is discussed that sets up an "indicator" type of slider. A program called "MOUSEPTR" will be discussed shortly (before PROGRESS is discussed) because it sets up a more typical, more capable type of slider control than is set up by the PROGRESS program.

TABLE 12.1   The slider style flags

SLS_HORIZONTAL	Position the slider horizontally
SLS_VERTICAL	Position the slider vertically
SLS_CENTER	Center the shaft in window
SLS_BOTTOM	Position a horizontal shaft towards the bottom
SLS_TOP	Position a horizontal shaft towards the top
SLS_LEFT	Position a vertical shaft towards the left
SLS_RIGHT	Position a vertical shaft towards the right
SLS_SNAPTOINCREMENT	Set increment positions for slider arm
SLS_BUTTONSBOTTOM	Place buttons below the shaft
SLS_BUTTONSTOP	Place buttons above the shaft
SLS_BUTTONSLEFT	Place buttons to the left of the shaft
SLS_BUTTONSRIGHT	Place buttons to the right of the shaft
SLS_OWNERDRAW	Some fields are owner-drawn
SLS_READONLY	Provide a read-only slider
SLS_RIBBONSTRIP	Provide a ribbon strip
SLS_HOMEBOTTOM	Set the home position to be the bottom
SLS_HOMETOP	Set the home position to be the top
SLS_HOMELEFT	Set the home position to the left
SLS_HOMERIGHT	Set the home position to the right
SLS_PRIMARYSCALE1	Set scale 1 as the primary scale
SLS_PRIMARYSCALE2	Set scale 2 as the primary scale

TABLE 12.2   Slider control
window messages

```
SLM_ADDDETENT
SLM_QUERYDETENTPOS
SLM_QUERYSCALETEXT
SLM_QUERYSLIDERINFO
SLM_QUERYTICKPOS
SLM_QUERYTICKSIZE
SLM_REMOVEDETENT
SLM_SETSCALETEXT
SLM_SETSLIDERINFO
SLM_SETTICKSIZE
```

SLIDER CONTROL WINDOW MESSAGES

Before turning to discussions of the MOUSEPTR and PROGRESS programs, the subject of messages, as this subject applies to sliders, needs to be treated, at least briefly.

Table 12.2 lists the set of slider messages applications can use to communicate with a slider to do such things as query and set characteristics of the slider. Table 12.3 lists the set of messages that a slider can send to its owner window to update it regarding changes in the status of the slider.

THE MOUSEPTR PROGRAM

The MOUSEPTR program, whose source code is presented in this section, sets up a slider control that provides a user control for adjusting mouse tracking speed. The mouse tracking speed is increased or decreased as the slider arm is moved to the left or right along its shaft. Each time the slider arm is moved, the MOUSEPTR program communicates directly with the PM mouse device driver to implement a new tracking speed.

Two buttons are provided beneath the slider for selectively saving or canceling new tracking speed settings that are made by using the MOUSEPTR program. To implement (save) a changed speed setting and exit the MOUSEPTR program, the user clicks on the button labeled "Exit." To undo (cancel with-

TABLE 12.3   Slider control
notification messages

```
SLN_CHANGE
SLN_SLIDERTRACK
SLN_SETFOCUS
SLN_KILLFOCUS
```

out implementing) any changes made in mouse tracking speed and exit the
program, the user clicks on the button labeled "Cancel."

The MOUSEPTR program's source code is made up of the following
seven files:

MOUSEPTR.C

```
#define INCL_WIN
#define INCL_WINSTDSLIDER
#define INCL_DOS
#define INCL_DOSPROCESS
#include <os2.h>
#include "mouseptr.h"


/* function prototypes */
MRESULT EXPENTRY MyDlgProc( HWND, ULONG, MPARAM, MPARAM );
VOID SetAcceleration( USHORT );


/* Acceleration Table
 *     The slider arm position is used as an index into this table.
 *     The table contains the level 1 and level 2 multipliers.
 */
                       /* M1 M2 */
ATABLE aTable[] = {     1,  1,
                        1,  1,
                        1,  2,
                        1,  3,
                        2,  3,
                        2,  4,
                        3,  5,
                        4,  6,
                        5,  7,
                        6,  8,
                        7, 10,
                   };


INT main( VOID )
{
    HAB    hab;
    HMQ    hmq;
    QMSG   qmsg;
    HWND   hwndDlg;
    SWP    swp;

    hab = WinInitialize( 0 );

    hmq = WinCreateMsgQueue( hab, 0 );

    hwndDlg = WinLoadDlg( HWND_DESKTOP,   /* set the desktop as parent   */
                          NULLHANDLE,     /* no owner                    */
```

```
                              MyDlgProc,        /* address of dialog procedure */
                              NULLHANDLE,       /* use .EXE fill for resources */
                              ID_MYDIALOG,      /* ID of the dialog box resource */
                              NULL );           /* no control data */

    /* find where system would place dialog box */
    WinQueryTaskSizePos( hab, 0, &swp );

    /* place dialog box at position given by the shell */
    WinSetWindowPos( hwndDlg,          /* change the dialog window's position */
                     NULLHANDLE,       /* ignored, SWP_ZORDER not set */
                     swp.x, swp.y,     /* position of lower left corner */
                     0, 0,             /* ignored SWP_SIZE not set */
                     SWP_SHOW          /* show dialog box */
                     | SWP_MOVE );     /* do not ignore swp.x and swp.y */

    if (hwndDlg)
        while (WinGetMsg( hab, &qmsg, NULLHANDLE, 0, 0 ))
            WinDispatchMsg( hab, &qmsg );

    WinDestroyMsgQueue( hmq );
    WinTerminate( hab );

    return 0;
} /* End of main */


MRESULT EXPENTRY MyDlgProc( HWND hwndDlg, ULONG msg, MPARAM mp1, MPARAM mp2 )
{
    CHAR szBuffer[50];
    USHORT usArmPos;

    switch (msg) {

        case WM_INITDLG:

            WinPostMsg( hwndDlg,
                        WM_SETICON,
                        (MPARAM)WinLoadPointer( HWND_DESKTOP,
                                                NULLHANDLE,
                                                IDI_MYICON ),
                        NULL);

            /* Set the slider arm to the center position (5) */
            WinSendDlgItemMsg ( hwndDlg,
                                ID_SLIDER,
                                SLM_SETSLIDERINFO,
                                MPFROM2SHORT( SMA_SLIDERARMPOSITION,
                                              SMA_INCREMENTVALUE ),
                                (MPARAM)CENTER_TICK );

            /* Set all of the tick marks 7 pixels high */
            WinSendDlgItemMsg ( hwndDlg,
                                ID_SLIDER,
                                SLM_SETTICKSIZE,
```

```
                              MPFROM2SHORT( SMA_SETALLTICKS, 7 ),
                              (MPARAM)NULL );

        /* Pad this ticks text or else it will get clipped */
        WinSendDlgItemMsg( hwndDlg,
                           ID_SLIDER,
                           SLM_SETSCALETEXT,
                           MPFROMSHORT( 0 ),
                           MPFROMP( "Slow" ) );

        WinSendDlgItemMsg( hwndDlg,
                           ID_SLIDER,
                           SLM_SETSCALETEXT,
                           MPFROMSHORT( CENTER_TICK ),
                           MPFROMP( "Default" ) );

        WinSendDlgItemMsg( hwndDlg,
                           ID_SLIDER,
                           SLM_SETSCALETEXT,
                           MPFROMSHORT( 10 ),
                           MPFROMP( "Fast" ) );

        /* Get the number of pixels to the center of the shaft */
        usArmPos = (USHORT)WinSendDlgItemMsg(
                           hwndDlg,
                           ID_SLIDER,
                           SLM_QUERYSLIDERINFO,
                           MPFROM2SHORT( SMA_SLIDERARMPOSITION, SMA_RANGEVALUE ),
                           NULL );

        /* Place a detent in the exact center of the shaft */
        WinSendDlgItemMsg( hwndDlg,
                           ID_SLIDER,
                           SLM_ADDDETENT,
                           MPFROMSHORT( usArmPos ),
                           NULL );

    break;

case WM_CONTROL:

    if (SHORT1FROMMP( mp1 ) == ID_SLIDER) {

        if (SHORT2FROMMP( mp1 ) == SLN_CHANGE)
            SetAcceleration( (USHORT)WinSendDlgItemMsg(
                           hwndDlg,
                           ID_SLIDER,
                           SLM_QUERYSLIDERINFO,
                           MPFROM2SHORT( SMA_SLIDERARMPOSITION,
                                         SMA_INCREMENTVALUE ),
                           (MPARAM)NULL ));
        break;
    } else
        return WinDefDlgProc( hwndDlg, msg, mp1, mp2 );
```

```
      case WM_COMMAND:
         switch (LOUSHORT( mp1 ) ) {

            case ID_CANCEL:
               SetAcceleration( CENTER_TICK );
               WinPostMsg( hwndDlg, WM_QUIT, 0, 0 );
               return FALSE;

            case ID_EXIT:
               WinPostMsg( hwndDlg, WM_QUIT, 0, 0 );
               return FALSE;

         } break;

      case WM_CLOSE:
         WinPostMsg( hwndDlg, WM_QUIT, 0, 0 );
         return FALSE;

      default:
         return WinDefDlgProc( hwndDlg, msg, mp1, mp2 );

   }

   return (MRESULT)FALSE;
} /* end of MyDlgProc */


VOID SetAcceleration( USHORT usIndex )
{
   HFILE hMouse;
   ULONG ulAction, ulParmInOut = 0, ulDataInOut = 0;
   THRESHOLD th;

   DosOpen( (PSZ)"MOUSE$",
            (PHFILE)&hMouse,
            (PULONG)&ulAction,
            (ULONG)0L,
            (ULONG)FILE_READONLY,
            (ULONG)FILE_OPEN,
            (ULONG)OPEN_SHARE_DENYNONE,
            (PVOID)NULL );

   th.Length = 10;
   th.Level1 = 5;
   th.Level2 = 10;

   th.Mult1 = aTable[usIndex].m1;
   th.Mult2 = aTable[usIndex].m2;

   /*  This IOCTL will set the new threshold values */

   DosDevIOCtl( (HFILE)hMouse,
                (ULONG)0x0007,
                (ULONG)0x0055,
                (PVOID)&th,
```

```
                    (ULONG)sizeof(THRESHOLD),
                    (PULONG)&ulParmInOut,
                    (PVOID)NULL,
                    (ULONG)0L,
                    (PULONG)&ulDataInOut ) ;

   DosClose( hMouse ) ;
} /* end of SetAcceleration */
```

MOUSEPTR.H

```
#define ID_MYDIALOG     200
#define IDI_MYICON      201
#define ID_SLIDER       202
#define ID_CANCEL       203
#define ID_EXIT         204
#define CENTER_TICK       5

/* The following structure is used for the Set/Get Threshold IOCTL call */

typedef struct _TH {
   USHORT Length;                /* Length of packet in bytes (10) */
   USHORT Level1;               /* Level 1 movement value */
   USHORT Mult1;                /* Level 1 multiplier value */
   USHORT Level2;               /* Level 2 movement value */
   USHORT Mult2;                /* Level 2 multiplier value */
} THRESHOLD;

typedef struct _ATABLE {
   USHORT m1;                   /* Level 1 multiplier value */
   USHORT m2;                   /* Level 2 multiplier value */
} ATABLE;
```

MOUSEPTR.RC

```
#include <os2.h>
#include "mouseptr.h"

ICON IDI_MYICON mouseptr.ico

rcinclude mouseptr.dlg
```

MOUSEPTR.DLG

```
DLGINCLUDE 1 "MOUSEPTR.H"

DLGTEMPLATE ID_MYDIALOG LOADONCALL MOVEABLE DISCARDABLE
BEGIN
   DIALOG  "Mouse Accelerator", ID_MYDIALOG, -43, -28, 264, 102, 0,
           FCF_SYSMENU | FCF_TITLEBAR | FCF_MINBUTTON | FCF_TASKLIST
```

```
    BEGIN
        CONTROL        "", ID_SLIDER, 32, 24, 208, 53, WC_SLIDER,
                       SLS_HORIZONTAL | SLS_CENTER | SLS_SNAPTOINCREMENT |
                       SLS_BUTTONSTOP | SLS_HOMELEFT | SLS_PRIMARYSCALE1 |
                       WS_GROUP | WS_TABSTOP | WS_VISIBLE
                       CTLDATA 12, 0, 11, 25, 0, 0
        PUSHBUTTON     "Cancel", ID_CANCEL, 74, 8, 40, 14
        PUSHBUTTON     "Exit", ID_EXIT, 129, 8, 40, 14
        ICON IDI_MYICON, IDI_MYICON, 115, 80, 21, 16, WS_GROUP
    END
END
```

MOUSEPTR.DEF

```
NAME MOUSEPTR WINDOWAPI

DESCRIPTION 'Slider Control Example Program'

CODE    MOVEABLE
DATA    MOVEABLE MULTIPLE

HEAPSIZE  10240
STACKSIZE 24576
```

MOUSEPTR.MAK

```
all : mouseptr.exe

mouseptr.exe : mouseptr.obj  mouseptr.def mouseptr.res
        link386 /PM:PM mouseptr,,,,mouseptr.def;
        rc mouseptr.res

mouseptr.res: mouseptr.rc mouseptr.ico mouseptr.h mouseptr.dlg
        rc -r mouseptr.rc

mouseptr.obj:mouseptr.c mouseptr.h
        icc /C /Ss /W3 .$*.c
```

MOUSEPTR.ICO

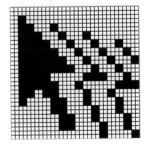
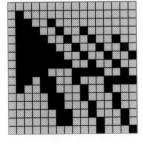
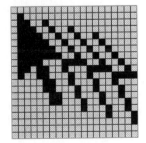

VGA Independent   16 x 16   20 x 20

MOUSEPTR.ICO file, containing various icons of different sizes.

Using Dialog Boxes with Sliders

The MOUSEPTR program uses a dialog box as its main window. The layout of the dialog box can be handled by a utility known as DLGEDIT, which is provided as a component of the OS/2 tool kit that is available from IBM.

Using DLGEDIT, a slider control can easily be added to a dialog window. When you first add a slider control to a dialog window by using DLGEDIT, you will be prompted for the number of increments in scale 1 (the primary scale) and scale 2 (the secondary scale). DLGEDIT will use these values to set values that are contained in a SLDCDATA structure, which is used as control data to create a slider window and formatted as follows:

```
typedef struct _SLDCDATA {
    ULONG   cbSize;                /* size in bytes of control block     */
    USHORT  usScale1Increments;    /* number of divisions to be used     */
    USHORT  usScale1Spacing;       /* space in pixels between increments  */
    USHORT  usScale2Increments;    /* number of divisions on scale        */
    USHORT  usScale2Spacing;       /* space in pixels between increments  */
} SLDCDATA;
```

Values that describe increments in the primary and secondary scales are stored in the fields named usScale1Increments and usScale2-Increments of the SLDCDATA data structure. The usScale1Spacing and usScale2Spacing fields of the SLDCDATA structure will be initialized to zero by DLGEDIT. A zero value in these fields tells the slider control to calculate the spacing between the slider increments.

A slider created by the DLGEDIT utility will use the following default slider style flags: SLS_HORIZONTAL, SLS_CENTER, SLS_SNAPTOINCREMENT, SLS_HOMELEFT, and SLS_PRIMARYSCALE1. However, these flags can be changed by changing the properties that are specified in a dialog box that is made to appear by double clicking on the slider window that is displayed by DLGEDIT.

The DLGEDIT utility does not set up a slider that has buttons. This is in contrast to the MOUSEPTR program, which sets up a pair of slider buttons positioned to the right of the shaft. In the MOUSEPTR program, the right-located set of buttons was added to the slider by simply including the slider style flag SLS_BUTTONSRIGHT.

The DLGEDIT utility stores descriptions of MOUSEPTR's main window and of the controls that are to appear in the main window. The MOUSEPTR.DLG file, which is set out with the rest of the source code, is used for this purpose. To inform the RC compiler to access the MOUSEPTR window template, the following line of code needs to be added to the file MOUSEPTR.RC:

```
rcinclude mouseptr.dlg
```

INITIALIZING THE SLIDER

The MOUSEPTR program uses the `WinLoadDlg` API to load its main window. The main window of the MOUSEPTR program is a dialog box that contains the slider control. One of the parameters to the `WinLoadDlg` API is the address (`MyDlgProc`) of the dialog window procedure. This procedure will receive a `WM_INITDLG` message after the dialog box has been created but before it becomes visible.

Adding Tick Marks, Detents, and Text

The MOUSEPTR program processes a `WM_INITDLG` message by carrying out the following steps:

- Initializing the position of the slider arm so that the slider arm will initially reside at the center of the shaft
- Adding tick marks to represent incremental slider arm positions that are to be selectable
- Adding a detent for the default position, midway along the length of the slider shaft, which will replace the tick mark that otherwise would appear at the midlength position
- Adding scale text to label opposite end regions of the slider shaft and the default

In the MOUSEPTR program there are eleven possible positions (representing eleven selectable values) for the slider arm. The positions range from position 0 (far left) to position 10 (far right). The default position for the slider arm is directly in the center of the slider shaft at increment value 5. The MOUSEPTR program initializes the slider arm to occupy the default position by using the `SLM_SETSLIDERINFO` message, which is illustrated in the following code:

```
/* Set the slider arm to the center position (5) */
WinSendDlgItemMsg ( hwndDlg,
                    ID_SLIDER,
                    SLM_SETSLIDERINFO,
                    MPFROM2SHORT( SMA_SLIDERARMPOSITION,
                                  SMA_INCREMENTVALUE ),
                    (MPARAM)CENTER_TICK );
```

Tick marks are initialized by the slider control to have a size of zero, which means that the tick marks are set to be invisible. To make the tick marks visible, a `SLM_SETTICKSIZE` message must be sent to change the size of the tick marks to a value greater than zero. The message is formatted to place the tick position number in the high portion of the first message parameter (`mp1`) and the tick size, measured in pixels, in the low portion of `mp1`.

The MOUSEPTR example sets the size of all of its tick marks by sending a single `SLM_SETTICKSIZE` message to the slider control accompanied by a special attribute, called `SMA_SETALLTICKS`, which is set instead of a tick position number in the high portion of mp1. All 11 tick marks are set to a size of seven pixels high by using the following code excerpt:

```
WinSendDlgItemMsg( hwndDlg,
                   ID_SLIDER,
                   SLM_SETTICKSIZE,
                   MPFROM2SHORT ( SMA_SETALLTICKS, 7 ),
                   (MPARAM)NULL );
```

The MOUSEPTR program places text above the left, center, and right tick marks. The scale text items "Slow," "Default," and "Fast" are set by sending `SLM_SETSCALETEXT` messages to the slider window, using the following code:

```
WinSendDlgItemMsg( hwndDlg,
                   ID_SLIDER,
                   SLM_SETSCALETEXT,
                   MPFROMSHORT( 0 ),
                   MPFROMP( "Slow" ) );

WinSendDlgItemMsg( hwndDlg,
                   ID_SLIDER,
                   SLM_SETSCALETEXT,
                   MPFROMSHORT( CENTER_TICK ),
                   MPFROMP( "Default" ) );

WinSendDlgItemMsg( hwndDlg,
                   ID_SLIDER,
                   SLM_SETSCALETEXT,
                   MPFROMSHORT( 10 ),
                   MPFROMP( "Fast" ) );
```

A detent is added to the slider by sending a `SLM_ADDDETENT` message that includes the number of pixels from the home position to where the detent is to appear. The MOUSEPTR example places the detent in the center of the slider shaft. Since the slider arm already occupies the center position due to its being set at the location of the default, a `SLM_QUERYSLIDERINFO` message can be issued to retrieve the number of pixels from the home position to the center of the shaft. The code excerpt that queries the number of pixels from the home position to the center of the slider shaft is as follows:

```
/* Get the number of pixels to the center of the shaft */
usArmPos = (USHORT)WinSendDlgItemMsg(
            hwndDlg,
            ID_SLIDER,
```

```
SLM_QUERYSLIDERINFO,
MPFROM2SHORT( SMA_SLIDERARMPOSITION, SMA_RANGEVALUE ),
NULL );
```

The SMA_RANGEVALUE attribute is used in this code to get the slider arm position in pixels. Later the SLM_QUERYSLIDERINFO message is used again, but with the attributes SMA_RANGEVALUE and SMA_INCREMENTVALUE to query the tick mark position (incremental value) after the slider arm has been moved by the user.

It is important to note that when a slider is created using the DLGEDIT utility, the usScale1Spacing and usScale2Spacing fields of the SLDCDATA data structure are set to zero. This tells the slider control to figure out the number of pixels that are to be present between such incremental values as are to be designated by tick marks along the slider shaft. To control this number of pixels, the MOUSEPTR.DLG file can be changed to force the usScale1Spacing and usScale2Spacing values to designate a desired number of pixels that are to be present between tick marks.

The number of pixels from the home position to the center of the shaft can be used to set the position of the detent by sending the SLM_ADDDETENT message to the slider window. The following code excerpt accomplishes this objective:

```
/* Place a detent in the exact center of the shaft */
WinSendDlgItemMsg( hwndDlg,
                   ID_SLIDER,
                   SLM_ADDDETENT,
                   MPFROMSHORT( usArmPos ),
                   NULL );
```

HANDLING THE SLN_CHANGE MESSAGE

If the user changes the position of the slider arm, a WM_CONTROL message will be sent to MOUSEPTR's dialog window procedure (MyDlgProc). A WM_CONTROL message is processed by checking whether it was a SLN_CHANGE notification. If a SLN_CHANGE notification was received, this indicates that the slider arm has been moved.

To handle a SLN_CHANGE notification message, the MOUSEPTR program queries the slider arm's incremental position by sending a SLM_QUERYSLIDERINFO message to the slider. When the new position of the slider arm is obtained, the internal function SetAcceleration is called to use the slider arm's position as an index into an array of tracking speed values (aTable). The array stores associated values, with each increment describing a new tracking speed that is to be used with the mouse device driver.

Following is a code excerpt that handles WM_CONTROL messages in the MOUSEPTR program:

```
case WM_CONTROL:

    if ( SHORT1FROMMP( mp1 ) == ID_SLIDER ) {

        if (SHORT2FROMMP( mp1 ) == SLN_CHANGE)
            SetAcceleration( (USHORT)WinSendDlgItemMsg(
                             hwndDlg,
                             ID_SLIDER,
                             SLM_QUERYSLIDERINFO,
                             MPFROM2SHORT( SMA_SLIDERARMPOSITION,
                                           SMA_INCREMENTVALUE ),
                             (MPARAM)NULL ));
    break;
    } else
        return WinDefDlgProc( hwndDlg, msg, mp1, mp2 );
```

The SetAcceleration Function

In the foregoing code excerpt the `SetAcceleration` function is called to change mouse tracking speed, using a device I/O control API called `DosDevIOCtl`, which allows OS/2 applications to communicate directly with a device driver. A device driver will typically provide a set of services that are each identified by a unique function number. `DosDevIOCtl` services are very hardware-dependent and generally should be avoided by PM applications. Their use should be limited to applications that require specific features that are only made available by a particular device driver.

To use a `DosDevIOCtl` call to communicate with a device driver, an application must use the `DosOpen` API to obtain a handle to the device driver. The `DosOpen` API requires the name of the device driver in order to obtain a handle to it. The MOUSEPTR program uses the name MOUSE$ to identify the mouse device driver. When access to a device driver is no longer needed, an application should return the device handle using the `DosClose` API.

THE PROGRESS INDICATOR PROGRAM

An example program called PROGRESS, whose source code for which is presented in this section, sets up a slider for use as a progress indicator. This example program creates a slider by using the `WinCreateWindow` API. The PROGRESS program creates a vertical slider that is of a "read-only" character in that the user cannot change the value that it displays. The owner window draws the level of the indicator in a blue color instead of the default dark gray color. The read-only slider created by the PROGRESS program is shown in Figure 12.2.

The PROGRESS program's source code is listed in the following three files:

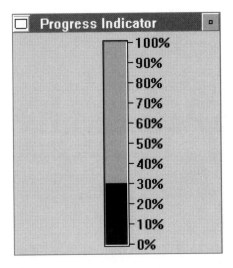

FIGURE 12.2 Slider created by the PROGRESS program.

PROGRESS.C

```
#define INCL_WIN
#include <os2.h>
#define ID_SLIDER 1
#define ID_TIMER  2


/* function prototypes */
INT main( VOID );
MRESULT EXPENTRY ClientWndProc( HWND, ULONG, MPARAM, MPARAM );


/* global variables */
HAB  hab;
HWND hwndSlider;


INT main( VOID )
{
   HMQ  hmq;
   HWND hwndFrame;
   HWND hwndClient;
   QMSG qmsg;
```

```
SLDCDATA sldcdata;
ULONG ulSliderStyle;
CHAR szTickText[5];
ULONG i;
HDC   hdc;
RECTL rcl ;
LONG  alScreen[2];
CHAR  szClientClass[] = "Client Window";
ULONG flCreateFlags = FCF_TITLEBAR        /* create: title bar control     */
                    | FCF_SYSMENU         /*            system menu control */
                    | FCF_MINBUTTON       /*            minimize button      */
                    | FCF_BORDER          /* draw borders                    */
                    | FCF_SHELLPOSITION   /* shell decides window position  */
                    | FCF_TASKLIST;       /* title added to switch list      */


hab = WinInitialize( 0 );

hmq = WinCreateMsgQueue( hab, 0 );

WinRegisterClass( hab,              /* anchor block handle */
                  szClientClass,    /* class name */
                  ClientWndProc,    /* pointer to window procedure */
                  CS_SIZEREDRAW,    /* class style */
                  0 );              /* number of class data bytes */

hwndFrame = WinCreateStdWindow(
                HWND_DESKTOP,     /* parent */
                0,                /* make window visible */
                &flCreateFlags,   /* creation flags for frame window */
                szClientClass,    /* client window class name */
                "Progress Indicator", /* title bar text */
                0,                /* use default client window style  */
                                  /*    WS_VISIBLE is not needed here */
                NULLHANDLE,       /* resource ID's are in rc file */
                0,                /* no ID for frame window */
                &hwndClient );    /* address to place client window handle */

WinSendMsg( hwndFrame,
            WM_SETICON,
            (MPARAM)WinQuerySysPointer( HWND_DESKTOP, SPTR_APPICON, FALSE ),
            NULL);

hdc = WinOpenWindowDC( hwndFrame );

DevQueryCaps( hdc,
              CAPS_WIDTH,
              2L,
              alScreen );

WinSetWindowPos( hwndFrame,
                 NULLHANDLE,                           /* Z-order */
                 0,                                    /* X coordinate */
                 0,                                    /* Y coordinate */
                 alScreen[0]/3,                        /* X size */
```

```
                alScreen[1]/2,                         /* Y size */
                SWP_SHOW | SWP_SIZE) ;

WinQueryWindowRect( hwndClient, &rcl ) ;

sldcdata.cbSize = sizeof(SLDCDATA);
sldcdata.usScale1Increments = 11;      /* # of divisions on scale */
sldcdata.usScale1Spacing = (rcl.yTop - rcl.yBottom - 20)/10;

ulSliderStyle = WS_VISIBLE       |
                SLS_RIBBONSTRIP  |     /* Fill with different color */
                SLS_VERTICAL     |     /* Shaft will be vertical */
                SLS_HOMEBOTTOM   |     /* Start on bottom */
                SLS_OWNERDRAW    |     /* We will draw the ribbon */
                SLS_READONLY;          /* Visual purposes only */

hwndSlider = WinCreateWindow(
                hwndClient,            /* parent window handle */
                WC_SLIDER,             /* Window class */
                (PSZ)NULL,             /* title text */
                ulSliderStyle,         /* style */
                0,                     /* X position */
                0,                     /* Y position */
                rcl.xRight,            /* X size */
                rcl.yTop,              /* Y size */
                hwndClient,            /* owner */
                HWND_TOP,              /* z-order */
                ID_SLIDER,             /* id */
                &sldcdata,             /* control data */
                NULL );                /* Presentation parms */

WinSendMsg ( hwndSlider,
             SLM_SETTICKSIZE,
             MPFROM2SHORT( SMA_SETALLTICKS, 5 ),
             (MPARAM) NULL );

for (i = 0; i <= 10; i++) {

    _itoa( i*10, szTickText, 10 );
    strcat( szTickText, "%" );

    WinSendMsg( hwndSlider,
                SLM_SETSCALETEXT,
                MPFROMSHORT( i ),
                MPFROMP( szTickText ) );
} /* endfor */

WinSendMsg( hwndSlider,
            SLM_SETSLIDERINFO,
            MPFROM2SHORT( SMA_SHAFTDIMENSIONS, 0 ),
            MPFROMLONG( rcl.xRight / 8 ) );

i = CLR_YELLOW;
WinSetPresParam( hwndSlider,
                 PP_BACKGROUNDCOLORINDEX,
```

```
                            (ULONG)sizeof(LONG),
                            (PVOID)&i);

   if ( hwndFrame )
      while (WinGetMsg( hab, &qmsg, NULLHANDLE, 0, 0 ))
         WinDispatchMsg( hab, &qmsg );

   WinDestroyWindow( hwndFrame ); /* clean up */
   WinDestroyMsgQueue( hmq );
   WinTerminate( hab );

   return 0;
} /* end main */


MRESULT EXPENTRY ClientWndProc( HWND hwnd, ULONG msg, MPARAM mp1, MPARAM mp2 )
{
   static USHORT usPercentDone = 0;

   switch( msg ) {

   case WM_CREATE:
      WinStartTimer( hab,
                     hwnd,
                     ID_TIMER,
                     1000 );             /* Time in millisecs */
      break;

   case WM_DRAWITEM:

      if (((POWNERITEM)mp2)->idItem == SDA_RIBBONSTRIP) {
         WinFillRect(  ((POWNERITEM)mp2)->hps,
                       &((POWNERITEM)mp2)->rclItem,
                       CLR_BLUE );
         return (MRESULT)TRUE;
      }
      else
         return (MRESULT)FALSE;

   case WM_TIMER:

      if(SHORT1FROMMP( mp1 ) == ID_TIMER) {

         if(++usPercentDone > 10) {
            usPercentDone = 0;
         }

         WinSendMsg ( hwndSlider,
                      SLM_SETSLIDERINFO,
                      MPFROM2SHORT(SMA_SLIDERARMPOSITION, SMA_INCREMENTVALUE),
                      MPFROMSHORT( usPercentDone ) );

         return (MRESULT)FALSE;
      }
      break;
```

```
    default:
        return WinDefWindowProc( hwnd, msg, mp1, mp2 );
    }

    return (MRESULT)FALSE;
} /* end of ClientWndProc */
```

PROGRESS.DEF

```
NAME PROGRESS WINDOWAPI

DESCRIPTION 'Slider Control Example Program'

CODE    MOVEABLE
DATA    MOVEABLE MULTIPLE

HEAPSIZE  10240
STACKSIZE 24576
```

PROGRESS.MAK

```
all : progress.exe

progress.exe : progress.obj  progress.def
        link386 /PM:PM progress,,,,progress.def;

progress.obj : progress.c
        icc /C /Ss /W3 .\$*.c
```

Using WinCreateWindow for Sliders

The PROGRESS program creates a slider using the `WinCreateWindow` API. However, before `WinCreateWindow` is called, the slider control data structure (`SLDCDATA`) must be initialized.

To create the slider control, the `usScale1Increments` field in a `SLDCDATA` structure must be initialized to describe the number of increments the slider will use. The PROGRESS program sets `usScale1Increments` to equal eleven possible positions labeled from 0 percent to 100 percent, in increments of 10 percent.

The PROGRESS example sets several style flags in order to define the characteristics of the resulting slider. The following slider style flags are set for the slider window of PROGRESS:

- `SLS_RIBBONSTRIP`   Instructs the slider control to fill the area between the home position and the current slider arm position, whereby an "indicator" is formed.
- `SLS_VERTICAL`   Orients the slider so that it will extend vertically rather than horizontally.
- `SLS_HOMEBOTTOM`   Sets the home position of the slider at the bottom of the slider's shaft. This is the default state for a vertical slider.

- SLS_OWNERDRAW   Instructs the slider control to notify the owner's window procedure by using a WM_DRAWITEM message when the slider shaft, the ribbon strip, the slider arm, and the background of the slider need to be updated.
- SLS_READONLY   Instructs the slider to be read-only so that the user cannot change the value represented by the slider. Slider buttons and detents are not supported by read-only sliders.

The following code excerpt illustrates how the PROGRESS program uses the WinCreateWindow API to create a slider window:

```
sldcdata.cbSize = sizeof(SLDCDATA);
sldcdata.usScale1Increments = 11;     /* # of divisions on scale */
sldcdata.usScale1Spacing = (rcl.yTop - rcl.yBottom - 20)/10;

ulSliderStyle = WS_VISIBLE          |
                SLS_RIBBONSTRIP |    /* Fill with different color */
                SLS_VERTICAL    |    /* Shaft will be vertical */
                SLS_HOMEBOTTOM  |    /* Start on bottom */
                SLS_OWNERDRAW   |    /* We will draw the ribbon */
                SLS_READONLY;        /* Visual purposes only */

hwndSlider = WinCreateWindow(
             hwndClient,                 /* parent window handle */
             WC_SLIDER,                  /* Window class */
             (PSZ)NULL,                  /* title text */
             ulSliderStyle,              /* style */
             0,                          /* X position */
             0,                          /* Y position */
             rcl.xRight,                 /* X size */
             rcl.yTop,                   /* Y size */
             hwndClient,                 /* owner */
             HWND_TOP,                   /* z-order */
             ID_SLIDER,                  /* id */
             &sldcdata,                  /* control data */
             NULL );                     /* Presentation parms */
```

The above WinCreateWindow call sets a slider window to be the child of a standard window's client window. The window class name is WC_SLIDER; the window ID is ID_SLIDER. The slider style flags and a pointer to the SLDCDATA structure are also provided. The slider window is set to occupy the client window fully.

Setting the Tick Mark Size

The WinCreateWindow API will return a window handle to the newly created slider window. Using this handle, the PROGRESS program will add tick marks and scale text. The following SLM_SETTICKSIZE message is used to set all of the tick marks to five pixels in width:

```
WinSendMsg ( hwndSlider,
              SLM_SETTICKSIZE,
              MPFROM2SHORT( SMA_SETALLTICKS, 5 ),
              (MPARAM) NULL );
```

Setting the Scale Text

The PROGRESS example will set scale text associated with each of the eleven tick marks by sending `SLM_SETSCALETEXT` messages to the slider window accompanied by a corresponding percentage label. The following code loops through the list of tick marks to set their labels:

```
for (i = 0; i <= 10; i++) {
    _itoa( i*10, szTickText, 10 );
    strcat( szTickText, "%" );

    WinSendMsg( hwndSlider,
                SLM_SETSCALETEXT,
                MPFROMSHORT( i ),
                MPFROMP( szTickText ) );
}
```

Widening the Slider Shaft

The width of a vertical slider (height of a horizontal slider) is referred to by the term *slider breadth*. By default, slider breadth is quite narrow. Moreover, a read-only slider has a slider shaft even thinner than normal. In the PROGRESS program, slider breadth (shaft width) is set by a `SLM_SETSLIDERINFO` message to one-eighth of the total client width.

The following code excerpt sets slider breadth:

```
WinSendMsg( hwndSlider,
            SLM_SETSLIDERINFO,
            MPFROM2SHORT( SMA_SHAFTDIMENSIONS, 0 ),
            MPFROMLONG( rcl.xRight / 8 ) );
```

Using the SLS_OWNERDRAW Style Flag

By default the slider "ribbon strip" color is a dark gray. A more interesting color for the ribbon strip is used in the PROGRESS program, namely blue. When set, the slider control style `SLS_OWNERDRAW` will cause the slider window to notify its owner whenever the slider's shaft, ribbon strip, arm, and background are to be drawn. The slider sends the `WM_DRAWITEM` message to notify the owner of such an event.

Handling WM_DRAWITEM Messages

Upon receiving the WM_DRAWITEM message, the client window procedure of the PROGRESS program will look for changes that should be reflected by the length of the ribbon strip. The first message parameter (mp1) of WM_DRAWITEM is set equal to the window ID of the slider that sent the WM_DRAWITEM message. The second message parameter (mp2) contains a pointer to an OWNERITEM data structure, defined in the PMWIN.H header file and formatted as follows:

```
typedef struct _OWNERITEM {
    HWND     hwnd;
    HPS      hps;
    ULONG    fsState;
    ULONG    fsAttribute;
    ULONG    fsStateOld;
    ULONG    fsAttributeOld;
    RECTL    rclItem;
    LONG     idItem;
    ULONG    hItem;
} OWNERITEM;
```

The identity of the item to be drawn is determined from the idItem field of the OWNERITEM data structure. If idItem has been set equal to the window identity of the ribbon strip (SDA_RIBBONSTRIP), the PROGRESS example will fill the rectangle provided by the rclItem field of the OWNERITEM data structure. The WinFillRect API uses the presentation space handle from the OWNERITEM structure to fill the ribbon strip. The CLR_BLUE color index value is used to fill the rectangle (the ribbon strip) using the color blue. The window procedure returns a value of TRUE after processing a WM_DRAWITEM message to notify the slider that the message has been handled by the owner.

If the WM_DRAWITEM message is not intended for the ribbon strip, the PROGRESS program will return a value of FALSE, informing the slider that it must draw the ribbon strip.

The following code excerpt handles the WM_DRAWITEM message for the PROGRESS program:

```
case WM_DRAWITEM:
    if (((POWNERITEM)mp2)->idItem == SDA_RIBBONSTRIP) {
        WinFillRect(   ((POWNERITEM)mp2)->hps,
                       &((POWNERITEM)mp2)->rclItem,
                       CLR_BLUE );
        return((MRESULT)TRUE);
    }
    else
        return((MRESULT)FALSE);
```

Changing the PROGRESS Indicator

During the processing of the WM_CREATE message, the PROGRESS program will start a one-second timer, which sends WM_TIMER messages with the passage of each second of time to notify the PROGRESS program when to increment the slider position. The indicator adds to its value by 10 percent upon receiving each new timer message until a total of 100 percent is reached. Once 100 percent is reached, the slider arm will be reset to indicate a value of zero. The SLM_SETSLIDERINFO is used once again to set the slider arm position. The SMA_INCREMENTVALUE attribute indicates that an incremental value for the new slider position is being used as a parameter.

Following is a code excerpt that uses the SLM_SETSLIDERINFO message to update the slider arm positions:

```
case WM_TIMER:

    if(SHORT1FROMMP( mp1 ) == ID_TIMER) {

        if(++usPercentDone > 10) {
            usPercentDone = 0;
        }

        WinSendMsg( hwndSlider,
                    SLM_SETSLIDERINFO,
                    MPFROM2SHORT( SMA_SLIDERARMPOSITION, SMA_INCREMENTVALUE ),
                    MPFROMSHORT( usPercentDone ) );

        return (MRESULT)FALSE;
    }
    break;
```

Working Around Text Clipping Problems

When a slider is created by a PM application, the application can specify the spacing, in pixels, between all of the incremental values along the slider shaft. The usScale1Spacing and usScale2Spacing fields of the SLDCDATA structure can be initialized with the pixel spacings between increments to be used to set the primary and secondary scales of the slider. Applications have the option to initialize the usScale1Spacing and usScale2Spacing values equal to zero, thereby instructing the slider control to calculate both the spacing between increments and the size of the slider shaft.

By default a slider will be provided that has a shaft length that is sized to fill the slider window. However, default sizing may cause problems when an application tries to add scale text to label tick marks at the beginning and end of the slider shaft. In processing the SLM_SETSCALETEXT message, the slider will try to center scale text adjacent to its corresponding tick mark. If the text extends beyond the bounds of the slider window, the slider control will clip it.

The example programs that are presented in this chapter avoid the problem of "scale text clipping" by sizing the slider shaft manually. Both of the example programs that are set out in this chapter initialize the `usScale1Spacing` field to a value, in pixels, that ensures that the slider shaft is kept well within the boundaries of the slider window. By using such a technique, a PM application can ensure that scale text will not be clipped.

CHAPTER 13
Value Set Controls

Many PM applications require a capability, which is provided by *value set controls*, to display a set of bitmaps, icons, colors, or text strings graphically in an array representing choices that are available to a user.

Value set controls are designed to help applications to set out items that may be selected from a value set window, clearly and graphically in an array of rows and columns. Items are identified by their row and column numbers in a window-displayed array. Because value set control windows handle the sizing and positioning of their value set items, an application that uses value set controls needs only to handle the messages that are generated when value set items are selected.

Workplace Shell uses value set controls in its palette windows for the selection of fonts and colors. A value set control can display a set of commonly chosen items in an easily accessible manner, similar to a tool bar. A value set control can give a PM application an orderly method of selecting items, easier to understand than the more conventional approach of using a cumbersome set of menus and submenus.

VALUE SET CONTROL STYLES

Value set style flags are used to define characteristics of a value set window and its value set items. Style flags are listed in Table 13.1.

Each individual value set item is associated with a *value item attribute*. The value item attribute informs a value set control whether a particular value set item contributes a bitmap, an icon, a text string, an RGB color, or a color index.

When a value set is created, all items within it are initialized to have an attribute that is associated with the style of the newly created value set window. However, once the window has been created, the attributes of any item within the window can be changed. The following attributes are available: VIA_BITMAP, VIA_ICON, VIA_TEXT, VIA_RGB, and VIA_COLORINDEX. The styles that are

195

TABLE 13.1 The value set
style flags

VS_BITMAP	0x0001
VS_ICON	0x0002
VS_TEXT	0x0004
VS_RGB	0x0008
VS_COLORINDEX	0x0010
VS_BORDER	0x0020
VS_ITEMBORDER	0x0040
VS_SCALEBITMAPS	0x0080
VS_RIGHTTOLEFT	0x0100
VS_OWNERDRAW	0x0200

associated with these attributes are VS_BITMAP, VS_ICON, VS_TEXT, VS_RGB, and VS_COLORINDEX, respectively. If no window style is specified, value set items are given a VIA_BITMAP attribute, which corresponds to a VS_BITMAP style.

VALUE SET CONTROL MESSAGES

Messages allow items of a value set window to be queried and changed, if needed. Table 13.2 lists value set control window messages, which can be used by applications to communicate with the value set control window procedure. Table 13.3 lists messages that a value set window can send to its owner window to update the owner window regarding changes in the status of the value set.

THE VSET EXAMPLE

An example program called VSET, whose source code is presented in this section, uses a value set control to display system bitmaps. When a bitmap is selected, the VSET title bar is updated with row and column information about

TABLE 13.2 Value set control
window messages

VM_QUERYITEM	0x0375
VM_QUERYITEMATTR	0x0376
VM_QUERYMETRICS	0x0377
VM_QUERYSELECTEDITEM	0x0378
VM_SELECTITEM	0x0379
VM_SETITEM	0x037a
VM_SETITEMATTR	0x037b
VM_SETMETRICS	0x037c

TABLE 13.3 Value set
control notification messages

VN_SELECT	120
VN_ENTER	121
VN_DRAGLEAVE	122
VN_DRAGOVER	123
VN_DROP	124
VN_DROPHELP	125
VN_INITDRAG	126
VN_SETFOCUS	127
VN_KILLFOCUS	128
VN_HELP	129

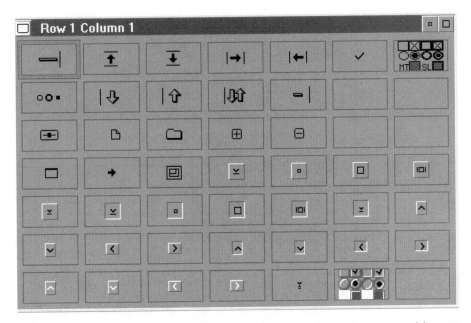

FIGURE 13.1   VSET window with value set control displaying system bitmaps.

the location of the selected bitmap. Figure 13.1 shows the value set window that is created by the VSET program.

The source code used to compile the VSET program is listed in the following three files:

VSET.C

```
#define INCL_WIN
#include <os2.h>
#define NUM_SYSBMAPS 48
```

```
/* function prototypes */
INT main( VOID );
MRESULT EXPENTRY MyFrameProc( HWND, ULONG, MPARAM, MPARAM );


/* global variables */
PFNWP OldFrameProc;
HWND hwndVSet;


INT main( VOID )
{
   HAB  hab;
   HMQ  hmq;
   HWND hwndFrame;
   QMSG qmsg;
   USHORT row = 1, col = 1;
   VSCDATA vscData;
   ULONG ulVSetStyle;
   ULONG i;
   FRAMECDATA fcd;

   fcd.cb = sizeof( FRAMECDATA );        /* length of structure        */
   fcd.flCreateFlags =   FCF_TITLEBAR    /* create: title bar control  */
                       | FCF_SYSMENU     /*         system menu control */
                       | FCF_SIZEBORDER  /*         sizeborders         */
                       | FCF_MINMAX      /*         min and max buttons */
                       | FCF_SHELLPOSITION /* shell decides window pos  */
                       | FCF_TASKLIST;   /* title added to switch list */
   fcd.hmodResources = NULLHANDLE;       /* Handle to a module         */
   fcd.idResources   = 0;                /* identifier for the frame   */

   hab = WinInitialize( 0 );
   hmq = WinCreateMsgQueue( hab, 0 );

   hwndFrame = WinCreateWindow(
            HWND_DESKTOP,      /* parent window is the desktop    */
            WC_FRAME,          /* class name                      */
            "System Bitmaps",  /* text added to title bar         */
            0,                 /* window style                    */
            0, 0, 0, 0,        /* ignored, FCF_SHELLPOSITION set  */
            NULLHANDLE,        /* no owner window                 */
            HWND_TOP,          /* on top of Desktop's children    */
            0,                 /* ID number for frame resources   */
            &fcd,              /* data unique for frame windows   */
            NULL );            /* no presentation parameters      */

   WinSendMsg ( hwndFrame,
            WM_SETICON,
            (MPARAM)WinQuerySysPointer( HWND_DESKTOP,
                                        SPTR_APPICON,
                                        FALSE),
            NULL);
```

```
      vscData.cbSize = sizeof(VSCDATA);
      vscData.usRowCount = 7;
      vscData.usColumnCount = 7;

   ulVSetStyle = VS_BITMAP | VS_ITEMBORDER;

   /* Now create the value set window. */
   hwndVSet = WinCreateWindow(
                  hwndFrame,      /* parent window handle     */
                  WC_VALUESET,    /* window class             */
                  NULL,           /* no window text           */
                  ulVSetStyle,    /* style                    */
                  0, 0, 0, 0,     /* ignored, frame will pos  */
                  hwndFrame,      /* owner                    */
                  HWND_BOTTOM,    /* Z-order                  */
                  FID_CLIENT,     /* ID                       */
                  &vscData,       /* control data             */
                  NULL );         /* no presentation parms    */

   for (i = 1; i <= NUM_SYSBMAPS; i++) {

      WinSendMsg( hwndVSet,
                  VM_SETITEM,
                  MPFROM2SHORT( row, col ),
                  MPFROMLONG( WinGetSysBitmap( HWND_DESKTOP, i ) ) );

      if(++col >= 8) {
          col = 1;
          ++row;
      }
   }

   OldFrameProc = WinSubclassWindow( hwndFrame, MyFrameProc );

   WinSetWindowText( hwndFrame, "Row 1 Column 1");

   WinShowWindow( hwndFrame, TRUE );

   if ( hwndFrame )
      while( WinGetMsg( hab, &qmsg, NULLHANDLE, 0, 0 ))
         WinDispatchMsg( hab, &qmsg );

   WinDestroyWindow( hwndFrame );
   WinDestroyMsgQueue( hmq );
   WinTerminate( hab );

} /* End of main */


MRESULT EXPENTRY MyFrameProc( HWND hwnd, ULONG msg, MPARAM mp1, MPARAM mp2 )
{

   switch( msg ) {

      case WM_CONTROL:
```

```
        if (SHORT2FROMMP( mp1 ) == VN_SELECT) {
            ULONG ulRowCol;
            CHAR szBuffer[20];

            ulRowCol = (ULONG)WinSendMsg( hwndVSet,
                                          VM_QUERYSELECTEDITEM,
                                          NULL,
                                          NULL );

            sprintf( szBuffer, "Row %d Column %d",
                     SHORT1FROMMP( ulRowCol ),
                     SHORT2FROMMP( ulRowCol ) );

            WinSetWindowText( hwnd, szBuffer);

            return (MRESULT)FALSE;
        }
    }

    return (MRESULT)(*OldFrameProc)( hwnd, msg, mp1, mp2 );
} /* end of MyFrameProc */
```

VSET.DEF

```
NAME VSET WINDOWAPI

DESCRIPTION 'Value Set Example Program'

CODE    MOVEABLE
DATA    MOVEABLE MULTIPLE

HEAPSIZE  10240
STACKSIZE 24576
```

VSET.MAK

```
all : vset.exe

vset.exe : vset.obj vset.def
        link386 /PM:PM vset,,,,vset.def;

vset.obj : vset.c
        icc /C /O+ /Ss /W3 ./$*.c
```

Using WinCreateWindow for Value Sets

The VSET program creates a value set using the WinCreateWindow API.
Before issuing the WinCreateWindow API, the value set control data structure

(VSCDATA) must be initialized. The VSCDATA data structure is defined in the PMSTDDLG.H public header file as follows:

```
typedef struct _VSCDATA {
    ULONG   cbSize;
    USHORT  usRowCount;
    USHORT  usColumnCount;
} VSCDATA;
```

The cbSize field of the VSCDATA data structure is set to the total size of a VSCDATA data structure, in bytes. In the VSET program, the usRowCount and the usColumnCount fields are both set to seven. The selection of a 7 × 7 matrix is acceptable because it provides 49 positions, more than adequate to accommodate the 44 system bitmaps that are made available by OS/2 Version 2.0. A 4 × 11 or 11 × 4 matrix could also have been selected, to more precisely accommodate the need for locations to store 44 system bitmaps. Regardless of what sort of matrix is selected, a value set control will make use of the entire window area to display the items of the value set. Any items not assigned a system bitmap will appear as rectangles with a standard background color (typically light gray).

The VSET program uses the following value set style flags for its value set window:

- VS_BITMAP   Instructs the value set control that all value set items will be bitmaps. The value set control will assume a value item attribute of VIA_BITMAP for all value set items unless otherwise instructed. VS_BITMAP is the default style for a value set window.
- VS_ITEMBORDER   Instructs the value set control to draw a border around each value set item.

The value set control used in the VSET program is created as a client to a frame window. The frame window is subclassed to handle messages from the value set control. Any other messages are sent to the original frame window procedure.

In the VSET program, a value set control is created by using a VSCDATA structure as control data in a call to the WinCreateWindow API. The VSET program takes advantage of the fact that its items will be given a VIA_BITMAP attribute, based on the VS_BITMAP style. To override the default attributes of a particular item, an application may use a VM_SETITEMATTR message to specify a new attribute for the item.

Setting Value Set Items

The WinCreateWindow API that creates the VSET value set returns a handle to the value set window. Using this handle, the VSET program will assign system bitmaps to the items in its value set window. A value set item is assigned a bitmap by changing its contents with a VM_SETITEM message that is sent to the value set window.

The following code excerpt from the VSET program sets up system bitmaps in its value set control:

```
for (i = 1; i <= NUM_SYSBMAPS; i++) {

    WinSendMsg( hwndVSet,
                VM_SETITEM,
                MPFROM2SHORT( row, col ),
                MPFROMLONG( WinGetSysBitmap( HWND_DESKTOP, i ) ) );

    if (++col >= 8) {
       col = 1;
       ++row;
    }
}
```

The VM_SETITEM message in this code uses a row value and a column value in the first message parameter to identify the item that is being changed. A handle to a system bitmap, obtained from WinGetSysBitmap, is used as the second parameter in the message.

Selecting Items

Messages from the value set control, indicating that an item has been selected, are sent in the format of a WM_CONTROL message. The VSET program processes WM_CONTROL messages and sets the title bar text to indicate which item has been selected. If any other types of messages are received, the VSET program sends such messages to the original frame procedure for processing.

WM_CONTROL messages contain a VN_SELECT notification code in the low word of the first message parameter (mp1). Once a VN_SELECT notification is received, the VSET program will query the row and column of a selected item by sending a VM_QUERYSELECTEDITEM message to the value set window. The return code is a long integer value whose upper and lower words indicate the row and column numbers, respectively. The VSET program will update the title bar text with the new row and column numbers by using the WinSetWindowText API.

CHAPTER 14
File Dialog Controls

Because the need to prompt a user to provide or select a file name is common to so many programs, PM provides a standard dialog box that allows a user either to select an existing file name or to specify a new file name. This standard dialog box that PM provides is referred to as the *file dialog control*.

Before OS/2 Version 2.0 introduced the file dialog control, each program needed to include code of its own to a create a file dialog box. The various forms of file dialog boxes that were provided by various programs differed principally in the positions and sizes of such components as buttons, list boxes, and entry fields. The file dialog control that is now provided by PM saves programmers the need to write hundreds of lines of code, and it provides a consistent "look and feel" among PM programs.

A file dialog box can be displayed for the purpose of opening a file (commonly used by "Open" menu items) or for the purpose of saving a file under a new name (commonly used by "Save as" menu items). A list of available subdirectories and files is displayed within the file dialog box, as well as an entry field for directly entering a file name. Standard file dialog controls that are provided by PM for opening and saving files are shown in Figures 14.1 and 14.2, respectively.

USING THE FILE DIALOG

PM applications display the file dialog by calling the `WinFileDlg` API. An application must specify the parent and owner window handles as parameters to this API. The last parameter to the `WinFileDlg` API is a pointer to a FILEDLG

203

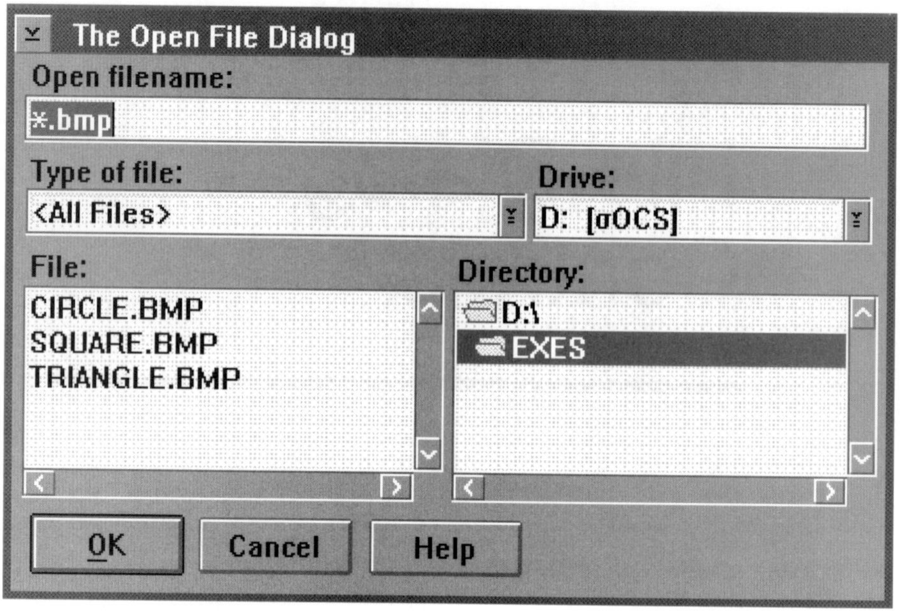

FIGURE 14.1 The "Open" file dialog.

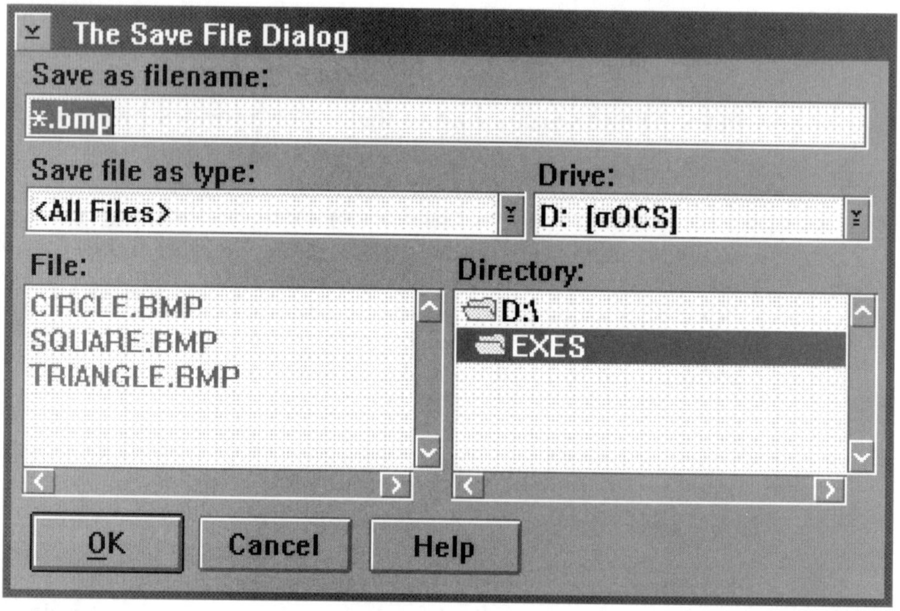

FIGURE 14.2 The "Save As" file dialog.

data structure, which is formatted as follows:

```
typedef struct _FILEDLG {
    ULONG    cbSize;
    ULONG    fl;
    ULONG    ulUser;
    LONG     lReturn;
    LONG     lSRC;
    PSZ      pszTitle;
    PSZ      pszOKButton;
    PFNWP    pfnDlgProc;
    PSZ      pszIType;
    PAPSZ    papszITypeList;
    PSZ      pszIDrive;
    PAPSZ    papszIDriveList;
    HMODULE  hMod;
    CHAR     szFullFile[CCHMAXPATH];
    PAPSZ    papszFQFilename;
    ULONG    ulFQFCount;
    USHORT   usDlgId;
    SHORT    x;
    SHORT    y;
    SHORT    sEAType;
} FILEDLG;
```

Many of the fields in a FILEDLG structure have default values and do not need to be initialized. A PM application needs to initialize only certain fields of the FILEDLG structure before calling the WinFileDlg API. An example program called BITVIEW, presented later in this chapter, shows the minimum code that is needed to initialize a FILEDLG data structure and to display a typical file dialog.

Like most dialog boxes, the file dialog can appear as a modal or modeless (nonmodal) dialog box. As a modal dialog box, a file dialog does not allow the other windows of its associated program to receive user input until the file dialog has been closed. If the file dialog is set up as a modeless dialog box, the message loop of its associated program directs user input to the file dialog or to other specified windows of the program.

The WinFileDlg API returns a value of TRUE if a modal file dialog has been successfully created. If an application requests the file dialog to be modeless, the return value from WinFileDlg will be the window handle of the newly created file dialog. In either case, a return value equal to NULLHANDLE will indicate that the file dialog was not successfully created.

Most applications will use the file dialog control as a modal dialog box, which causes the WinFileDlg API to create, handle, and close the file dialog. If a modeless file dialog is used, the WinFileDlg API merely creates and displays the file dialog. Most PM programs use a modal file dialog because a call to WinFileDlg handles the entire operation of the file dialog. Completion of the call to `WinFileDlg`, which modifies the `FILEDLG` structure, gives notice that the modal file dialogue has been closed.

An application using a modeless file dialog must handle an additional `WM_COMMAND` message that indicates that the file dialog was dismissed. Dismissing a modeless file dialog is not handled by the `WinFileDlg` API; therefore, the program must wait for a `WM_COMMAND` message that is accompanied by the value `CMDSRC_FILEDLG` to indicate that the file dialog was closed and that the `FILEDLG` structure has been updated.

When a `FILEDLG` structure is updated to reflect a current file selection, the `szFullFile` field of the `FILEDLG` structure will contain a path and file name of the current user-selected file. The `szFullFile` field can be used as input to the `DosOpen` API to obtain a file handle to read and write to the file.

The `lReturn` field of the `FILEDLG` data structure contains the window ID of a button that is pressed to close the file dialog. The window ID will equal either `DID_OK` (the window ID of the "OK" push button) or `DID_CANCEL` (the window ID of the "Cancel" push button).

An application can easily alter the appearance of a file dialog by using a substitute dialog template. The use of a substitute dialog template permits additional controls to be incorporated into a file dialog. If an application does not use the default file dialog, the `lReturn` field may be equal to the window ID of an added control rather than the window ID `DID_OK` or `DID_CANCEL`.

THE BITVIEW EXAMPLE

The BITVIEW program allows the user to select a bitmap file to be displayed in the client window area. BITVIEW uses a pull-down menu option called "Open" to display a file dialog that prompts the user to supply the name of a bitmap file. BITVIEW includes another pull-down option known as "Save As," which brings up a slightly different file dialog that uses the `FDS_SAVEAS_DIALOG` style. Since the sole purpose of the "Save As" option is to illustrate differences between the "Open" and "Save As" file dialogs, the BITVIEW program does not save the file.

The following six files are used to compile the BITVIEW program:

BITVIEW.C

```
#define INCL_WIN
#define INCL_GPI
#include <os2.h>
#include "bitview.h"


/* function prototypes */
INT main( VOID );
MRESULT EXPENTRY ClientWndProc( HWND, ULONG, MPARAM, MPARAM );
APIRET GetBMPFile( HWND, PHFILE );
APIRET ReadBitmap( HWND, HFILE );
```

```
VOID SaveFile( HWND );
VOID MessageBox ( HWND, PSZ );


/* global variables */
HAB hab;
HBITMAP hbm = 0;


INT main( VOID )
{
   HMQ    hmq;
   HWND   hwndFrame;
   HWND   hwndClient;
   CHAR   szClientClass[] = "Client Window";
   QMSG   qmsg;
   ULONG flCreateFlags = FCF_TITLEBAR       /* create: title bar control    */
                       | FCF_SYSMENU        /*          system menu control . */
                       | FCF_MENU           /*             action bar        */
                       | FCF_MINMAX         /*          min and max buttons   */
                       | FCF_SIZEBORDER     /* draw sizeborders              */
                       | FCF_SHELLPOSITION /* shell decides window position */
                       | FCF_TASKLIST       /* title added to switch list    */
                       | FCF_ICON;          /* frame has an icon             */

   hab = WinInitialize( 0 );
   hmq = WinCreateMsgQueue( hab, 0 );

   WinRegisterClass( hab,           /* anchor block handle */
                     szClientClass, /* class name */
                     ClientWndProc, /* pointer to window procedure */
                     CS_SIZEREDRAW, /* class style */
                     0 );           /* number of class data bytes */

   hwndFrame = WinCreateStdWindow(
                     HWND_DESKTOP,     /* Desktop window is parent     */
                     WS_VISIBLE,       /* window styles                */
                     &flCreateFlags,   /* frame control flag           */
                     szClientClass,    /* client window class name     */
                     "Bitmap Viewer",  /* title bar text               */
                     0,                /* no special class style       */
                     NULLHANDLE,       /* resource is in .EXE file      */
                     ID_FRAME_RES,     /* frame window identifier       */
                     &hwndClient       /* client window handle          */
                     );

   if (hwndFrame)
      while(WinGetMsg( hab, &qmsg, NULLHANDLE, 0, 0 ))
         WinDispatchMsg( hab, &qmsg );

   WinDestroyWindow( hwndFrame );
   WinDestroyMsgQueue( hmq );
   WinTerminate( hab );
```

```
      return 0;
} /* end of main */


MRESULT EXPENTRY ClientWndProc( HWND hwnd, ULONG msg, MPARAM mp1, MPARAM mp2 )
{
    static SHORT sClientX, sClientY;   /* client window X and Y dimensions */
    switch(msg) {

    case WM_COMMAND:

        switch (SHORT1FROMMP( mp1 )) {

        case IDM_OPEN:
          { HFILE FileHandle;
            APIRET rc;

            rc = GetBMPFile( hwnd, &FileHandle );
            if (rc == NO_ERROR) {
               rc = ReadBitMap( hwnd, FileHandle );
               if (rc == NO_ERROR)
                  WinInvalidateRect( hwnd, NULL, FALSE );
               else
                  MessageBox( hwnd, "Error reading bitmap." );
            }
          } break;

        case IDM_SAVE:
            SaveFile( hwnd );
            break;

        default:
            return WinDefWindowProc( hwnd, msg, mp1, mp2 );
        }
        break;

    case WM_ERASEBACKGROUND:
        return (MRESULT)TRUE;

    case WM_PAINT:
      { HPS     hps;
        RECTL   rcl;

        hps = WinBeginPaint( hwnd, NULLHANDLE, &rcl );
        rcl.yBottom = rcl.xLeft = 0;
        rcl.xRight = (LONG)sClientX;
        rcl.yTop = (LONG)sClientY;
        WinDrawBitmap( hps,
                       hbm,
                       NULL,
                       (PPOINTL)&rcl,
                       0L,                    /* Fgnd color */
                       0L,                    /* Bkgd color */
                       DBM_STRETCH );
```

```
         WinEndPaint( hps );
      } break;

   case WM_SIZE:
      sClientX = SHORT1FROMMP( mp2 );
      sClientY = SHORT2FROMMP( mp2 );
      break;
   case WM_HELP:
      MessageBox( hwnd, "Help has been requested!" );
      sClientY = SHORT2FROMMP( mp2 );
      break;

   default:
      return WinDefWindowProc( hwnd, msg, mp1, mp2 );
   }

   return (MRESULT)FALSE;
} /* end of ClientWndProc */


APIRET GetBMPFile( HWND hwndClient, PHFILE pFileHandle )
{
   FILEDLG FileDlg;
   HWND hwndDlg;
   HFILE FileHandle;
   ULONG ulAction;
   APIRET rc = 1;

   memset( &FileDlg, 0, sizeof(FILEDLG) );  /* Init all fields to zero */
   FileDlg.cbSize = sizeof(FILEDLG);
   FileDlg.fl = FDS_CENTER | FDS_HELPBUTTON | FDS_OPEN_DIALOG;
   FileDlg.pszTitle = "The Open File Dialog";
   strcpy( FileDlg.szFullFile, "*.bmp" );

   hwndDlg = WinFileDlg( HWND_DESKTOP, hwndClient, (PFILEDLG)&FileDlg );

   if (hwndDlg && (FileDlg.lReturn == DID_OK)) {

      rc = DosOpen(
           FileDlg.szFullFile,                    /* File name       */
           &FileHandle,                           /* Returned to us  */
           &ulAction,                             /* Action taken    */
           0,                                     /* File size (N/A) */
           FILE_NORMAL,                           /* File attributes */
           FILE_OPEN,
           OPEN_ACCESS_READONLY | OPEN_SHARE_DENYNONE,
           NULL );                                /* EA buffer (N/A) */
      if(rc == NO_ERROR)
         *pFileHandle = FileHandle;

   }

   return rc;
} /* end of GetBMPFile */
```

```
APIRET ReadBitmap( HWND hwndClient, HFILE FileHandle )
{
    FILESTATUS FileInfo;
    PBYTE  pFileBegin = NULL;          /* beginning of bitmap file data    */
    ULONG  cbRead;                     /* Number of bytes read by DosRead. */
    HPS hps;
    PBITMAPFILEHEADER2 pbfh2;          /* can address any file types       */
    PBITMAPINFOHEADER2 pbmp2;
    ERRORID err;
    CHAR szBuffer[50];
    APIRET      rc;                    /* API return code                  */

    rc = DosQueryFileInfo( FileHandle,
                           FIL_STANDARD,         /* File information level  */
                           &FileInfo,
                           sizeof(FileInfo) );
    if (rc)
        return(rc);

    rc = DosAllocMem( (PPVOID) &pFileBegin,
                      (ULONG)  FileInfo.cbFile,
                      (ULONG)  PAG_READ | PAG_WRITE | PAG_COMMIT );

    if (rc)
        return(rc);

    rc = DosRead( FileHandle,
                  (PVOID)pFileBegin,
                  FileInfo.cbFile,
                  &cbRead );

    if (rc)
        return(rc);

    if (*((PUSHORT)pFileBegin) == BFT_BITMAPARRAY)
        pbfh2 = (PBITMAPFILEHEADER2)
                   &((PBITMAPARRAYFILEHEADER2)pFileBegin)->bfh2;

    else
        pbfh2 = (PBITMAPFILEHEADER2)pFileBegin;

    pbmp2 = &pbfh2->bmp2;       /* pointer to info header (readability) */

    hps = WinGetPS( hwndClient );
    hbm = GpiCreateBitmap(
            hps,
            pbmp2,                             /* BITMAPINFOHEADER2    */
            CBM_INIT,                          /* options              */
            (PBYTE)pFileBegin + pbfh2->offBits,  /* addr of bitmap data  */
            (PBITMAPINFO2)pbmp2 );             /* clr and format info  */

    if (!hbm)
```

```
      {
         err = WinGetLastError( hab );
         sprintf( szBuffer, "GpiLoadBitmap failed with a rc of %ld", err );
         MessageBox( hwndClient, szBuffer );
      }

   WinReleasePS( hps );
   DosFreeMem( pFileBegin );
   DosClose( FileHandle );

   return NO_ERROR;
} /* end of ReadBitmap */


VOID SaveFile( HWND hwndClient )
{
   FILEDLG FileDlg;
   HWND hwndDlg;

   memset( &FileDlg, 0, sizeof(FILEDLG) );  /* Init all fields to zero */
   FileDlg.cbSize = sizeof(FILEDLG);
   FileDlg.fl = FDS_HELPBUTTON | FDS_SAVEAS_DIALOG | FDS_CENTER;
   FileDlg.pszTitle = "The Save File Dialog";
   strcpy( FileDlg.szFullFile, "*.bmp" );

   hwndDlg = WinFileDlg( HWND_DESKTOP, hwndClient, (PFILEDLG)&FileDlg );

   if (hwndDlg && (FileDlg.lReturn == DID_OK))
      MessageBox( hwndClient, "Code to save BMP file not implemented." );

} /* end of SaveFile */


VOID MessageBox( HWND hwndOwner, PSZ pszText )
{

   WinMessageBox ( HWND_DESKTOP,
                   hwndOwner,
                   pszText,
                   "Bitview Example",        /* Message box title */
                   0,                        /* Message box ID    */
                   MB_OK );
} /* end of MessageBox */
```

BITVIEW.H

```
#define ID_FRAME_RES    100

#define IDM_FILE        101
```

```
#define IDM_OPEN       102
#define IDM_SAVE       103

#define NO_ERROR         0
```

BITVIEW.RC

```
#include <os2.h>
#include "bitview.h"
ICON    ID_FRAME_RES bitview.ico

MENU    ID_FRAME_RES
{
    SUBMENU  "~File",  IDM_FILE, MIS_TEXT
    {
        MENUITEM "~Open...",   IDM_OPEN
        MENUITEM "~Save...",   IDM_SAVE
    }
}
```

BITVIEW.DEF

```
NAME BITVIEW WINDOWAPI

DESCRIPTION 'File Dialog Example Program'

CODE    MOVEABLE
DATA    MOVEABLE MULTIPLE

HEAPSIZE  10240
STACKSIZE 24576
```

BITVIEW.MAK

```
all : bitview.exe

bitview.exe : bitview.obj bitview.def bitview.res
        link386 /PM:PM bitview,,,,bitview.def;
        rc bitview.res

bitview.res : bitview.rc bitview.ico bitview.h
        rc -r bitview.rc

bitview.obj : bitview.c bitview.h
        icc /C /O+ /Ss /W3 .\$*.c
```

BITVIEW.ICO

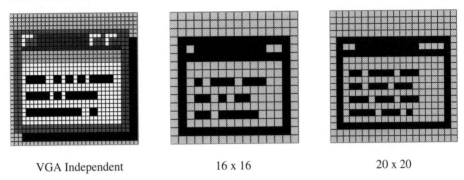

VGA Independent   16 x 16   20 x 20

BITVIEW.ICO file, containing various icons of different sizes.

Setting Up the FILEDLG Structure

Before issuing the `WinFileDlg` API, a PM application must initialize the `FILEDLG` data structure. The following is a code excerpt taken from the BITVIEW program for initializing a `FILEDLG` data structure:

```
memset( &FileDlg, 0, sizeof(FILEDLG) );   /* Init all fields to zero */
FileDlg.cbSize = sizeof(FILEDLG);
FileDlg.fl = FDS_CENTER | FDS_HELPBUTTON | FDS_OPEN_DIALOG;
FileDlg.pszTitle = "The Open File Dialog";
strcpy( FileDlg.szFullFile, "*.bmp" );
```

All fields of the `FILEDLG` data structure are initialized to zero using the `memset` function that is found in the standard C runtime library. The `cbSize` field is set to the total size of the `FILEDLG` data structure, in bytes. The `fl` field of the `FILEDLG` data structure is expected to contain a list of style flags, each of which is prefixed by `FDS_`. These style flags are used to set certain characteristics of the file dialog that is being created. The following are the style flags used by the BITVIEW program, together with their respective definitions:

- `FDS_CENTER` Causes the dialog window to be positioned in the center of its parent window.
- `FDS_HELPBUTTON` Causes a "Help" button to be added to the bottom of the file dialog window. When this push button is pressed, a `WM_HELP` message will be sent to the owner window.
- `FDS_OPEN_DIALOG` Specifies an "Open" file dialog.
- `FDS_SAVEAS_DIALOG` Specifies a "Save As" file dialog.

The BITVIEW program sets up the `pszTitle` field of the `FILEDLG` data structure to set text that is to be displayed in the title bar of the file dialog. If the `pszTitle` field is set to a `NULL` string, the title bar text will default to

"Open" for dialogs of type `FDS_OPEN_DIALOG` or to "Save as" for dialogs of type `FDS_SAVEAS_DIALOG`.

The `szFullFile` field of the `FILEDLG` data structure can be used to filter a listing of files that will appear in the "Files" list box. Since the BITVIEW program is interested only in bitmap files, the string `*.BMP` is used in the `szFullFile` field to filter out file names that do not end with a `.BMP` file extension.

Using WinFileDlg

Once the `FILEDLG` data structure has been initialized, BITVIEW will issue the `WinFileDlg` API to bring up the file dialog. The following code excerpt is used to call `WinFileDlg`:

```
hwndDlg = WinFileDlg( HWND_DESKTOP, hwndClient, (PFILEDLG)&FileDlg );
```

In this code, `HWND_DESKTOP` (the handle for the desktop window) is used to specify the parent window. The client window handle, `hwndClient`, is used to specify the owner of the file dialog window. The owner will be given the focus after a modal file dialog is closed or a `WM_COMMAND` is sent after a modeless file dialog is closed.

After calling the `WinFileDlg` API, the BITVIEW program executes the following code to open a specified bitmap file:

```
if (hwndDlg && (FileDlg.lReturn == DID_OK)) {

    rc = DosOpen(
        FileDlg.szFullFile,                         /* File name      */
        &FileHandle,                                /* Returned to us */
        &ulAction,                                  /* Action taken   */
        0,                                          /* File size (N/A) */
        FILE_NORMAL,                                /* File attributes */
        FILE_OPEN,
        OPEN_ACCESS_READONLY | OPEN_SHARE_DENYNONE,
        NULL );                                     /* EA buffer (N/A) */

    if (rc == NO_ERROR)
        *pFileHandle = FileHandle;
}
```

The `hwndDlg` parameter that `WinFileDlg` returns is checked for a value of `TRUE`. Since BITVIEW uses a modal file dialog, a return value of `TRUE` indicates that the creation of the file dialog was successful. Likewise, the `lReturn` field of the `FILEDLG` structure is checked for a value of `DID_OK`. If the "OK" button was pressed by the user, the `lReturn` field will be found to equal `DID_OK`, which indicates that a path and filename properly reside in the `szFullFile` field of the `FILEDLG` data structure.

The BITVIEW program uses the `szFullFile` field as a parameter to the `DosOpen` API. If the file specified by `szFullFile` is valid, the `DosOpen` API will return a file handle that allows BITVIEW to read and write to the file. If the file contains a valid bitmap, the BITVIEW program will display the bitmap in the client window.

"Save As" and "Open" File Dialogs

The BITVIEW program can display both an "Open" and a "Save As" file dialog. The steps that are involved in creating the "Save As" and the "Open" file dialogs differ in using an `FDS_SAVEAS_DIALOG` or an `FDS_OPEN_DIALOG` style flag, respectively. The `pszTitle field` is set either to the text string "Open a BMP file" (for the "Open" file dialog) or to the text string "Save the BMP file" (for the "Save As" file dialog).

The two file dialogs used in the BITVIEW program differ in a number of ways, including the way in which file names are selected. Unlike the "Open" file dialog, which can select from the list box that displays available file names, the "Save As" file dialog does not allow the user to select any of the file names that are displayed. The default title bar text and some of the static text differ between the two types of file dialogs.

Similarities also exist between the two file dialogs used in the BITVIEW program. For example, the look and feel provided by the "Open" and "Save As" file dialogs remains substantially the same. Moreover, the "Save As" file dialog behaves like the "Open" file dialog in that both update their `szFullFile` field with a path and file name of a user-selected file.

Supporting Help Screens

Before issuing the `WinFileDlg` API, an application can specify that a "Help" button should appear in the file dialog, by using the `FDS_HELPBUTTON` style flag in the `fl` field of the `FILEDLG` structure. When the "Help" button is pressed, the file dialog will send a `WM_HELP` message to its owner window. The client window of the BITVIEW program is set as the owner window, and it processes `WM_HELP` messages by displaying a message box when the user presses the "Help" push button.

CHAPTER 15
Font Dialog Controls

PM provides a *font dialog control,* which is a dialog box that lists available PM fonts and provides a *preview area* for displaying the appearance of a selected font. The font dialog control can be used not only to select a font but also to select the font's point size, style, and emphasis. An advantage of using a font dialog control is that it eliminates the need, which PM applications otherwise have, to include many lines of extra code to implement their font dialog controls.

A font dialog control, created by an example program called "FONT" whose source code is presented later in this chapter, appears in Figure 15.1.

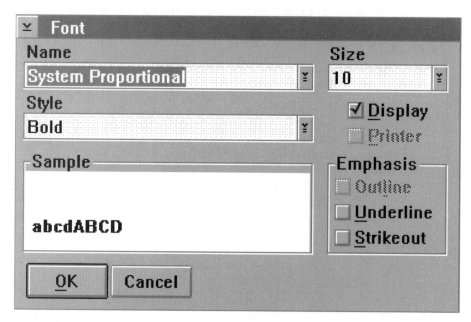

FIGURE 15.1 An example of a font dialog created by the FONT program.

USING THE FONT DIALOG

To access the font dialog, PM applications use the WinFontDlg API, which is quite similar to the WinFileDlg API that is used to handle file dialogs and is discussed in Chapter 14. To call the WinFontDlg API, an application must specify the handles of the parent and owner windows as parameters to the API. The last parameter of the WinFontDlg API is a pointer to a FONTDLG data structure, which is one of the larger data structures to be encountered in PM programming. To make use of this data structure, many of its fields only need to be initialized to a value of zero (to instruct the font dialog to use default values).

In the FONT example program that is presented later in this chapter, such fields of the FONTDLG data structure as are initialized to values other than zero indicate fields that programmers will typically want to set in order to override the use of default values. Following is the FONTDLG data structure; the fields that are usually set to nonzero values are presented in bold print for emphasis:

```
typedef struct _FONTDLG {
    ULONG    cbSize;
    HPS      hpsScreen;
    HPS      hpsPrinter;
    PSZ      pszTitle;
    PSZ      pszPreview;
    PSZ      pszPtSizeList;
    PFNWP    pfnDlgProc;
    PSZ      pszFamilyname;
    FIXED    fxPointSize;
    ULONG    fl;
    ULONG    flFlags;
    ULONG    flType;
    ULONG    flTypeMask;
    ULONG    flStyle;
    ULONG    flStyleMask;
    LONG     clrFore;
    LONG     clrBack;
    ULONG    ulUser;
    LONG     lReturn;
    LONG     lSRC;
    LONG     lEmHeight;
    LONG     lXHeight;
    LONG     lExternalLeading;
    HMODULE  hMod;
    FATTRS   fAttrs;
    SHORT    sNominalPointSize;
    USHORT   usWeight;
    USHORT   usWidth;
    SHORT    x;
    SHORT    y;
```

```
    USHORT  usDlgId;
    USHORT  usFamilyBufLen;
    USHORT  usReserved;
} FONTDLG;
```

A PM application must initialize certain fields of the FONTDLG data structure before calling the WinFontDlg API. The fields that need to be initialized are cbSize, hpsScreen, pszFamilyname, fl, fAttrs, and usFamilyBufLen. The large number of fields that are included in the FONTDLG data structure correctly suggests that a large number of possibilities exist for customizing the font dialog.

Like the WinFileDlg API that is discussed in Chapter 14, the WinFontDlg API can create either a modal or a modeless dialog box. When the dialog box is closed, the FONTDLG structure that was used to create it is updated with information about the font selected by the user. The lReturn field of the FONTDLG structure contains the window ID of a button that is used to close the dialog box. If controls have been added to the font dialog, possible window IDs that may be returned include those of the added controls as well as the standard IDs DID_OK and DID_CANCEL.

THE FONT PROGRAM

The FONT program utilizes the WinFontDlg API to bring up a font dialog window that can be used to select not only a font but also such attributes as the font's point size, style, and emphasis. The FONT program will display a text string using the font and selected font attributes. A text string showing the name of the font is presented in the center of the client window. The text string provides "visual feedback" to the user in that it employs the selected font and makes use of selected font attributes.

If an outline font was chosen, the FONT program will automatically scale the font to the correct point size. Several GPI calls are needed to handle outline fonts. A number of the more significant GPI calls that are used to handle outline fonts will be discussed later.

The following six files were used to compile the FONT example program:

FONT.C

```
#define INCL_WIN
#define INCL_GPI
#include <os2.h>
#include "font.h"


/* function prototypes */
INT main( VOID );
MRESULT EXPENTRY ClientWndProc( HWND, ULONG, MPARAM, MPARAM );
```

```
VOID SetFont( HWND, PFONTDLG, HPS, HDC );
VOID DefaultOutput( SHORT, SHORT, HPS, HDC );


/* global variables */
HAB    hab;
CHAR   achFontname[FACESIZE];  /* buffer needed for Font dlg  */
LONG   lyFontResolution;


INT main( VOID )
{
   HMQ    hmq;
   HWND   hwndFrame;
   HWND   hwndClient;
   CHAR   szClientClass[] = "Client Window";
   QMSG   qmsg;
   ULONG  flCreateFlags = FCF_TITLEBAR       /* create: title bar control    */
                     | FCF_SYSMENU       /*              system menu control */
                     | FCF_MENU          /*              action bar          */
                     | FCF_MINMAX        /*              min and max buttons  */
                     | FCF_SIZEBORDER    /* draw sizeborders                 */
                     | FCF_SHELLPOSITION /* shell decides window position    */
                     | FCF_TASKLIST      /* title added to switch list       */
                     | FCF_ICON;         /* frame has an icon                */

   hab = WinInitialize( 0 );
   hmq = WinCreateMsgQueue( hab, 0 );

   WinRegisterClass( hab,             /* anchor block handle */
                  szClientClass,   /* class name */
                  ClientWndProc,   /* pointer to window procedure */
                  CS_SIZEREDRAW,   /* class style */
                  0 );             /* number of class data bytes */


   hwndFrame = WinCreateStdWindow(
                  HWND_DESKTOP,          /* Desktop window is parent     */
                  WS_VISIBLE,            /* window styles                */
                  &flCreateFlags,        /* frame control flag           */
                  szClientClass,         /* client window class name     */
                  "Font Dialog Example", /* title bar text               */
                  0,                     /* no special class style       */
                  NULLHANDLE,            /* resource is in .EXE file      */
                  ID_FRAME_RES,          /* frame window identifier      */
                  &hwndClient );         /* client window handle         */

   if (hwndFrame)
      while (WinGetMsg( hab, &qmsg, NULLHANDLE, 0, 0 ))
         WinDispatchMsg( hab, &qmsg );

   WinDestroyWindow( hwndFrame );
   WinDestroyMsgQueue( hmq );
   WinTerminate( hab );
   return 0;
} /* end of main */
```

```
MRESULT EXPENTRY ClientWndProc( HWND hwnd, ULONG msg, MPARAM mp1, MPARAM mp2 )
{
   static HPS hps;                    /* Presentation Space handle      */
   static HDC hdc;                    /* Device Context handle          */
   static SHORT sClientX, sClientY;   /* Client wnd X and Y dimensions  */
   static USHORT  fPaint = 0;         /* Paint default string           */
   static FONTDLG fontdlg;

   switch( msg ) {

   case WM_CREATE:
    { SIZEL  sizel = { 0L, 0L };  /* presentation page size */
      hdc = WinOpenWindowDC( hwnd );
      hps = GpiCreatePS ( hab,
                          hdc,
                          &sizel,
                          PU_PELS
                          | GPIT_MICRO
                          | GPIA_ASSOC );

      memset( &fontdlg, 0, sizeof(FONTDLG) );
      fontdlg.cbSize = sizeof(FONTDLG);

      fontdlg.hpsScreen = hps;

      achFontname[0] = '\0';

      fontdlg.pszFamilyname = achFontname;
      fontdlg.usFamilyBufLen = FACESIZE;
      fontdlg.clrFore = SYSCLR_WINDOWTEXT;
      fontdlg.clrBack = SYSCLR_WINDOW;
      fontdlg.fl = FNTS_CENTER | FNTS_INITFROMFATTRS;
      fontdlg.fAttrs.usRecordLength = sizeof(FATTRS);
    } break;

   case WM_COMMAND:

      switch (SHORT1FROMMP( mp1 )) {

      case ID_FONT:
         fPaint = 0;
         SetFont( hwnd, &fontdlg, hps, hdc );
         WinInvalidateRect( hwnd, NULL, FALSE );
         break;

      default:
         return WinDefWindowProc( hwnd, msg, mp1, mp2 );
      }
      break;

   case WM_ERASEBACKGROUND:
      return (MRESULT)TRUE;
```

```
   case WM_SIZE:
      sClientX = SHORT1FROMMP(mp2);
      sClientY = SHORT2FROMMP(mp2);
      break;

   case WM_PAINT:
    { RECTL   rcl;

      WinBeginPaint( hwnd, hps, &rcl );
      DefaultOutput( sClientX, sClientY, hps, hdc );
      WinEndPaint( hps );
    } break;

   case WM_DESTROY:
      GpiDestroyPS( hps );
      DevCloseDC( hdc );
      break;

   default:
      return WinDefWindowProc( hwnd, msg, mp1, mp2 );
   }

   return (MRESULT)FALSE;
} /* end of ClientWndProc */


VOID SetFont( HWND hwndOwner, PFONTDLG pfontdlg, HPS hps, HDC hdc )
{
   HWND        hwndFontDlg;
   CHAR        szFamilyname[FACESIZE];
   RECTL       rc;
   POINTL      pt;
   LONG        lMatch;
   BOOL        fSuccess;
   SIZEF       sizef;
   CHAR        achBuff[50];
   LONG        lxFontResolution;

   GpiErase( hps );

   hwndFontDlg = WinFontDlg( HWND_DESKTOP, hwndOwner, pfontdlg );

   if ((hwndFontDlg) && (pfontdlg->lReturn == DID_OK)) {

      GpiCreateLogFont( pfontdlg->hpsScreen,
                        NULL,
                        LCID_MYFONT,
                        &pfontdlg->fAttrs );

      GpiSetCharSet( pfontdlg->hpsScreen, LCID_MYFONT );

      if ( pfontdlg->fAttrs.fsFontUse == FATTR_FONTUSE_OUTLINE ) {
         DevQueryCaps( hdc, CAPS_HORIZONTAL_FONT_RES,
                       (LONG)1, &lxFontResolution );
```

```
          DevQueryCaps( hdc, CAPS_VERTICAL_FONT_RES,
                        (LONG)1, &lyFontResolution );

          /*  Calculate the size of the character box, based on the
           *  point size selected and the resolution of the device
           *  Pixels = Inches * pixels/inch
           */
          sizef.cx = (FIXED)(((pfontdlg->fxPointSize) / 72 ) *
                             lxFontResolution);
          sizef.cy = (FIXED)(((pfontdlg->fxPointSize) / 72 ) *
                             lyFontResolution);

          GpiSetCharBox( pfontdlg->hpsScreen, &sizef );

      }
   }
} /* end of SetFont */


VOID DefaultOutput( SHORT sTotalX, SHORT sTotalY, HPS hps, HDC hdc )
{
   FONTMETRICS fm;
   CHAR szStyle[20];
   LONG lPtSize;
   CHAR szString[80];
   POINTL aptl[TXTBOX_COUNT] ;
   POINTL pt;

   GpiErase( hps );

   GpiQueryFontMetrics( hps, sizeof(FONTMETRICS), &fm );

   if (fm.fsDefn & FM_DEFN_OUTLINE)
      strcpy( szStyle, "Outline" );
   else
      strcpy( szStyle,"Image" );

   DevQueryCaps( hdc, CAPS_VERTICAL_FONT_RES, (LONG)1, &lyFontResolution );

   lPtSize = ((fm.lEmHeight * 72) + 71) / lyFontResolution;
   sprintf( szString, "%s, %s, %ld point",
            fm.szFamilyname,
            szStyle,
            lPtSize );

   GpiQueryTextBox ( hps, strlen( szString ), szString, TXTBOX_COUNT, aptl );

   if ((aptl[TXTBOX_BOTTOMRIGHT].x - aptl[TXTBOX_BOTTOMLEFT].x) < sTotalX)
      pt.x = (sTotalX / 2) -
             ((aptl[TXTBOX_BOTTOMRIGHT].x - aptl[TXTBOX_BOTTOMLEFT].x) /2);
   else
      pt.x = 1;
```

```
    pt.y = sTotalY / 2;
    GpiCharStringAt( hps, &pt, (LONG)strlen( szString ), szString );

} /* end of DefaultOutput */
```

FONT.H

```
#define   ID_FRAME_RES    200
#define   ID_FONT         201
#define   LCID_MYFONT     1L
#define   DEFAULT_WIDTH   8
#define   DEFAULT_HEIGHT  13
```

FONT.RC

```
#include <os2.h>
#include "font.h"

ICON ID_FRAME_RES font.ico

MENU    ID_FRAME_RES
BEGIN
    MENUITEM "~Font...",  ID_FONT, MIS_TEXT
END
```

FONT.DEF

```
NAME       FONT  WINDOWAPI

DESCRIPTION 'OS/2 Presentation Manager Sample'

CODE       MOVEABLE
DATA       MOVEABLE MULTIPLE

HEAPSIZE  10240
STACKSIZE 24576
```

FONT.MAK

```
all : font.exe

font.exe : font.obj  font.def font.res
        link386 /PM:PM font,,,,font.def;
        rc font.res

font.res : font.rc font.ico font.h
        rc -r font.rc

font.obj : font.c font.h
        icc /C /Ss /W3 \.$*.c
```

FONT.ICO

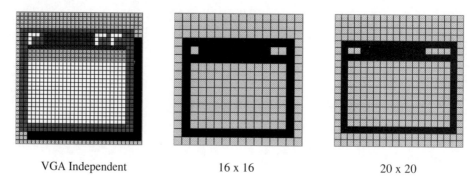

| VGA Independent | 16 x 16 | 20 x 20 |

FONT.ICO file, containing various icons of different sizes.

Creating a Micro Presentation Space

During the processing of the WM_CREATE message, the FONT program creates a micro presentation space. A micro presentation space differs from a cached-micro presentation space in that the micro presentation space needs to be created only once in order for it to be available for an application to utilize repeatedly, whereas a cached-micro presentation space is released once the processing of a paint message has been completed.

The FONT program uses a micro presentation space to store font attributes that are selected by the font dialog. If a cached-micro presentation space were to be used instead of a micro presentation space, the font attributes could not be "stored" in the presentation space; rather, the font attributes would need to be set (reset) each time that the FONT program redrew the client window.

The code in the FONT program that is used to create a micro presentation space is as follows:

```
SIZEL  sizel = { 0L, 0L };  /* presentation page size */

hdc = WinOpenWindowDC( hwnd );

hps = GpiCreatePS ( hab,
                    hdc,
                    &sizel,
                    PU_PELS
                    | GPIT_MICRO
                    | GPIA_ASSOC );
```

Every presentation space is associated with a device context (DC) that defines the output device that the presentation space is using. For example, a presentation space for a PM window is associated with the DC of the PM screen.

The FONT program creates a presentation space that is associated with a screen DC. A handle to a screen DC can be obtained by using the `WinOpenWindowDC` API. The FONT program assigns the handle that is returned by the `WinOpenWindowDC` API to a variable called `hdc`.

The `hdc` variable is used as the first parameter in a call to the `GpiCreatePS` API. The parameter that follows the `hdc` variable is a pointer to a `SIZEL` data structure. The `SIZEL` data structure includes two `LONG` values containing the `x` and `y` dimensions of the presentation page. A *presentation page* defines the rectangular area that is usable by a presentation space.

The `GpiCreatePS` API can be called with a presentation page size of zero and with a `GPIA_ASSOC` flag, which instructs `GpiCreatePS` to use default dimensions and units that correspond to the screen DC that is specified by the variable `hdc`. The default units for a screen DC are pixels.

Initializing the FONTDLG Data Structure

The FONT program allocates a `FONTDLG` data structure as a static variable to contain its information in an unchanged form during the processing of several messages. The `FONTDLG` structure is initialized during the processing of the `WM_CREATE` message.

The following code excerpt from the FONT program initializes the `FONTDLG` structure:

```
CHAR achFontname[FACESIZE];        /* Buffer needed for Font dlg */

memset(&fontdlg, 0, sizeof(FONTDLG));
fontdlg.cbSize = sizeof(FONTDLG);
fontdlg.hpsScreen = hps;
achFontname[0] = '\0';
fontdlg.pszFamilyname = achFontname;
fontdlg.usFamilyBufLen = FACESIZE;
fontdlg.clrFore = SYSCLR_WINDOWTEXT;
fontdlg.clrBack = SYSCLR_WINDOW;
fontdlg.fl = FNTS_CENTER | FNTS_INITFROMFATTRS;
fontdlg.fAttrs.usRecordLength = sizeof(FATTRS);
```

In this code, all fields are initially set to zero by using the `memset` C runtime library function. In most cases a zero in a given field tells PM to use a predefined default for that field. The `cbSize` field is set to the size of the `FONTDLG` structure in bytes. The `hpsScreen` field contains the micro presentation space that is associated with a screen DC.

The `pszFamilyname` field must point to a data area that `WinFontDlg` will use to store the font family name that is selected by the user. The FONT program sets `pszFamilyname` to point to a previously allocated data area, called `achFontname`, which is an array of a size equal to the value known as `FACESIZE`, because the size of the `pszFamilyname` buffer should equal the size of the `szFamilyname` field in a `FONTMETRICS` data structure.

An application can set the initial font family name that will be used as the default font name in the font dialog. The default name is set by pointing `pszFamilyname` to a string that contains a valid font family name. If the `pszFamilyname` is initialized to point to a NULL string, the font dialog will use the default system font family name. The FONT program does not specify a name in `pszFamilyname`, so the default is used. The `usFamilyBufLen` field holds the size, in bytes, of the buffer that is pointed to by `pszFamilyname`. In the FONT program, `usFamilyBufLen` is set equal to the value of FACESIZE.

Continuing with a discussion of the initialization code already set out, the `clrFore` field sets the foreground color that is used by the font dialog. The FONT program sets the foreground color equal to the system-defined color for window text, `SYSCLR_WINDOWTEXT`. The `clrBack` field sets the background color used by the font dialog. The FONT program sets the background equal to the system-defined color for a window background, `SYSCLR_WINDOW`.

The `fl` field contains the font dialog style flags, which are characterized by `FNTS_` prefixes. The FONT program uses the `FNTS_CENTER` flag to inform the `WinFontDlg` API to center the font dialog window about its parent window. The `FNTS_INITFROMFATTRS` flag is also used to set up a font dialog that initializes itself by using information that is supplied in the `fAttrs` field of the `FONTDLG` structure. The `fAttrs` field is a `FATTRS` data structure, the format of which is as follows:

```
typedef struct _FATTRS {
    USHORT   usRecordLength;
    USHORT   fsSelection;
    LONG     lMatch;
    CHAR     szFacename[FACESIZE];
    USHORT   idRegistry;
    USHORT   usCodePage;
    LONG     lMaxBaselineExt;
    LONG     lAveCharWidth;
    USHORT   fsType;
    USHORT   fsFontUse;
} FATTRS;
```

The `fAttrs.usRecordLength` field is initialized to the size of a `FATTRS` structure by the FONT program.

Stack Requirements

The `WinFontDlg` API requires a stack space much larger than normal. The FONT program uses a stack size of 24K. The stack size given to a PM application corresponds to the `STACKSIZE` parameter in its module definition file FONT.DEF. The stack size declaration from the `FONT.DEF` file is:

```
STACKSIZE 24576
```

The WinFontDlg API

The FONT program initially uses the default font with its default attributes. If the user selects the "Font" menu option, the FONT program calls `WinFontDlg` to display a font dialog. The following code excerpt is the call that FONT program makes to `WinFontDlg`:

```
hwndFontDlg = WinFontDlg( HWND_DESKTOP, hwndOwner, pfontdlg );
```

The FONT program uses the `HWND_DESKTOP` (the handle for the desktop window) as the parent window. The client window handle, `hwndClient`, is used to specify the owner of the font dialog window.

After the `WinFontDlg` API has been called, the FONT program checks whether the font dialog was created; if so, this confirms that the user selected either the "OK" button or "Cancel" button to complete the `WinFontDlg` call. If the user selected the "Cancel" button, the FONT program assumes that no font changes were requested by the user.

The `hwndFontDlg` parameter is used to determine whether the file dialog was successfully displayed and was accessible to the user. The `lReturn` field of the `FONTDLG` is used to check which button was used to close the font dialog. If `lReturn` has the value `DID_OK`, the user pressed the "OK" button. If `lReturn` has the value `DID_CANCEL`, the user pressed the "Cancel" button.

Setting Fonts with GPI Calls

After a font dialog is used to retrieve a font, the application must set matching font attributes so that the selected font can be used. The attributes are set by creating a logical font and by setting a character box size.

A logical font is a collection of associated font attributes. A character box is a rectangle that is used to determine the size of an outline font (the outline font is scaled to fit). The application must set the proper character box size in order to display fonts properly at a specified point size.

The following code is used in the FONT program to set the font attributes:

```
GpiCreateLogFont( pfontdlg->hpsScreen,
                  NULL,
                  LCID_MYFONT,
                  &pfontdlg->fAttrs );

GpiSetCharSet( pfontdlg->hpsScreen, LCID_MYFONT );

if ( pfontdlg->fAttrs.fsFontUse == FATTR_FONTUSE_OUTLINE ) {
   DevQueryCaps( hdc, CAPS_HORIZONTAL_FONT_RES,
                 (LONG)1, &lxFontResolution);
```

```
            DevQueryCaps( hdc, CAPS_VERTICAL_FONT_RES,
                          (LONG)1, &lyFontResolution);

    /*  Calculate the size of the character box, based on the
     *  point size selected and the resolution of the device
     *  Pixels = Inches * pixels/inch
     */
    sizef.cx = (FIXED)(((pfontdlg->fxPointSize) / 72 ) *
                        lxFontResolution );
    sizef.cy = (FIXED)(((pfontdlg->fxPointSize) / 72 ) *
                        lyFontResolution );

    GpiSetCharBox( pfontdlg->hpsScreen, &sizef );

}
```

The GpiCreateLogFont API is called to create a logical font that will be associated with the micro presentation space of the FONT program. The local identifier value provided to this API can be used at a later time to refer to the newly created font. The FATTRS portion of the FONTDLG data structure that is pointed to by the fAttrs field is updated by the WinFontDlg API to contain new font information. Using the pfontdlg->fAttrs pointer, the FONT program provides the new font information to the GpiCreateLogFont API, which in turn sets the attributes that are used by all text output that is directed to the micro presentation space. The attributes are specified by the fAttrs field of the FontDLG data structure.

The GpiSetCharSet API is called to set the micro presentation space to use the logical font that is created by GpiCreateLogFont. Text displayed in the micro presentation space will be drawn with font attributes that are defined by the logical font.

If the user has chosen an outline font, an appropriate character box size must be set that is based on the point size that has been selected. Font sizes are defined in units called *points*. A point is equal to 1/72 of an inch. Using the DevQueryCaps API, the FONT program determines the horizontal and vertical number of pixels per inch. Using these values, the character box size is calculated with the following formulas:

Char box X (*in pixels*) = (Point size/72) × X font resolution (*pixels/inch*)

Char box Y (*in pixels*) = (Point size/72) × Y font resolution (*pixels/inch*)

The GpiSetCharBox API is called to set the character box size, which is calculated with the formulas that are set out above. This causes text that is directed to the micro presentation space to have correct font attributes that correspond with those that have been specified by the user.

CHAPTER 16

Notebook Controls

PM provides a *notebook control*, which, when displayed, resembles a bound notebook and is formed from several *pages* that are arranged in a stack, one atop another. A *binding* is provided along a selected edge of the stack of pages that comprises the notebook. The appearance of the binding can be set to have the appearance of a plain black border or a spiral ring binding. *Page buttons* and *tabs* are provided to permit a user to scroll or to "flip" through the pages of the notebook. A status line is usually presented at the bottom of each page and typically displays text that labels the pages with such information as page numbers.

Each page of a notebook control permits a number of controls that are related to a specific category of information to be grouped together. By this arrangement, many controls can be organized into related groups that are presented on separate notebook pages so that they can be accessed with ease. Workplace Shell makes heavy use of notebook controls to provide easy access to hundreds of controls that are used to change system settings.

NOTEBOOK CONTROL COMPONENTS

Tab and page button components provide easy ways to move from page to page. Tabs permit the user to move among groups of related pages. Page buttons permit the user to scroll through pages one at a time.

Each page of a notebook control typically presents a window within which are displayed several controls that have selectable settings. Tabs may be displayed along the edges of the pages to assist in leafing among various groups of pages or in scrolling from page to page. A *major tab* provides a label that can be used to move rapidly to the first of a group of related pages, which are pages that present controls that are related to the label that appears on the tab. A *minor tab* provides a label that can be used to move rapidly among pages of a related group. A *forward page button* and a *backward page button* are provided to selectively permit forward or backward scrolling of the pages within the stack of pages that constitutes the notebook.

While major tabs can be placed on any one of the four sides of the stack of pages that form a notebook, the positioning of the major tabs and the selection of a location for the page buttons cooperate to determine which edges will be occupied by the binding and by the minor tabs. The binding is always placed opposite the edge that is occupied by the major tabs. The minor tabs are always placed perpendicular to the edge that is occupied by the major tabs.

Each major or minor tab contains either a bitmap or text. Corner portions of the tabs of a notebook can be drawn in a selected one of the following styles: *square, rounded,* or *polygonal.* If a tab includes text, the text can be set to one of the following: *right-justified, left-justified,* or *centered.*

The optional status line of a notebook page typically includes text that is set when the notebook page is created. Status line text can be changed at any time after its associated page has been created. Each page can have its own unique status line text. Status line text can provide a brief description of the associated notebook page, or other selected information.

SETTING UP A NOTEBOOK

PM provides several style flags to set the appearance of a notebook control. The names of the notebook style flags have a BKS_ prefix. The BKS style flags are used to override default settings of a notebook control to set the positions and appearances of the tabs, page buttons, and binding. When a notebook is set up, the style flags BKS_BACKPAGESBR, BKS_BACKPAGESBL, BKS_BACKPAGESTR, and BKS_BACKPAGESTL determine the positions of the page buttons and the minor tabs.

The last two characters of the style flag names have special meanings. The use of a "B" or "T" (as the first of the last two characters) indicates "bottom" or "top," respectively. The use of an "R" or "L" (as the second of the last two characters) indicates "right" or "left," respectively. A combination of one of each of these characters designates a corner region where the pages are located. For example, "BR" indicates that the page buttons are located in a bottom right corner region of all of the pages of a notebook.

Similar style flags are used to determine the position of the major tabs: BKS_MAJORTABRIGHT, BKS_MAJORTABLEFT, BKS_MAJORTABTOP, and BKS_MAJORTABBOTTOM. The major tabs are placed on one of the two edges that intersect to form a corner region that is occupied by the page buttons. The minor tabs occupy the other of these two intersecting edges.

Inserting Pages

After the notebook is created with features set by the BKS style flags, each page of a notebook control can be inserted (is created) using a `BKM_INSERTPAGE` message. While the `BKS_` style flags will control many characteristics of the pages that are inserted into the notebook, characteristics that are unique to each individual page can be set by using attributes that have a `BKA_` prefix. The `BKA_` attributes are sent with a `BKM_INSERTPAGE` message and serve to set such page characteristics as the type of tab (major or minor) that a page will exhibit. For example, using a `BKA_MAJOR` attribute associates a major tab with a page being inserted. Likewise, using a `BKA_MINOR` attribute associates a minor tab with a page being inserted.

The order in which notebook pages are arranged can be selected by setting the `BKA_` attributes that are sent with a `BKM_INSERTPAGE` message. A page can be inserted in front of or behind all pages that presently form the notebook by using a `BKA_FIRST` or a `BKA_LAST` attribute, respectively. A page can be inserted in front of or behind a particular page of a notebook by using a `BKA_PREV` or a `BKA_NEXT` attribute, respectively.

An optional status line can be added to a notebook page by using the `BKA_STATUSTEXTON` attribute when the page is inserted. The alignment of the status line text is common to all pages of a notebook, because it is set when the notebook is created by using one of the following style flags: `BKS_STATUSTEXTLEFT` (left-justified), `BKS_STATUSTEXTRIGHT` (right-justified), and `BKS_STATUSTEXTCENTER` (centered).

After a page is inserted in a notebook, an *application page window* may be associated with the page by sending a `BKM_SETPAGEWINDOWHWND` message. An application page window is displayed on top of a page when the page is being displayed, and it provides space to contain controls or to allow an application to draw within the window. The application can choose to let the notebook handle the task of properly sizing an application page window, by setting a `BKA_AUTOPAGESIZE` attribute.

THE GEOSHAPE PROGRAM

An example program called "GEOSHAPE," whose source code for which appears later in this chapter, uses a notebook control with a left-located spiral type binding, three right-located major tabs, and two bottom-located minor tabs. Figure 16.1 shows the notebook control that is created by the GEOSHAPE example program, with its topmost page displaying a blue-colored circle that is located within the bounds of an associated window.

The GEOSHAPE notebook has three major tabs for permitting the user to move among groups of related pages that display a circle, a square, or a triangle, respectively. Each group of pages consists of a page that has a major tab followed by two pages that have minor tabs. The minor tabs are provided

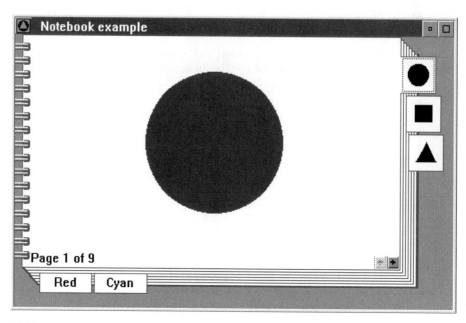

FIGURE 16.1 Notebook control created by the GEOSHAPE program.

to assist the user in selecting a color for each group's geometric shape from among the pages of the group. The three major tabs have bitmaps that display their associated geometric shapes. The minor tabs have text that labels the colors of the shapes that are displayed on their associated pages. A status line appears on each page to display the page number of the page being displayed.

The GEOSHAPE program illustrates how a notebook control typically is set up and communicates with a PM application. The GEOSHAPE program's source code is listed in the following nine files:

GEOSHAPE.C

```
#define INCL_WIN
#define INCL_GPI
#include <os2.h>
#include "geoshape.h"


/* function prototypes */
INT main( VOID );
MRESULT EXPENTRY PgWindowProc( HWND, ULONG, MPARAM, MPARAM );
ULONG SetupPage ( USHORT );
MRESULT EXPENTRY MyNBProc( HWND, ULONG, MPARAM, MPARAM );


/* global variables */
PFNWP   RealNBProc;
```

```
HWND     hwndNotebook;
HWND     hwndPage;


MYPAGEINFO aPageInfo[NUM_PAGES] = {
    0,  BKA_MAJOR, "",        NULLHANDLE, ID_CIRCLE,   CLR_BLUE,
    0,  BKA_MINOR, "Red",     NULLHANDLE, ID_CIRCLE,   CLR_RED,
    0,  BKA_MINOR, "Cyan",    NULLHANDLE, ID_CIRCLE,   CLR_CYAN,
    0,  BKA_MAJOR, "",        NULLHANDLE, ID_SQUARE,   CLR_PINK,
    0,  BKA_MINOR, "Brown",   NULLHANDLE, ID_SQUARE,   CLR_BROWN,
    0,  BKA_MINOR, "Gray",    NULLHANDLE, ID_SQUARE,   CLR_PALEGRAY,
    0,  BKA_MAJOR, "",        NULLHANDLE, ID_TRIANGLE, CLR_GREEN,
    0,  BKA_MINOR, "Yellow",  NULLHANDLE, ID_TRIANGLE, CLR_YELLOW,
    0,  BKA_MINOR, "Black",   NULLHANDLE, ID_TRIANGLE, CLR_BLACK
};



INT main(VOID)
{
    HAB  hab;                                /* anchor block handle       */
    HMQ  hmq;                                /* message queue handle      */
    HWND hwndFrame;                          /* frame window handle       */
    HWND hwndClient;                         /* client area window handle */
    CHAR szPageWindow[] = "PageWindow";
    QMSG qmsg;                               /* message from message queue */
    HPS  hps;                                /* presentation Space handle  */
    POINTL  ptl;
    USHORT  usTabX, usTaby;
    USHORT  i;

    FRAMECDATA fcd;
    fcd.cb = sizeof(FRAMECDATA);             /* length of structure          */
    fcd.flCreateFlags =  FCF_TITLEBAR        /* create: title bar control    */
                      |  FCF_SYSMENU         /*          system menu control */
                      |  FCF_MINMAX          /*          min and max buttons  */
                      |  FCF_SIZEBORDER      /* draw sizeborders             */
                      |  FCF_SHELLPOSITION   /* shell decides window position */
                      |  FCF_TASKLIST        /* title added to switch list   */
                      |  FCF_ICON;           /* frame has an icon            */

    fcd.hmodResources = NULLHANDLE;          /* handle to a module           */
    fcd.idResources   = ID_FRAMEWND;         /* identifier for the frame     */

    hab = WinInitialize( 0 );
    hmq = WinCreateMsgQueue( hab, 0 );

    WinRegisterClass( hab,                   /* anchor block handle          */
                (PSZ)szPageWindow,           /* window class name            */
                (PFNWP)PgWindowProc,         /* address of window procedure  */
                CS_SIZEREDRAW,               /* class style                  */
                0 );                         /* no extra window words        */

    hwndFrame = WinCreateWindow(
                HWND_DESKTOP,                /* parent window handle         */
```

```
                WC_FRAME,                    /* window class                */
                "Notebook example",          /* title text                  */
                0,                           /* style                       */
                0, 0, 0, 0, /* ignored, FCF_SHELLPOSITION was set           */
                NULLHANDLE,                  /* owner                       */
                HWND_TOP,                    /* z-order                     */
                ID_FRAMEWND,                 /* id                          */
                &fcd,                        /* control data                */
                NULL );                      /* presentation parms          */

hwndNotebook = WinCreateWindow(
                hwndFrame,                   /* parent window handle        */
                WC_NOTEBOOK,                 /* window class                */
                (PSZ)NULL,                   /* title text                  */
                BKS_SPIRALBIND,              /* style                       */
                0, 0, 0, 0,                  /* ignored, frame will pos     */
                hwndFrame,                   /* owner                       */
                HWND_BOTTOM,                 /* z-order                     */
                FID_CLIENT,                  /* id                          */
                NULL,                        /* control data                */
                NULL );                      /* presentation parms          */

RealNBProc = WinSubclassWindow( hwndNotebook, (PFNWP)MyNBProc );

hwndPage = WinCreateWindow(
                hwndFrame,                   /* parent window handle        */
                (PSZ)szPageWindow,           /* window class                */
                (PSZ)NULL,                   /* title text                  */
                0,                           /* style                       */
                0, 0, 0, 0,                  /* ignored, nbook will pos     */
                hwndFrame,                   /* owner                       */
                HWND_BOTTOM,                 /* z-order                     */
                ID_BOOKPAGE,                 /* id                          */
                NULL,                        /* control data                */
                NULL );                      /* presentation parms          */

hps = WinGetPS( hwndNotebook );

aPageInfo[0].hbm = GpiLoadBitmap(
                    hps,
                    NULLHANDLE,      /* use the current EXE file */
                    ID_CIRCLE,
                    0L, 0L );        /* no X/Y stretching */

aPageInfo[3].hbm = GpiLoadBitmap(
                    hps,
                    NULLHANDLE,      /* use the current EXE file */
                    ID_SQUARE,
                    0L, 0L );        /* no X/Y stretching */

aPageInfo[6].hbm = GpiLoadBitmap(
                    hps,
                    NULLHANDLE,      /* use the current EXE file */
                    ID_TRIANGLE,
                    0L, 0L );        /* no X/Y stretching */
```

```c
    WinReleasePS( hps );

    for (i = 0; i < NUM_PAGES; i++)
        aPageInfo[i].ulPageID = SetupPage(i);

    ptl.x = 4;  /* average width of a character in dialog coordinates */
    ptl.y = 8;  /* average height of a character in dialog coordinates */

    WinMapDlgPoints( hwndNotebook,          /* get pels per character        */
                     &ptl,
                     1,                      /* # of coordinate points        */
                     TRUE );                 /* dialog to window              */

    usTabX = usTabY = ptl.x * 7;

    WinSendMsg( hwndNotebook,
                BKM_SETDIMENSIONS,
                MPFROM2SHORT( usTabX, usTabY ),   /* width and height pels    */
                MPFROMSHORT( BKA_MAJORTAB ) );    /* all major tabs           */

    usTabX = ptl.x * 10;                          /* 10 characters wide       */
    usTabY = (ptl.y * 2) - (ptl.y / 2);           /* 1.5 characters high      */

    WinSendMsg( hwndNotebook,
                BKM_SETDIMENSIONS,
                MPFROM2SHORT ( usTabX, usTabY ),  /* width and height pels    */
                MPFROMSHORT( BKA_MINORTAB ) );    /* all minor tabs           */

  WinShowWindow( hwndFrame, TRUE);

    if ( hwndFrame )
        while( WinGetMsg( hab, &qmsg, NULLHANDLE, 0, 0 ) )
            WinDispatchMsg( hab, &qmsg );

    WinDestroyWindow( hwndFrame );
    WinDestroyMsgQueue( hmq );
    WinTerminate( hab );

    return 0;
} /* end of main */

ULONG SetupPage ( USHORT cPage )
{
    ULONG   ulNewPageID;
    USHORT  usPageStyle;
    CHAR    szStatusLineText[15];

    usPageStyle = aPageInfo[cPage].usTabAttr
                | BKA_AUTOPAGESIZE
                | BKA_STATUSTEXTON;

    ulNewPageID = LONGFROMMR( WinSendMsg(
                                hwndNotebook,
                                BKM_INSERTPAGE,
```

```
                              (MPARAM)0,
                              MPFROM2SHORT( usPageStyle, BKA_LAST ) ) );

   if (aPageInfo[cPage].hbm == NULLHANDLE)
      WinSendMsg( hwndNotebook,
                  BKM_SETTABTEXT,
                  MPFROMLONG( ulNewPageID ),
                  MPFROMP( aPageInfo[cPage].pszTabText ) );

   else                                    /* if not text then bitmap tab */

      WinSendMsg( hwndNotebook,
                  BKM_SETTABBITMAP,
                  MPFROMLONG( ulNewPageID ),
                  MPFROMLong( (LONG)aPageInfo[cPage].hbm ) );

   sprintf( szStatusLineText,  "Page %d of 9", (cPage + 1) );
   WinSendMsg( hwndNotebook,
               BKM_SETSTATUSLINETEXT,
               MPFROMLONG( ulNewPageID ),
               MPFROMP( szStatusLineText ) );

   WinSendMsg( hwndNotebook,
               BKM_SETPAGEWINDOWHWND,
               MPFROMLONG( ulNewPageID ),
               MPFROMHWND( hwndPage ) );

   return ( ulNewPageID );
} /* end of SetupPage */

MRESULT EXPENTRY PgWindowProc( HWND hwnd, ULONG msg, MPARAM mp1, MPARAM mp2 )
{
   static SHORT sPageX, sPageY;       /* page window X and Y dimensions */
   static ARCPARAMS arcp = { 1, 1, 0, 0 };

   switch (msg) {
      case WM_PAINT:
       { HPS      hps;
         RECTL    rcl;
         POINTL   ptl;
         ULONG    ulCurPgID;
         PMYPAGEINFO pMyPageInfo;

         hps = WinBeginPaint( hwnd, NULLHANDLE, &rcl );

         ulCurPgID = (ULONG)WinSendMsg(
                        hwndNotebook,
                        BKM_QUERYPAGEID,
                        (MPARAM)0,                        /* reference page */
                        MPFROM2SHORT( BKA_TOP, 0 ) ); /* order, style   */

         pMyPageInfo = (PMYPAGEINFO)aPageInfo;

         while (pMyPageInfo->ulPageID != ulCurPgID)
            ++pMyPageInfo;
```

```
        if (pMyPageInfo->ulShape == ID_CIRCLE) {
           SHORT x, y, Radius;

           x = sPageX / 3;
           y = sPageY / 3;
           Radius = ( x > y ? y : x );
           arcp.lQ = arcp.lP = Radius;
           GpiSetArcParams( hps, &arcp );

           ptl.x = sPageX / 2;
           ptl.y = sPageY / 2;
           GpiMove( hps, &ptl );

           GpiSetColor( hps, pMyPageInfo->lColor );

           GpiFullArc( hps, DRO_FILL, MAKEFIXED( 1, 0 ) );
        }
        else if (pMyPageInfo->ulShape == ID_SQUARE) {
           SHORT w;

           if (sPageX > sPageY)
              w = sPageY / 2;
           else
              w = sPageX / 2;

           rcl.xLeft = (sPageX / 2) - (w / 2);
           rcl.xRight = rcl.xLeft + w;
           rcl.yBottom = (sPageY / 2 ) - (w / 2);
           rcl.yTop = rcl.yBottom + w;

           WinFillRect( hps,
                        &rcl,
                        pMyPageInfo->lColor );
        }
        else if (pMyPageInfo->ulShape == ID_TRIANGLE) {

           GpiSetColor( hps, pMyPageInfo->lColor );
           GpiBeginArea( hps, BA_NOBOUNDARY );
           ptl.x = sPageX / 4;
           ptl.y = sPageY / 4;
           GpiMove( hps, &ptl );

           ptl.x *= 3;
           GpiLine( hps, &ptl );

           ptl.x = sPageX / 2;
           ptl.y *= 3;
           GpiLine( hps, &ptl );

           ptl.x /= 2;
           ptl.y /= 3;
           GpiLine( hps, &ptl );
           GpiEndArea( hps );
        }
```

```
        WinEndPaint( hps );
    } break;

    case WM_SIZE:
        sPageX = SHORT1FROMMP( mp2 );
        sPageY = SHORT2FROMMP( mp2 );
        break;

    case WM_ERASEBACKGROUND:
        return (MRESULT)TRUE;

    default:
        return WinDefWindowProc( hwnd, msg, mp1, mp2 );
    }
    return (MRESULT)FALSE;
} /* end of PgWindowProc */


MRESULT EXPENTRY MyNBProc( HWND hwnd, ULONG msg, MPARAM mp1, MPARAM mp2 )
{
    if (msg == WM_CLOSE) {
        WinPostMsg( hwnd, WM_QUIT, (MPARAM)0, (MPARAM)0 );
        RealNBProc( hwnd, msg, mp1,mp2 );
    }
    else
        return RealNBProc( hwnd, msg, mp1, mp2 );
} /* end of MyNBProc */
```

GEOSHAPE.H

```
#define ID_FRAMEWND 256

#define ID_CIRCLE   257
#define ID_SQUARE   258
#define ID_TRIANGLE 259

#define ID_BOOKPAGE 260
#define NUM_PAGES   9

typedef struct _MYPAGEINFO {
    ULONG   ulPageID;
    USHORT  usTabAttr;
    PSZ     pszTabText;
    HBITMAP hbm;
    ULONG   ulShape;
    LONG    lColor;
} MYPAGEINFO;
typedef MYPAGEINFO *PMYPAGEINFO;
```

GEOSHAPE.RC

```
#include <os2.h>
#include "geoshape.h"
```

```
ICON ID_FRAMEWND geoshape.ico

BITMAP ID_CIRCLE    circle.bmp
BITMAP ID_SQUARE    square.bmp
BITMAP ID_TRIANGLE  triangle.bmp
```

GEOSHAPE.DEF

```
NAME GEOSHAPE WINDOWAPI

DESCRIPTION 'Notebook Control Example'

CODE MOVEABLE
DATA MOVEABLE MULTIPLE

HEAPSIZE 10240
STACKSIZE 24576
```

GEOSHAPE.MAK

```
all : geoshape.exe

geoshape.exe : geoshape.obj geoshape.def geoshape.res
        link386 /PM:PM geoshape,,,,geoshape.def;
        rc geoshape.res

geoshape.res : geoshape.rc geoshape.ico geoshape.h circle.bmp square.bmp \
            triangle.bmp
        rc -r geoshape.rc

geoshape.obj : geoshape.c geoshape.h
        icc /C /Ss /W3 .\ $*.c
```

GEOSHAPE.ICO

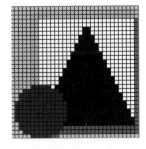  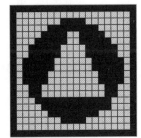

VGA Independent   16 x 16   20 x 20

GEOSHAPE.ICO file, containing various icons of different sizes.

CIRCLE.BMP

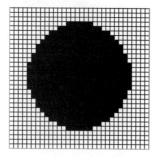

SQUARE.BMP

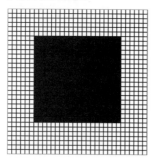

TRIANGLE.BMP

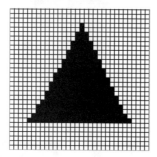

Creating a Notebook Window

The GEOSHAPE example creates a notebook control window by using the `WinCreateWindow` API with the `BKS_SPIRALBIND` style flag to set a spiral ring binding style. The `WC_NOTEBOOK` class and a `FID_CLIENT` window ID are used as parameters in the `WinCreateWindow` call to create a window of the notebook class as a client window. The owner and parent are set to the GEOSHAPE frame window by specifying the variable `hwndFrame` twice as a parameter. The GEOSHAPE program uses all default styles for a notebook window, except that the default solid binding style is overridden by specifying that a spiral binding style is to be used.

GEOSHAPE Notebook Pages

Once a notebook has been created by the GEOSHAPE program, the program inserts pages into the notebook by sending `BKM_INSERTPAGE` messages to the notebook window. In the GEOSHAPE program, a total of nine pages are inserted into the notebook. Rather than to duplicate code for inserting one notebook page after another, the GEOSHAPE program uses a function called `SetupPage`, which inserts and initializes notebook pages. The following code excerpt is taken from the SetupPage function of the GEOSHAPE program:

```
usPageStyle = aPageInfo[cPage].usTabAttr
            | BKA_AUTOPAGESIZE
            | BKA_STATUSTEXTON;

ulNewPageID = LONGFROMMR( WinSendMsg(
                    hwndNotebook,
                    BKM_INSERTPAGE,
                    (MPARAM)0,
                    MPFROM2SHORT( usPageStyle, BKA_LAST ) ) );
```

This code excerpt sends the `BKM_INSERTPAGE` message. The first message parameter (`mp1`) can be used to specify the ID of an existing page in front of which, or behind which, the page being inserted is to be placed. The GEOSHAPE program uses only the `BKA_LAST` attribute to insert its pages; therefore, the GEOSHAPE program does not need to set the value of `mp1` to indicate a page ID. The value in `mp1` is set to zero, because it is ignored unless `BKA_PREV` or `BKA_NEXT` are used.

The `usPageStyle` field is used to specify the attributes of a page that is being inserted. All pages used by the GEOSHAPE program have status text, because the `BKA_STATUSTEXTON` attribute is used. Since no `BKS_` style flag is used to position the status text, the default, left justification (`BKS_STATUSTEXTLEFT`), is used. PM is allowed to automatically handle the sizing of the page window, because the `BKA_AUTOPAGESIZE` attribute is used.

In the GEOSHAPE program the `usTabAttr` variable is set with either of the attributes `BKA_MAJOR` or `BKA_MINOR`. The `BKM_INSERTPAGE` message will return the page ID of the newly created notebook page. A page ID is the mechanism that is used to distinguish among the pages of a notebook.

GEOSHAPE Page Tabs

Each of the notebook pages used in the GEOSHAPE program is provided with either a major or a minor tab attribute. When a tab is pressed, the corresponding page is brought to the top of the notebook. Not all of the minor tabs are displayed at a particular time. The only minor tabs that are visible are those corresponding to the major section of the notebook that is associated with the currently displayed page.

In the GEOSHAPE program, each of the major tabs contains a bitmap that provides a graphical representation of the major section to which the notebook has been opened. The minor tabs contain text that describes subsections within a major section. The following code excerpt from GEOSHAPE.C is used for setting major tab bitmaps or minor tab text:

```
if (aPageInfo[cPage].hbm == NULLHANDLE)
    WinSendMsg( hwndNotebook,
             BKM_SETTABTEXT,
             MPFROMLONG( ulNewPageID ),
             MPFROMP( aPageInfo[cPage].pszTabText ) );

else                                      /* if not text then bitmap tab */
    WinSendMsg( hwndNotebook,
             BKM_SETTABBITMAP,
             MPFROMLONG( ulNewPageID ),
             MPFROMLONG( (LONG)aPageInfo[cPage].hbm ) );
```

Each notebook page inserted by the SetupPage routine is described by a MYPAGEINFO data structure. The MYPAGEINFO data structure is displayed below:

```
typedef struct _MYPAGEINFO {
    ULONG    ulPageID;
    USHORT   usTabAttr;
    PSZ      pszTabText;
    HBITMAP hbm;
    ULONG    ulShape;
    LONG     lColor;
} MYPAGEINFO;
typedef MYPAGEINFO *PMYPAGEINFO;
```

The hbm field of the above structure will contain a valid bitmap handle if the notebook page is associated with a major tab. If a notebook page is associated with a minor tab, the hbm field will be set to a value of NULLHANDLE.

The SetupPage function will check for a valid bitmap handle to determine whether it should issue a BKM_SETTABTEXT or BKM_SETTABBITMAP message. The BKM_SETTABTEXT message includes the ID of the corresponding notebook page and the actual tab text. The BKM_SETTABBITMAP includes the ID of the corresponding notebook page along with a bitmap handle for the bitmap that is to be drawn into the tab.

The shape of all of the tabs of a notebook is determined by the style flags that are set when the notebook window is created. The GEOSHAPE program does not specify a control style flag for a tab shape when it creates the notebook window. When no style flag is set, the tabs will be drawn with default square edges (BKS_SQUARETABS). The BKS_ROUNDEDTABS or BKS_POLYGONTABS could have been specified to cause the tabs to be drawn with rounded or polygon edges, respectively.

Tab dimensions are set using the BKM_SETDIMENSIONS message. The following code excerpt sets the dimensions of the major and minor tabs:

```
ptl.x = 4;   /* average width of a character in dialog coordinates */
ptl.y = 8;   /* average height of a character in dialog coordinates */

WinMapDlgPoints( hwndNotebook,            /* get pels per character     */
                 &ptl,
                 1,                       /* # of coordinate points     */
                 TRUE );                  /* dialog to window           */

usTabX = usTabY = ptl.x * 7;

WinSendMsg( hwndNotebook,
            BKM_SETDIMENSIONS,
            MPFROM2SHORT( usTabX, usTabY ),   /* width and height pels */
            MPFROMSHORT( BKA_MAJORTAB ) );    /* all major tabs        */

usTabX = ptl.x * 10;                     /* 10 characters wide         */
usTabY = (ptl.y * 2) - (ptl.y / 2);      /* 1.5 characters high        */

WinSendMsg( hwndNotebook,
            BKM_SETDIMENSIONS,
            MPFROM2SHORT( usTabX, usTabY ),   /* width and height pels */
            MPFROMSHORT( BKA_MINORTAB ) );    /* all minor tabs        */
```

The first message parameter (mp1) of the BKM_SETDIMENSIONS message contains tab width and height. The second message parameter (mp2) specifies whether major or minor tab dimensions are being set. The BKM_SETDIMENSIONS message will set the dimensions of all major or all minor tabs. The dimensions of tabs cannot be individually set.

Status Line Text

The status line of the GEOSHAPE notebook is located at the bottom of each notebook page. Status text, presented on the status line of each page, is used to provide information about the current geometric shape of the page that is being displayed.

The following code excerpt is used by the `SetupPage` function of the GEOSHAPE program to set status text:

```
WinSendMsg( hwndNotebook,
            BKM_SETSTATUSLINETEXT,
            MPFROMLONG( ulNewPageID ),
            MPFROMP( szStatusLineText ) );
```

The `BKM_SETSTATUSLINETEXT` message is used to set status line text. The first message parameter (`mp1`) contains the ID of the page that is being updated. The second message parameter (`mp2`) contains a pointer to the text string. The page specified by `mp1` must have the `BKA_STATUSTEXTON` attribute set in order for the status text to be visible.

Associating a Window with a Page

Whenever a notebook page is displayed, the notebook sends a `BKN_PAGE-SELECTED` notification message, containing the ID of the notebook page that is being displayed. The page window associated with the page is sized and positioned automatically if the `BKA_AUTOPAGESIZE` attribute is set.

The GEOSHAPE program associates all nine of its pages with the same window handle. The following code excerpt, taken from the `SetupPage` function of the GEOSHAPE program, uses the `BKM_SETPAGEWINDOWHWND` message to associate a notebook page with a window handle:

```
WinSendMsg( hwndNotebook,
            BKM_SETPAGEWINDOWHWND,
            MPFROMLONG( ulNewPageID ),
            MPFROMHWND( hwndPage ) );
```

The first message parameter (`mp1`) contains the ID of the notebook page that will be associated with the window handle contained in second message parameter (`mp2`). In the GEOSHAPE program, all nine pages are associated with the same page window.

The BKM_QUERYPAGEID Message

Since the GEOSHAPE program uses the same page window for all nine of its pages, the program needs to know which page currently is being displayed so that it can display the appropriate information when the page window receives a `WM_PAINT` message. The GEOSHAPE program utilizes the `BKM_QUERYPAGEID` message to query the present page ID each time a `WM_PAINT` message is received.

In the following code excerpt, GEOSHAPE queries the current page ID:

```
ulCurPgID = (ULONG) WinSendMsg(
                    hwndNotebook,
                    BKM_QUERYPAGEID,
                    (MPARAM)0,                       /* reference page */
                    MPFROM2SHORT( BKA_TOP, 0 ) ); /*   order, style */
```

The BKM_QUERYPAGEID message can be used to retrieve the page ID that is in front of or behind some known page. The first message parameter (mp1) typically contains the ID of a reference page. The GEOSHAPE program is only interested in the page which is currently displayed, so mp1 is not needed. The page being displayed is specified using the BKA_TOP definition in the high word of the second message parameter (mp2). The low word of mp2 can be used to filter the page IDs that are returned (based on their tab attributes BKA_MAJOR or BKA_MINOR). The GEOSHAPE program does not set mp2, because it is querying the page presently being displayed and does not want tab attributes to interfere with the page query message.

The **BKN_PAGESELECTED** Notification Message

The notebook control window sends a BKN_PAGESELECTED notification message whenever a new page is brought to the top of the notebook. The GEOSHAPE program could intercept this message to keep track of which page is currently being displayed; however, the GEOSHAPE program has been written instead to query the ID of the presently displayed page when needed (as explained in the foregoing discussion of the BKM_QUERYPAGEID message).

The following code could be used to handle the BKN_PAGESELECTED notification message sent from a notebook control:

```
case WM_CONTROL:
    if (SHORT2FROMMP( mp1 ) == BKN_PAGESELECTED) {
        ulCurPgID = ((PPAGESELECTNOTIFY)PVOIDFROMMP( mp2 ))->ulPageIdNew;
        return (MRESULT)FALSE;
    }
```

In this code, the ulCurPgID variable is updated with the ID of the currently displayed page. The GEOSHAPE program could have used a ulCurPgID value found this way, instead of by a BKM_QUERYPAGEID message, during the processing of WM_PAINT messages.

To use the ulCurPgID variable to hold the current page that is being displayed, the GEOSHAPE program would need to make the ulCurPgID variable static, and the foregoing code would need to be added to intercept WM_CONTROL messages with an ID of BKN_PAGESELECTED.

Possible Problems with Closing Notebook Controls

The only PM controls that should handle WM_CLOSE messages are the file and font dialog boxes. These dialog boxes are stand-alone windows and are allowed to process the WM_CLOSE message when they are closed. During the processing of a WM_CLOSE message, a window will post a WM_QUIT message to terminate the handling of its message loop. When an application's message loop receives a WM_QUIT message, the application's windows are destroyed and the program exits.

Controls are typically children of a frame window and should not handle WM_CLOSE messages. A frame window will typically create and close many controls, and it is inappropriate for one of these controls to process a WM_CLOSE message. A WM_CLOSE message typically is intercepted to release resources; however, a control should process a WM_DESTROY message to handle any necessary "clean-up."

Unlike any of the other PM controls (except the file and font dialogs), in some versions of OS/2 the notebook control has been found to intercept WM_CLOSE messages. This does not cause problems with most uses that are made of notebook controls, except when the notebook control is used as a client window.

A frame will give control of the processing of a WM_CLOSE message to its client window. The notebook control intercepts the WM_CLOSE message and does not properly post a WM_QUIT message during the processing of the WM_CLOSE message. A frame window assumes that a WM_CLOSE message is properly handled by its client window, so it does not post its own WM_QUIT message when a client window is available to receive a WM_CLOSE message.

While the GEOSHAPE program has a control as a client window like many other programs presented in this book, it was found that the GEOSHAPE program needed to subclass its notebook control, because the notebook control is set up as a client window. A WM_CLOSE message sent to the notebook is intercepted and a WM_QUIT message is posted. Without the WM_QUIT message the GEOSHAPE window would remain on the desktop, because the program cannot be closed in a standard way.

CHAPTER 17
Container Controls

Another highly capable type of control that PM provides is a *container control*. A container control "contains" a set of *objects* or *container items*. Each object or container item has a *record* of data associated with it. The items and selected portions of their associated data can be displayed in a variety of *views*. The types of views that the container control makes available to provide different graphical formats for presenting items and data are *icon views*, *name views*, *text views*, *tree views*, and *details views*.

The container control handles all of the work that needs to be done to keep items and data organized within its container window. The container control allows the user to size its container window and will rearrange items and data as may be needed to accommodate a new window size. If a container window is not large enough to display all of the selected items and data, the container control will provide scroll bars to permit all of the selected items and data to be viewed. While a PM application can specify the spacing in pixels between adjacent container items, it is more common for the application to simply let the container control attend to such spacing calculations as need to be performed to provide a suitable display of items in a container window.

SELECTION, MANIPULATION, AND EDITING OF ITEMS

The container control provides a very robust interface for permitting the user to select one or more container items for use by a PM application. More than one item appearing in a container can be selected, regardless of whether they are displayed contiguously. Selected items are highlighted (drawn using a different color background) to indicate *selected state emphasis*.

247

The container control provides support for *direct manipulation* of selected items (commonly called "drag and drop"). Using direct manipulation, selected container items can be "dragged" from one container and "dropped" either into another container or onto one of the items of a container. During a drag and drop, a target container or item is often given *target emphasis* (typically a black border that is drawn around the target container or item).

The container control permits direct editing of any text data that is presented within a container window. Direct editing also can be used to modify column headings and container titles. To initiate direct editing, a common default permits the user simply to click on a text field while holding down the ALT key. Alternatively, an application can change the mouse and keyboard event sequences that initiate direct editing.

TYPES OF CONTAINER VIEWS

The various types of container views that are available for use by containers have different capabilities associated with them. However, in many basic respects, the various types of views behave quite similarly, as will become apparent in the following discussion, which deals with the characteristics of icon views, name views, text views, tree views, and details views individually.

Icon View

The icon view is the default view that the container control uses. The icon view displays icons or bitmaps, either of which can be labeled with text. The text consists of one or more lines located beneath the icons or bitmaps. The text typically explains the meaning of its associated icon or bitmap.

An icon view that contains system icons and pointers is shown in Figure 17.1. This view is generated by an example program called ICONS, discussed later in this chapter. The ICONS program can display views other than the default icon view, such as the name view and the text view that are shown in subsequent figures in this section.

When an application uses an icon view, it can choose to let the container arrange all of the items that are to appear within a container window. The container will arrange the items horizontally across the container window, with equal spacing between adjacent items. If all of the items cannot fit within a single row, additional rows will be used as needed.

Name View

The name view is very similar to the icon view in that it displays either icons or bitmaps, together with corresponding text fields. Text is presented to the right of the icon or bitmap.

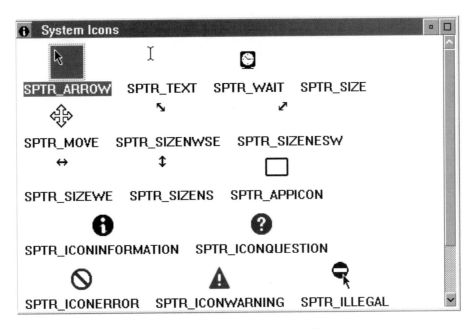

FIGURE 17.1 An icon view displayed by the ICONS program.

A PM application that uses a name view can elect to display the items using a *flowed name view* or a *nonflowed name view*. In a nonflowed view, items will be arranged from top to bottom. Figure 17.2 illustrates a nonflowed name view that is generated by the ICONS program. In a flowed view, items are arranged horizontally across the container window, with equal spacing between adjacent items. If all of the items cannot fit within a single row, additional rows will be used as needed. Figure 17.3 illustrates a flowed name view that is generated by the ICONS program.

Text View

The text view permits only text strings to be presented as container items. There is no set limit on the number of characters or lines in each text string. All text strings are left-justified.

Like the name view, the text view supports both flowed and nonflowed arrangements of items. In a nonflowed view, text strings will be displayed in a single column (top to bottom), even if scroll bars must be added to "extend" the view. Figure 17.4 illustrates a nonflowed text view that is generated by the ICONS program. In a flowed view, text strings are arranged from the top of the window and extending downward until the bottom of the window is reached, whereupon additional columns will be used as needed. Figure 17.5 illustrates a flowed text view that is generated by the ICONS program.

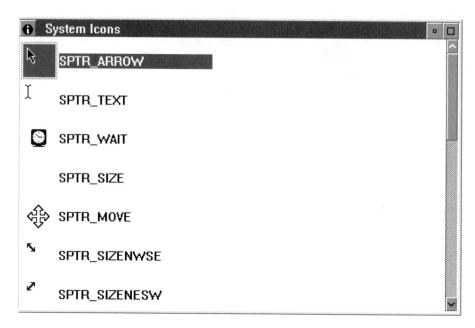

FIGURE 17.2   A nonflowed name view displayed by the ICONS program.

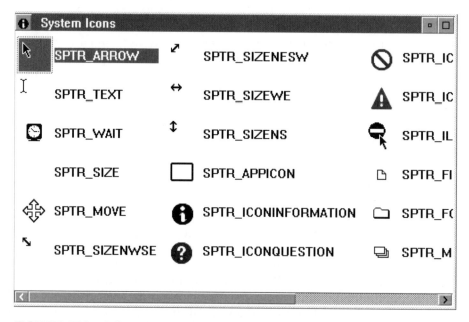

FIGURE 17.3   A flowed name view displayed by the ICONS program.

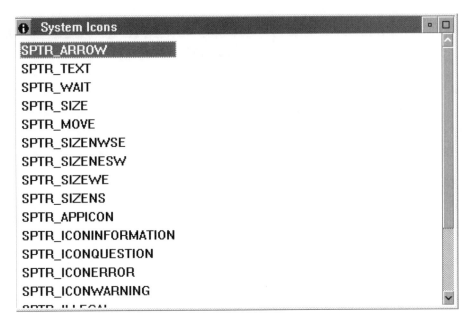

FIGURE 17.4 A nonflowed text view displayed by the ICONS program.

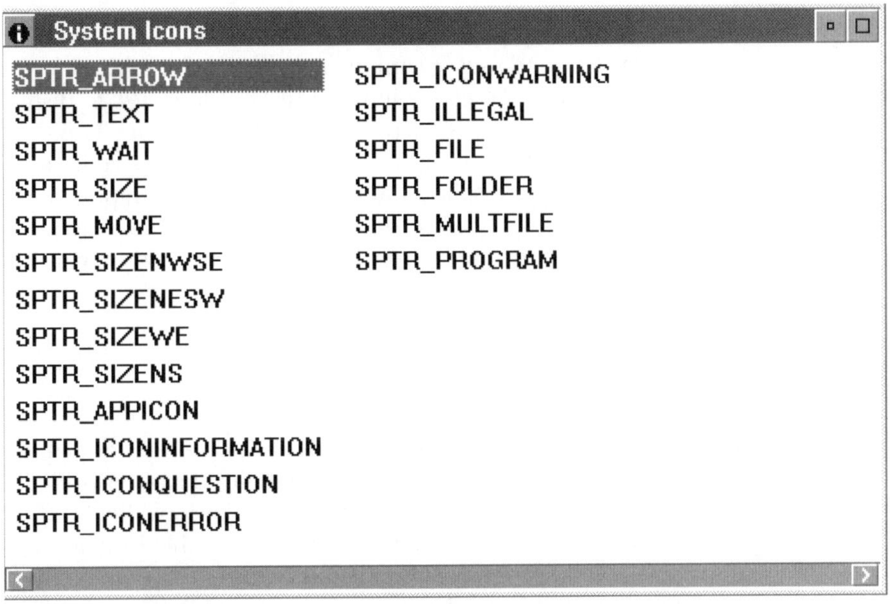

FIGURE 17.5 A flowed text view displayed by the ICONS program.

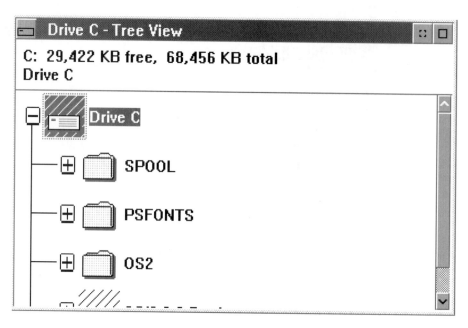

FIGURE 17.6 Workplace Shell drive folder presenting a tree icon view of directories and files.

Tree View

The tree view can be used by applications that need to display items that have a hierarchical nature. An example that utilizes a tree view to display files that are located on a particular disk drive is presented in Figure 17.6.

An advantage of using a tree view is that it permits an application to expand and collapse displayed items to enhance or simplify the display of data. The tree view supports three different ways to display data: a *tree icon view*, a *tree text view*, and a *tree name view*. Figure 17.6 uses a tree icon view to create its display of directories and files.

Details View

The details view is the most powerful and flexible view available to a container control. The additional power and flexibility that is provided by the details view comes from its ability to display the various fields of an item's data simultaneously, regardless of the character of the format that is needed to display each field properly. The various fields of data can be displayed as icons, bitmaps, text, numbers, dates, or times. In addition to supporting the most diverse set of data formats, the details view permits data items to be drawn in columns that are given unique headings.

Index	Color	RGB	
7		0	
9		80	
12		8000	
13		8080	
10		800000	
11		800080	
14		808000	
8		808080	
15		cccccc	
1		ff	
4		ff00	
5		ffff	

FIGURE 17.7 A details view displayed by the OWNERDR program.

A details view presenting a list of colors that are made available by a system's graphics adapter is shown in Figure 17.7. This view is generated by an example program called OWNERDR, discussed later in this chapter.

An advantage of working with a details view is that an application can set up many columns that contain different types of data. An application can place a *split bar* between any two adjacent columns. A container control is allowed to have only one split bar.

The presence of a split bar causes a container control to treat the two areas that are segregated by the split bar separately, as if the segregated areas comprise "separate windows." Each of these windows can have its own scroll bars, if needed.

A further advantage of working with a details view is that an application can directly draw an item into a specified column (rather than having the item drawn automatically by the container). The direct drawing of an item uses the same owner-drawn item techniques that are discussed in Chapter 10, wherein the container sends WM_DRAWITEM messages to notify its owner window when and where to draw owner-drawn items.

THE ICONS PROGRAM

The ICONS example program uses a container control to display system icons and pointers, together with their corresponding ID names. The ICONS program initializes the container control to use an icon view. The ICONS program uses a context menu to permit a user to change the view that is displayed by the container. Views that are supported by the ICONS program include the icon, name, and text. Flowed or nonflowed arrangements can be used if either name or text views are selected.

The source code for the ICONS program is listed in the following five files:

ICONS.C

```
#define INCL_WIN
#include <os2.h>
#include "icons.h"


/* function prototypes */
INT main( VOID );
MRESULT EXPENTRY MyFrameProc( HWND, ULONG, MPARAM, MPARAM );
VOID InitCnr( HWND );

/* global variables */
PFNWP       OldFrameWndProc;
HWND        hwndCnr;  /* container window handle */
HWND        hwndMenu; /* context menu window handle */
SYSICONINFO aIconInfo[NUM_SYS_ICONS] = {
    SPTR_ARROW,          "SPTR_ARROW",
    SPTR_TEXT,           "SPTR_TEXT",
    SPTR_WAIT,           "SPTR_WAIT",
    SPTR_SIZE,           "SPTR_SIZE",
    SPTR_MOVE,           "SPTR_MOVE",
    SPTR_SIZENWSE,       "SPTR_SIZENWSE",
    SPTR_SIZENESW,       "SPTR_SIZENESW",
    SPTR_SIZEWE,         "SPTR_SIZEWE",
    SPTR_SIZENS,         "SPTR_SIZENS",
    SPTR_APPICON,        "SPTR_APPICON",
    SPTR_ICONINFORMATION, "SPTR_ICONINFORMATION",
    SPTR_ICONQUESTION,   "SPTR_ICONQUESTION",
    SPTR_ICONERROR,      "SPTR_ICONERROR",
    SPTR_ICONWARNING,    "SPTR_ICONWARNING",
    SPTR_ILLEGAL,        "SPTR_ILLEGAL",
    SPTR_FILE,           "SPTR_FILE",
    SPTR_FOLDER,         "SPTR_FOLDER",
    SPTR_MULTFILE,       "SPTR_MULTFILE",
    SPTR_PROGRAM,        "SPTR_PROGRAM"
};

INT main( VOID )
{
    HAB hab;                              /* PM anchor block handle     */
    HMQ hmq;                              /* Message queue handle       */
    HWND hwndFrame;                       /* Frame window handle        */
    QMSG qmsg;                            /* Message from message queue */
    FRAMECDATA fcd;
```

```
fcd.cb = sizeof(FRAMECDATA);              /* length of structure        */
fcd.flCreateFlags = FCF_TITLEBAR          /* create: title bar control  */
                  | FCF_SYSMENU           /* system menu control        */
                  | FCF_SIZEBORDER        /* sizeborders                */
                  | FCF_MINMAX            /* min and max buttons        */
                  | FCF_SHELLPOSITION     /* shell decides window pos   */
                  | FCF_TASKLIST;         /* title added to switch list */
fcd.hmodResources = NULLHANDLE;           /* handle to a module         */
fcd.idResources = 0;                      /* identifier for the frame   */


hab = WinInitialize( 0 );

hmq = WinCreateMsgQueue( hab, 0 );

hwndFrame = WinCreateWindow(
            HWND_DESKTOP,      /* parent window is the desktop          */
            WC_FRAME,          /* class name                            */
            "System Icons",    /* text added to title bar               */
            0,                 /* window style                          */
            0, 0, 0, 0,        /* ignored, FCF_SHELLPOSITION was set    */
            NULLHANDLE,        /* no owner window                       */
            HWND_TOP,          /* top of Desktop's children             */
            0,                 /* ID number for frame resources         */
            &fcd,              /* control data                          */
            NULL );            /* no presentation parameters            */

WinSendMsg(
   hwndFrame,
   WM_SETICON,
   (MPARAM)WinQuerySysPointer( HWND_DESKTOP, SPTR_ICONINFORMATION, FALSE ),
   NULL );

hwndCnr = WinCreateWindow(
            hwndFrame,        /* parent window handle         */
            WC_CONTAINER,     /* Window class                 */
            NULL,             /* no window text               */
            CCS_AUTOPOSITION  /* window style                 */
            | CCS_READONLY,
            0, 0, 0, 0,       /* frame formats client         */
            hwndFrame,        /* owner                        */
            HWND_BOTTOM,      /* Z-order                      */
            FID_CLIENT,       /* ID                           */
            NULL,             /* no control data              */
            NULL);            /* no presentation parms        */

InitCnr( hwndCnr );

OldFrameWndProc = WinSubclassWindow( hwndFrame, MyFrameProc );

/* load context menu */
hwndMenu = WinLoadMenu( HWND_OBJECT, NULLHANDLE, ID_CONTEXTMENU );

WinShowWindow( hwndFrame, TRUE );
```

```
    if ( hwndFrame && hwndCnr )
        while (WinGetMsg( hab, &qmsg, NULLHANDLE, 0, 0 ))
            WinDispatchMsg( hab, &qmsg );

    WinDestroyWindow( hwndFrame );
    WinDestroyMsgQueue( hmq );
    WinTerminate( hab );

    return 0;
} /* end of main */


MRESULT EXPENTRY MyFrameProc( HWND hwnd, ULONG msg, MPARAM mp1, MPARAM mp2 )
{
    switch (msg) {

    case WM_COMMAND:
      { CNRINFO cnrinfo;

        switch (SHORT1FROMMP( mp1 )) {

        case IDM_ICONVIEW:
            cnrinfo.flWindowAttr = CV_ICON;
            break;

        case IDM_NAME_FLOWED:
            cnrinfo.flWindowAttr = CV_NAME | CV_FLOW;
            break;

        case IDM_NAME_NONFLOWED:
            cnrinfo.flWindowAttr = CV_NAME;
            break;

        case IDM_TEXT_FLOWED:
            cnrinfo.flWindowAttr = CV_TEXT | CV_FLOW;
            break;

        case IDM_TEXT_NONFLOWED:
            cnrinfo.flWindowAttr = CV_TEXT;
            break;

        default:
            return (MRESULT)(*OldFrameWndProc)( hwnd, msg, mp1, mp2 );
        }

        WinSendMsg( hwndCnr,
                    CM_SETCNRINFO,
                    &cnrinfo,
                    MPFROMLONG( CMA_FLWINDOWATTR ) );
      } break;

    case WM_CONTROL:

        switch (SHORT2FROMMP( mp1 )) {
```

```
        case CN_CONTEXTMENU:
          { POINTL pt;

            WinQueryPointerPos( HWND_DESKTOP, &pt );
            WinPopupMenu( HWND_DESKTOP,
                          hwnd,
                          hwndMenu,
                          (SHORT)pt.x,
                          (SHORT)pt.y,
                          IDM_ICONVIEW,
                          PU_NONE | PU_SELECTITEM | PU_MOUSEBUTTON1 |
                          PU_MOUSEBUTTON2 | PU_KEYBOARD );


          } return (MRESULT)FALSE;
        }
        break;
      }

    return (MRESULT)(*OldFrameWndProc)( hwnd, msg, mp1, mp2 );
} /* end of MyFrameProc */


VOID InitCnr(HWND hwnd)
{

    PRECORDCORE     pRecordCore, pStartingRecordCore;
    RECORDINSERT    recordInsert;
    PSYSICONINFO    pIconInfo;
    ULONG           i;

    pRecordCore = WinSendMsg(
                    hwnd,
                    CM_ALLOCRECORD,
                    0,                              /* No additional bytes */
                    MPFROMLONG( NUM_SYS_ICONS ) );

    pStartingRecordCore = pRecordCore;
    pIconInfo = (PSYSICONINFO)&aIconInfo;

    for (i = 0; i < NUM_SYS_ICONS; i++) {

        pRecordCore->cb = sizeof(RECORDCORE);

        pRecordCore->hptrIcon = WinQuerySysPointer( HWND_DESKTOP,
                                                    pIconInfo->lIconID,
                                                    FALSE );

        pRecordCore->pszIcon = pRecordCore->pszName
            = pRecordCore->pszText = pIconInfo->pszIconName;

        pRecordCore = pRecordCore->preccNextRecord;
        ++pIconInfo;
    }
```

```
    recordInsert.cb = sizeof(RECORDINSERT);
    recordInsert.pRecordParent= NULL;
    recordInsert.pRecordOrder = (PRECORDCORE)CMA_END;
    recordInsert.zOrder = (USHORT)CMA_TOP;
    recordInsert.cRecordsInsert= NUM_SYS_ICONS;
    recordInsert.fInvalidateRecord = TRUE;

    WinSendMsg( hwnd,
            CM_INSERTRECORD,
            (PRECORDCORE)pStartingRecordCore,
            &recordInsert );

} /* end of InitCnr */
```

ICONS.H

```
#define ID_CONTEXTMENU      100

#define IDM_ICONVIEW        200
#define IDM_NAMEVIEW        201
#define IDM_TEXTVIEW        202

#define IDM_NAME_FLOWED     204
#define IDM_NAME_NONFLOWED  205

#define IDM_TEXT_FLOWED     206
#define IDM_TEXT_NONFLOWED  207

#define NUM_SYS_ICONS       19

typedef struct _SYSICONINFO
{
   LONG lIconID;
   PSZ  pszIconName;
} SYSICONINFO;
typedef SYSICONINFO *PSYSICONINFO;
```

ICONS.RC

```
#include <os2.h>
#include "icons.h"

MENU ID_CONTEXTMENU
   BEGIN
      MENUITEM "Icon View", IDM_ICONVIEW
      SUBMENU "Name View",  IDM_NAMEVIEW
         BEGIN
            MENUITEM "Flowed",     IDM_NAME_FLOWED
            MENUITEM "Non-flowed", IDM_NAME_NONFLOWED
         END
```

```
        SUBMENU "Text View", IDM_TEXTVIEW
            BEGIN
                MENUITEM "Flowed",      IDM_TEXT_FLOWED
                MENUITEM "Non-flowed", IDM_TEXT_NONFLOWED
            END
    END
```

ICONS.DEF

```
NAME ICONS WINDOWAPI

DESCRIPTION 'Container Control Example Program'

CODE    MOVEABLE
DATA    MOVEABLE MULTIPLE

HEAPSIZE  10240
STACKSIZE 24576
```

ICONS.MAK

```
all : icons.exe

icons.exe : icons.obj icons.def icons.res
        link386 /PM:PM icons,,,,icons.def;
        rc icons.res

icons.res : icons.rc icons.h
        rc -r icons.rc

icons.obj : icons.c icons.h
        icc /C /O+ /Ss /W3 .\$*.c
```

Creating a Container Window

The ICONS program creates a notebook container using the `WinCreate-Window` API. Among the parameters used by this API call is the value `WC_CONTAINER`, which identifies the name of the container window class. The `CCS_AUTOPOSITION` and `CCS_READONLY` window style flags are used also. The `CCS_AUTOPOSITION` style flag tells the container control to rearrange container data items automatically when one of the following events takes place: the window size changes, the data items within the container window change, a font change takes place, or the window title text changes. The `CCS_AUTOPOSITION` flag applies only when the icon view is being used. The `CCS_READONLY` flag informs the container control that this container is to be read-only. When the `CCS_READONLY` flag is set, the direct editing facilities of the container are turned off.

The following code excerpt shows the call made by the ICONS program to create a container window:

```
hwndCnr = WinCreateWindow(
           hwndFrame,              /* parent window handle   */
           WC_CONTAINER,           /* Window class           */
           NULL,                   /* no window text         */
           CCS_AUTOPOSITION        /* window style           */
           | CCS_READONLY,
           0, 0, 0, 0,             /* frame formats client   */
           hwndFrame,              /* owner                  */
           HWND_BOTTOM,            /* Z-order                */
           FID_CLIENT,             /* ID                     */
           NULL,                   /* no control data        */
           NULL );                 /* no presentation parms  */
```

Notice that in this API call `FID_CLIENT` is used as a window ID. This allows the frame to position the container window as if it were a client window.

Once a container window has been created, the application must set up the items that are to be displayed in the container. Each item is stored in a record and is added to the container by using the `CM_INSERTRECORD` message.

Allocating Container Records

Container records are stored in a `RECORDCORE` data structure, which is defined as follows in the public header file `PMSTDDLG.H`:

```
typedef struct _RECORDCORE {
    ULONG                 cb;
    ULONG                 flRecordAttr;
    POINTL                ptlIcon;
    struct _RECORDCORE    *preccNextRecord;
    PSZ                   pszIcon;
    HPOINTER              hptrIcon;
    HPOINTER              hptrMiniIcon;
    HBITMAP               hbmBitmap;
    HBITMAP               hbmMiniBitmap;
    PTREEITEMDESC         pTreeItemDesc;
    PSZ                   pszText;
    PSZ                   pszName;
    PSZ                   pszTree;
} RECORDCORE;
```

The ICONS program uses system icons and pointers as items for its container window. Each icon and pointer is paired with its ID name. The ICONS program allocates one record—a `RECORDCORE` data structure—for each system icon and pointer. The ICONS program allocates all of the needed RECORDCORE structures by sending a single CM_ALLOCRECORD message to the container window, as is illustrated by the following ICONS program code excerpt:

```
pRecordCore = WinSendMsg(
              hwnd,
              CM_ALLOCRECORD,
              0,                              /* No additional bytes */
              MPFROMLONG( NUM_SYS_ICONS ) );
```

The second message parameter (mp2) in this code excerpt uses a constant, NUM_SYS_ICONS, to specify the number of needed RECORDCORE structures. The NUM_SYS_ICONS value equals the number of system icons plus the number of pointers that are used by the ICONS program as container items. Presently NUM_SYS_ICONS is set equal to 19, since there are a total of 19 available system icons and pointers.

The first message parameter (mp1) to the foregoing call is intended to be used to specify an additional allocation of bytes for each record. This parameter is useful when the container data items have more information associated with them than can be held in a RECORDCORE data structure. However, the ICONS program uses a value of zero for the mp1 parameter, because no additional space is required.

The CM_ALLOCRECORD message will return a pointer to the starting RECORDCORE data structure. The RECORDCORE data structures are linked together in a linked list through the preccNextRecord field of the RECORDCORE data structure. The last RECORDCORE data structure in the linked list contains a NULL pointer in the preccNextRecord field.

Storing Information in Container Records

The ICONS program updates each RECORDCORE structure in the linked list that is returned by the CM_ALLOCRECORD message so that it contains a handle to an icon or pointer, together with a text string that represents the corresponding ID name. Once the linked list is updated, a pointer to the first RECORDCORE structure of the linked list is given to the container window with a CM_INSERTRECORD message. The container goes through the linked list and sets up a separate item for each RECORDCORE structure that is contained in the list.

The following code excerpt illustrates how the ICONS program updates each RECORDCORE data structure in the linked list that was returned by sending the CM_ALLOCRECORD message:

```
for (i = 0; i < NUM_SYS_ICONS; i++) {

    pRecordCore->cb = sizeof(RECORDCORE);
```

```
    pRecordCore->hptrIcon = WinQuerySysPointer( HWND_DESKTOP,
                                                pIconInfo->lIconID,
                                                FALSE );
    pRecordCore->pszIcon = pRecordCore->pszName
       = pRecordCore->pszText = pIconInfo->pszIconName;

    pRecordCore = pRecordCore->preccNextRecord;
    ++pIconInfo;
}
```

A handle to each icon or pointer is obtained by using the `WinQuerySysPointer` API, which will return a handle to the icon or pointer that is associated with the ID that was used as a parameter to the API.

The ICONS program defines a data structure called `SYSICONINFO` in its `ICONS.H` file. An array of `SYSICONINFO` data structures is used to store descriptions of available system icons and pointers. The `SYSICONINFO` data structure is defined as follows:

```
typedef struct _SYSICONINFO {
    LONG         lIconID;
    PSZ          pszIconName;
} SYSICONINFO;
```

The `SYSICONINFO` data structure contains an integer icon ID that is used by PM (an `SPTR_` constant) and a pointer to a text string that represents an icon ID name. The array of the `SYSICONINFO` data structures is stored as global data as follows:

```
SYSICONINFO aIconInfo[NUM_SYS_ICONS] = {
    SPTR_ARROW,              "SPTR_ARROW",
    SPTR_TEXT,               "SPTR_TEXT",
    SPTR_WAIT,               "SPTR_WAIT",
    SPTR_SIZE,               "SPTR_SIZE",
    SPTR_MOVE,               "SPTR_MOVE",
    SPTR_SIZENWSE,           "SPTR_SIZENWSE",
    SPTR_SIZENESW,           "SPTR_SIZENESW",
    SPTR_SIZEWE,             "SPTR_SIZEWE",
    SPTR_SIZENS,             "SPTR_SIZENS",
    SPTR_APPICON,            "SPTR_APPICON",
    SPTR_ICONINFORMATION,    "SPTR_ICONINFORMATION",
    SPTR_ICONQUESTION,       "SPTR_ICONQUESTION",
    SPTR_ICONERROR,          "SPTR_ICONERROR",
    SPTR_ICONWARNING,        "SPTR_ICONWARNING",
    SPTR_ILLEGAL,            "SPTR_ILLEGAL",
    SPTR_FILE,               "SPTR_FILE",
    SPTR_FOLDER,             "SPTR_FOLDER",
    SPTR_MULTFILE,           "SPTR_MULTFILE",
    SPTR_PROGRAM,            "SPTR_PROGRAM"
};
```

The ICONS programs uses this array when updating each RECORDCORE structure in the linked list that was returned by the CM_ALLOCRECORD message. The value in the lIconId field of the aIconInfo array is used in a call to WinQuerySysPointer. The pszIconName field of the aIconInfo array is stored in the pszIcon, pszName, and pszText fields of the RECORDCORE structure that is currently being updated. The pszIcon, pszName, and pszText fields are used for the icon, name, and text views, respectively.

Inserting Container Records

Once all of the records have been updated in the linked list, the ICONS program inserts them into the container, using a CM_INSERTRECORD message. Because a pointer to the linked list (pStartingRecordCore) is used as a parameter in the message, only one message is needed to insert all of the items into the ICONS container. The following code excerpt inserts the container records into the ICONS container:

```
recordInsert.cb = sizeof(RECORDINSERT);
recordInsert.pRecordParent= NULL;
recordInsert.pRecordOrder = (PRECORDCORE)CMA_END;
recordInsert.zOrder = (USHORT)CMA_TOP;
recordInsert.cRecordsInsert= NUM_SYS_ICONS;
recordInsert.fInvalidateRecord = TRUE;


WinSendMsg( hwnd,
            CM_INSERTRECORD,
            (PRECORDCORE)pStartingRecordCore,
            &recordInsert );
```

The second message parameter (mp2) is a pointer to a RECORDINSERT data structure. The RECORDINSERT data structure contains general information about the records that are being inserted as well as a count of the number of records that are being inserted. The ICONS program uses NUM_SYS_ICONS for the number of items being inserted.

Once items have been inserted into a container, the items will be displayed as soon as the container window is made visible. By default, the container data items are displayed using the icon view. The system icons used by the ICONS program will be displayed with corresponding text string icon IDs directly beneath them.

Using a Context Menu

The ICONS program allows the user to dynamically change views by using a pop-up menu that lists icon, name, and text views as menu items. The ICONS program uses the pop-up menu as a *context menu* to present the list of views that are available to the user. A context menu is a pop-up menu that contains a list of actions that are applicable to selected container items.

When the user requests a context menu by using the mouse or keyboard, PM sends a WM_CONTEXTMENU message. The system value SV_CONTEXTMENU defines a mouse event that instructs a context menu to be displayed. The keyboard event that instructs a context menu to be displayed is defined by the system value SV_CONTEXTMENUB. By default, the user can either click on "button two" of the mouse or press Shift-F10 to bring up a context menu.

When a context menu is instructed to appear, the container control receives a WM_CONTEXTMENU message. In response, the container sends its owner window a WM_CONTROL message with a CN_CONTEXTMENU notification code as a parameter.

Handling CN_CONTEXTMENU Messages

Upon receiving a CN_CONTEXTMENU notification message from the container control, the ICONS program will display a pop-up menu that allows the user to change container views. The following code excerpt from ICONS.C is used to handle CN_CONTEXTMENU notifications:

```
case WM_CONTROL:

    switch (SHORT2FROMMP( mp1 )) {

        case CN_CONTEXTMENU:
        { POINTL pt;

            WinQueryPointerPos( HWND_DESKTOP, &pt );

            WinPopupMenu( HWND_DESKTOP,
                          hwnd,
                          hwndMenu,
                          (SHORT)pt.x,
                          (SHORT)pt.y,
                          IDM_ICONVIEW,
                          PU_NONE | PU_SELECTITEM | PU_MOUSEBUTTON1 |
                          PU_MOUSEBUTTON2 | PU_KEYBOARD );

        } return (MRESULT)FALSE;
    }
    break;
```

In this code the menu handle hwndMenu was set using a call to WinLoadMenu in the main function. The WinLoadMenu API creates a menu from a menu template that is specified by the resource ID number ID_CONTEXTMENU in the ICONS.RC resource file, shown in the following code excerpt:

```
MENU ID_CONTEXTMENU
   BEGIN
      MENUITEM "Icon View", IDM_ICONVIEW
      SUBMENU  "Name View",  IDM_NAMEVIEW
         BEGIN
            MENUITEM "Flowed",      IDM_NAME_FLOWED
            MENUITEM "Non-flowed", IDM_NAME_NONFLOWED
         END
      SUBMENU "Text View",        IDM_TEXTVIEW
         BEGIN
            MENUITEM "Flowed",      IDM_TEXT_FLOWED
            MENUITEM "Non-flowed", IDM_TEXT_NONFLOWED
         END
   END
```

The `WinPopupMenu` API is used to display the context menu. The context menu allows the user to select an icon view, a name view, or a text view. If the chosen view is a name or text view, the user also must pick either a flowed or nonflowed arrangement for the container items.

Changing the Container View

When a context menu is used to select a view that is to be displayed by the ICONS program, a `WM_COMMAND` message is sent that contains the ID of the menu item selected. The ICONS program uses the following code to change the container view:

```
case WM_COMMAND:
 { CNRINFO cnrinfo;

    switch (SHORT1FROMMP( mp1 )) {

       case IDM_ICONVIEW:
          cnrinfo.flWindowAttr = CV_ICON;
          break;

       case IDM_NAME_FLOWED:
          cnrinfo.flWindowAttr = CV_NAME | CV_FLOW;
          break;

       case IDM_NAME_NONFLOWED:
          cnrinfo.flWindowAttr = CV_NAME;
          break;

       case IDM_TEXT_FLOWED:
          cnrinfo.flWindowAttr = CV_TEXT | CV_FLOW;
          break;
```

```
        case IDM_TEXT_NONFLOWED:
            cnrinfo.flWindowAttr = CV_TEXT;
            break;

        default:
            return (MRESULT)(*OldFrameWndProc)( hwnd, msg, mp1, mp2 );
    }

    WinSendMsg( hwndCnr,
                CM_SETCNRINFO,
                &cnrinfo,
                MPFROMLONG( CMA_FLWINDOWATTR ) );
} break;
```

A CM_SETCNRINFO message is used in this code to change the current container view. The first message parameter (mp1) is a pointer to a CNRINFO data structure, which is defined in PMSTDDLG.H, as follows:

```
typedef struct _CNRINFO {
    ULONG       cb;
    PVOID       pSortRecord;
    PFIELDINFO  pFieldInfoLast;
    PFIELDINFO  pFieldInfoObject;
    PSZ         pszCnrTitle;
    ULONG       flWindowAttr;
    POINTL      ptlOrigin;
    ULONG       cDelta;
    ULONG       cRecords;
    SIZEL       slBitmapOrIcon;
    SIZEL       slTreeBitmapOrIcon;
    HBITMAP     hbmExpanded;
    HBITMAP     hbmCollapsed;
    HPOINTER    hptrExpanded;
    HPOINTER    hptrCollapsed;
    LONG        cyLineSpacing;
    LONG        cxTreeIndent;
    LONG        cxTreeLine;
    ULONG       cFields;
    LONG        xVertSplitbar;
} CNRINFO;
```

The CM_SETCNRINFO message is sent by the ICONS program to change many aspects of a container window. The first message parameter (mp1) is set to point to the updated CNRINFO data structure. The ICONS program uses such a message to change window attributes. Based on the menu item selected, the ICONS program updates the flWindowAttr field of the CNRINFO data structure with flags that correspond to the view selected. The CMA_FLWINDOWATTR flag is used in the second message parameter (mp2) to inform the container control that the flWindowAttr field has been given new window attributes and that the container window should be repainted.

THE OWNERDR PROGRAM

The OWNERDR program uses a container control with a details view to display a table containing color indexes, color samples, and corresponding RGB values for physical colors that are available on a video adapter. The RGB values are displayed in hexadecimal notation so that intensities of the red, green, and blue color components are distinguishable.

The OWNERDR program utilizes the owner draw capabilities that are provided by the container control to permit the owner window to handle the drawing of the color samples. Each color sample is a filled rectangle that displays an available color. The owner window draws color samples, because container controls do not support a data type that permits different color samples to be displayed. An impractical alternative to the use of owner-drawn color samples is the use of separate bitmaps to represent each available color. While a bitmap is a data type that can be used to represent a color sample, assigning a bitmap to each available color sample is not practical on systems that have 256 colors or more, due to the enormous amount of memory that would be allocated.

The OWNERDR program's source code is listed in the following six files:

OWNERDR.C

```c
#define INCL_WIN
#define INCL_GPI
#include <os2.h>
#include "ownerdr.h"


/* function prototypes */
INT main( VOID );
MRESULT EXPENTRY MyFrameProc( HWND, ULONG, MPARAM, MPARAM );
VOID InitCnr( HWND );


/* global variables */
PFNWP OldFrameWndProc;
    LONG    alColors[256*2]; /* array holds index and RGB values */
    CHAR    aRGBs[256][10];  /* array to hold ascii RGBs          */

INT main( VOID )
{
    HAB  hab;
    HMQ  hmq;
    QMSG qmsg;
    HWND hwndFrame; /* frame window handle */
    HWND hwndCnr  ; /* container window handle */
    FRAMECDATA fcd;

    fcd.cb = sizeof(FRAMECDATA);           /* length of structure      */
    fcd.flCreateFlags = FCF_TITLEBAR       /* create: title bar control */
                    | FCF_SYSMENU          /*          system menu control */
                    | FCF_SIZEBORDER       /*          sizeborders       */
```

```
                    | FCF_MINMAX        /*          min and max buttons */
                    | FCF_SHELLPOSITION /* shell decides window pos     */
                    | FCF_ICON          /* frame has an icon            */
                    | FCF_TASKLIST;     /* title added to switch list   */

    fcd.hmodResources = NULLHANDLE;     /* Handle to a module           */
    fcd.idResources   = ID_FRAMEWND;    /* identifier for the frame     */

    hab = WinInitialize( 0 );
    hmq = WinCreateMsgQueue( hab, 0 );

    hwndFrame = WinCreateWindow(
                HWND_DESKTOP,            /* parent window is the desktop  */
                WC_FRAME,                /* class name                    */
                "Container Example",     /* text added to title bar       */
                0,                       /* window style                  */
                0,0,0,0,                 /* ignored, FCF_SHELLPOSITION used */
                NULLHANDLE,              /* no owner window               */
                HWND_TOP,                /* Top of Desktop's children     */
                ID_FRAMEWND,             /* ID number for frame resources */
                &fcd,                    /* data unique for frame windows */
                NULL );                  /* no presentation parameters    */

    /* Now create the container window. */
    hwndCnr = WinCreateWindow(
                hwndFrame,       /* parent window handle    */
                WC_CONTAINER,    /* window class            */
                NULL,            /* no window text          */
                CCS_AUTOPOSITION /* window style            */
                | CCS_READONLY,
                0, 0, 0, 0,      /* frame formats client    */
                hwndFrame,       /* owner                   */
                HWND_TOP,        /* Z-order                 */
                FID_CLIENT,      /* ID                      */
                NULL,            /* no control data         */
                NULL );          /* no presentation parms   */

    InitCnr( hwndCnr );

    OldFrameWndProc = WinSubclassWindow( hwndFrame, MyFrameProc );

    WinShowWindow( hwndFrame, TRUE );

    if (hwndFrame && hwndCnr)
       while (WinGetMsg( hab, &qmsg, NULLHANDLE, 0, 0 ))
          WinDispatchMsg( hab, &qmsg );

    WinDestroyWindow( hwndFrame );
    WinDestroyMsgQueue( hmq );
    WinTerminate( hab );

    return 0;
} /* end of main */
```

```
MRESULT EXPENTRY MyFrameProc( HWND hwnd, ULONG msg, MPARAM mp1, MPARAM mp2 )
{

   if (msg == WM_DRAWITEM) {
      PCNRDRAWITEMINFO pCnrDrawItemInfo;
      PUSERRECORD pUserRecord;

      pCnrDrawItemInfo = (PCNRDRAWITEMINFO)((POWNERITEM)mp2)->hItem;
      pUserRecord = (PUSERRECORD)(pCnrDrawItemInfo->pRecord);

      /* NOTE: pUserRecord will be NULL if this message is for */
      /* the column heading.                                   */
      if ((ULONG)pUserRecord) {

         /* Put the PS into RGB mode */
         GpiCreateLogColorTable( ((POWNERITEM)mp2)->hps,
                                 LCOL_RESET,
                                 LCOLF_RGB,
                                 0L,
                                 0L,
                                 NULL ) ;

         WinFillRect(
             ((POWNERITEM)mp2)->hps,
             &((POWNERITEM)mp2)->rclItem,
             ((PUSERRECORD)(pCnrDrawItemInfo->pRecord))->ur_rgbValue );

         return 0;
      }
   }

   return (MRESULT)(*OldFrameWndProc)( hwnd, msg, mp1, mp2 );
} /* end of MyFrameProc */


VOID InitCnr( HWND hwnd )
{
   CNRINFO   cnrinfo;
   PUSERRECORD      pStartingUserRecord, pUserRecord;
   RECORDINSERT     recordInsert;
   PFIELDINFO       pStartingFieldInfo, pFieldInfo;
   FIELDINFOINSERT  fieldInfoInsert;
   PCOLORINFO       pci;
   HPS   hps;
   LONG  lColors;
   ULONG i;


   hps = WinGetPS( hwnd );

   lColors = GpiQueryRealColors(
              hps,
              LCOLOPT_INDEX,       /* Return index and RGB */
```

```
                     0L,                    /* Start color index   */
                     (LONG)256*2,           /* Max array elements   */
                     (PLONG)alColors );     /* Area to fill         */

    WinReleasePS( hps );

    lColors /= 2;

    cnrinfo.cb = sizeof(CNRINFO);
    cnrinfo.pszCnrTitle = "Physical Color Table";
    cnrinfo.cFields = 3;

    cnrinfo.flWindowAttr = CV_DETAIL
                         | CA_CONTAINERTITLE
                         | CA_TITLESEPARATOR
                         | CA_DETAILSVIEWTITLES;

    WinSendMsg( hwnd,
                CM_SETCNRINFO,
                &cnrinfo,
                MPFROMLONG( CMA_FLWINDOWATTR | CMA_CNRTITLE ) );

    pUserRecord = WinSendMsg(
                    hwnd,
                    CM_ALLOCRECORD,
                    MPFROMLONG( (LONG)(sizeof(USERRECORD) -
                                       sizeof(RECORDCORE)) ),
                    MPFROMLONG( lColors ) );

    /* Save pointer to the first record */
    pStartingUserRecord = pUserRecord;

    pci = (PCOLORINFO)&alColors;

    for(i = 0; i < lColors; i++) {

        pUserRecord->recordCore.cb = sizeof(RECORDCORE);
        pUserRecord->ur_lIndex = pci->ci_lIndex;
        pUserRecord->ur_rgbValue = pci->ci_rgbValue;

        /***********************************************************************/
        /* Currently, the container will only display integer values in    */
        /* decimal format. We use "sprintf" to convert the decimal value   */
        /* into an ascii string. The ascii string will display the RGB     */
        /* in HEX format.                                                  */
        /***********************************************************************/
        sprintf( aRGBs[i], "%lx", pci->ci_rgbValue );
        pUserRecord->pszRGB = aRGBs[i];

        pUserRecord = (PUSERRECORD)pUserRecord->recordCore.preccNextRecord;
        ++pci;

    }
```

```
    recordInsert.cb = sizeof(RECORDINSERT);
    recordInsert.pRecordParent= NULL;
    recordInsert.pRecordOrder = (PRECORDCORE)CMA_END;
    recordInsert.zOrder = (USHORT)CMA_TOP;
    recordInsert.cRecordsInsert=(USHORT)lColors;
    recordInsert.fInvalidateRecord = TRUE;

    WinSendMsg( hwnd,
                CM_INSERTRECORD,
                (PRECORDCORE)pStartingUserRecord,
                &recordInsert );

    pFieldInfo = WinSendMsg( hwnd,
                            CM_ALLOCDETAILFIELDINFO,
                            MPFROMLONG(3),
                            NULL );

    pStartingFieldInfo = pFieldInfo;

    pFieldInfo->cb = sizeof(FIELDINFO);

    pFieldInfo->flData = CFA_HORZSEPARATOR | CFA_CENTER |
                        CFA_SEPARATOR | CFA_ULONG;
    pFieldInfo->flTitle = CFA_CENTER;
    pFieldInfo->pTitleData = "Index";
    pFieldInfo->offStruct = FIELDOFFSET( USERRECORD, ur_lIndex );
    pFieldInfo = pFieldInfo->pNextFieldInfo;

    pFieldInfo->cb = sizeof(FIELDINFO);
    pFieldInfo->flData = CFA_HORZSEPARATOR | CFA_CENTER |
                        CFA_SEPARATOR | CFA_OWNER;
    pFieldInfo->flTitle = CFA_CENTER;
    pFieldInfo->pTitleData = "Color";
    pFieldInfo = pFieldInfo->pNextFieldInfo;

    pFieldInfo->cb = sizeof(FIELDINFO);
    pFieldInfo->flData = CFA_HORZSEPARATOR | CFA_CENTER |
                        CFA_SEPARATOR | CFA_STRING;
    pFieldInfo->flTitle = CFA_CENTER;
    pFieldInfo->pTitleData = "RGB";
    pFieldInfo->offStruct = FIELDOFFSET( USERRECORD, pszRGB );

    fieldInfoInsert.cb = (ULONG)(sizeof(FIELDINFOINSERT));
    fieldInfoInsert.pFieldInfoOrder = (PFIELDINFO)CMA_FIRST;
    fieldInfoInsert.cFieldInfoInsert = (SHORT)(3);
    fieldInfoInsert.fInvalidateFieldInfo = TRUE;

    WinSendMsg( hwnd,
                CM_INSERTDETAILFIELDINFO,
                MPFROMP(pStartingFieldInfo),
                MPFROMP(&fieldInfoInsert) );

} /* end of InitCnr */
```

OWNERDR.H

```
#define ID_FRAMEWND      100

typedef struct _COLORINFO
{
   LONG ci_lIndex;
   LONG ci_rgbValue;
} COLORINFO;
typedef COLORINFO *PCOLORINFO;

typedef struct _USERRECORD
{
  RECORDCORE recordCore;
  LONG       ur_lIndex;
  LONG       ur_rgbValue;
  PSZ        pszRGB;
} USERRECORD;


typedef USERRECORD *PUSERRECORD;
```

OWNERDR.RC

```
#include <os2.h>
#include "ownerdr.h"

ICON ID_FRAMEWND ownerdr.ico
```

OWNERDR.DEF

```
NAME OWNERDR WINDOWAPI

DESCRIPTION 'Owner Drawn Container Example'

CODE MOVEABLE
DATA MOVEABLE MULTIPLE

HEAPSIZE  10240
STACKSIZE 24576
```

OWNERDR.MAK

```
all : ownerdr.exe

ownerdr.exe : ownerdr.obj ownerdr.def ownerdr.res
        link386 /PM·PM ownerdr,,,,ownerdr.def;
        rc ownerdr.res
```

```
ownerdr.res : ownerdr.rc ownerdr.ico ownerdr.h
        rc -r ownerdr.rc

ownerdr.obj : ownerdr.c ownerdr.h
        icc /C /O+ /Ss /W3 .$*.c
```

OWNERDR.ICO

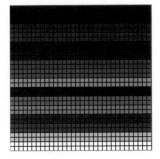

VGA Independent

OWNERDR.ICO file, containing the icon for the OWNERDR program.

Starting Up in Details View

Unless changed, a container window will use the icon view by default. To change the default view, the OWNERDR program overrides the default icon view by setting the flag CV_DETAIL in the CNRINFO structure that is used in a CM_SETCNRINFO message. The OWNERDR program uses this message in the same manner as does the ICONS program when it switches views.

The following code excerpt, taken from the OWNERDR program, initializes the container window to use a details view:

```
cnrinfo.cb = sizeof(CNRINFO);
cnrinfo.pszCnrTitle = "Physical Color Table";
cnrinfo.cFields = 3;

cnrinfo.flWindowAttr = CV_DETAIL
                     | CA_CONTAINERTITLE
                     | CA_TITLESEPARATOR
                     | CA_DETAILSVIEWTITLES;

WinSendMsg( hwnd,
          CM_SETCNRINFO,
          &cnrinfo,
          MPFROMLONG( CMA_FLWINDOWATTR | CMA_CNRTITLE ) );
```

The flags that are used to set the `flWindowAttr` field in this code are the following:

- `CV_DETAIL`   Displays container items using a details view.
- `CA_CONTAINERTITLE`   Displays a title at the top of the container window. Title text is taken from the `pszCnrTitle` field of the `CNRINFO` data structure.
- `CA_TITLESEPARATOR`   Includes a horizontal line to separate the container title and columns.
- `CA_DETAILSVIEWTITLES`   Displays column headings, the text for which is taken from the `pTitleData` field of the `FIELDINFO` data structure that is associated with each column.

Message parameter two (mp2) contains the `CMA_FLWINDOWATTR` and `CMA_CNRTITLE` flags. The `CMA_FLWINDOWATTR` flag tells the container control to update the window attributes. The `CMA_CNRTITLE` flag tells the container to update the title text.

Allocating Larger Container Records

The OWNERDR program needs to store the color index and RGB values for each color in a record. The default data structure that is used to hold container records is the `RECORDCORE` data structure. Because the `RECORDCORE` data structure is not sufficient to accommodate the needs of the OWNERDR program, a `CM_ALLOCRECORD` message is used to allocate container records that have extended bytes.

The OWNERDR program defines its own record data structure, called `USERRECORD`, that is a superset of the standard `RECORDCORE` structure. The `USERRECORD` data structure is defined in `OWNERDR.H`, as follows:

```
typedef struct _USERRECORD {
    RECORDCORE    recordCore;
    LONG          ur_lIndex;
    LONG          ur_rgbValue;
    PSZ           pszRGB;
} USERRECORD;
```

The `ur_lIndex` field of the `USERRECORD` data structure holds a color index value. The `ur_rgbValue` field of the `USERRECORD` data structure holds an RGB value that corresponds to the color index value. The RGB value is displayed in hexadecimal format so that the user can easily see the red, green, and blue intensities of a given color.

Because a container will always display integer values in a decimal format, the OWNERDR program overcomes this shortcoming by using the `sprintf` C runtime library function to print the RGB value in hexadecimal format to a buffer. OWNERDR retrieves the contents of the buffer and displays the RGB value as a text string that is stored in the `pszRGB` field of the `USERRECORD` data structure.

The following code excerpt is used by the OWNERDR program to provide needed record data structures that are large enough to hold extended data:

```
pUserRecord = WinSendMsg(
                hwnd,
                CM_ALLOCRECORD,
                MPFROMLONG( (LONG)(sizeof(USERRECORD) -
                                    sizeof(RECORDCORE)) ),
                MPFROMLONG( lColors ) );
```

In this code, the first message parameter (`mp1`) represents the amount of additional memory, in bytes, that is needed for each record. The second message parameter (`mp2`) is the number of record structures that are allocated. The `lColors` variable contains the number of physical colors that are supported by the system.

Allocating FIELDINFO Data Structures

When using the details view, an application must allocate one `FIELDINFO` data structure for each column that it plans to support. The `FIELDINFO` data structure is defined in `PMSTDDLG.H`, as follows:

```
typedef struct _FIELDINFO {
    ULONG               cb;
    ULONG               flData;
    ULONG               flTitle;
    PVOID               pTitleData;
    ULONG               offStruct;
    PVOID               pUserData;
    struct _FIELDINFO   *pNextFieldInfo;
    ULONG               cxWidth;
} FIELDINFO;
```

The `FIELDINFO` data structures are allocated by using a `CM_ALLOC-DETAILFIELDINFO` message. The OWNERDR program contains three columns: a column for the color index value, a column that contains individual rectangles that will be filled with the different available colors, and a third column that contains RGB values. The following code excerpt allocates three `FIELDINFO` data structures for the three columns of data that are presented by the OWNERDR program:

```
pFieldInfo = WinSendMsg( hwnd,
                         CM_ALLOCDETAILFIELDINFO,
                         MPFROMLONG( 3 ),
                         NULL );
```

The `CM_ALLOCDETAILFIELDINFO` message returns a pointer to the first
`FIELDINFO` data structure in a linked list. The `pNextFieldInfo` field of
the `FIELDINFO` data structure points to the next `FIELDINFO` data structure.
The last `FIELDINFO` data structure in the linked list contains a `NULL` pointer in
the `pNextFieldInfo` field.

Initializing the FIELDINFO Data Structures for Every Column

Once the `FIELDINFO` data structures have been allocated, they must be initialized. The following code initializes the three `FIELDINFO` data structures that
are used by the OWNERDR program:

```
pFieldInfo->cb = sizeof(FIELDINFO);

pFieldInfo->flData = CFA_HORZSEPARATOR | CFA_CENTER |
                     CFA_SEPARATOR | CFA_ULONG;
pFieldInfo->flTitle = CFA_CENTER;
pFieldInfo->pTitleData = "Index";
pFieldInfo->offStruct = FIELDOFFSET( USERRECORD, ur_lIndex );
pFieldInfo = pFieldInfo->pNextFieldInfo;

pFieldInfo->cb = sizeof(FIELDINFO);
pFieldInfo->flData = CFA_HORZSEPARATOR | CFA_CENTER |
                     CFA_SEPARATOR | CFA_OWNER;
pFieldInfo->flTitle = CFA_CENTER;
pFieldInfo->pTitleData = "Color";
pFieldInfo = pFieldInfo->pNextFieldInfo;

pFieldInfo->cb = sizeof(FIELDINFO);
pFieldInfo->flData = CFA_HORZSEPARATOR | CFA_CENTER |
                     CFA_SEPARATOR | CFA_STRING;
pFieldInfo->flTitle = CFA_CENTER;
pFieldInfo->pTitleData = "RGB";
pFieldInfo->offStruct = FIELDOFFSET( USERRECORD, pszRGB );
```

The `cb` field of the `FIELDINFO` data structure is initialized with the size of
a `FIELDINFO` data structure, expressed in bytes. The `flData` field is set with
attributes of the fields data. The following attributes are used in the OWNERDR
program to influence the appearance of one of the three columns:

- `CFA_CENTER`   Indicates that items are to be drawn in the center of the
  column.
- `CFA_HORZSEPARATOR`   Indicates that a horizontal line is to be drawn
  beneath each item in the column.

- CFA_SEPARATOR   Indicates that vertical lines are to appear to the right of each item in the column.
- CFA_ULONG   Identifies items in the column as being of the type ULONG.
- CFA_STRING   Identifies items in the column as being text strings.
- CFA_OWNER   Instructs the container to send WM_DRAWITEM messages to the owner window whenever an item in the column needs to be drawn.

The flTitle field sets column headings by using CFA flags in the same manner in which they are used in the flData field. The OWNERDR program sets the flTitle field that is associated with each column heading to have the CFA_CENTER flag, which causes the text of the column heading to be centered. The pTitleData field of the FIELDINFO data structure is updated with a text string that appears in the column heading.

The offStruct field of the FIELDINFO data structure is updated to contain the number of bytes from the begining of the USERRECORD structure to where the data to be displayed by the FIELDINFO structure's column is stored. The color index column requires its FIELDINFO structure to have an offStruct equal to the offset from the beginning of the USERRECORD structure to the ur_lIndex. The RGB column requires its offStruct to be equal to the offset from the beginning of the USERRECORD structure to the pszRGB field.

The color samples column does not need its offStruct field set to any value, because the items in its column are drawn by the owner window. The container does not need to access the data that is associated with an owner-drawn item, since the owner-drawn window handles the drawing of the data. Therefore, offStruct does not need to be set to describe the location of data that is to be drawn in the color samples column of the OWNERDR program.

Inserting FIELDINFO Data Structures

Once all of the FIELDINFO data structures have been updated, the OWNERDR program inserts the updated data into the container. The FIELDINFO data structures are inserted into the container by using the CM_INSERTDETAILFIELDINFO container message. The following code is used for inserting FIELDINFO data structures into the container:

```
fieldInfoInsert.cb = (ULONG)(sizeof(FIELDINFOINSERT));
fieldInfoInsert.pFieldInfoOrder = (PFIELDINFO)CMA_FIRST;
fieldInfoInsert.cFieldInfoInsert = (SHORT)(3);
fieldInfoInsert.fInvalidateFieldInfo = TRUE;

WinSendMsg( hwnd,
            CM_INSERTDETAILFIELDINFO,
            MPFROMP( pStartingFieldInfo ),
            MPFROMP( &fieldInfoInsert ) );
```

The CM_INSERTDETAILFIELDINFO message requires a pointer to the FIELDINFO data structure that starts the linked list of FIELDINFO structures, which contains one for each column. The second message parameter (mp2) contains a pointer to a FIELDINFOINSERT data structure, which contains general information about all of the FIELDINFO data structures that are being inserted as well as a count of the number of FIELDINFO data structures that are being inserted.

Handling the WM_DRAWITEM Message for a Details View Column

The container control issues the WM_DRAWITEM message to the OWNERDR program whenever any item in the second column needs to be painted. The second column is the column that OWNERDR uses to display a rectangle containing a sample of each unique color that is available.

The following code excerpt is used in the OWNERDR program to handle a WM_DRAWITEM message:

```
if (msg == WM_DRAWITEM) {
    PCNRDRAWITEMINFO pCnrDrawItemInfo;
    PUSERRECORD pUserRecord;

    pCnrDrawItemInfo = (PCNRDRAWITEMINFO)((POWNERITEM)mp2)->hItem;
    pUserRecord = (PUSERRECORD)(pCnrDrawItemInfo->pRecord);

    /* NOTE: pUserRecord will be NULL if this message is for */
    /* the column heading.                                   */
    if ((ULONG)pUserRecord) {

        /* Put the PS into RGB mode */
        GpiCreateLogColorTable ( ((POWNERITEM)mp2)->hps,
                                 LCOL_RESET,
                                 LCOLF_RGB,
                                 0L,
                                 0L,
                                 NULL ) ;

    WinFillRect(
        ((POWNERITEM)mp2)->hps,
        &((POWNERITEM)mp2)->rclItem,
        ((PUSERRECORD)(pCnrDrawItemInfo->pRecord))->ur_rgbValue );

    return 0;
    }
}
```

When the OWNERDR program receives the WM_DRAWITEM message, the second message parameter (mp2) contains a pointer to an OWNERITEM data structure, which is defined in the PMWIN.H public header file, as follows:

```
typedef struct _OWNERITEM {
    HWND    hwnd;
    HPS     hps;
    ULONG   fsState;
    ULONG   fsAttribute;
    ULONG   fsStateOld;
    ULONG   fsAttributeOld;
    RECTL   rclItem;
    LONG    idItem;
    ULONG   hItem;
} OWNERITEM;
```

The hItem field of the OWNERITEM data structure contains a pointer to a CNRDRAWITEMINFO data structure, which is defined in the PMLSTDDLG.H public header file as follows:

```
typedef struct _CNRDRAWITEMINFO {
    PRECORDCORE pRecord;
    PFIELDINFO  pFieldInfo;
} CNRDRAWITEMINFO;
```

The pRecord field of the CNRDRAWITEMINFO data structure points to the USERRECORD data structure for one of the items in the column that OWNERDR has chosen to draw. If the pRecord field contains a NULL pointer, OWNERDR knows that this WM_DRAWITEM message was intended to be a column heading, so OWNERDR lets the container control draw it. If pRecord contains a valid pointer, the presentation space given by the WM_DRAWITEM message is placed into RGB mode so that the rectangle can be filled with the RGB value that resides in the USERRECORD data structure.

CHAPTER 18
Formatting Frame Controls

Frame windows are designed to give PM applications the capability to change the way that frame controls are sized and positioned. A PM application can position frame controls, such as a title bar or system menu, literally anywhere within a frame window. The process of arranging a set of frame controls within a frame window is called *formatting the frame* or *formatting the frame controls.*

PM applications typically choose the frame controls that are to be created for a frame window and turn to PM to handle the task of formatting the frame controls automatically. Regardless of the frame controls that are made available to a frame window, PM will try to arrange the frame controls so that the resulting frame window will have the appearance of a standard window. However, PM *does* allow applications to alter the "standard look" of a frame window, so a novel, nonstandard appearance can be created by rearranging the standard controls, by adding controls that normally are not used as frame controls, or both.

This chapter addresses how PM normally formats standard frame controls and how to change the method that PM uses to format a frame window. Chapter 19 builds on the techniques that are discussed in this chapter by explaining how nonstandard frame controls can be added to a frame window and treated as standard frame controls. The methods that are discussed in this chapter and in Chapter 19 show how PM does not limit applications to mundane, standard appearances.

280

CHANGING THE STANDARD FRAME FORMAT

Figure 18.1 shows a frame window that is created by an example program called FRAMEWND, the source code for which is presented shortly. The FRAMEWND program subclasses a frame window to effectively turn the positions of its frame controls upside down.

The frame window of Figure 18.1 illustrates how standard frame controls can be entirely rearranged by using only a few lines of additional code. The dramatically different look of the upside-down window effect of the FRAMEWND program exemplifies the flexibility that PM provides to programmers so that they can write code that will give their applications a very distinctive appearance.

Assembling the Pieces

Formatting a frame is a process that essentially involves assembling frame controls that are configured to fit within the boundaries of a frame window. When PM formats a frame, it assembles frame controls to make each control as accessible as the size of the frame permits. Regardless of whether an application takes charge of formatting the controls of a frame, or whether the task of formatting controls is turned over to PM, the formatting process involves arranging controls as if they were pieces of a jigsaw puzzle.

Formatting takes place whenever a frame is resized or has a control removed or added. Although the term *formatting* is used in reference to a

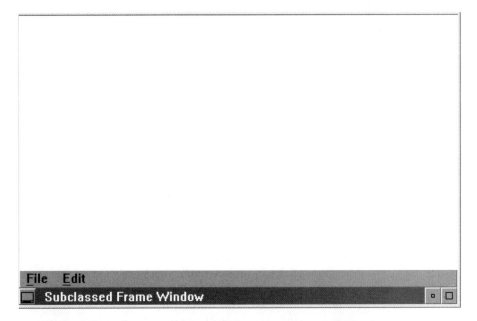

FIGURE 18.1   Frame window created by the FRAMEWND program.

set of frame controls, the process of formatting a frame window's controls necessitates that the frame window's client window also be formatted when the frame controls are formatted. During the formatting of a frame window, a client window is treated simply as if it were another frame control.

Frame controls are child windows of a frame window that are formatted to appear as parts of the frame window. Without the process of formatting frame windows, the frame controls would behave as normal child windows. When a frame is being formatted, its child windows are checked for special window ID numbers, called *frame ID numbers* (FID numbers). The FID numbers that are queried include FID_SYSMENU, FID_TITLEBAR, FID_MENU, FID_VERTSCROLL, FID_HORZSCROLL, and FID_CLIENT. Each of these FID numbers can be assigned to only one child window of a frame. If two or more windows exist that have the same FID number, problems may result when PM formats the frame. Typically, PM will use the first window it finds with an FID number that matches the number being queried. To make certain that PM uses the intended window, each child window should be given a unique ID number.

During the process of formatting a frame window, a list of the available frame controls is assembled. If a client window (FID_CLIENT) exists, it will be included in the assembled list of available frame controls, just as if it were a frame control. After the frame has created a list of available frame controls, the frame specifies an appropriate size and position for each item in the list. These size and position assignments are made by taking many factors into account, including the space that is available within a frame window and the space that needs to be occupied by the various types of controls in the list. If a frame is too small, some controls may be designated to be hidden rather than to attempt to fit all of the available controls within the space that is provided by the frame window.

Unless instructed to do otherwise, PM always tries to assign to available controls such sizes and positions as will assist in creating the appearance of a standard window. It is typical for applications *not* to create all of the frame controls that are available. If a frame control is not created, PM may choose to expand the sizes of one or more of the frame controls that are created, so that space is filled that otherwise might be left "empty" by a missing control. For example, if a frame has a title bar but does not have a system menu, PM normally will elect to expand the title bar to include the space that would have been occupied by the system menu. Although PM tries to avoid creating "gaps" between controls, if a system menu, minmax buttons, or both exist without a title bar being present, the resulting excessive amount of empty but normally occupied space will be provided with a background-colored rectangle where the missing title bar should be located.

PM applications are permitted to remove or add frame controls at selected times after a frame has been displayed on the desktop. If a frame control has been removed or added, the frame must be notified to reformat the frame controls so that suitable steps will be taken, both to fill gaps created when frame controls are removed and to make room for frame controls that are added.

Changing the Standard Format

Frame windows typically use the default size, position, and Z-order that PM provides for frame controls. However, each time a frame window is resized or repositioned, the frame receives messages that allow the frame to reformat its frame controls properly to fit within the new size of the frame window. Because PM vigilantly maintains the format of frame controls, a frame control cannot be repositioned by a simple call to `WinSetWindowPos`. The `WinSetWindowPos` API might happen to change a frame control temporarily; however, the change will be undone the next time the frame window is formatted in response to such actions as being resized.

The default Z-order that is used by a frame window to arrange its frame controls places the system menu as the topmost window and places the client window as the bottommost window. The default Z-order of frame controls, including the client window, has the following top-to-bottom arrangement:

- Title bar (`FID_TITLEBAR`)
- System menu (`FID_SYSMENU`)
- Minmax buttons (`FID_MINMAX`)
- Action bar (`FID_MENU`)
- Vertical scroll bar (`FID_VERTSCROLL`)
- Horizontal scroll bar (`FID_HORZSCROLL`)
- Client window (`FID_CLIENT`)

Each time a frame is formatted, the size, position, and Z-order of the available frame controls are described in an array. Once the array is set up, it is given to an API to handle the formatting of the frame controls that are described by the array. Changing the contents of an array before the array is used in formatting permits the manner in which PM formats a frame to be controlled and changed as may be desired.

The array that is used to describe a set of frame controls is an array of `SWP` data structures. Each `SWP` data structure describes a single available frame control and how it is to be sized and positioned. The order of the `SWP` data structures in the array represents the Z-order that the frame controls will have when formatted. By default, the order follows the frame control Z-order just described. Switching the order of the contents within the `SWP` structures will change the Z-order of frame controls. Changing the size and position values that are stored in the `SWP` structures changes the sizes and positions of frame controls.

When a frame window is starting to format its frame controls, the frame window allocates memory that is large enough to store an `SWP` array that describes the frame controls. The size of the `SWP` array is determined by the return code of a `WM_QUERYFRAMECTLCOUNT` message, which the frame sends to itself. Once the memory for an `SWP` array is allocated, the frame sends yet another message, `WM_FORMATFRAME`, to itself to fill the contents of the array. Controlling how `WM_FORMATFRAME` messages are processed allows an `SWP` array that is being used to format a frame to be changed, thereby changing the manner which a frame window is to be formatted.

When a window procedure receives a WM_FORMATFRAME message, the first message parameter (mp1) is a pointer to an empty SWP array. The WM_FORMATFRAME message sets the values in the SWP array and gives a return code that equals the number of frame controls that are described in the SWP array. After the SWP array has been set up by sending a WM_FORMATFRAME message, the array is used as a parameter in an API call to WinSetMultWindowPos, which handles the arranging of the frame controls that are listed in the SWP array.

There are many ways to cause a frame to send itself a WM_FORMATFRAME message. The most common ways are to resize the frame, to unhide the frame, or to send the frame a WM_UPDATEFRAME message. A WM_UPDATEFRAME message instructs a frame window to format its frame controls and should be sent by an application after frame controls have been removed or added from a frame window.

THE FRAMEWND PROGRAM

The frame window shown in Figure 18.1 was created by subclassing a standard frame window and by altering how WM_FORMATFRAME messages are processed. The FRAMEWND program goes through the given array of frame controls and changes the position of each frame control to produce the "upside-down" effect that is shown in Figure 18.1.

The following six files provide the code that is needed to compile the FRAMEWND program:

FRAMEWND.C

```
#define INCL_GPI
#define INCL_WIN
#include <os2.h>
#include "framewnd.h"


/* function prototypes */
INT main( VOID );
MRESULT EXPENTRY NewFrameProc( HWND, ULONG, MPARAM, MPARAM );
MRESULT EXPENTRY MyClientWndProc( HWND, ULONG, MPARAM, MPARAM );


/* global variables */
PFNWP OldFrameProc;


INT main( VOID )
{
    HAB hab;
    HMQ hmq;
    QMSG qmsg;
    HWND hwndFrame, hwndClient;
```

```
        ULONG flCreateFlags = FCF_TITLEBAR        /* create: title bar control   */
                            | FCF_SYSMENU         /*          system menu control */
                            | FCF_MENU            /*          action bar          */
                            | FCF_MINMAX          /*          min and max buttons  */
                            | FCF_SIZEBORDER      /* draw sizeborders             */
                            | FCF_SHELLPOSITION   /* shell decides window position */
                            | FCF_TASKLIST        /* title added to switch list    */
                            | FCF_ICON;           /* frame has an icon            */
        CHAR szClientClass[] = "Client Window";

        hab = WinInitialize( 0 );
        hmq = WinCreateMsgQueue( hab, 0 );

        WinRegisterClass( hab,
                          szClientClass,
                          MyClientWndProc,
                          CS_SIZEREDRAW,
                          0 );

        hwndFrame = WinCreateStdWindow(
                        HWND_DESKTOP,     /* parent */
                        0,                /* frame window style */
                        &flCreateFlags,   /* creation flags for frame window */
                        szClientClass,    /* client window class name */
                        "Subclassed Frame Window", /* text added to title */
                        0,                /* client window style */
                        NULLHANDLE,       /* resource ID's are in rc file */
                        ID_FRAMEWND,      /* ID for frame window */
                        &hwndClient );    /* address to place client window handle */

        OldFrameProc = WinSubclassWindow( hwndFrame, NewFrameProc );

        WinShowWindow( hwndFrame, TRUE );

        if (hwndFrame)
           while (WinGetMsg( hab, &qmsg, NULLHANDLE, 0, 0 ))
              WinDispatchMsg( hab, &qmsg );

        WinDestroyWindow( hwndFrame );
        WinDestroyMsgQueue( hmq );
        WinTerminate( hab );

        return 0;
} /* end main */


MRESULT EXPENTRY NewFrameProc( HWND hwnd, ULONG msg, MPARAM mp1, MPARAM mp2 )
{
    switch (msg) {
    case WM_FORMATFRAME:
      { USHORT i, rc;
        PSWP pswp;
        SWP swpFrame;
```

```
      /* have the old frame procedure format the frame's windows */
      rc = (USHORT)OldFrameProc( hwnd, msg, mp1, mp2 );

      /* query the frame size to get the frame height swpFrame.cy */
      WinQueryWindowPos( hwnd, &swpFrame );

      /*
       * go through the frame's windows, and change the way the
       *   old frame procedure formatted the windows
       */
      for (i = 0, pswp = (PSWP)mp1; i < rc; i++, pswp++)
          pswp->y = swpFrame.cy - (pswp->y + pswp->cy);

      /* return the number of frame controls */
      return (MRESULT)rc;
    } break;
  default:
    return (MRESULT)(*OldFrameProc)( hwnd, msg, mp1, mp2 );
  } /* endswitch */
  return FALSE;
} /* NewFrameProc */


MRESULT EXPENTRY MyClientWndProc( HWND hwnd, ULONG msg, MPARAM mp1, MPARAM mp2)
{
  switch (msg) {

  // place message handling for client window here

  case WM_COMMAND:
    if (SHORT1FROMMP(mp2) == CMDSRC_MENU)
      WinAlarm( HWND_DESKTOP, WA_NOTE );
    break;
  case WM_ERASEBACKGROUND:
    return (MRESULT)TRUE;
  default:
    return(WinDefWindowProc( hwnd, msg, mp1, mp2 ));
  } /* endswitch */

  return FALSE;
} /* MyClientWndProc */
```

FRAMEWND.H

```
#define ID_FRAMEWND    1
#define MY_PULLDOWN1   101
#define MY_PULLDOWN2   102
#define MY_MENUITEM1   201
#define MY_MENUITEM2   202
#define MY_MENUITEM3   203
#define MY_MENUITEM4   204
#define MY_MENUITEM5   205
#define MY_MENUITEM6   206
```

FRAMEWND.RC

```
#include <os2.h>
#include "framewnd.h"

ICON ID_FRAMEWND framewnd.ico


MENU ID_FRAMEWND
    BEGIN
        SUBMENU "~File", MY_PULLDOWN1
            BEGIN
                MENUITEM "~New",                    MY_MENUITEM1
                MENUITEM "~Open",                   MY_MENUITEM2
                MENUITEM "~Close",                  MY_MENUITEM3
            END
        SUBMENU "~Edit", MY_PULLDOWN2
            BEGIN
                MENUITEM "Cu~t\tShift+Delete",      MY_MENUITEM4
                MENUITEM "~Copy\tCtrl+Insert",      MY_MENUITEM5
                MENUITEM "~Paste\tShift+Insert",    MY_MENUITEM6
            END
    END
```

FRAMEWND.DEF

```
NAME       FRAMEWND      WINDOWAPI

DESCRIPTION 'FRAMEWND OS/2 PM Example Program'

STUB         'OS2STUB.EXE'

DATA         MULTIPLE

STACKSIZE   16348
HEAPSIZE    16348

PROTMODE
```

FRAMEWND.MAK

```
all : framewnd.exe

framewnd.exe : framewnd.obj framewnd.def framewnd.res
        link386 /PM:PM framewnd,,,,framewnd.def;
        .rc framewnd.res

framewnd.res: framewnd.rc framewnd.ico framewnd.h
        rc -r framewnd.rc

framewnd.obj:framewnd.c framewnd.h
        icc /C /Ss /W3 .\$*.c
```

FRAMEWND.ICO

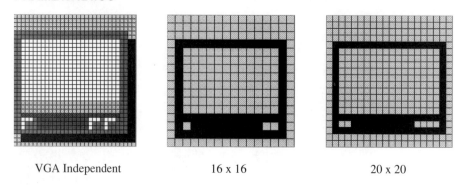

VGA Independent   16 x 16   20 x 20

FRAMEWND.ICO file, containing various icons of different sizes.

Creating the FRAMEWND Window

The FRAMEWND program creates a standard window that is subclassed with a window procedure called `newFrameProc`. The address of the original frame window procedure is stored in a pointer called `oldFrameProc`, and it is called by the `newFrameProc` procedure as the procedure to handle unmodified messages. The only messages that are modified by the `newFrameProc` procedure are WM_FORMATFRAME messages. To handle WM_FORMATFRAME messages, the `newFrameProc` procedure first calls the `oldFrameProc` procedure, but the results are altered to create the nonstandard look of the FRAMEWND program.

The FRAMEWND program creates a subclassed frame window by calling `WinCreateStdWindow` followed by a call to `WinSubclassWindow`. It is important that the WS_VISIBLE flag not be used in the call to `WinCreateStdWindow`; otherwise, the FRAMEWND window will be displayed before it is subclassed.

The "upside-down" arrangement of the frame controls depends on the subclassing procedure `newFrameProc` intercepting all WM_FORMATFRAME messages. If the FRAMEWND were to be created as a visible window, the first WM_FORMATFRAME message would be missed. If the FRAMEWND window misses the first WM_FORMATFRAME message, when the FRAMEWND is made visible, its frame controls will assume their standard arrangement rather than the intended inverted arrangement. Only after the FRAMEWND window is resized will the `newFrameProc` procedure be given a WM_FORMATFRAME message, whereupon the desired inverted arrangement of controls will take effect.

The FRAMEWND program relies on the fact that when a frame window is created as invisible, the frame does not format its controls by sending itself a WM_FORMATFRAME message. Rather, the frame window will send itself a WM_FORMATFRAME message when the window is displayed for the first time. Therefore, the FRAMEWND program creates its frame in an invisible state, subclasses the frame to intercept WM_FORMATFRAME messages, and then makes the window visible. It is not until the window becomes visible that the first WM_FORMATFRAME message is sent.

The WM_FORMATFRAME Message

The WM_FORMATFRAME message in the FRAMEWND program is intercepted by the newFrameProc procedure to change the positions of frame controls. When handling a WM_FORMATFRAME message, the newFrameProc first calls the oldFrameProc to initially handle the message, and then modifies the result. When subclassing WM_FORMATFRAME messages, it is important to call the original window procedure first and then make modifications to the result.

One of the reasons for calling the original window procedure (oldFrameProc) is that the PM frame class may already be subclassed. It is possible to reregister a public window class during the initialization of PM that takes place while OS/2 is loading on a system. Because a reregistered public class is a subclass, the reregistered public class can use an alternate technique for handling WM_FORMATFRAME messages. The technique of reregistering a public class is discussed in Chapter 23.

The first message parameter of WM_FORMATFRAME is a pointer to an array of SWP data structures. When a WM_FORMATFRAME message is received, the SWP array is empty and must be initialized with information describing how each frame control is to be sized and positioned. The FRAMEWND program initializes the array by calling the oldFrameProc procedure. The oldFrameProc procedure sets up the array with the standard arrangement of frame controls that PM gives to all frame windows.

The second message parameter (mp2) of WM_FORMATFRAME is set to the value of NULL, despite assertions in a number of OS/2–related publications that mp2 is a pointer to a RECTL data structure that describes a recommended position for the client window. PM does not need information about the client window to format a frame; however, if a program that formats a set of frame controls needs a recommended size and position for the client window, the WM_CALCFRAMERECT message can be used.

While FRAMEWND is processing WM_FORMATFRAME, the WinQueryWindowPos API is called to query the height of the frame window. The API places frame window height and other information about the FRAMEWND frame window into an SWP variable called swpFrame. The value swpFrame.cy is used as the height of the FRAMEWND frame window. It is valid to use WinQueryWindowPos to get information about the frame window, because WM_FORMATFRAME messages are sent after the frame has assumed the size and position that it will have when the frame controls are fully formatted. It is the resizing or displaying of a frame window that causes WM_FORMATFRAME messages to be sent.

Although querying the size of the frame is valid during a WM_FORMATFRAME message, querying the size of the frame controls is not. During a WM_FORMATFRAME message, the present height and width of the frame controls that are being formatted will have arbitrary values, such as zero if the frame is being formatted for the first time.

After the call to `WinQueryWindowPos`, the FRAMEWND program uses a `for` loop to go through the `SWP` array that has been initialized by the `oldFrameProc` procedure. The loop alters the result of the `oldFrameProc` procedure by changing the vertical position of each frame control in the `SWP` array. The following code shows the `for` loop:

```
for (i = 0, pswp = (PSWP)mp1; i < rc; i++, pswp++ )
    pswp->y = swpFrame.cy - (pswp->y + pswp->cy);
```

In this code the pointer `pswp` goes through the `SWP` array. The vertical position of each frame control is changed by altering the `y` field of each `SWP` structure in the array. The altered vertical position of each frame control is set to the height of the frame window (`swpFrame.cy`) minus the sum of the frame control's position and height (`pswp->y + pswp->cy`). The changes that are made in the vertical positions of the frame controls are what creates the "upside-down" window effect of the FRAMEWND program.

When the FRAMEWND program has completed processing a `WM_FORMATFRAME` message, the `WM_FORMATFRAME` message must be returned with a value equal to the number of frame controls that were formatted. The FRAMEWND program uses the `oldFrameProc` procedure to initialize the `SWP` array, and the `oldFrameProc` returns the number of controls that it formatted. The FRAMEWND program stores the returned number in a variable called `rc`, which is the value that is used as the return code.

While the `oldFrameProc` procedure is attempting to calculate the number of frame controls that are to be formatted, it checks all of the child windows of the FRAMEWND window for FID numbers. The child windows that are assigned FID numbers are considered to be frame controls and are described in an `SWP` structure in the `SWP` array.

Calculating the Client Area

The area that a client window occupies is called the *client area*. While the FRAMEWND program does not need to do so, other PM applications may need to calculate the client area to format their frame controls properly. PM provides the `WinCalcFrameRect` API to calculate the client area or the area occupied by the frame of the client. A Boolean value is used as a parameter to determine which type of area is being calculated by the API `WinCalcFrameRect`. The `WinCalcFrameRect` API calculates client or frame areas by sending a `WM_CALCFRAMERECT` message to the frame of the client window.

To calculate a client area, the `WM_CALCFRAMERECT` message uses a `RECTL` data structure to accept information describing the frame. During the processing of the `WM_CALCFRAMERECT` message, the `RECTL` structure is modified to contain information describing a frame window that is properly sized to fit around the client.

If code is added to the FRAMEWND program to use `WinCalcFrameRect` or `WM_CALCFRAMERECT` to calculate the client area, the code will return a client area that is calculated by the `oldFrameProc` and does not take into consideration the inverted positions of the FRAMEWND frame controls. Therefore, if a program needs to determine the modified client area that is used by the `newFrameProc` procedure, the following code should be added to the `newFrameProc` procedure to intercept `WM_CALCFRAMERECT` messages:

```
case WM_CALCFRAMERECT:
{ RECTL  rcl;
  BOOL   rc;
  LONG   FrameHeight;
  LONG   ClientHeight;

  /* copy the RECTL structure pointed to by mp1 */
  rcl = *(PRECTL)mp1;

  /* set mp1 to be the old position of the client window */
  rc = (BOOL)(*oldFrameProc)( hwnd, msg, mp1, mp2 );

  /* if mp2 is TRUE,
   *    oldFrameProc just calculated the client RECTL, therefore
   *    modify the calculation of the client RECTL
   */
  if (SHORT1FROMMP( mp2 )) {
      ClientHeight = ((PRECTL)mp1)->yTop - ((PRECTL)mp1)->yBottom;

      /* the new yBottom value for the client window */
      ((PRECTL)mp1)->yBottom = rcl.yBottom +
                          (rcl.yTop - ((PRECTL)mp1)->yTop);

      /* the new yTop value for the client window */
      ((PRECTL)mp1)->yTop = ((PRECTL)mp1)->yBottom + ClientHeight;

      rc = TRUE;
  }
  return (MRESULT)rc;
} break;
```

This code intercepts `WM_CALCFRAMERECT` messages, and if a client area is being calculated, the code changes the result to match the client area given to a client window that is formatted by the `newFrameProc` procedure.

The first message parameter (`mp1`) in the foregoing code points to a `RECTL` data structure that describes an area for a frame or a client. Regardless of which type of window area is being calculated, the values in the `RECTL` structure describe the area in coordinates that are relative to the lower left corner of the desktop window. The RECTL structure may not necessarily describe the present area that is occupied by a frame window or by a client window, because the WM_CALCFRAMERECT message is commonly used to calculate an area before either window has been positioned on the desktop.

The second message parameter (mp2) of the WM_CALCFRAMERECT message is TRUE if a client area is being calculated. In the foregoing code, oldFrameProc is given the WM_CALCFRAMERECT message, and if mp2 is TRUE (signaling that a client area is being calculated), the result of oldFrameProc is altered to describe the client area that the newFrameProc procedure will set for the client window after modifying the format that is given by the oldFrameProc procedure.

CHAPTER 19
Creating New Frame Controls

Although PM supplies a very capable set of standard frame controls, PM further enhances the capabilities of its frame windows by permitting them to use nonstandard controls and by permitting frame windows to be formatted in nonstandard ways. A frame window can include nonstandard controls just as if they were a part of the standard selection of frame controls. Moreover, because it can format its controls in nonstandard ways, a frame window has the ability both to position standard frame controls in almost any desired manner and to use and selectively position nonstandard controls to supplement the standard frame controls. PM gives programs the ability to provide frame windows that feature novel appearances and that incorporate precisely such controls as meet the needs of specific applications.

In this chapter, an example program is presented that adds a menu button between a frame window's system menu button and its title bar. The menu button emulates the three-dimensional appearance and behavior of a system menu button. By subclassing the normal operations of a frame window, the menu button is incorporated as a seamless addition to the frame window.

STANDARD FRAME CONTROLS

PM provides several ways to add or remove standard frame controls from a frame window. Many PM applications offer options to change their available frame controls, for instance to provide a window of simplified appearance. For example, the system clock that is provided by Workplace Shell allows a user to remove frame controls, including the title bar, the system menu, and the minmax buttons, so that the associated client window can be expanded to present more information.

One approach that a PM application can take to selectively add or remove frame controls is to selectively create and destroy the controls. PM provides the

293

WinCreateFrameControls API to permit any of the standard controls to be created with ease. Likewise, the WinDestroyWindow API can be used to destroy a standard control. However, a more efficient method than these APIs can be used that does not require windows to be destroyed and created.

Most PM applications that can add and remove frame controls can, instead, take the preferred alternative approach of simply creating a standard window that includes all of the frame controls that may be needed by particular programs and then selectively hiding unwanted controls by changing the parent of the unwanted controls to PM's object window (HWND_OBJECT). Thus, rather than create and destroy frame controls, the preferred approach is to use the WinSetParent API both to add and to remove existing frame control windows. By using the WinSetParent API, a control can be moved from a frame window to PM's invisible object window, thereby quickly and easily removing the control from the frame. To return the control to the frame window with equal efficiency, WinSetParent can be called once again, this time to set the frame window as the control's parent.

The WM_UPDATEFRAME Message

Regardless of the method that may be used to add or remove frame controls, the frame must be reformated each time a control is added or removed. The WM_UPDATEFRAME message is designed to format frame windows that have had frame controls removed or added. The WM_UPDATEFRAME message automatically handles the many steps that are needed to format a frame window. The first message parameter (mp1) of a WM_UPDATEFRAME can contain a set of FCF flags, listing frame controls that may have been added or removed.

Most applications take the simple approach of using a value of zero for mp1, which causes a frame window that receives the message to go through the following steps:

- Send a WM_QUERYFRAMECTLCOUNT message to query the number of available frame controls (including nonstandard controls)
- Set up an SWP array large enough to describe all available frame controls
- Send a WM_FORMATFRAME message to initialize the SWP array
- Call the WinSetMultWindowPos API to position the frame controls by using the data that is stored in the SWP array

The WM_UPDATEFRAME message is also used to update a frame window when its action bar window has had a menu item added or removed. The size of the window of the action bar may need to be changed to compensate for an added or removed menu item. If a change in size is needed, the frame must be reformated. In some cases, however, an action bar window may not need to be resized because its existing menu items can be drawn within the present size of the window.

To avoid unnecessary formatting of a frame window, it is desirable for a WM_UPDATEFRAME message to be sent using FCF flags that list frame controls that have been added, removed, or changed. When a frame receives such a WM_UPDATEFRAME message (accompanied by appropriate FCF flags), the frame determines what formatting is needed. If no formatting is needed, the FCF flags are invalidated, causing the necessary frame controls to simply be redrawn.

Most PM applications will not bother to set FCF flags when sending a WM_UPDATEFRAME message, because when a frame control is added or removed, the frame window will need to be formatted.

ADDING A NONSTANDARD FRAME CONTROL

PM allows nonstandard frame controls to be incorporated into a frame window and to be treated as if they are standard frame controls. To add nonstandard controls to a frame, the controls must be created as children of a frame window, and the frame must be subclassed to alter how the WM_QUERYFRAMECTLCOUNT and WM_FORMATFRAME messages are processed.

A frame that receives a WM_QUERYFRAMECTLCOUNT message returns a value that indicates the total number of frame controls that are available. To add nonstandard frame controls to a frame window, the value that is returned by a WM_QUERYFRAMECTLCOUNT message must be properly incremented to take into account the number of added nonstandard frame controls. Also, the WM_FORMATFRAME message must be altered to reserve space for both standard and added nonstandard frame controls.

THE FRMMENU PROGRAM

Figure 19.1 shows a frame window that is created by an example program called FRMMENU, whose source code is presented in this section. The FRMMENU

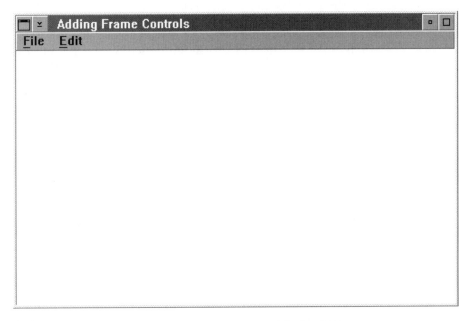

FIGURE 19.1   Frame window created by the FRMMENU program.

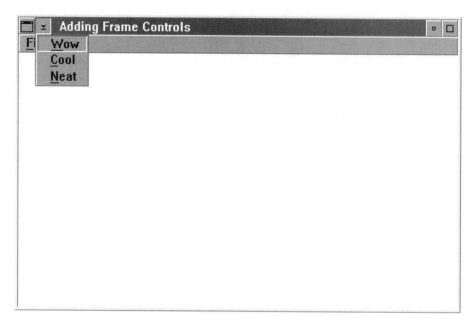

FIGURE 19.2 The FRMMENU window with its menu button in a "pressed" state and with its pull-down menu displayed.

program adds a nonstandard control, placed between its system menu and title bar. The added nonstandard control is a menu button that has the appearance of a title bar button (the same appearance exhibited by a system menu button or a minmax button).

The FRMMENU menu button is a menu class window with an "owner-drawn menu item" that has a pull-down menu. The menu button can appear either in a "pressed" state or in its normal "unpressed" state. Figure 19.1 shows the menu button in its normal "unpressed" state. Figure 19.2 shows the FRMMENU menu button in its "pressed" state and with its pull-down menu displayed.

The following six files are used to compile the FRMMENU program:

FRMMENU.C

```
#define INCL_DOSRESOURCES
#define INCL_GPI
#define INCL_WIN
#include <os2.h>
#include <string.h>
#include "frmmenu.h"

/* function protypes */
INT main( VOID );
MRESULT EXPENTRY MyClientWndProc( HWND, ULONG, MPARAM, MPARAM );
MRESULT EXPENTRY MyFrameWndProc( HWND, ULONG, MPARAM, MPARAM );

/* global variables */
CLASSINFO fci;
```

```
CHAR szMyFrameClass[]  = "My Frame Window" ;
CHAR szMyClientClass[] = "My Client Window";


INT main( VOID )
{
    HAB  hab;
    HMQ  hmq;
    QMSG qmsg;
    HWND hwndFrame;
    HWND hwndClient;
    SWP  swp;
    FRAMECDATA fcd;

    fcd.cb = sizeof(FRAMECDATA);  /* length of structure */
    fcd.flCreateFlags = FCF_TITLEBAR        /* create: title bar control  */
                    | FCF_SYSMENU       /*          system menu control  */
                    | FCF_MENU          /*          action bar control   */
                    | FCF_SIZEBORDER    /*          sizeborders          */
                    | FCF_MINMAX        /*          min and max buttons   */
                    | FCF_SHELLPOSITION /* shell decides window position */
                    | FCF_TASKLIST      /* title added to switch list    */
                    | FCF_ICON;         /* frame has an icon             */
    fcd.hmodResources = NULLHANDLE;  /* no DLLs used for resources  */
    fcd.idResources   = ID_FRMMENU;  /* ID number for frame resources  */

    hab = WinInitialize( 0 );
    hmq = WinCreateMsgQueue( hab, 0 );

    WinQueryClassInfo( hab, WC_FRAME, &fci );

    WinRegisterClass( hab,                  /* anchor block handle */
                    szMyFrameClass,     /* class name */
                    MyFrameWndProc,     /* pointer to window procedure */
                    CS_FRAME            /* class style */
                    | CS_HITTEST
                    | CS_SYNCPAINT
                    | CS_CLIPSIBLINGS,
                    fci.cbWindowData ); /* number of class data bytes */

    WinRegisterClass( hab,              /* anchor block handle */
                    szMyClientClass,  /* class name */
                    MyClientWndProc,  /* pointer to window procedure */
                    CS_SIZEREDRAW,    /* class style */
                    0 );              /* no class data bytes needed */

    hwndFrame = WinCreateWindow(
                    HWND_DESKTOP,     /* parent window is the desktop */
                    szMyFrameClass,   /* use public frame class */
                    "Adding Frame Controls", /* text added to title bar */
                    0,                /* window style */
                    0, 0, 0, 0,       /* ignored, FCF_SHELLPOSITION was set */
                    NULLHANDLE,       /* no owner window */
                    HWND_TOP,         /* place on top of Desktop's children */
```

```
                        ID_FRMMENU,          /* window ID of the frame    */
                        &fcd,                /* data unique to frame windows */
                        NULL );              /* no presentation parameters */

    hwndClient = WinCreateWindow(
                        hwndFrame,           /* parent window is the frame */
                        szMyClientClass,     /* privately registered client class */
                        NULL,                /* window name not used by client */
                        0,                   /* window style */
                        0, 0, 0, 0,          /* ignored, client window */
                        hwndFrame,           /* owner window is the frame */
                        HWND_BOTTOM,         /* standard Z-order of client windows */
                        FID_CLIENT,          /* ID number recognized by the frame */
                        NULL,                /* no control data */
                        NULL );              /* no presentation parameters */

    WinShowWindow( hwndFrame, TRUE );

    if (hwndFrame)
        while (WinGetMsg( hab, &qmsg, NULLHANDLE, 0, 0 ))
            WinDispatchMsg( hab, &qmsg );

    WinDestroyWindow( hwndFrame );
    WinDestroyMsgQueue( hmq );
    WinTerminate( hab );

    return 0;
} /* end main */

MRESULT MyFrameWndProc( HWND hwnd, ULONG msg, MPARAM mp1, MPARAM mp2 )
{
    static HWND       hwndMyMenu;          /* handle to the added frame control */
    static HWND       hwndSysMenu;         /* frame window's system menu */
    static HWND       hwndActionBar;       /* frame window's FID_MENU window */
    static HBITMAP    hbmBtn;              /* button bitmap not pressed down */
    static HBITMAP    hbmBtnDep;           /* button bitmap pressed down */
    static SHORT      cxBitmap, cyBitmap;  /* width & height of menu bitmap */

    switch (msg) {
    case WM_CREATE:
    { PVOID pmt; /* pointer to a menu template */
      BITMAPINFOHEADER bmpinfo;

      /* call the frame class window procedure */
      (*fci.pfnWindowProc)( hwnd, msg, mp1, mp2 );

      /*  - load the menu template from the exe's resources
       *  - create a menu class window with ID number MY_FID
       *  - release the resource
       */
      DosGetResource( NULLHANDLE, RT_MENU, MY_FID, &pmt );
      hwndMyMenu = WinCreateWindow( hwnd,
                                    WC_MENU,
                                    NULL,
```

```
                               MS_ACTIONBAR | MS_TITLEBUTTON,
                               0, 0, 0, 0,
                               hwnd,
                               HWND_BOTTOM,
                               MY_FID,
                               pmt,
                               NULL );
    DosFreeResource( pmt );

    /* load the bitmaps of a button both pressed and not pressed */
    hbmBtn    = WinGetSysBitmap( HWND_DESKTOP, SBMP_CHILDSYSMENU );
    hbmBtnDep = WinGetSysBitmap( HWND_DESKTOP, SBMP_CHILDSYSMENUDEP );

    /* get the height and width of the child menu bitmap */
    GpiQueryBitmapParameters( hbmBtn, &bmpinfo );
    cxBitmap = bmpinfo.cx;
    cyBitmap = bmpinfo.cy;

    /* get the following handles for the WM_NEXTMENU message */
    hwndSysMenu   = WinWindowFromID( hwnd, FID_SYSMENU );
    hwndActionBar = WinWindowFromID( hwnd, FID_MENU );
  } break;

case WM_MEASUREITEM:
    if (((POWNERITEM)mp2)->idItem == MY_MENUBUTTON) {
        ((POWNERITEM)mp2)->rclItem.xRight = cxBitmap;
        ((POWNERITEM)mp2)->rclItem.yTop   = cyBitmap;
        return (MRESULT)cyBitmap;
    } else
        return (MRESULT)(*fci.pfnWindowProc)( hwnd, msg, mp1, mp2 );

case WM_DRAWITEM:
  { POINTL ptl;

    if (((POWNERITEM)mp2)->idItem == MY_MENUBUTTON) {
        ptl.x=((POWNERITEM)mp2)->rclItem.xLeft;
        ptl.y=((POWNERITEM)mp2)->rclItem.yBottom;
        WinDrawBitmap( ((POWNERITEM)mp2)->hps,
            ( (((POWNERITEM)mp2)->fsAttribute && MIA_HILITED)
               ? hbmBtnDep
               : hbmBtn ),
           NULL, &ptl,
           0,0, DBM_NORMAL | DBM_IMAGEATTRS );
        ((POWNERITEM)mp2)->fsAttribute = ((POWNERITEM)mp2)->fsAttributeOld
           &= ~(MIA_CHECKED | MIA_HILITED | MIA_FRAMED );
        return (MRESULT)TRUE;
    } else
          return (MRESULT)(*fci.pfnWindowProc)( hwnd, msg, mp1, mp2 );
  } break;

case WM_NEXTMENU:
    if ((BOOL)mp2) {                        /* if beginning of menu */
      if ( (HWND)mp1 == hwndMyMenu )   /* if menu is the menu button   */
        return (MRESULT)hwndSysMenu;   /* goto system menu next        */
```

```
        if ( (HWND)mp1 == hwndActionBar ) /* if menu is the action bar    */
            return (MRESULT)hwndMyMenu;    /* goto menu button next        */
    } else {                               /* else end of menu */
        if ( (HWND)mp1 == hwndMyMenu )     /* if menu is the menu button   */
            return (MRESULT)hwndActionBar; /* goto action bar next         */
        if ( (HWND)mp1 == hwndSysMenu )    /* if menu is the system menu   */
            return (MRESULT)hwndMyMenu;    /* goto menu button next        */
    } /* endif */
    /* let the original frame procedure handle the other cases */
    return (MRESULT)(*fci.pfnWindowProc)( hwnd, msg, mp1, mp2);

case WM_QUERYFRAMECTLCOUNT:
    /* return the number of controls plus 1 for the added menu button */
    return (MRESULT)((LONG)(*fci.pfnWindowProc)(hwnd, msg, mp1, mp2) + 1);

case WM_FORMATFRAME:
{ PSWP  aswp;  /* pointer to SWP structures describing frame controls */
  SWP   swp;   /* temporary storage for FID_CLIENT's SWP structure    */
  PSWP  pswpTitleBar;  /* pointer to FID_TITLEBAR's SWP structure      */
  LONG  cxMenu, cyMenu; /* width and height of the added menu button   */
  LONG  xMenu, yMenu;  /* position of menu button                      */
  LONG  NumberOfSWPs;  /* number of controls formatted so far          */
  LONG  i;             /* index through aswp                           */

    NumberOfSWPs = (LONG)(*fci.pfnWindowProc)( hwnd, msg, mp1, mp2 );
    aswp = mp1;

    /* (NumberOfSWPs - 1) should be the index to SWP of FID_CLIENT */
    NumberOfSWPs--; /* make NumberOfSWPs index to FID_CLIENT */

    /* copy FID_CLIENT's SWP structure */
    swp = aswp[NumberOfSWPs];

    /* go through the array to find the desired frame controls */
    for ( i=0; i < NumberOfSWPs; i++ )
        if ( WinQueryWindowUShort( aswp[i].hwnd, QWS_ID ) == FID_TITLEBAR ) {
            pswpTitleBar = &aswp[i];
            break;
        }

    cxMenu = cxBitmap;
    cyMenu = pswpTitleBar->cy;
    xMenu  = pswpTitleBar->x;
    yMenu  = pswpTitleBar->y;
    pswpTitleBar->cx -= cxMenu;
    pswpTitleBar->x  += cxMenu;

    /* position menu button where the left side of the title bar used to be
     *   and set the width and height of the menu button
     */
    aswp[ NumberOfSWPs ].fl =  SWP_MOVE
                             | SWP_SIZE
                             | SWP_SHOW;
```

```
         aswp[NumberOfSWPs].cx = cxMenu;
         aswp[NumberOfSWPs].cy = cyMenu;
         aswp[NumberOfSWPs].x  = xMenu;
         aswp[NumberOfSWPs].y  = yMenu;
         aswp[NumberOfSWPs].hwnd = hwndMyMenu;
         aswp[NumberOfSWPs].hwndInsertBehind = NULLHANDLE;
         aswp[NumberOfSWPs].ulReserved1 = 0;
         aswp[NumberOfSWPs].ulReserved2 = 0;

         /* done filling MY_FID's SWP structure, increment NumberOfSWPs to */
         /*    point to the next SWP structure                            */
         NumberOfSWPs++;

         /* place FID_CLIENT last by copying it from swp to the end of aswp */
         aswp[NumberOfSWPs] = swp;

         /* account for new menu button being added to aswp */
         NumberOfSWPs++;

         /* return the number of frame controls formatted */
         return (MRESULT)NumberOfSWPs;
       } break;

     case WM_DESTROY:
       /* release the two system bitmaps used for the menu button */
       GpiDeleteBitmap( hbmBtn );
       GpiDeleteBitmap( hbmBtnDep );

       /* call the original frame procedure */
       return (MRESULT)(*fci.pfnWindowProc)( hwnd, msg, mp1, mp2);

     default:
       return (*fci.pfnWindowProc)( hwnd, msg, mp1, mp2 );
     } /* endswitch */
   return FALSE;
} /* MyFrameWndProc */


MRESULT EXPENTRY MyClientWndProc( HWND hwnd, ULONG msg, MPARAM mp1, MPARAM mp2 )
{
   switch (msg) {

   // place message handling for client window here

   case WM_COMMAND:
     if (SHORT1FROMMP(mp2) == CMDSRC_MENU)
        WinAlarm( HWND_DESKTOP, WA_NOTE );
     break;
   case WM_ERASEBACKGROUND:
     return (MRESULT)TRUE;
   default:
     return(WinDefWindowProc( hwnd, msg, mp1, mp2 ));
   } /* endswitch */
   return FALSE;
} /* MyClientWndProc */
```

FRMMENU.H

```
#define ID_FRMMENU      1
#define MY_FID          2
#define MY_MENUBUTTON   3
#define MY_PULLDOWN1    101
#define MY_PULLDOWN2    102
#define MY_MENUITEM1    201
#define MY_MENUITEM2    202
#define MY_MENUITEM3    203
#define MY_MENUITEM4    204
#define MY_MENUITEM5    205
#define MY_MENUITEM6    206
#define MY_MENUITEM7    207
#define MY_MENUITEM8    208
#define MY_MENUITEM9    209
```

FRMMENU.RC

```
#include <os2.h>
#include "frmmenu.h"

ICON ID_FRMMENU frmmenu.ico


MENU MY_FID
   BEGIN
      SUBMENU "",  MY_MENUBUTTON, MIS_OWNERDRAW
         BEGIN
            MENUITEM "~Wow",  MY_MENUITEM1
            MENUITEM "~Cool", MY_MENUITEM2
            MENUITEM "~Neat", MY_MENUITEM3
         END
   END

MENU ID_FRMMENU
   BEGIN
      SUBMENU "~File", MY_PULLDOWN1
         BEGIN
            MENUITEM "~New",   MY_MENUITEM4
            MENUITEM "~Open",  MY_MENUITEM5
            MENUITEM "~Close", MY_MENUITEM6
         END
      SUBMENU "~Edit", MY_PULLDOWN2
         BEGIN
            MENUITEM "Cu~t\tShift+Delete",   MY_MENUITEM7
            MENUITEM "~Copy\tCtrl+Insert",   MY_MENUITEM8
            MENUITEM "~Paste\tShift+Insert", MY_MENUITEM9
         END
   END
```

FRMMENU.DEF

```
NAME     FRMMENU    WINDOWAPI

DESCRIPTION  'Adding Nonstandard Frame Controls'

STUB        'OS2STUB.EXE'

DATA        MULTIPLE

STACKSIZE   16348

HEAPSIZE    16348

PROTMODE
```

FRMMENU.MAK

```
all : frmmenu.exe

frmmenu.exe : frmmenu.obj  frmmenu.def frmmenu.res
       link386 /PM:PM frmmenu,,,,frmmenu.def;
       rc frmmenu.res

frmmenu.res: frmmenu.rc frmmenu.ico frmmenu.h
       rc -r frmmenu.rc

frmmenu.obj:frmmenu.c frmmenu.h
       icc /C /Ss /W3 .$*.c
```

FRMMENU.ICO

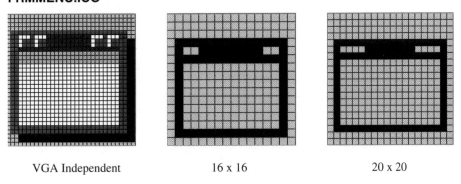

VGA Independent   16 x 16   20 x 20

FRMENU.ICO file, containing various icons of different sizes.

Creating the Menu Button

The FRMMENU program registers a private frame class called szMyFrame-Class. The window of the FRMMENU menu button is created by using the

WinCreateWindow API together with a menu template, which is loaded from the resources of the FRMMENU program:

```
        DosGetResource( NULLHANDLE, RT_MENU, MY_FID, &pmt);
        hwndMyMenu = WinCreateWindow( hwnd,
                                      WC_MENU,
                                      NULL,
                                      MS_ACTIONBAR | MS_TITLEBUTTON,
                                      0, 0, 0, 0,
                                      hwnd,
                                      HWND_BOTTOM,
                                      MY_FID,
                                      pmt,
                                      NULL );
        DosFreeResource( pmt );
```

This code uses the DosGetResource API to load a menu template that describes the menu button and its pull-down menu. The pointer pmt is set to point to a menu template and is used as control data in the call that is made to the WinCreateWindow API. The menu template is described in the FRMMENU.RC file and has the ID number MY_FID. The call to WinCreateWindow creates the window of the menu button with a window ID of MY_FID. The window ID of the menu button (MY_FID) must be set to a value that is not equal to any of the FID numbers; otherwise the frame window will format the menu button as one of the standard controls.

To create the FRMMENU menu button, the window style flags MS_ACTIONBAR and MS_TITLEBUTTON are used to give the menu button the behavior of an action bar while avoiding drawing borders, which are not desired for a title bar button. The MS_ACTIONBAR flag also affects how menu items are arranged, because if this flag is not set, PM will try to draw the menu button as a pull-down or pop-up menu with items that are arranged in a column. The MS_ACTIONBAR style instructs PM to place menu items horizontally across the window and to omit the extra borders that are normally used by pull-down and pop-up menus.

After the menu button window has been created, the menu template that was loaded by DosGetResource can be released by calling DosFreeResource. The menu template is used to create the needed menu items and submenus, but once the menu has been created, the menu template is no longer needed.

To draw the menu button, two system bitmaps, SBMP_CHILDSYSMENU and SBMP_CHILDSYSMENUDEP, are used to draw the menu button when it is pressed or released. The following code is used to load the two needed bitmaps:

```
/* load the bitmaps of a button both pressed and not pressed */
hbmBtn    = WinGetSysBitmap( HWND_DESKTOP, SBMP_CHILDSYSMENU );
hbmBtnDep = WinGetSysBitmap( HWND_DESKTOP, SBMP_CHILDSYSMENUDEP );
```

```
/* get the height and width of the child menu bitmap */
GpiQueryBitmapParameters( hbmBtn, &bmpinfo );
cxBitmap = bmpinfo.cx;
cyBitmap = bmpinfo.cy;
```

This code includes a call to `GpiQueryBitmapParameters`, which is used to query the size of the button bitmaps. Because these two bitmaps are the same size, only one of the bitmaps is queried, and its width and height are stored in the variables `cxBitmap` and `cyBitmap`, respectively. These two variables are used when the menu button size is set with a `WM_MEASUREITEM` message sent to the frame by the window of the menu button.

The WM_QUERYFRAMECTLCOUNT Message

Because the FRMMENU program adds one nonstandard control to its frame window, the frame window needs to be notified, each time it is formatted, that the additional control exists. During the formatting of the FRMMENU controls, a `WM_QUERYFRAMECTLCOUNT` message is sent to the frame to query the number of frame controls. The sending of this message provides an appropriate opportunity to specify that the frame has an added nonstandard control.

When the FRMMENU program receives a `WM_QUERYFRAMECTLCOUNT` message, the window procedure (`fci.pfnWindowProc`) used by the frame window class is called. The frame window procedure returns the number of controls with FID window IDs. The FRMMENU program then increments this value by one to notify PM about the existence of an added control. When the `fci.pfnWindowProc` procedure handles a `WM_QUERYFRAMECTLCOUNT` message, the procedure will not register the menu button as a frame control, because the menu button does not have an FID number as a window ID. Giving the menu button an FID number as a window ID is not a proper solution, because even though the `fci.pfmWindowProc` procedure would automatically count the menu button when it handled a `WM_QUERYFRAMECTLCOUNT` message, the `WM_FORMATFRAME` message will cause the menu button to be improperly formatted as a standard frame control associated with the FID number.

The WM_FORMATFRAME Message

The FRMMENU program sets the values in the `SWP` arrays that the first parameters of the `WM_FORMATFRAME` messages point to. Such values are set by first calling the `fci.pfnWindowProc` procedure to initially set the data in the `SWP` array for the standard controls and then altering the result to format the menu button. The following code shows how FRMMENU uses a call to PM to initially handle `WM_FORMATFRAME` messages:

```
NumberOfSWPs = (LONG)(*fci.pfnWindowProc)( hwnd, msg, mp1, mp2 );
```

In this code, the first parameter of the WM_FORMATFRAME message (mp1) points to an SWP array that is of sufficient size to handle the number of available controls. PM allocates the SWP array, and the FRMMENU program specifies the needed size of the array with the return code of the WM_QUERYFRAMECTLCOUNT message.

The NumberOfSWPs variable contains the number of standard controls that the frame procedure fci.pfnWindowProc has formatted. In the FRMMENU program, the value of NumberOfSWPs is initially one less than the actual number of controls, because PM is unaware of the FRMMENU menu button. The FRMMENU program must format the menu button itself by adding information about it to the SWP array and returning the WM_FORMATFRAME message with the value (NumberOfSWPs + 1)—a value that equals the number of standard frame controls plus the additional nonstandard menu button.

When PM initializes the SWP array, the array typically describes the controls in the following standard order: FID_TITLEBAR, FID_SYSMENU, FID_MINMAX, FID_MENU, and FID_CLIENT. The next-to-last SWP structure in the array describes the size of the client window. The last SWP structure in the array is empty, because PM has no code to carry out the formatting of the added menu button control.

The order of the controls in the SWP array represents the Z-order that the controls will have in the frame window. It is important to position the slowly drawn client window last in the SWP array to ensure that the more-quickly drawn windows are drawn before the drawing of the client window is undertaken when the frame window is repainted.

To maintain the proper Z-order, the FRMMENU program must insert the added menu button in the SWP array before the SWP structure that describes the client window. The client window is described in the next-to-last element in the SWP array. The FRMMENU program moves the contents of the client window SWP element into the last SWP element. The SWP element that originally described the client window is overwritten with information describing the menu button. This procedure inserts the menu button before the client window.

To reorder the SWP array, the FRMMENU program temporarily copies the contents of the SWP of the client window into a variable called swp. The following line of code performs the copying:

```
/* copy FID_CLIENT's SWP structure */
swp = aswp[NumberOfSWPs];
```

After this line, the FRMMENU program will overwrite the aswp[NumberOfSWPs] variable with information describing the position and size of the menu button. To calculate size and position, the FRMMENU button must reposition the title bar to make room for the menu button. To change the title bar, the structure in the SWP array that describes the title bar must be changed.

Except for the uniformly correct assumption that the position of the client window is last, a program should not assume that the order of the SWP array matches the standard order that is used by PM, for the order of the SWP array may have been altered by a subclassing window procedure. In Chapter 23 a method is discussed that reregisters a public window class before any applications have been started. A program that alters how a standard frame control is formatted should search through the SWP array for an SWP structure that has a matching FID value that identifies the control.

The following code is used by the FRMMENU program to search the array for the SWP structure that describes the title bar:

```
/* go through the array to find the desired frame controls */
for (i=0; i < NumberOfSWPs; i++)
    if (WinQueryWindowUShort( aswp[i].hwnd, QWS_ID ) == FID_TITLEBAR ) {
        pswpTitleBar = &aswp[i];
        break;
    }
```

The following code is used by the FRMMENU program to alter the title bar to make room for the menu button:

```
        cxMenu = cxBitmap;
        cyMenu = pswpTitleBar->cy;
        xMenu  = pswpTitleBar->x;
        yMenu  = pswpTitleBar->y;
        pswpTitleBar->cx -= cxMenu;
        pswpTitleBar->x  += cxMenu;
```

The FRMMENU program sets the next-to-last SWP structure to contain data regarding the size and position of the menu button control. The following code shows how the last SWP structure is initialized:

```
/* position menu button where the left side of the title bar used to be
 *      and set the width and height of the menu button
 */
aswp[NumberOfSWPs].fl =  SWP_MOVE
                       | SWP_SIZE
                       | SWP_SHOW;
aswp[NumberOfSWPs].cx = cxMenu;
aswp[NumberOfSWPs].cy = cyMenu;
aswp[NumberOfSWPs].x  = xMenu;
aswp[NumberOfSWPs].y  = yMenu;
aswp[NumberOfSWPs].hwnd = hwndMyMenu;
aswp[NumberOfSWPs].hwndInsertBehind = NULLHANDLE;
aswp[NumberOfSWPs].ulReserved1 = 0;
aswp[NumberOfSWPs].ulReserved2 = 0;
```

It is important to note that the SWP_NOADJUST flag was not added to the variable aswp[NumberOfSWPs].fl. The SWP_NOADJUST flag will prevent WM_ADJUSTWINDOWPOS messages being sent to a window. Most windows have no need for a WM_ADJUSTWINDOWPOS message except for menu windows.

A menu window, such as the FRMMENU menu button, requires a WM_ADJUSTWINDOWPOS message to be sent to it when the window is being repositioned. The WM_ADJUSTWINDOWPOS notifies a window being resized of the size it may be given. If the new size is not appropriate for the window, it can alter the data given by the WM_ADJUSTWINDOWPOS message. A frame window will use this feature to get a size for its action bar.

When a menu window receives a WM_ADJUSTWINDOWPOS message, the menu window will calculate the new positions for its menu items and the sizes that are needed to contain them. A menu will adjust only the height that is given by the WM_ADJUSTWINDOWPOS message; the width suggested by the message will be left untouched. A frame window formatting an action bar will use the size calculated by a menu window's reply to WM_ADJUSTWINDOWPOS and will position its action bar to have the full width of its client area. The height can expand as may be needed and can even expand to fill the area where a client window normally is placed.

One property unique to menus is that a menu window relies on the WM_ADJUSTWINDOWPOS message not only to suggest an appropriate size, but also to calculate the positions of its menu items. Without a WM_ADJUSTWINDOWPOS message, a menu window would be unable to position its items. The result would be a solid-colored rectangle with no menu items. If a SWP_NOADJUST message were used in the foregoing code, the FRMMENU menu button would not properly draw the three-dimensional button.

Once the FRMMENU program has placed information describing its menu button in the next-to-last structure of the SWP array, the last structure is set with information that describes the client window. During the formatting of the frame, the variable NumberOfSWPs is used as an index for the next-to-last and final structures in the SWP array. When information describing the client window is copied to the final SWP structure, NumberOfSWPs is set to be an index for the final structure. The following line of code places the client window back onto the SWP array after it has been temporarily stored in the swp variable:

```
/* place FID_CLIENT last by copying it from swp to the end of aswp */
aswp[NumberOfSWPs] = swp;
```

The techniques that are discussed in Chapter 18 and in this chapter can be used in a wide variety of ways to provide sets of controls in frame windows that are tailored to meet the unique needs of a wide variety of PM applications. A creatively designed set of controls can be provided in a frame window essentially by creating a new class of frame window, as has been described in this chapter.

CHAPTER 20
Dynamic Link Libraries

A dynamic link library (DLL) provides a module that OS/2 applications can use to store resources and executable code. Any process can load a DLL and can take advantage of its functions and resources. A DLL can be used to provide a library of functions that can be called by a program just as if the functions were APIs. In fact, all of PM's APIs are made accessible to programs through the use of DLLs, with a majority of the APIs residing in PMWIN.DLL.

The object-oriented capabilities of DLLs render them very useful for developing almost any type of system software. Collecting common functions in a DLL facilitates code reusability, encourages the writing of good compact code, and makes it relatively easy to hide and encapsulate information. The functions that are contained within a DLL can be enhanced, modified or updated at any time without requiring that client applications be recompiled.

When providing a library of functions in a DLL, it is common for programmers to fail to take full advantage of OS/2's *exception handling*. With exception handling, a function can be made more "bulletproof" by giving it an ability to catch such errors as invalid parameters before OS/2 is forced to end a program because the program is behaving improperly. If a DLL is supplying a set of APIs, each of its functions should be able to recover from a set of invalid parameters without ultimately causing a program to terminate abnormally. Exception handling can protect DLLs from ill-behaved programs.

In this chapter a DLL called QBOX is presented that provides its own API function and makes use of OS/2's built-in exception handling. A program called TESTAPP is used to test the QBOX API with functions that use valid and invalid parameters. The invalid parameters cause errors from which many programs would not be able to recover. However, the QBOX DLL is capable of making a graceful recovery from these errors and returns an appropriate error code.

309

DYNAMIC VS. STATIC LINKING

Application programs can gain access to the functions, data, and resources of a DLL by using a process called dynamic linking. By using dynamic linking, an application can avoid containing large static libraries. By storing a library of functions in a DLL, a program can have a more compact, more efficient size, and the code that is included in the DLL can be shared with other programs that need to implement its functions.

DLLs save memory, because programs that share the same functions can store a single statement of such functions in a single location, where it can be accessed as needed. Both hard disk space and system memory are saved from storing redundant code.

While the dynamic link process is similar to the static link process, the resulting modules (`.DLL` files and `.EXE` files, respectively) are quite different. Unlike statically linked library functions, dynamically linked library functions are not stored in the modules that reference them. Instead, information about the dynamically linked library function and its corresponding DLL file are stored in the module header. At run time, the DLL information that is stored in the module header is used by the operating system to load the necessary DLLs and to execute the functions stored within these DLLs.

THE LIBPATH STATEMENT

Whenever a program starts to execute, OS/2 loads the DLLs that are needed to run the program. The `LIBPATH` statement, which is located in the `CONFIG.SYS` file, determines the search path and search order that are used by the operating system to locate a DLL at program execution time. Following is a sample `LIBPATH` statement:

```
LIBPATH=.;C:\OS2\DLL;C:\OS2\MDOS;C:\OS2\APPS\DLL;D:\TOOLKT20\DLL;D:\IBMC\DLL
```

The period immediately following the equal sign in this `LIBPATH` statement tells the operating system to begin by searching the current directory for the DLL in question. If the DLL is not found in the current directory, the operating system will check the next directory that is specified in the `LIBPATH` statement. While a user can modify the `LIBPATH` statement at any time, any changes that are made by the user will not take effect until the system is rebooted to load the updated `CONFIG.SYS` file.

THE QBOX DLL

An example DLL called QBOX, the source code for which is presented in this section, illustrates how to build a DLL. QBOX exports a library function called `QBox` that can be called to display a message-box–like dialog that queries the user

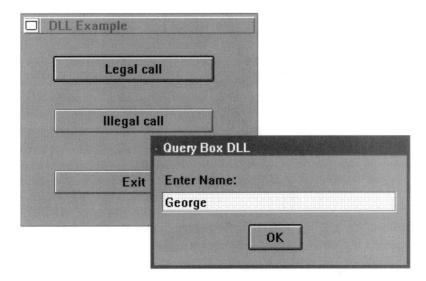

FIGURE 20.1 The QBOX dialog created by using the TESTAPP program.

for a text string. The QBOX dialog displays an entry field and an "OK" button for use in closing the dialog box. Labels for the dialog's title bar and entry field can be specified when calling the QBox function.

Figure 20.1 shows the QBOX dialog as it appears with a given title and entry field label. The program that is shown using the QBOX dialog is called TESTAPP and is presented later in this chapter.

When a user clicks on the "OK" button, the text in the entry field is copied to a buffer that is specified by a pointer when the QBox function is called. If the pointer to the buffer is invalid, the QBox function is able to return an error code, because it uses OS/2's exception handling. Without exception handling, a program that uses the QBOX DLL would be terminated by OS/2 as the result of a bad address being detected by a hardware trap.

The source code for the QBOX DLL is listed in the following five files:

QBOX.C

```
#define INCL_WIN
#define INCL_DOS
#define INCL_DOSEXCEPTIONS
#define INCL_ERRORS
#include <os2.h>
#include <string.h>
#include <setjmp.h>
#include "qbox.h"
```

```
/* function prototypes */
ULONG EXPENTRY XHandler( PEXCEPTIONREPORTRECORD,
                         PEXCEPTIONREGISTRATIONRECORD,
                         PCONTEXTRECORD,
                         PVOID );
MRESULT EXPENTRY MyDlgProc( HWND, ULONG, MPARAM, MPARAM );


/* global variables */
jmp_buf env;

APIRET EXPENTRY QBox( HWND hwndParent,
                      HWND hwndOwner,
                      PSZ pszTitle,
                      PSZ pszLabel,
                      PSZ pszBuffer,
                      ULONG ulLen )
{
   HMODULE hmod;
   HWND hwndDlg, hwndEF;
   PVOID pMem;
   EXCEPTIONREGISTRATIONRECORD XRegRec;

   XRegRec.ExceptionHandler = (_ERR * volatile)XHandler ;
   DosSetExceptionHandler( (PEXCEPTIONREGISTRATIONRECORD)&XRegRec );

   if (setjmp( env )) {
       DosUnsetExceptionHandler( &XRegRec ) ;
       return (APIRET)ERROR_INVALID_PARAMETER;
   }

   DosQueryModuleHandle( "QBOX", &hmod );
   hwndDlg = WinLoadDlg( hwndParent,      /* parent            */
                         hwndOwner,       /* owner             */
                         MyDlgProc,       /* dialog window proc */
                         hmod,            /* module handle     */
                         IDD_QBOX,        /* dialog template ID */
                         NULL );          /* no app data       */

   WinSetWindowText( hwndDlg, pszTitle );
   WinSetDlgItemText( hwndDlg, IDD_TEXT, pszLabel );

   hwndEF = WinWindowFromID( hwndDlg, IDD_EF );

   WinSendMsg( hwndEF,
               EM_SETTEXTLIMIT,
               MPFROMSHORT( (SHORT)ulLen ),
               0 );

   WinProcessDlg( hwndDlg );

   DosAllocMem( (PPVOID)&pMem,
                (ULONG)ulLen,
                (ULONG)PAG_READ | PAG_WRITE | PAG_COMMIT );
```

```
   WinQueryWindowText( hwndEF, ulLen, pMem );
   strcpy( pszBuffer, pMem );
   DosFreeMem( pMem );
   DosUnsetExceptionHandler( &XRegRec ) ;

   return (APIRET)NO_ERROR;
} /* end of QBox */


ULONG EXPENTRY XHandler( PEXCEPTIONREPORTRECORD pXRepRec,
                         PEXCEPTIONREGISTRATIONRECORD pRegRec,
                         PCONTEXTRECORD pContextRecord,
                         PVOID pUnk )
{
   if ( pXRepRec->ExceptionNum == XCPT_ACCESS_VIOLATION )
      longjmp( env,1 );
   else
      return XCPT_CONTINUE_SEARCH;
} /* end of XHandler */


MRESULT EXPENTRY MyDlgProc( HWND hwndDlg, ULONG msg, MPARAM mp1, MPARAM mp2 )
{

   switch (msg) {

      case WM_COMMAND:
         switch (LOUSHORT( mp1 )) {

            case IDD_OK:
               return(MRESULT)( WinDismissDlg( hwndDlg, TRUE ) );
         }
         break;

      default:
         return WinDefDlgProc( hwndDlg, msg, mp1, mp2 );
   }

   return (MRESULT)FALSE;
} /* end of MyDlgProc */
```

QBOX.H

```
/*  function declaration */
APIRET EXPENTRY QBox( HWND, HWND, PSZ, PSZ, PSZ, ULONG );


#define IDD_QBOX 101
#define IDD_TEXT 102
#define IDD_EF   103
#define IDD_OK   104
```

QBOX.DEF

```
LIBRARY      QBOX

DESCRIPTION  'DLL and Exception Handling Example'

PROTMODE

DATA         LOADONCALL
CODE         LOADONCALL

EXPORTS      QBox
```

QBOX.RC

```
#include <os2.h>
#include "qbox.h"

DLGTEMPLATE IDD_QBOX LOADONCALL MOVEABLE DISCARDABLE
BEGIN
    DIALOG  "", IDD_QBOX, 33, 27, 188, 59, WS_VISIBLE, FCF_TITLEBAR
    BEGIN
        LTEXT            "",   IDD_TEXT,  9, 42, 170,  8
        ENTRYFIELD       "",   IDD_EF,    9, 30, 170,  8, ES_MARGIN
        DEFPUSHBUTTON    "OK", IDD_OK,   71,  8,  40, 14
    END
END
```

QBOX.MAK

```
all : qbox.dll

qbox.dll : qbox.obj qbox.def qbox.res
        link386 /NOI qbox,qbox.dll,,DDE4NBS+os2386.lib,qbox.def
        rc qbox.res qbox.dll

qbox.res : qbox.rc
        rc -r qbox.rc

qbox.obj : qbox.c qbox.h
        icc /C+ /Ge- /Gm+ /Gd- /Ms $*.c
```

Exporting Library Functions and Data

A DLL makes library functions available to application programs and to other DLLs by "exporting" them. This is accomplished by using the EXPORT statement in a module definition file (.DEF file).

The QBox function is exported by using its name in the following statement:

```
EXPORTS       QBox
```

This statement could have been exported using *ordinals*. An ordinal defines an index value that can be used to reference a library function or a data item that is being exported. The following statement shows how the QBox function could have been exported using an ordinal value:

```
EXPORTS       QBox  @1
```

If an ordinal value has been assigned, programs have the option of calling the QBox function not by name but rather by calling the function number (@1). While this form of function call does not change how the C code for a program is written, it does change how the module definition file is set up for the program.

Ensuring Appropriate Linkage

By default, the C SET/2 compiler uses the *optlink* linkage convention for putting parameters on a stack. The optlink convention is an optimized calling convention that uses some of the general-purpose registers for parameter passing; corresponds to the /Mp compiler option. The alternative linkage convention is the *system* linkage convention, which corresponds to the /Ms compiler option.

Applications and DLLs that dynamically link to functions that reside in a DLL must ensure that there are no conflicts with the manner in which parameters are placed on the stack. The optlink option cannot be used for functions stored in a DLL; such functions need the system linkage to have parameters placed on the stack correctly.

The QBOX DLL uses the following function prototypes to assist in avoiding linkage convention conflicts:

```
/* function declaration */
APIRET EXPENTRY QBox( HWND, HWND, PSZ, PSZ, PSZ, ULONG );
```

The EXPENTRY macro is used in this declaration and should be used for all DLL-exported entry points. EXPENTRY is defined in the public header file OS2DEF.H and is equal to the _System keyword, which will force the compiler to use the system linkage convention for the function that is listed in the prototype. This keyword will override the /Mp compiler switch.

The function prototype for QBox is listed in the file QBOX.H. Applications and DLLs that dynamically link to the QBox function need to include the QBOX.H header file to avoid possible linkage convention conflicts.

EXCEPTION HANDLING

OS/2 is a protected operating system that prevents a program from overwriting areas of memory that are being used to store executable code, or code and data that belong to another program. For example, if an executing program attempts to reference a piece of data that it does not own, the operating system will flag this condition and will interrupt the execution of the ill-behaved program. This interruption of program execution is called an *exception*. OS/2 supports many different types of exceptions. When an exception (sometimes referred to as a *trap*) occurs, the operating system passes control to one of several provided exception handlers. The type of exception that is encountered determines which exception handler will be called by the operating system.

The OS/2 operating system supplies a default exception handler for each of the possible exceptions. DLLs and application programs can override the default exception handler by registering their own exception handler, using the DosSetExceptionHandler API.

The C programming language makes heavy use of pointers. It is quite common for C programs to have a parameter for a function that points to a location in memory. If a pointer is invalid, or if a memory address is encountered that is not accessible by the executing program, a memory access exception will occur. Under this condition, the default exception handler will prevent the program from proceeding.

The default exception handler is usually sufficient for application programs. Exceptions caused by application programs usually are found and corrected in the development stage of the application. DLLs, on the other hand, have little control over the parameters that are used. DLLs can use the exception-handling capabilities of OS/2 to allow the calling program to proceed by returning an error code instead of letting the operating system terminate the program.

In the QBOX DLL, the following code is used to set up exception handling before the QBox function uses any of its given parameters:

```
XRegRec.ExceptionHandler = (_ERR * volatile)XHandler ;
DosSetExceptionHandler( (PEXCEPTIONREGISTRATIONRECORD)&XRegRec );
```

In this code the DosSetExceptionHandler API is used to set up a function called XHandler as the exception handler for the QBOX DLL. The address of XHandler is specified in an ExceptionHandler field of the EXCEPTIONREGISTRATIONRECORD data structure.

After the foregoing code is executed by a program, traps that are caused by invalid parameters being given to the QBox function are handled by the XHandler function. The QBox function makes the following call to a standard C function, setjmp, to store information about the present state of the executing program:

```
if (setjmp( env )) {
    DosUnsetExceptionHandler( &XRegRec ) ;
    return(APIRET)ERROR_INVALID_PARAMETER;
}
```

When `setjmp` is called, the return code is zero and the code in the `if` statement is not executed. The `setjmp` function stores such information as the present address of the machine code instruction that is being executed. By calling a function called `longjmp`, the program can be made to jump back to the address stored by `setjmp`, except that the return code is set to 1. The altered return code causes the code in the `if` statement to be executed.

If the `XHandler` function receives a trap, it checks to determine whether the trap was caused by an illegal access to memory. The handler function also calls `longjmp` to cause the present program to return to the call that was made to `setjmp` in the `QBox` function. By this arrangement, the environment is set up so that a return code of 1 is set and the `QBox` function exits with an error code. Once the `QBox` function has finished using the parameters it is given, the exception handler is released by using the `DosUnsetExceptionHandler` API.

THE TESTAPP PROGRAM

To test the QBOX DLL and its exception handling, a program called TESTAPP (the source code for which is presented in this section) can be used. The TESTAPP program displays a dialog box with two buttons that, if pressed, will call the `QBox` function. The first button is labeled "Legal call" and causes a QBOX dialog to appear.

The second button is labeled "Illegal call" and causes a QBOX dialog to appear, but at the same time it causes a given pointer to intentionally be set so that it is invalid. When the QBOX dialog is closed, the QBOX DLL will receive an exception when it tries to store data at the address given by the invalid pointer. Since the QBOX DLL has exception handling, it returns an error code to TESTAPP rather than let the TESTAPP program be terminated by default.

The TESTAPP program's source code is listed in the following five files:

TESTAPP.C

```
#define INCL_WIN
#define INCL_DOS
#define INCL_ERRORS
#include <os2.h>
#include "testapp.h"
#include "qbox.h"


/* function prototypes */
INT main( VOID );
MRESULT EXPENTRY MyDlgProc( HWND, ULONG, MPARAM, MPARAM );
```

```
/* global variables */
CHAR szBuffer[TEXT_LIMIT];
INT main( VOID )
{
   HAB       hab;
   HMQ       hmq;
   HWND      hwndDlg;
   HMODULE   hMod;
   SWP       swp;

   hab = WinInitialize( 0 );

   hmq = WinCreateMsgQueue( hab, 0 );

   DosLoadModule( NULL, 0, "QBOX", &hMod );

   hwndDlg = WinLoadDlg( HWND_DESKTOP,   /* parent             */
                         NULLHANDLE,     /* no owner           */
                         MyDlgProc,      /* dialog window proc */
                         NULLHANDLE,     /* module handle      */
                         IDD_MYDLG,      /* dialog template ID */
                         NULL);          /* no app data        */

   WinSendMsg( hwndDlg,
               WM_SETICON,
               (MPARAM)WinQuerySysPointer( HWND_DESKTOP,
                                           SPTR_APPICON,
                                           FALSE ),
               NULL );

   /* find where system would place dialog box */
   WinQueryTaskSizePos( hab, 0, &swp );

   /* place dialog box at position given by the shell */
   WinSetWindowPos( hwndDlg,        /* change the dialog window's position */
                    NULLHANDLE,     /* ignored, SWP_ZORDER not set */
                    swp.x, swp.y,   /* position of lower left corner */
                    0, 0,           /* ignored SWP_SIZE not set */
                    SWP_SHOW        /* show dialog box */
                    | SWP_MOVE );   /* do not ignore swp.x and swp.y */


   WinProcessDlg( hwndDlg );

   DosFreeModule( hMod );

   WinDestroyMsgQueue( hmq );
   WinTerminate( hab );

   return 0;
} \* end of main */
```

```
MRESULT EXPENTRY MyDlgProc( HWND hwndDlg, ULONG msg, MPARAM mp1, MPARAM mp2 )
{

    switch (msg) {

        case WM_COMMAND:
            switch (LOUSHORT( mp1 )) {

                case IDB_LEGAL:
                  { APIRET rc;

                      rc = QBox( HWND_DESKTOP,
                                 hwndDlg,
                                 "Query Box DLL",
                                 "Enter Name:",
                                 szBuffer,
                                 TEXT_LIMIT );

                      if (rc == NO_ERROR)
                          WinMessageBox( HWND_DESKTOP,
                                         HWND_DESKTOP,
                                         szBuffer,
                                         "Name Returned",
                                         0,
                                         MB_OK );
                  } break;

                case IDB_ILLEGAL:
                  { APIRET rc;

                      rc  = QBox( HWND_DESKTOP,
                                  hwndDlg,
                                  "Query Box DLL",
                                  "Enter name:",
                                  NULL,            /* NULL is an invalid parameter */
                                  TEXT_LIMIT );

                      if  (rc != NO_ERROR)
                          WinMessageBox( HWND_DESKTOP,
                                         HWND_DESKTOP,
                                         "Exception handler worked!",
                                         "Invalid Pointer Test",
                                         0,
                                         MB_OK );
                  } break;

                case IDB_EXIT:
                    WinDestroyWindow( hwndDlg );
                    break;
            }
            break;
                case WM_CLOSE:
                    Win Destroy Window ( hwndDlg );
                    break;
```

```
   default:
      return WinDefDlgProc( hwndDlg, msg, mp1, mp2 );
   }

   return (MRESULT)FALSE;
} /* end of MyDlgProc */
```

TESTAPP.H

```
#define IDD_MYDLG          201

#define IDB_LEGAL          202
#define IDB_ILLEGAL        203
#define IDB_EXIT           204

#define TEXT_LIMIT         50
```

TESTAPP.RC

```
#include <os2.h>
#include "testapp.h"

DLGTEMPLATE IDD_MYDLG LOADONCALL MOVEABLE DISCARDABLE
BEGIN
   DIALOG  "DLL Example", IDD_MYDLG, -1, -28, 170, 102, 0,
           FCF_SYSMENU | FCF_TITLEBAR | FCF_TASKLIST
   BEGIN
      DEFPUSHBUTTON  "Legal call",    IDB_LEGAL,   23, 76, 119, 14
      PUSHBUTTON     "Illegal call",  IDB_ILLEGAL, 23, 48, 119, 14
      PUSHBUTTON     "Exit",          IDB_EXIT,    23, 15, 119, 14
   END
END
```

TESTAPP.DEF

```
NAME          TESTAPP WINDOWAPI

DESCRIPTION   'DLL Example Program'

CODE          MOVEABLE
DATA          MOVEABLE MULTIPLE

HEAPSIZE      10240
STACKSIZE     24576

IMPORTS       QBOX.QBox
```

TESTAPP.MAK

```
all : testapp.exe

testapp.exe : testapp.obj testapp.def testapp.res
        link386 /NOI /PM:PM testapp,,,,testapp.def;
        rc testapp.res

testapp.res: testapp.rc testapp.h qbox.h
        rc -r testapp.rc

testapp.obj:testapp.c testapp.h
        icc /C /Ss /W3 .\$*.c
```

Importing Library Routines

The TESTAPP program imports the QBox function by using the IMPORTS statement in the TESTAPP.DEF file. The following code excerpt from TESTAPP is used to import the QBox library routine:

```
IMPORTS        QBOX.QBox
```

Any application program can import a DLL's functions so long as the library and function names are known. The foregoing example is referred to as *importing by name*. If QBOX exported these functions by ordinal, the TESTAPP program could have used the ordinal number that is associated with the QBox function to import it. The following statement is a sample of how an application can import library functions by ordinal:

```
IMPORTS        QBox = QBOX.1
```

Another alternative that can be used to access an exported library function or data contained in a DLL is to link with an import library. QBOX could have an import library created by adding the following line to the QBOX.MAK file:

```
implib qbox.lib qbox.def
```

In this code the implib utility (which comes with the OS/2 tool kit) uses a the QBOX.DEF file to create an import library called QBOX.LIB. Instead of having IMPORTS statements added to the TESTAPP.DEF file, the TESTAPP program can be linked to the QBOX.LIB file as if QBOX.LIB were a static library.

CHAPTER 21
System Hooks

PM provides a set of *hooks*, which give programs access to the inner workings of PM. Hooks are yet another way to extend the capabilities of PM. If a program needs to alter how PM handles certain operations, hooks provide a way of altering PM's behavior.

To use a hook, PM programs register a *hook procedure*, which is to be called by PM when a defined event or set of events takes place. The hook procedure is notified of the event before notice of the event has been dispatched to the rest of the system. This allows a hook procedure to add, modify, or filter events that are seen by the rest of the system.

Many hook procedures can be registered for the same hook. PM will call all hook procedures that are registered for a particular hook each time an event occurs that relates to the particular hook. While it is unusual to have more than one procedure registered for a hook, PM can maintain a chain of hooks and will always start with the hook procedure that has been registered most recently.

Toward the last half of this chapter, a program called PLAYBACK is presented that takes advantage of a specific set of hooks that can be used for recording and playing back keystrokes. The PLAYBACK program can store two sets of keystrokes that can be played back to any program running on the PM desktop. When the user presses one of the given "hot keys," PLAYBACK can trick a program into believing that a series of keystrokes are being entered at the keyboard. By using hooks, the PLAYBACK program gains access to the way PM notifies programs of keyboard events. Two of the types of hooks used by PLAYBACK are called *journal hooks*. A third type of hook used by PLAYBACK is called an *input hook*. These and other types of hooks are discussed in the section that follows.

TYPES OF HOOKS

PM supports several different types of hooks. Each individual hook type is identified by a name that has an HK_ prefix. To use a hook, a hook procedure must be registered with PM. The format of the parameters that are used when a hook procedure is called depends on the type of hook that is being used.

The sections that follow discuss the types of hooks that are supported by PM.

The Input Hook (HK_INPUT)

The input hook allows an application to monitor all messages that are to be received by the `WinGetMsg` or `WinPeekMsg` call. An application can register an input hook for a local message queue or for the system message queue. Once an input hook procedure has finished processing an event supplied by a hook, it can instruct PM either to continue through the hook chain or to end the processing of the event. By using a return code of `FALSE`, a procedure that uses an input hook can tell PM to continue to process a message. If the procedure returns a code of `TRUE`, the message will not continue to be processed.

The Journal-Record Hook (HK_JOURNALRECORD)

The journal-record hook allows applications to record a series of keyboard and pointing device events. By filtering out the other types of events, PM sends only keyboard and pointing device events to a journal-record hook procedure. The journal-record hook procedure can store a sequence of events it receives so that another type of hook procedure, namely the journal-playback hook, can be used to play the sequence of events back.

Journal-record hooks must always be associated with the system message queue. Unlike the input hook, PM does not allow a journal-record hook procedure to determine whether a message should not continue through the hook chain. The journal-record hook only allows a procedure to monitor events, so no return code is used to indicate whether PM should continue to handle an event.

The Journal-Playback Hook (HK_JOURNALPLAYBACK)

The journal-playback hook allows applications to insert messages into the system message queue. This hook is usually used in conjunction with the journal-record hook to play back a series of previously recorded keystrokes, pointing device events, or both. Like the journal-record hook, a journal-playback hook must always be associated with the system message queue.

The Message-Filter Hook (HK_MSGFILTER)

The message-filter hook allows applications to monitor messages that are received by PM when it is in a *system-modal* message loop. A system-modal message loop is simply a while loop that repeatedly calls `WinGetMsg`. The difference between a normal message loop and PM's modal message loop is the accessibility of changing the way the loop dispatches messages. Since the loop is built into PM, a hook must be provided if programs are to be allowed access to a message that is received by PM's message loop.

Several system-modal loops are used by PM to handle such operations as the movement of the tracking rectangle for windows and the display of dialog and message boxes. The message-filter hook procedure provides a parameter to identify which system-modal loop PM currently is running. The following are the values that are used to identify the origin of a message received by a message-filter hook:

- MSGF_DIALOGBOX   The dialog box message loop.
- MSGF_MESSAGEBOX   The message box message loop.
- MSGF_TRACK   The tracking rectangle message loop, used for a sizing or tracking operation.
- MSGF_DRAG   The direct manipulation (drag-drop) message loop.
- MSGF_DDEPOSTMSG   Dynamic Data Exchange (DDE) message loop.

Like the input hook, the message-filter hook procedure can specify a return code to indicate whether the event gets passed to the next hook procedure.

The Send-Message Hook (HK_SENDMSG)

The send-message hook allows applications to monitor all messages that are sent, rather than posted, to a message queue. PM applications can call a window procedure directly, using the WinSendMsg API. The send-message hook will be called before the message is sent to the window procedure that is specified by the HWND parameter of the WinSendMsg API. The send-message hook can work in conjunction with the input hook to allow an application to monitor all messages that are being delivered to PM applications.

Applications can register a send-message hook for a local message queue or for the system message queue. The send-message hook procedure does not contain a return code and therefore cannot filter out messages that are sent to a window.

The Help Hook (HK_HELP)

The help hook allows applications to monitor WM_HELP messages that are being processed by the default message handler. PM will call a registered help hook procedure during the default processing of a WM_HELP message. The help hook procedure is provided with information that describes the context in which help was requested, such as the ID of the window from which help was requested and the window's screen coordinates.

A help hook procedure can return a value of FALSE, to instruct PM to pass the message to the next help hook procedure in the chain, or TRUE, to end the processing of the message.

The Find-Word Hook (HK_FINDWORD)

The find-word hook allows applications to control the formatting of a character string that is displayed by using the `WinDrawText` API. When the `WinDrawText` API has been called, PM will check whether the caller has the `DT_WORDBREAK` flag set. The `DT_WORDBREAK` flag tells the `WinDrawText` API to draw only such words as fit within a provided rectangle. If the `DT_WORDBREAK` flag is set during a `WinDrawText` operation, PM will call the registered find-word hook procedure. The find-word hook procedure returns a value of `TRUE`, to instruct PM to draw the text string starting at a specific character within the string, or `FALSE`, to instruct PM to use the default text-formatting algorithm.

The Code-Page-Changed Hook (HK_CODEPAGECHANGED)

The code-page-changed hook allows applications to receive notification when the code page changes for a given message queue. This hook is purely for notification purposes and can be used by applications with language dependencies.

A *code page* defines the set of characters that are available at any given time. The raw scan codes that are generated by the keyboard hardware are translated to ASCII characters using a *keyboard translate table*. The translate table is always based off a particular code page, because code pages are usually designed to meet the requirements of a particular language. The default code page for OS/2 is code page 850, which is considered the universal code page, since it meets the requirements of many languages.

The code-page-changed hook handler does not have a return code; hence, each code-page-changed hook procedure in the chain will be notified of all code page changes.

The Destroy-Window Hook (HK_DESTROYWINDOW)

The destroy-window hook notifies applications whenever a window is destroyed. The handle of the window being destroyed is provided to the hook procedure. All destroy-window hook procedures in the hook chain will receive this notification.

The Loader Hook (HK_LOADER)

The loader hook notifies applications of the loading and unloading of DLLs and of procedures within those DLLs. The loader hook procedure is given a value that corresponds to the function requesting that the DLL be loaded. Possible origins of the loader hook event are the `WinLoadLibrary`, `WinDeleteLibrary`, `WinLoadProcedure`, and `WinDeleteProcedure` APIs. One of the parameters to the loader hook procedure is a success indicator of type `PBOOL`. If the loader hook procedure chooses to handle the loading or deleting of the library procedure, it must return a value to inform PM if the operation was successful (TRUE) or if a failure occurred (FALSE). The loader hook procedure returns a value of TRUE to instruct PM to bypass the rest of the loader hook procedures in the chain. A return value of FALSE instructs PM to call the next loader hook procedure in the chain.

Registering a Hook Procedure Using WinSetHook

Applications register a hook procedure with PM by using the WinSetHook API. The HK_ identifier determines the type of hook that is being registered. Each individual hook type may have several hook procedures registered for it. All of the hook procedures that are associated with a particular hook type form a *hook chain*. The last hook procedure registered for a particular hook type will be the first one called by PM when an appropriate event occurs. Some of the hook types allow the individual hook procedures to determine whether the event should proceed down to and through the rest of the hook chain. Other hook types do not provide this choice; rather, they ensure that all hook procedures in the chain will be called.

One of the parameters to the WinSetHook API is a message queue handle. WinSetHook allows an application to install a hook for a system queue or a message queue of the current thread by calling WinSetHook. If the value HMQ_CURRENT is used, the installed hook procedure will be associated with the message queue of the current thread. If a NULLHANDLE value is used, the hook procedure will be associated with the system message queue. In this case, the hook procedure must reside in a DLL so that it can be accessed by other threads that handle the hook for PM. Hook procedures registered for a local message queue can reside in the application, because the message queue is owned by the thread that called WinSetHook. It is important to note that some hooks, such as the journal hooks, can only be registered as system hooks. Such a requirement means that a program using the hook must have a DLL to contain the hook procedure.

Applications should issue the WinReleaseHook API to remove hook procedures from the chain when the hook procedure is no longer needed or when the application is terminating. When an application is about to be terminated, the operating system will release all hook procedures that were registered by that application.

THE PLAYBACK PROGRAM

The PLAYBACK example program allows the user to record a series of keystrokes that can be played back when a hot key is hit. To store a series of keystrokes, a button labeled "Start" must be pressed. When recording keystrokes, the

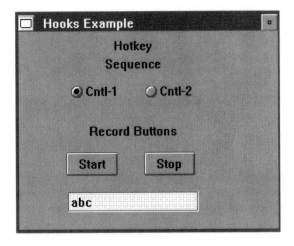

FIGURE 21.1 The PLAYBACK dialog box while recording keystrokes.

PLAYBACK program displays an entry field to show the letters of the keystrokes. Figure 21.1 shows the PLAYBACK window while the PLAYBACK program is recording a series of keystrokes.

PLAYBACK uses the record and playback journal hooks and an input hook of the system queue to accomplish its task. PLAYBACK allows the user to record two different keystroke sequences. One keystroke sequence will be assigned to the Ctrl-1 hot key sequence; the other will be assigned to the Ctrl-2 hot key sequence. The input hook is used to detect when one of the hot keys has been activated. By the use of the input hook, the system queue is filtered for the hot keys, and PLAYBACK can be activated regardless of the application that may presently have the focus.

The source code for the PLAYBACK program is listed in the following five files:

PLAYBACK.C

```
#define INCL_WIN
#include <os2.h>
#include "playback.h"
#include "hooks.h"

/* function prototypes */
INT main( VOID );
MRESULT EXPENTRY MyDlgProc( HWND, ULONG, MPARAM, MPARAM );

/* global variables */
HWND hwndEF;
```

```
INT main( VOID )
{
    HMQ  hmq;
    HAB  hab;
    QMSG Qmsg;
    HWND hwndDlg;
    SWP  swp;

    hab = WinInitialize( 0 );
    hmq = WinCreateMsgQueue( hab, 0 );

    MyInit( hab );
    SetInputHook();

    hwndDlg = WinLoadDlg( HWND_DESKTOP, /* parent              */
                          NULLHANDLE,   /* no owner            */
                          MyDlgProc,    /* dialog window proc */
                          NULLHANDLE,   /* module handle       */
                          IDD_DLG,      /* dialog template ID */
                          NULL );       /* no app data         */

    hwndEF = WinWindowFromID( hwndDlg, IDD_EF );
    WinShowWindow( hwndEF, FALSE );

    WinSendMsg( hwndDlg,
                WM_SETICON,
                (MPARAM)WinQuerySysPointer( HWND_DESKTOP,
                                            SPTR_APPICON,
                                            FALSE ),
                NULL );

    /* find where system would place dialog box */
    WinQueryTaskSizePos( hab, 0, &swp );

    /* place dialog box at position given by the shell */
    WinSetWindowPos( hwndDlg,         /* change the dialog window's position */
                     NULLHANDLE,      /* ignored, SWP_ZORDER not set */
                     swp.x, swp.y,    /* position of lower left corner */
                     0, 0,            /* ignored SWP_SIZE not set */
                     SWP_SHOW         /* show dialog box */
                     | SWP_MOVE );    /* do not ignore swp.x and swp.y */


    WinProcessDlg( hwndDlg );
    ReleaseInputHook();

    WinDestroyMsgQueue( hmq );
    WinTerminate( hab );

    return 0;
} /* end of main */

MRESULT EXPENTRY MyDlgProc( HWND hwnd, ULONG msg, MPARAM mp1, MPARAM mp2 )
{
    static USHORT usCurQ;
```

```
switch (msg) {

case WM_CONTROL:

    if (SHORT2FROMMP( mp1 ) == BN_CLICKED) {

        if (SHORT1FROMMP( mp1 ) == IDD_RAD1)
            usCurQ = 1;
        else if (SHORT1FROMMP( mp1 ) == IDD_RAD2)
            usCurQ = 2;
        break;
    }

    else if (SHORT2FROMMP( mp1 ) == EN_KILLFOCUS) {
        WinShowWindow( hwndEF, FALSE );
        WinSendMsg( hwndEF,                      /* Select all of the */
                    EM_SETSEL,                   /* text so it can be */
                    MPFROM2SHORT( 0, 0x7fff ),   /* deleted.  */
                    0 );
        WinSendMsg( hwndEF,
                    EM_CLEAR,
                    0,
                    0 );
        ReleaseRecordHook();
        break;
    }
    return WinDefDlgProc( hwnd, msg, mp1, mp2 );

case WM_COMMAND:

    switch (SHORT1FROMMP( mp1 )) {

        case IDD_START:
            WinShowWindow( hwndEF, TRUE );
            WinSetFocus( HWND_DESKTOP, hwndEF );  /* Give Entry fld focus */
            SetRecordHook( usCurQ );
            break;

        case IDD_STOP:
            WinShowWindow( hwndEF, FALSE );
            WinSendMsg( hwndEF,                      /* Select all of the */
                        EM_SETSEL,                   /* text so it can be */
                        MPFROM2SHORT( 0, 0x7fff ),   /* deleted.  */
                        0 );
            WinSendMsg( hwndEF,
                        EM_CLEAR,
                        0,
                        0 );
            ReleaseRecordHook();
            break;

        case DID_CANCEL:
            return FALSE;
            break;
```

```
            default:
                return WinDefDlgProc( hwnd, msg, mp1, mp2 );

        }

        break;

    case WM_CLOSE:
        WinDestroyWindow( hwnd );
        break;

    default:
        return WinDefDlgProc( hwnd, msg, mp1, mp2 );
    }

    return FALSE;
} /* end of MyDlgProc */
```

PLAYBACK.H

```
#define IDD_DLG      200
#define IDD_RAD1     201
#define IDD_RAD2     202
#define IDD_START    203
#define IDD_STOP     204
#define IDD_EF       205
```

PLAYBACK.RC

```
#include <os2.h>
#include "playback.h"

DLGTEMPLATE IDD_DLG LOADONCALL MOVEABLE DISCARDABLE
BEGIN
    DIALOG "Hooks Example", IDD_DLG, 40, -3, 195, 109, 0,
            FCF_SYSMENU | FCF_TITLEBAR | FCF_MINBUTTON | FCF_TASKLIST
    BEGIN
        LTEXT           "Hotkey", 206, 74, 97, 34, 8
        LTEXT           "Sequence", 207, 67, 87, 47, 8
        AUTORADIOBUTTON "Ctrl-1", IDD_RAD1, 42, 71, 39, 10, WS_TABSTOP
        AUTORADIOBUTTON "Ctrl-2", IDD_RAD2, 98, 71, 39, 10, WS_TABSTOP
        LTEXT           "Record Buttons", 208, 55, 50, 69, 8
        PUSHBUTTON      "Start", IDD_START, 37, 29, 40, 14
        PUSHBUTTON      "Stop", IDD_STOP, 96, 29, 40, 14
        ENTRYFIELD      "", IDD_EF, 41, 11, 95, 8, ES_MARGIN
    END
END
```

PLAYBACK.DEF

```
NAME        PLAYBACK WINDOWAPI

DESCRIPTION 'PM Hooks Example Program'
```

```
CODE          MOVEABLE
DATA          MOVEABLE MULTIPLE

HEAPSIZE      10240
STACKSIZE     24576

IMPORTS       HOOKS.MyInit
              HOOKS.SetInputHook
              HOOKS.ReleaseInputHook
              HOOKS.SetRecordHook
              HOOKS.ReleaseRecordHook
```

PLAYBACK.MAK

```
all : playback.exe

playback.exe : playback.obj playback.def playback.res
        link386 /NOI /PM:PM playback,,,,playback.def;
        rc playback.res

playback.res : playback.rc playback.h
        rc -r playback.rc

playback.obj : playback.c playback.h hooks.h
        icc /C /Ss /W3 \.$*.c
```

THE HOOKS DLL

Journal record and playback hooks are always associated with the system message queue. Due to this fact, the journal record and playback hook procedures must reside in a DLL. The input hook that is used by PLAYBACK to detect the hot key is also associated with the system message queue. All hooks that are used by PLAYBACK reside in HOOKS.DLL, which exports functions that the PLAYBACK program calls to set and release all hooks.

The source code for the HOOKS DLL is listed in the following four files:

HOOKS.C

```
#define INCL_WIN
#define INCL_DOS
#include <os2.h>
#include "hooks.h"


/* global variables */
HAB hab2;
HMODULE hMod;
PFN pInputHook, pRecordHook, pPlaybackHook;
QMSG aQmsg1[MAX_Q_ENTRIES], aQmsg2[MAX_Q_ENTRIES];
USHORT cQ1, cQ2, usInQ, usOutQ;
USHORT cOut = 0;
```

```
VOID EXPENTRY MyInit( HAB hab )
{
    hab2 = hab;

    DosLoadModule( NULL, 0, "HOOKS", &hMod );

    DosQueryProcAddr( hMod,
                      0,                     /* ordinal number not used   */
                      "InputHook",           /* procedure name            */
                      &pInputHook );         /* pointer to hook proc       */
    DosQueryProcAddr( hMod,
                      0,                     /* ordinal number not used   */
                      "JournalRecordHook",   /* procedure name            */
                      &pRecordHook );        /* pointer to hook proc       */

    DosQueryProcAddr( hMod,
                      0,                     /* ordinal number not used   */
                      "JournalPlaybackHook", /* procedure name            */
                      &pPlaybackHook );      /* pointer to hook proc       */

} /* end of MyInit */


VOID EXPENTRY SetInputHook( VOID )
{
    WinSetHook( hab2,
                NULLHANDLE,                  /* hook system msg Q          */
                HK_INPUT,                    /* hook type                  */
                pInputHook,                  /* our hook handler           */
                hMod );                      /* DLL needed for system hook */

} /* end of SetInputHook */


VOID EXPENTRY ReleaseInputHook( VOID )
{
    WinReleaseHook( hab2,
                    NULLHANDLE,              /* hook system msg Q          */
                    HK_INPUT,                /* hook type                  */
                    pInputHook,              /* our hook handler           */
                    hMod );                  /* DLL needed for system hook */
    DosFreeModule( hMod );
} /* end of ReleaseInputHook */


VOID EXPENTRY SetRecordHook( USHORT usQ )
{
    if (usQ == 1) {
        cQ1 = 0;
        usInQ = 1;
    }
    else {
        cQ2 = 0;
        usInQ = 2;
    }
```

```
    WinSetHook( hab2,
                NULLHANDLE,                    /* hook system msg Q        */
                HK_JOURNALRECORD,              /* hook type                */
                pRecordHook,                   /* our hook handler         */
                hMod );                        /* hook proc DLL            */

} /* end of SetRecordHook */


VOID EXPENTRY ReleaseRecordHook( VOID )
{
    WinReleaseHook( hab2,
                NULLHANDLE,                    /* system msg Q             */
                HK_JOURNALRECORD,              /* hook type                */
                pRecordHook,                   /* our hook handler         */
                hMod );                        /* hook proc DLL            */

} /* end of ReleaseRecordHook */


BOOL EXPENTRY InputHook( HAB hab, PQMSG pQmsg, ULONG fs )
{
    if((pQmsg->msg == WM_CHAR) &&
       (CHARMSG( &pQmsg->msg )->fs & KC_CTRL) &&
       (CHARMSG( &pQmsg->msg )->fs & KC_KEYUP) ) {

        if((CHARMSG( &pQmsg->msg )->scancode == SCAN_1) ||
           (CHARMSG( &pQmsg->msg )->scancode == SCAN_2) ) {
            usOutQ = CHARMSG( &pQmsg->msg )->scancode - 1;
            WinSetHook( hab2,
                    NULLHANDLE,                /* hook system msg Q        */
                    HK_JOURNALPLAYBACK,        /* hook type                */
                    pPlaybackHook,             /* our hook handler         */
                    hMod );                    /* hook proc DLL            */
        }
    }
    return (FALSE);                            /* pass the message down the chain */

} /* end of InputHook */


VOID EXPENTRY JournalRecordHook( HAB hab, PQMSG pQmsg )
{
    PQMSG pCurQmsg;

    if(pQmsg->msg == WM_CHAR) {

        if (usInQ == 1) {

            pCurQmsg = (PQMSG)(&aQmsg1[cQ1]);
            if (cQ1 >= MAX_Q_ENTRIES)
                cQ1 = 0;
            else
                ++cQ1;
        }
```

```
      else {
          pCurQmsg = (PQMSG)(&aQmsg2[cQ2]);
          if (cQ2 >= MAX_Q_ENTRIES)
             cQ2 = 0;
          else
             ++cQ2;
      }
      memcpy( pCurQmsg, pQmsg, sizeof(QMSG) );
   }
} /* end of JournalRecordHook */


ULONG EXPENTRY JournalPlaybackHook( HAB hab, BOOL fSkip, PQMSG pQmsg )
{
   PQMSG pCurQmsg;

   if(fSkip == FALSE) {
      if(usOutQ == 1)
         pCurQmsg = (PQMSG)(&aQmsg1[cOut]);
      else
         pCurQmsg = (PQMSG)(&aQmsg2[cOut]);

      pCurQmsg->time = pQmsg->time;

      memcpy( pQmsg, pCurQmsg, sizeof(QMSG) );
   }
   else {
      ++cOut;
      if (((usOutQ == 1) && (cOut >= cQ1)) ||
          ((usOutQ == 2) && (cOut >= cQ2))) {

         WinReleaseHook( hab2,
                         NULLHANDLE,          /* hook system msg Q    */
                         HK_JOURNALPLAYBACK,  /* hook type            */
                         pPlaybackHook,       /* our hook handler     */
                         hMod );              /* hook proc DLL        */
         cOut = 0;
      }
   }
   return 0L; /* time in millisecs */

} /* end of JournalPlaybackHook */
```

HOOKS.H

```
/* Prototype declarations */
VOID   EXPENTRY MyInit( HAB );
VOID   EXPENTRY SetInputHook( VOID );
VOID   EXPENTRY ReleaseInputHook( VOID );
VOID   EXPENTRY SetRecordHook( USHORT );
VOID   EXPENTRY ReleaseRecordHook( VOID );
BOOL   EXPENTRY InputHook ( HAB, PQMSG, ULONG );
VOID   EXPENTRY JournalRecordHook( HAB, PQMSG );
ULONG  EXPENTRY JournalPlaybackHook( HAB, BOOL, PQMSG );
```

```
#define MAX_Q_ENTRIES 100
#define SCAN_1          2
#define SCAN_2          3
```

HOOKS.DEF

```
LIBRARY        HOOKS

DESCRIPTION 'PM Hooks Example DLL'

PROTMODE

DATA           LOADONCALL
CODE           LOADONCALL

EXPORTS        MyInit
               SetInputHook
               ReleaseInputHook
               SetRecordHook
               ReleaseRecordHook
               InputHook
               JournalRecordHook
               JournalPlaybackHook
```

HOOKS.MAK

```
all : hooks.dll

hooks.dll : hooks.obj hooks.def
        link386 /NOI hooks,hooks.dll,,DDE4NBS+os2386.lib,hooks.def

hooks.obj : hooks.c hooks.h
        icc /C+ /Ge- /Gm+ $*.c
```

Hooking the System Queue

Most of the hooks that are used by the `WinSetHook` API can be associated either with a local message queue or with the system message queue. If an application is only hooking its local message queue, the corresponding hook procedure can reside in the executable (`.EXE`) file of the application. When an application hooks events to and from the system message queue, however, the hook procedure must reside in a DLL—an arrangement that allows the hook procedure to be called from under the context of any process.

The PLAYBACK program allows the user to send a keystroke sequence to any window on the desktop so long as the window has the focus. This is accomplished by using an input hook of the system message queue along with journal-record and journal-playback hooks. The hook procedure for each of these three hooks resides in the HOOKS DLL. Before these three hooks can be registered with PM, however, the module handle of the HOOKS DLL must be obtained along with the addresses of the hook procedures. PLAYBACK calls the `MyInit` function within the HOOKS DLL to obtain this information. The following code excerpt loads the HOOKS DLL and queries the needed addresses:

```
hab2 = hab;

DosLoadModule( NULL, 0, "HOOKS", &hMod );

DosQueryProcAddr( hMod,
                  0,                     /* ordinal number not used */
                  "InputHook",           /* procedure name          */
                  &pInputHook );         /* pointer to hook proc     */

DosQueryProcAddr( hMod,
                  0,                     /* ordinal number not used */
                  "JournalRecordHook",   /* procedure name          */
                  &pRecordHook );        /* pointer to hook proc     */

DosQueryProcAddr( hMod,
                  0,                     /* ordinal number not used */
                  "JournalPlaybackHook", /* procedure name          */
                  &pPlaybackHook );      /* pointer to hook proc     */
```

The variables `hab2`, `hMod`, `pInputHook`, `pRecord Hook`, and `pPlayback-Hook` are initialized with the code shown here and are used later for calls that are made to the `WinSetHook` and `WinReleaseHook` APIs.

Recording Messages

When the user presses the "Start" pushbutton, which is displayed in Figure 21.1, PLAYBACK records all keystrokes that the user types. PLAYBACK stops recording keystrokes either when the user presses the "Stop" button of Figure 21.1 or when the entry field window that displays the keystrokes loses focus. The following code excerpt (taken from PLAYBACK.C), illustrates the steps that PLAYBACK takes when the user presses the "Start" pushbutton:

```
case IDD_START:
    WinShowWindow( hwndEF, TRUE );
    WinSetFocus( HWND_DESKTOP, hwndEF ); /* Give Entry fld focus */
    SetRecordHook( usCurQ );
    break;
```

An entry field is used to allow the user to key in a text string. When the PLAYBACK dialog box is first created, the entry field is in an invisible state. The `WinShowWindow` API is used to make the entry field visible. The keyboard focus then is given to the entry field by using the `WinSetFocus` API.

The HOOKS DLL uses two queues to store the keystroke sequences for the two hot keys. When PLAYBACK is recording a series of keystrokes for one of the hot keys, the function `SetRecordHook` is called with a value of 1 or 2, which identifies which queue the HOOKS DLL should use to store the keystrokes.

PLAYBACK calls the `SetRecordHook`, exported by HOOKS, to activate the journal-record hook. `SetRecordHook` issues the following `WinSetHook` API call to achieve this task:

```
WinSetHook( hab2,
            NULLHANDLE,         /* hook system msg Q */
            HK_JOURNALRECORD,   /* hook type         */
            pRecordHook,        /* our hook handler  */
            hMod );             /* hook proc DLL     */
```

The `hab2`, `pRecordHook` and `hMod` variables all were initialized by the `MyInit` routine. After the `WinSetHook` API has been called, the journal hook procedure `JournalRecordHook` will be called whenever the system message queue receives a keyboard or pointing device event. The `JournalRecordHook` that resides in `HOOKS.C` is as follows:

```
VOID EXPENTRY JournalRecordHook( HAB hab, PQMSG pQmsg )
{
    PQMSG pCurQmsg;

    if(pQmsg->msg == WM_CHAR) {

        if(usInQ == 1) {
            pCurQmsg = (PQMSG)(&aQmsg1[cQ1]);
            if (cQ1 >= MAX_Q_ENTRIES)
                cQ1 = 0;
            else
                ++cQ1;
        }
        else {
            pCurQmsg = (PQMSG)(&aQmsg2[cQ2]);
            if (cQ2 >= MAX_Q_ENTRIES)
                cQ2 = 0;
            else
                ++cQ2;
        }
        memcpy( pCurQmsg, pQmsg, sizeof(QMSG) );
    }

} /* end of JournalRecordHook */
```

The PLAYBACK program will record only keystroke events. This is accomplished by ensuring that the `msg` field of the `QMSG` structure is equal to `WM_CHAR`. If the `QMSG` structure describes a `WM_CHAR` message, the whole `QMSG` structure is copied to the active record queue within the HOOKS DLL.

The number of keystroke messages contained within each internal record queue is kept in the cQ1 and cQ2 variables. The record queues have a limit of MAX_Q_ENTRIES (defined in HOOKS.H as 100) elements. When this limit is reached the queue counter is reset to zero.

Keystroke events will continue to be recorded until the user presses the "Stop" button. When the user presses the "Stop" button, the following code fragment will be executed:

```
case IDD_STOP:
   WinShowWindow( hwndEF, FALSE );
   WinSendMsg( hwndEF,                          /* Select all of the */
               EM_SETSEL,                       /* text so it can be */
               MPFROM2SHORT( 0, 0x7fff ),       /* deleted.          */
               0 );
   WinSendMsg( hwndEF,
               EM_CLEAR,
               0,
               0 );
   ReleaseRecordHook();
   break;
```

The entry field window will be hidden using the WinShowWindow API. The text that was entered in the entry field is cleared so that it does not appear the next time the entry field is displayed. This is attended to by sending an EM_CLEAR message to the entry field window. Before text in an entry field is cleared, it must be selected or highlighted. All of the text in the entry field is selected by sending an EM_SETSEL message to the entry field window. The starting and ending indexes into the text string are provided with the EM_SETSEL message.

The journal-record hook is released by calling the ReleaseRecordHook function, which is exported by the HOOKS DLL. The following code excerpt shows the syntax that is used by the ReleaseRecordHook routine to release the journal-record hook:

```
WinReleaseHook( hab2,
                NULLHANDLE,        /* system msg Q      */
                HK_JOURNALRECORD,  /* hook type         */
                pRecordHook,       /* our hook handler  */
                hMod );            /* hook proc DLL     */
```

Waiting for a Hot Key Sequence

Once a keystroke sequence has been recorded, it can be played back using one of the defined hot key sequences. The PLAYBACK program uses the Cntrl-1 and Cntrl-2 hot key sequences. An input hook of the system queue will monitor all keystroke events that occur.

The following is the input hook procedure that resides in the HOOKS DLL:

```
BOOL EXPENTRY InputHook( HAB hab, PQMSG pQmsg, ULONG fs )
{

   if ((pQmsg->msg == WM_CHAR) &&
       (CHARMSG( &pQmsg->msg )->fs & KC_CTRL) &&
       (CHARMSG( &pQmsg->msg )->fs & KC_KEYUP) ) {

       if ((CHARMSG( &pQmsg->msg )->scancode == SCAN_1) ||
           (CHARMSG( &pQmsg->msg )->scancode == SCAN_2) ) {
           usOutQ = CHARMSG( &pQmsg->msg )->scancode - 1;
           WinSetHook( hab2,
                       NULLHANDLE,                     /* hook system msg Q */
                       HK_JOURNALPLAYBACK,             /* hook type         */
                       pPlaybackHook,                  /* our hook handler  */
                       hMod );                         /* hook proc DLL     */
       }
   }
   return (FALSE);                              /* pass the message down the chain */

} /* end of InputHook */
```

The `InputHook` hook procedure filters out all nonkeystroke events. This is accomplished by comparing the `msg` field of the `QMSG` structure to the `WM_CHAR` message. If the event was a keystroke, the keyboard flags are checked to see whether the Ctrl key is currently depressed. If the Ctrl key is depressed, the keyboard scan code is checked against the scan codes for the "1" and "2" keys. If all tests pass, the playback queue, `usOutQ`, is set based on the current hot key. Ctrl-1 corresponds to output queue one, and Ctrl-2 corresponds to output queue two.

Playing Back the Keystrokes

The journal playback hook is activated by using the `WinSetHook` API. A successful return from the `WinSetHook` API will cause PM to call the `JournalPlaybackHook` routine until the journal playback hook is released through the use of the `WinReleaseHook` API.

The following code excerpt shows the `JournalPlaybackHook` procedure used by the HOOKS DLL:

```
ULONG EXPENTRY JournalPlaybackHook( HAB hab, BOOL fSkip, PQMSG pQmsg )
{
   PQMSG pCurQmsg;
```

```
if(fSkip == FALSE) {
   if(usOutQ == 1)
      pCurQmsg = (PQMSG)(&aQmsg1[cOut]);
   else
      pCurQmsg = (PQMSG)(&aQmsg2[cOut]);

   pCurQmsg->time = pQmsg->time;

   memcpy( pQmsg, pCurQmsg, sizeof(QMSG) );
}
else {
   ++cOut;
   if (((usOutQ == 1) && (cOut >= cQ1)) ||
       ((usOutQ == 2) && (cOut >= cQ2))) {

      WinReleaseHook( hab2,
                      NULLHANDLE,          /* hook system msg Q  */
                      HK_JOURNALPLAYBACK,  /* hook type          */
                      pPlaybackHook,       /* our hook handler   */
                      hMod );              /* hook proc DLL      */
      cOut = 0;
   }
}
return 0L; /* time in millisecs */
```

The `fSkip` parameter that is passed to `JournalPlaybackHook` is used to tell a journal-playback hook handler whether to skip to the next event. A value of `FALSE` indicates that the message at the top of the queue is to be returned. A value of `TRUE` tells the journal-playback hook procedure to advance to the next message in the queue.

If `fSkip` is equal to `FALSE`, PM is requesting the event that is currently on top of the playback queue. The journal-playback hook procedure is provided with a pointer to a `QMSG` structure. The `time` field of the `QMSG` structure contains the current value of the active millisecond counter. `JournalPlaybackHook` will stamp the current event with this time and copy the message currently at the top of its internal playback queue to the `QMSG` structure by using the `memcpy` C runtime library function.

If `fSkip` is equal to `TRUE`, `JournalPlaybackHook` will increment the count of elements that have been emptied from its internal playback queue. When there are no more elements left in the playback queue, `JournalPlaybackHook` will release the journal-playback hook by using the `WinReleaseHook` API.

While the `JournalPlaybackHook` procedure plays a series of recorded keystrokes, it returns a value of zero to PM for each stored keystroke it plays. This return value tells how long (in millisecs) that PM must wait before PM calls the `JournalPlaybackHook` again. This return value can be used to synchronize events and handle such messages as mouse events, which may be time-dependent. Since the PLAYBACK example simply deals with sequential keystroke streams, there is no need to postpone PM from calling back. When the `JournalPlaybackHook` procedure is finished with a series of keystrokes, it releases the hook and returns a value of zero. Once the hook is released, the `JournalPlaybackHook` procedure is no longer registered with PM and is no longer called.

CHAPTER 22
Initialization Files

PM programs can store a list of user selections and preferences in the form of *initialization files* (INI files). INI files essentially function as small databases that contain information that can range in complexity from simple text strings to large data structures. Although INI files can store almost any kind of information, their principal use is to store profile information that determines how applications should be set up and displayed (initialized) when they are started.

PM and Workplace Shell make use of two INI files, `os2.ini` and `os2sys.ini`, to store information that describes how they should appear when they are first loaded. These two files contain such information as the positions and colors to be used in drawing Workplace Shell folders and the system colors and border widths to be used by PM.

The APIs that are used to handle INI files are very similar to the standard library functions that are used to read and write text files. These APIs, supplied by a component of OS/2 called *Profile Manager*, are designed to handle the types of data that PM applications need to store to and retrieve from INI files. The complex data structures that most PM applications use to describe window positions and color schemes can be stored with a single call to Profile Manager.

USING AN INITIALIZATION FILE

Profile Manager handles INI files by using a set of APIs that have `Prf` prefixes. The `Prf` APIs are very much like the functions that are provided by the standard C library for writing and reading from files; however, the `Prf` APIs are designed to use the format of INI files. For example, such standard C functions as `fopen` and `fclose` have "equivalent" Profile Manager APIs, namely `PrfOpenProfile` and `PrfCloseProfile`, respectively. `Prf` APIs are also provided to write and read pieces of information that are stored either as text strings or as data structures.

To uniquely identify each piece of information that constitutes a data element of an INI file, each piece of information is assigned an *application name* and a *key name*, which are used together to create a unique label. The application name typically identifies the application to which a particular INI file relates. The key name is used to identify the various pieces of information that an application needs to have stored in an INI file.

Examples of typical strings that are used for application names and key names can be seen in the RC files `ini.rc` and `inisys.rc`, which describe the default contents of the system profiles `os2.ini` and `os2sys.ini`, respectively. The files `ini.rc` and `inisys.rc` contain tables of application names, key names, and associated values.

OS/2 provides a utility called MAKEINI to convert the ASCII files `ini.rc` and `inisys.rc` into the profiles `os2.ini` and `os2sys.ini`, respectively. By using the MAKEINI system utility, profiles easily can be changed to alter PM and Workplace Shell environments.

The os2.ini and os2sys.ini Profiles

PM makes heavy use of the system profiles `os2.ini` and `os2sys.ini` to store data such as system colors and border widths. Since these two INI files are accessed so frequently by PM, Profile Manager keeps the files constantly open, so the `Prf` calls to open and close these INI files need not be used each time access to one of these files is needed.

Like PM, applications are given easy access to the system profiles. Except when dealing with the `os2.ini` or `os2sys.ini` files, most INI files require that a handle to an INI file be obtained by calling `PrfOpenProfile`. However, the `os2.ini` and `os2sys.ini` files do not require that `PrfOpenProfile` be used, because the needed handles for these two files are already set up by PM, namely, the handles `HINI_USERPROFILE` and `HINI_SYSTEMPROFILE`, respectively. Because calls to `PrfOpenProfile` can be avoided by using one of these already established handles, many applications take the shortcut of using `HINI_USERPROFILE` to add data concerning their configurations to the `os2.ini` file. The `HINI_SYSTEMPROFILE` handle is seldom used, because the `os2sys.ini` profile has always been viewed as being provided for the exclusive use of the OS/2 system.

It is recommended that programs avoid the shortcut of directly storing data in the `os2.ini` file. Applications that ignore this recommendation cause the `os2.ini` file to be cluttered with data written by programs that a user will eventually upgrade or change. The recommended approach is for each application to create its own INI file. By calling `PrfOpenProfile`, an application can open an INI file (or create it if such a file does not exist), so that the `os2.ini` file will not become cluttered with information for this individual program.

Workplace Shell allows each application to specify a working subdirectory for its program objects. By the use of a name of a profile without specifying a path, an INI file that is created by `PrfOpenProfile` will be created in a working subdirectory that has been specified by the user.

Saving the Positions of Windows

Workplace Shell adds two `Win` APIs to PM for storing and restoring the size, position, and presentation parameters of a window. These two `Win` APIs, known as `WinStoreWindowPos` and `WinRestoreWindowPos`, are used by Workplace Shell to handle its folders when they are moved or altered by a user. While the `WinStoreWindowPos` and `WinRestoreWindowPos` APIs are easy to use, these APIs are limited to writing to the `os2.ini` file. An application should make its own `Prf` calls to save its window's present size and position in a separate INI file.

The following code shows a very simple way to store an `SWP` structure that describes a window's present size and position:

```
{
  HINI  hini;
  SWP   swp;
  ULONG ulSwp = sizeof(SWP);

  /* get the present window position */
  WinQueryWindowPos( hwndFrame, &swp );

  hini = PrfOpenProfile( hab, "MY.INI" );

  /* if window presently min or max, get restored size and position */
  if (swp.fl & (SWP_MAXIMIZE | SWP_MINIMIZE)) {
    swp.x  = WinQueryWindowUShort( hwndFrame, QWS_XRESTORE  );
    swp.y  = WinQueryWindowUShort( hwndFrame, QWS_YRESTORE  );
    swp.cx = WinQueryWindowUShort( hwndFrame, QWS_CXRESTORE );
    swp.cy = WinQueryWindowUShort( hwndFrame, QWS_CYRESTORE );
  }

  /* only concerned with maximized or minimized */
  swp.fl &= (SWP_MAXIMIZE | SWP_MINIMIZE);

  /* save swp structure to MY.INI file */
  PrfWriteProfileData( hini, "My_AppName", "My_KeyName", &swp, ulSwp );

  PrfCloseProfile( hini );
}
```

In this code, the `PrfOpenProfile` API is used to open (and if needed, to create) an INI file called `MY.INI`. The present window position of a frame window (`hwndFrame`) is queried and stored in an `SWP` structure called `swp`. The fact that the window may be maximized or minimized is stored in `swp.fl` by using the `WinQueryWindowPos` API. If the window is either maximized or minimized, the `swp` structure is not used to store the window's present position but rather the position that the window is given when it is not maximized or minimized.

The foregoing code saves the `hwndFrame` window position by using `PrfWriteProfileData` to store the data structure `swp`. Profile Manager does not concern itself with the character of the values that are stored in the `swp` structure. By treating a data structure as a buffer of given size that can be used to store binary data, Profile Manager has the capability to store substantially any type of contiguous data structure that is of a known length. The `PrfWriteProfileData` API creates an entry in the `MY.INI` file that uses the strings "My_AppName" and "My_KeyName" as the application and key names.

The following code restores the position of a window to a position that is stored in an INI file. This code also has a capability to handle a situation wherein no INI file yet exists because an application is being run for the first time:

```
{
    HINI  hini;
    SWP   swp;
    ULONG ulSwp = sizeof(SWP);

    hini = PrfOpenProfile( hab, "MY.INI" );

    /* if an swp structure has been saved, use it in WinSetWindowPos */
    if (PrfQueryProfileData( hini, "My_AppName", "My_KeyName",
                        &swp, &ulSwp )) {
        swp.fl |= SWP_ACTIVATE          /* make window active */
                | SWP_MOVE              /* do not ignore swp.x and swp.y */
                | SWP_SIZE              /* do not ignore swp.cx and swp.cy */
                | SWP_SHOW;             /* show window */

        WinSetWindowPos( hwndFrame,     /* change the window's position */
                    NULLHANDLE,         /* ignored, SWP_ZORDER not set */
                    swp.x, swp.y,       /* position of lower left corner */
                    swp.cx, swp.cy,     /* width and height */
                    swp.fl );           /* saved swp flags */

    /* else swp structure not saved, show window with size set when created */
    } else
        WinShowWindow( hwndFrame, TRUE );

    PrfCloseProfile( hini );
}
```

This code checks whether a call to `PrfQueryProfileData` finds an `swp` structure stored in `MY.INI`. The code assumes both that the `FCF_SHELLPOSITION` flag was used to create the frame window `hwndFrame` and that the `WS_VISIBLE` style flag was not used (resulting in `hwndFrame` being created but remaining hidden). If an application uses this code for the first time, the needed `MY.INI` file may not exist, and the code defaults to using the size and position information that has been set by the `FCF_SHELLPOSITION` flag.

An advantage that arises from using the two foregoing sections of code is the control that such code provides over precisely what kind of data is stored. In addition to window position data, an application can also store user option data, which identifies options that have been selected by a user simply by adding `Prf` calls to write and query the data.

In Chapter 23, more example code is presented that uses `Prf` calls to alter a value that appears in the `os2.ini` file. The example code is used in a utility that allows a user to query and change data that PM uses to list DLLs that are to be loaded once PM has been loaded.

CHAPTER 23
Registering Public Classes

One of the most powerful features for customizing PM is the ability to register a public window class. Not only can new public classes be added, but a behavior of an existing public class can be entirely changed by reregistering it.

By replacing any of PM's built-in window procedures, programmers can control almost every aspect of how PM works. The appearance and function of substantially any of PM's controls can be changed or supplemented by adding new controls. The key to implementing these powerful changes resides in registering and reregistering public window classes.

To register a public class, a system DLL must be created that contains a function that PM can call to register the needed public class. A public class must be registered at a specific time: namely, after PM has registered its public classes but before PM has created any windows. To assure that a system DLL is loaded at the correct time, the DLL must be added to a list that PM maintains in the os2.ini profile. By changing the list to include a new system DLL, PM will be caused to load the DLL at an appropriate time so that a function within the DLL can be called, when needed, to register public classes.

In this chapter, the code that is needed to create a DLL called TITLEBAR is presented. The TITLEBAR DLL reregisters the public class that defines a title bar (WC_TITLEBAR). The TITLEBAR DLL changes all title bars on the desktop to provide each title bar with a pop-up menu that lists items that alter the size and position of the title bar's frame window. To add TITLEBAR to the list of system DLLs that PM loads, a utility called SYSDLLS is presented to alter the list of DLLs that is maintained in the os2.ini file.

347

HAVING PM LOAD A SYSTEM DLL

During the loading of OS/2 onto a system, PM registers public window classes and loads system DLLs that are listed in certain entries of the os2.ini file. After a system DLL is loaded, PM calls the DLL to have it perform such tasks as adding one or more new public window classes and reregistering one or more existing public window classes.

To reregister a public class so that all applications will use the modified (reregistered) class, WinRegisterClass must be called from a system DLL that has been loaded by PM. The call to WinRegisterClass is made before PM has created any windows on the desktop. This allows all windows that are created thereafter to use the modified PM class. The use of a DLL is required to give all applications access to the same window procedure that defines the modified class. Since DLLs are designed to be loaded and shared by any number of OS/2 processes, they provide the best way available in OS/2 for permitting PM programs to access a function such as a window procedure.

In the os2.ini file, one entry lists DLLs that are to be loaded only one time, and a second entry lists DLLs that are to be loaded again and again, as needed on a per-process basis for each new process that is started. The file ini.rc that is used with the OS/2 MAKEINI utility shows the default contents of the os2.ini file.

The following two lines of code are from the ini.rc file and set the default values that are used by PM:

```
"SYS_DLLS"          "LoadOneTime"           "REXXINIT"
"SYS_DLLS"          "LoadPerProcess"        "PMCTLS"
```

In this code excerpt, the string "SYS_DLLS" is the application name, and the strings "LoadOneTime" and "LoadPerProcess" are key names. "REXXINIT" and "PMCTLS" are the names of DLLs that PM will load when the system is first initialized.

The DLL called "PMCTLS" contains code that handles the CUA controls, such as the notebook and container controls. Although PMCTLS is listed as a DLL that is to be loaded for each process, PM loads PMCTLS before loading any of the DLLs that are listed in the os2.ini file. This order of loading is appropriate, because PM's public classes are always registered before the system DLLs are loaded and given a chance to register their public classes. A DLL that is listed in the os2.ini file *can* assume that all public classes that are used by PM have been registered. PMCTLS is loaded by PM to handle many of PM's public classes. PMCTLS also appears in the os2.ini file so that it can handle some of its initialization code for each PM program.

By adding a name of a DLL to one or the other of the LoadOneTime or the LoadPerProcess lists, the added DLL can reregister any of the existing public window classes or can register new public window classes. The major difference between the code that is used for a DLL that is loaded once and the code that is used for a DLL that is loaded on a per-process basis is the way in which the module definition file (DEF file) for the DLL is set up. If a DLL is to be loaded only once, the flag INITGLOBAL is used in the definition file of the DLL. If a DLL is to be loaded on a per-process basis, an INITINSTANCE flag is used in the definition file of the DLL.

After PM has loaded a system DLL from the list of DLLs that is maintained in the os2.ini file, PM calls the DLL to register any public classes. To have PM properly call a system DLL, the DLL needs to export a function with an ordinal value of one. When the "ordinal one" function is called, the function can register any needed classes.

The C SET/2 Compiler and DLLs

OS/2 notifies each DLL when it is loaded by a program by calling an initialization function that is built into the DLL. An initialization function within a DLL is optional and is needed only if a DLL must set up variables or handle certain tasks before any of its other functions are called.

For DLLs that are compiled with the C SET/2 compiler, a function called _DLL_InitTerm can be set up to receive notice that a DLL has been loaded. The following code shows the format of the _DLL_InitTerm function:

```
unsigned long _System _DLL_InitTerm( unsigned long hmod, unsigned long ulFlag )
{
   /* if ulFlag is zero then initialize DLL else exiting DLL */
   if ( !ulFlag )

      // the DLL is being loaded, place any needed code here

   return 1;
} /* end _DLL_InitTerm */
```

By the use of _DLL_InitTerm, a DLL's variables and resources can be set up when the DLL is loaded. Depending on how the DLL is set up, a call to the _DLL_InitTerm function can indicate whether the DLL is being loaded for the first time by OS/2 or is being loaded for the first time for a particular process.

The C SET/2 compiler sets up _DLL_InitTerm to have two parameters. The first parameter is the handle to the module assigned by OS/2. The second parameter is a flag that indicates whether the DLL is being loaded (a value of zero) or is being unloaded (a nonzero value).

If the _DLL_InitTerm function that is set up by the C SET/2 compiler is to be used, a provision must be made to declare _DLL_InitTerm as a system function that works with parameters that are placed on a stack in a right-to-left order. Typically this is done by using a _System key word in the declaration for the _DLL_InitTerm function.

A SYSTEM DLL

When a system DLL for setting up a public class is being developed, it is preferable to use a test machine (a second computer) that has the OS/2 debugging kernel loaded so that the debugger can be used to check the operation of the newly written DLL. Although it is possible to develop code without using the debugging kernel, a bug in a DLL that is loaded by PM during initialization can hang the system. Unlike an application that is being debugged, system DLLs are loaded at a system level, long before any applications are started. If a bug in a system DLL prevents PM from running, removing the DLL from the system may require that the system be rebooted from a disk drive.

To debug problems at or near the system level, the kernel debugger is *the* tool that will provide the most useful, most detailed information. A C compiler development environment and its debugger cannot be used, because the debugger will not be loaded by the system, and so will not be active or available to monitor anything, when PM calls the DLL.

If you experiment with the programming of system DLLs, it is nearly inevitable that you will encounter a bug that will prevent your system from coming up. If this occurs, the DLL can be removed by rebooting the system from a diskette. The DLL should then be deleted or renamed so that it will not cause the system to hang when rebooted. If the DLL continues to be listed in the os2.ini file, this will pose no problem, because PM will simply ignore a nonexistent DLL listed in its os2.ini file.

THE SYSDLLS PROGRAM

An example program called SYSDLLS, the source code for which is presented in this section, serves as a utility to edit the LoadOneTime entry in the os2.ini file. The SYSDLLS program queries the os2.ini file and presents an entry field that contains the results of the query. By default, the entry field probably will contain "REXXINIT." If the user adds the name of a new DLL into the entry field and presses a button labeled "Write," the SYSDLLS utility will update the os2.ini file so that the next time the system is booted, PM will load the new DLL. The SYSDLLS utility also provides an additional button labeled "Query," which allows the contents of the entry field to be set to the present value that is stored in the os2.ini file.

The SYSDLLS utility provides a convenient way to alter the os2.ini file to include the TITLEBAR DLL that is described in this chapter. The following five files make up the SYSDLLS utility:

SYSDLLS.C

```
#define INCL_GPI
#define INCL_WIN
#include <os2.h>
#include "sysdlls.h"
```

```
/* function prototypes */
INT main( VOID );
MRESULT EXPENTRY MyDlgProc( HWND, ULONG, MPARAM, MPARAM );
VOID MyPrfQuery( HWND );
VOID MyPrfWrite( HWND );

/* global variables */
CHAR szAppName[] = "SYS_DLLS";
CHAR szKeyName[] = "LoadOneTime";

INT main( VOID )
{
   HAB  hab;
   HMQ  hmq;
   QMSG qmsg;
   HWND hwndDlg;
   SWP  swp;

   hab = WinInitialize( 0 );
   hmq = WinCreateMsgQueue( hab, 0 );

   hwndDlg = WinLoadDlg( HWND_DESKTOP, /* set the desktop as parent    */
                    NULLHANDLE,   /* no owner                     */
                    MyDlgProc,    /* address of dialog procedure  */
                    NULLHANDLE,   /* use .EXE fill for resources  */
                    ID_DLGBOX,    /* ID of the dialog box resource */
                    NULL );       /* no control data              */

   /* find where system would place dialog box */
   WinQueryTaskSizePos( hab, 0, &swp );

   /* place dialog box at position given by the shell */
   WinSetWindowPos( hwndDlg,           /* change the dialog window's position */
                NULLHANDLE,       /* ignored, SWP_ZORDER not set */
                swp.x, swp.y,     /* position of lower left corner */
                0, 0,             /* ignored SWP_SIZE not set */
                SWP_SHOW,         /* show dialog box */
                I SWP_MOVE );     /* do not ignore swp.x and swp.y */

   WinSendMsg( hwndDlg,
            WM_SETICON,
            (MPARAM)WinQuerySysPointer( HWND_DESKTOP,
                                        SPTR_APPICON,
                                        FALSE ),
            NULL );

   if (hwndDlg)
       while (WinGetMsg( hab, &qmsg, NULLHANDLE, 0, 0 ))
       WinDispatchMsg( hab, &qmsg );

   WinDestroyWindow( hwndDlg );
   WinDestroyMsgQueue( hmq );
   WinTerminate( hab );

   return 0;
} /* end main */
```

```
MRESULT EXPENTRY MyDlgProc( HWND hwnd, ULONG msg, MPARAM mp1, MPARAM mp2 )
{
    switch (msg) {

    case WM_INITDLG:
        WinSendMsg( hwnd, WM_SETICON,
                    (MPARAM)WinLoadPointer( HWND_DESKTOP,
                                            NULLHANDLE,
                                            ID_DLGBOX ),
                    NULL );
        WinSendDlgItemMsg( hwnd, ID_ENTRYFIELD, EM_SETTEXTLIMIT,
                           MPFROMSHORT( 1024 ), MPFROMLONG( 0 ) );


        /* place value of SYS_DLLS : LoadPerProcess into ID_ENTRYFIELD */
        MyPrfQuery( hwnd );

        break;


    case WM_COMMAND:
        switch (SHORT1FROMMP( mp1 )) {

            case ID_WRITE:
             /* place value in ID_ENTRYFIELD into SYS_DLLS : LoadPerprocess */
                MyPrfWrite( hwnd );
                break;

            case ID_QUERY:
             /* place value of SYS_DLLS : LoadPerProcess into ID_ENTRYFIELD */
                MyPrfQuery( hwnd );
                break;

            case DID_OK:
                WinPostMsg( hwnd, WM_QUIT, 0, 0 );
                return FALSE;
        }
        break;

    case WM_CLOSE:
        WinPostMsg( hwnd, WM_QUIT, 0, 0 );
        return FALSE;

    default:
        return( WinDefDlgProc( hwnd, msg, mp1, mp2 ));
    }
    return (MRESULT)FALSE;

} /* end MyDlgProc */

VOID MyPrfQuery( HWND hwnd )
{
    ULONG ulBuffer;
    CHAR szErrorMessage[] = "<VALUE NOT FOUND>";
    PSZ psz;
```

```
    PrfQueryProfileSize( HINI_USERPROFILE,
                         szAppName,
                         szKeyName,
                         &ulBuffer );

    /* allocate something at least big enough for szErrorMessage */
    psz = (PSZ)malloc( ulBuffer + sizeof(szErrorMessage) );

    if (psz != NULL) {
        PrfQueryProfileString( HINI_USERPROFILE,
                               szAppName,
                               szKeyName,
                               szErrorMessage,
                               psz,
                               ulBuffer );
        WinSetDlgItemText( hwnd, ID_ENTRYFIELD, psz );
    }

    free( psz );
    return;
} /* end MyPrfQuery */

VOID MyPrfWrite( HWND hwnd )
{
    ULONG  ulBuffer;
    USHORT rc;
    PSZ    psz;

    rc = WinMessageBox( HWND_DESKTOP, /* parent */
                hwnd,                 /* owner  */
                "This will change your os2.ini file.\nAre you sure?",
                "Writing to os2.ini",
                0,                              /* message box id */
                MB_ICONHAND | MB_YESNO ); /* yes and no button with icon */

    if (rc != MBID_YES)
        return;

    ulBuffer = WinQueryDlgItemTextLength( hwnd, ID_ENTRYFIELD ) + 1;

    /* allocate something to store the text */
    psz = (PSZ)malloc( ulBuffer );

    if (psz != NULL) {
        WinQueryDlgItemText( hwnd, ID_ENTRYFIELD, ulBuffer, psz );

        PrfWriteProfileString( HINI_USERPROFILE,
                               szAppName,
                               szKeyName,
                               psz );
    }

    free( psz );
    return;
} /* end MyPrfWrite */
```

SYSDLLS.H

```
#define ID_DLGBOX        100
#define ID_ENTRYFIELD    200
#define ID_TEXT1         301
#define ID_TEXT2         302
#define ID_TEXT3         303
#define ID_QUERY         401
#define ID_WRITE         402
```

SYSDLLS.RC

```
#include <os2.h>
#include "sysdlls.h"

DLGTEMPLATE ID_DLGBOX LOADONCALL MOVEABLE DISCARDABLE
BEGIN
    DIALOG "System DLL's", ID_DLGBOX, 0, 0, 182, 84, 0,
        FCF_TITLEBAR | FCF_SYSMENU | FCF_TASKLIST | FCF_DLGBORDER
    BEGIN
        LTEXT       "OS2.INI File:", ID_TEXT1, 8, 72, 144, 8
        LTEXT       "SYS_DLLS - Application Name", ID_TEXT2, 12, 60, 144, 8
        LTEXT       "LoadOneTime - Key Name", ID_TEXT3, 12, 48, 144, 8
        CONTROL     "", ID_ENTRYFIELD, 8, 28, 166, 14, WC_ENTRYFIELD,
                        ES_LEFT | ES_MARGIN |
                        WS_GROUP | WS_TABSTOP | WS_VISIBLE
                        PRESPARAMS PP_FONTNAMESIZE, "15.Helvetica"
        PUSHBUTTON "Write", ID_WRITE, 8, 4, 50, 16
                        PRESPARAMS PP_FONTNAMESIZE, "15.Times New Roman Italic"
        PUSHBUTTON "Query", ID_QUERY, 66, 4, 50, 16
                        PRESPARAMS PP_FONTNAMESIZE, "15.Times New Roman"
        PUSHBUTTON "Exit", DID_OK, 124, 4, 50, 16
                        PRESPARAMS PP_FONTNAMESIZE, "15.Times New Roman"
    END
END
```

SYSDLLS.DEF

```
NAME      SYSDLLS    WINDOWAPI

DESCRIPTION 'System DLL Utility'

STUB        'OS2STUB.EXE'

DATA        MULTIPLE

STACKSIZE   16348
HEAPSIZE    16348

PROTMODE
```

SYSDLLS.MAK

```
all : sysdlls.exe

sysdlls.exe : sysdlls.obj sysdlls.def sysdlls.res
        link386 /PM:PM sysdlls,,,,sysdlls.def;
        rc sysdlls.res

sysdlls.res : sysdlls.rc sysdlls.h
        rc -r sysdlls.rc

sysdlls.obj : sysdlls.c sysdlls.h
        ICC.EXE /C /Ss /W3 .\$*.c
```

THE TITLEBAR EXAMPLE DLL

A DLL called TITLEBAR, whose source code is presented in this section, is provided to illustrate how to reregister a public class to alter its behavior. The TITLEBAR DLL adds a pop-up menu to each title bar that appears on the desktop. The pop-up menu can be accessed by clicking the second mouse button when the pointer is on the title bar. The menu items in the pop-up menu match many of the items in the system menu, such as "restore," "move," "size," "maximize," "minimize," and "hide."

The pop-up menu is set up so that its items post the standard system command messages (WM_SYSCOMMAND) that are associated with menu items of the system menu. For instance, choosing "restore" from the pop-up menu functions in the exact manner as the "restore" item functions if it is selected from the system menu, namely by posting a WM_SYSCOMMAND message with SC_RESTORE as a message parameter.

The TITLEBAR DLL displays its pop-up menu so that the parent frame window receives any resulting messages. If a title bar is created without either a parent frame window or another window class as a parent, WM_SYSCOMMAND messages still are posted. This does not cause a problem, since windows that are not of the frame class will ignore system command messages that do not apply to them. If, for example, a title bar window is set up with the desktop as its parent, the TITLEBAR pop-up menu will cause WM_SYSCOMMAND messages to be sent to the desktop. However, the desktop simply ignores these messages.

A frame window will only respond to a WM_SYSCOMMAND message that it can perform. For example, if the TITLEBAR pop-up menu sends a WM_SYSCOMMAND message requesting a frame window to minimize, and if the frame window has no minimize button, the message is ignored.

The TITLEBAR DLL includes a very simple bit of code. Most DLLs that change public windows classes require much more code. The following five files are used to compile the TITLEBAR DLL:

TITLEBAR.C

```
#define INCL_DOS
#define INCL_WIN
#include <os2.h>
#include "titlebar.h"

#pragma data_seg( MY_SHARED_DATA )

/* prototypes */
INT main( VOID );
MRESULT EXPENTRY MyWndProc( HWND, ULONG, MPARAM, MPARAM );

/* globals */
static BOOL Init = FALSE;
static CLASSINFO fci;

INT main( VOID )
{
    if ( !Init ) {
        Init = TRUE;

        if (!WinQueryClassInfo( NULLHANDLE, WC_TITLEBAR, &fci )) {
            WinAlarm( HWND_DESKTOP, WA_ERROR );
            return 1; /* tell PM not to continue with this DLL */
        }

        if (!WinRegisterClass(
                NULLHANDLE,          /* anchor block handle */
                WC_TITLEBAR,         /* class name */
                MyWndProc,           /* pointer to window procedure */
                fci.flClassStyle | CS_PUBLIC,       /* class style */
                fci.cbWindowData + sizeof(HWND) ))   /* number of data bytes */
        {
            WinAlarm( HWND_DESKTOP, WA_ERROR );
            return 1; /* tell PM not to continue with this DLL */
        }
    }
    return 0;
} /* end main */

MRESULT EXPENTRY MyWndProc( HWND hwnd,
                            ULONG msg,
                            MPARAM mp1,
                            MPARAM mp2 )
{

    switch (msg) {

    case WM_CREATE:
      { HMODULE hmod;
        HWND    hwndMenu;

        DosLoadModule( NULL, 0, "TITLEBAR", &hmod );
        hwndMenu = WinLoadMenu( HWND_OBJECT, hmod, ID_TITLEBAR );
```

```
            DosFreeModule( hmod );

            /* change the window ID from FID_MENU to ID_TITLEBAR */
            WinSetWindowUShort( hwndMenu, QWS_ID, ID_TITLEBAR );

            /* store hwndMenu in title bar window data */
            WinSetWindowULong( hwnd, fci.cbWindowData, (ULONG)hwndMenu);

            return (MRESULT)(*fci.pfnWindowProc)( hwnd, msg, mp1, mp2);
        } break;

    case WM_COMMAND:
        switch (SHORT1FROMMP(mp1)) {
        default:
            return (MRESULT)(*fci.pfnWindowProc)( hwnd, msg, mp1, mp2 );
        }
        return FALSE;

    case WM_BUTTON2DOWN:
        { POINTL ptl;
          HWND hwndMenu;

          WinQueryPointerPos( HWND_DESKTOP, &ptl );

          hwndMenu = (HWND)WinQueryWindowULong( hwnd, fci.cbWindowData );

          WinPopupMenu( HWND_DESKTOP,

                        WinQueryWindow( hwnd, QW_PARENT ),
                        hwndMenu,
                        ptl.x,
                        ptl.y,
                        0,
                        PU_NONE
                        | PU_HCONSTRAIN | PU_VCONSTRAIN
                        | PU_MOUSEBUTTON1 | PU_MOUSEBUTTON2
                        | PU_KEYBOARD );

          return FALSE;
        } break;

    case WM_DESTROY:
        { POINTL ptl;
          HWND   hwndMenu;

          hwndMenu = (HWND)WinQueryWindowULong( hwnd, fci.cbWindowData );

          WinDestroyWindow( hwndMenu );
        } /* fall through to default */

    default:
        return (MRESULT)(*fci.pfnWindowProc)( hwnd, msg, mp1, mp2);
    }
    return FALSE;
} /* MyWndProc */
```

TITLEBAR.H

```
#define ID_TITLEBAR 101
```

TITLEBAR.RC

```
#include <os2.h>
#include "titlebar.h"

MENU ID_TITLEBAR
   BEGIN
      MENUITEM "~Restore",   SC_RESTORE,   MIS_SYSCOMMAND
      MENUITEM "~Move",      SC_MOVE,      MIS_SYSCOMMAND
      MENUITEM "~Size",      SC_SIZE,      MIS_SYSCOMMAND
      MENUITEM "Mi~nimize",  SC_MINIMIZE,  MIS_SYSCOMMAND
      MENUITEM "Ma~ximize",  SC_MAXIMIZE,  MIS_SYSCOMMAND
      MENUITEM "~Hide",      SC_HIDE,      MIS_SYSCOMMAND
   END
```

TITLEBAR.DEF

```
LIBRARY TITLEBAR INITGLOBAL

DESCRIPTION 'TITLEBAR PM Example Program'

PROTMODE

CODE LOADONCALL MOVEABLE DISCARDABLE
DATA LOADONCALL MULTIPLE NOIOPL NONSHARED READWRITE

SEGMENTS
     DDE4_DATA32     CLASS 'DATA' LOADONCALL SHARED READWRITE NOIOPL
     MY_SHARED_DATA CLASS 'DATA' LOADONCALL SHARED READWRITE NOIOPL

EXPORTS
        main @1
```

TITLEBAR.MAK

```
LFLAGS = /noi /map /nol /exepack /packcode /packdata# \
         /farcalltranslat /align:4 /nod /NOE
LIBS = dde4nbs.lib+os2386.lib

all : titlebar.dll

titlebar.dll : titlebar.obj titlebar.def titlebar.res
    link386 $(LFLAGS) titlebar,titlebar.dll,,$(LIBS),titlebar;
    rc titlebar.res titlebar.dll
    mapsym titlebar
```

```
titlebar.res : titlebar.rc titlebar.h
    rc -r titlebar.rc

titlebar.obj : titlebar.c
    ICC.EXE /C /Ge- /Ms /O+ /Rn /Sp1 /Ss /W3 .\$*.c
```

Using the TITLEBAR DLL

When PM loads the TITLEBAR DLL, a function called `main` in `TITLEBAR.C` is
called, because it is given an ordinal value of one in the `TITLEBAR.DEF` file.
The reason that the function is called `main` is not to obtain any special form
of treatment from the C compiler, but rather because this has become a traditional way of naming the ordinal one function that is called by PM.

When `main` is called by PM, a variable called `Init` is set to `TRUE`. `Init`
acts as a "safety net" to prevent the code in the `main` function from accidentally
getting called more than once. The variable `Init` is placed in a segment called
`MY_SHARED_DATA` as the result of the following `#pragma` that appears before
`Init` is declared:

```
#pragma data_seg( MY_SHARED_DATA )
```

The `MY_SHARED_DATA` segment is defined in the `TITLEBAR.DEF` file as being
shared by all processes. This sets up `Init` to be shared by all processes that use
TITLEBAR.

Calling WinRegisterClass

The function `main` handles the registration of the new title bar class. The
following code is employed by TITLEBAR both to query the present title bar
class and to use the queried information to reregister the title bar class. As a
result, the function `MyWndProc` is set up as the new window procedure for all
title bars:

```
if (!WinQueryClassInfo( NULLHANDLE, WC_TITLEBAR, &fci )) {
    WinAlarm( HWND_DESKTOP, WA_ERROR );
    return 1; /* tell PM not to continue with this DLL */
}

if (!WinRegisterClass(
        NULLHANDLE,         /* anchor block handle */
        WC_TITLEBAR,        /* class name */
        MyWndProc,          /* pointer to window procedure */
        fci.flClassStyle | CS_PUBLIC,       /* class style */
        fci.cbWindowData + sizeof(HWND) ))  /* number of data bytes */
{
```

```
          WinAlarm( HWND_DESKTOP, WA_ERROR );
          return 1; /* tell PM not to continue with this DLL */
}
```

In this code, space is added to the standard amount of class data made available for title bars by using the value `fci.cbWindowData + sizeof(HWND)`, in which `fci.cbWindowData` specifies the normal amount of memory that is needed for a title bar and `sizeof(HWND)` is added so that more memory is allocated to permit a handle for a title bar's pop-up menu to be stored.

As a part of setting up a modified title bar class, TITLEBAR adds a `CS_PUBLIC` flag to the default title bar class style by ORing `CS_PUBLIC` with `fci.flClassStyle`. This makes certain that the class is registered as public class, even though the value `fci.flClassStyle` should already contain `CS_PUBLIC`.

Handling Class Data

TITLEBAR adds an `HWND` value to the class data of each title bar that is created. The following code sets the class data to store a handle to a menu that is created for a title bar:

```
          /* store hwndMenu in title bar window data */
          WinSetWindowULong( hwnd, fci.cbWindowData, (ULONG)hwndMenu );
```

In this code, the value `fci.cbWindowData` is used by `WinSetWindowULong` as the offset into the class data to store a handle to a menu (`hwndMenu`). Storing a handle to menus in the class data of each title bar allows the window procedure to use PM as a vehicle for storing a database of menu handles without having to write extra code to handle memory allocation for each handle.

Although it is tempting to use zero as the offset to store the menu handle while using the `WinSetWindowULong` API, the value `fci.cdWindowData` is the proper offset to use. If another base offset is used, this risks the possibility that TITLEBAR will overwrite data that has been set up by PM or by another window procedure in a system DLL that was loaded before TITLEBAR.

By querying the size of the existing window data, TITLEBAR simply adds to the end of the stored data by using `fci.cbWindowData` as an offset. If an application subclasses the public title bar class and adds more class data, it is required that the application use an offset that is equal to the class data size that is returned by a call to `WinQueryClassInfo`.

Some window classes reserve a long integer value in their class data for use by applications. An application can access the long integer value by using an offset `QWL_USER` (equal to zero), which offsets to the beginning of the class data. Even if the window class for the title bar had such a value, it could not be used by TITLEBAR to store a window handle, because an application may be storing a value in the `QWL_USER` space that has been set aside for the `ULONG` value.

Index

Companion Software to

Advanced OS/2 Presentation Manager Programming

The PM source code presented in this book is available on a 3 1/2″ 1.4 Mb disk for $29.95 plus postage and handling. Florida residents add 6% sales tax. U.S. orders add $2.50 for shipping and handling. Orders outside of the U.S. add $5.00 for shipping and handling. Allow 4 to 6 weeks for delivery.

Send check or money order to:

Advanced PM Example Programs

P.O. Box 4534

Boynton Beach, FL 33424–4534

Please, send me _____ copy(ies) of the companion disk for use with the book *Advanced OS/2 Presentation Manager Programming* to:

Name: _____

Company: _____ **Phone:** _____

Address: _____

City: _____ **State:** _____ **Zip:** _____